Experience the Ministry of Jesus in a Spiritually Captivating Way

JOURNEY WITH

JESUS

THROUGH THE MESSAGE OF

MARK

Insightful & Engaging

Kieran Beville

JOURNEY WITH JESUS THROUGH THE MESSAGE OF MARK

Experience the Ministry of Jesus in a Spiritually Captivating Way

Kieran Beville

Christian Publishing House
Cambridge, Ohio

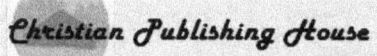
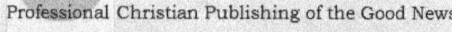

Professional Christian Publishing of the Good News

Copyright © 2015 Kieran Beville

All rights reserved. Except for brief quotations in articles, other publications, book reviews, and blogs, no part of this book may be reproduced in any manner without prior written permission from the publishers. For information, write, support@christianpublishers.org

Unless otherwise stated, scripture quotations are from *The Holy Bible, English Standard Version®*, copyright © 2001 by Crossway Bibles, a publishing ministry of Good News Publishers. Used by permission. All rights reserved.

JOURNEY WITH JESUS THROUGH THE MESSAGE OF MARK Experience the Ministry of Jesus in a Spiritually Captivating Way

Publishing by Christian Publishing House

ISBN-13: 978-0692398197

ISBN-10: 0692398198

ENDORSEMENTS

What other Christian Leaders are Saying About: *JOURNEY WITH JESUS THROUGH THE MESSAGE OF MARK Experience the Ministry of Jesus in a Spiritually Captivating Way*

New Christians and mature Christians will greatly benefit from reading this commentary on the Gospel of Mark. Simply, powerfully, with great precision, and exegetical accuracy, Dr. Kieran Beville masterfully brings us on a journey with Jesus that will transform our lives. I guarantee that you will be both challenged and changed as you hear the words of Jesus speaking afresh from the page of Scripture. You will see and experience the ministry of Jesus in a spiritually captivating and life changing way.

Kieran has a pastor's heart, a theologian's mind, and a writer's gift. His style is gripping, as he beautifully explains and illustrates Mark's Gospel. Kieran has done a great service to the church, and especially to true believers, who desire to grow in grace, increase in their knowledge of truth, and experience the intimacy, joy, and undeserved and unspeakable privilege of walking, as disciples, with Jesus. I unreservedly recommend and endorse this wonderful book.

It is a rich resource. May God mightily use "Journey with Jesus through the Message of Mark" throughout the world for His eternal glory!

Dr. Vincent Price
International Director
European Christian Mission – North America (ECM - NA)

I recently completed a sermon series in the Gospel of Mark, and I wish I'd had a copy of this book in hand as I was preparing messages. *Journey with Jesus through the Message of Mark* is an interesting and helpful survey of Mark's Gospel, exploring each major section of the text along with the key themes and insights from the text. Kieran Beville has written a book that can be enjoyed by laypersons as well as pastors and teachers. Pastors will find the abundant use of illustrations to be helpful in preparing their own messages. Journey with Jesus through the Message of Mark will find a welcome spot on the preacher's bookshelf.

Michael Duduit
Executive Editor, *Preaching*, and Dean of the College of Christian Studies, Anderson University, South Carolina

Journey with Jesus through the Message of Mark is an expository study of the Gospel of Mark by experienced pastor and teacher Kieran Beville. Originally preached as sermons at the Lee Valley Bible Church in Cork, Ireland, they are now in the form of short devotional reflections.

This book is ideal as a study companion for the personal study of the Gospel of Mark. One can read a section from the Gospel and then read the corresponding section to receive a fresh viewpoint and a practical application. The comments provide depth but they are usually between 3-4 pages in length and thus manageable for a lay reader.

In the author's comments, he often helpfully refers to background and historical information from the Ancient Near East that would not otherwise be easily understood by modern western readers. Many times there will be cross references to other passages of Scripture, thereby connecting Mark's writing with other important passages from the Bible. Other times Kieran Beville provides insights from current events, history, church life, or his rich personal experience. These draw out the ongoing relevance of the Gospel of Mark.

Journey with Jesus is coordinated with the chapters of Mark. Each section is divided appropriately with the modern scholarly understanding of the Gospel. The volume concludes with helpful essays on who killed Jesus, Judas Iscariot, and Pontius Pilate.

I commend these sermons, which are now well thought-out chapters to your reading. By using this book in your studies may you be helped in your own spiritual journey with the Savior!

H. H. Drake Williams, III

Professor of New Testament
Academic Dean
Tyndale Theological Seminary
Badhoevedorp, the Netherlands

Table of Content

ENDORSEMENTS 4
Foreword 12
Introduction 14
CHAPTER 1 17
   John the Baptist prepares the way (1:1-8) 17
   The baptism and temptation of Jesus (1:9-12) 21
   The calling of the first disciples (1:14-20) 29
   Jesus drives out an evil spirit (1:21-29) 34
   Jesus heals many (1:29-34) 42
   Jesus prays in a solitary place (1:35-39) 46
   Jesus cleanses a leper (1: 40-45) 52
CHAPTER 2 60
   Authority to forgive sin (2:1-12) 60
   Jesus calls Levi (2:13-17) 65
   Jesus questioned about fasting (2:18-22) 70
   Lord of the Sabbath (2:23-28) 78
CHAPTER 3 84
   The man with the shriveled hand (3:1-6) 84
   A great crowd follows Jesus (3:7-12) 89
   1 Kings 11:1-8 91
   The choosing of the twelve apostles (3:13-21) 93
   Family opposition (3:20-21) 95
   The unpardonable sin (3:22-30) 96
   Jesus' mother and brothers (3:31-36) 98
CHAPTER 4 101

The parable of the sower (4:1-20) 101
A lamp under a basket or on a stand (4:21-25)........106
The parable of the measure (4:21-25).......................107
The parable of the seed growing (4:26-29) 107
The parable of the mustard seed (4:30-34)...............108
Jesus calms a storm (4:35-41) 108
CHAPTER 5 112
Jesus heals a man with a demon (5:1-20) 112
Jairus' daughter (5:21-24; 35-43)...............................117
Jesus heals a woman with an issue of blood (Mark 5:25-34)..122
CHAPTER 6 128
Jesus rejected at Nazareth (6:1-6) 128
Jesus sends out the twelve apostles (6:7-13) 133
The death of John the Baptist (6:14-29) 137
The feeding of the five thousand (6:30-44) 143
Jesus walks on water (6:45-56) 149
Chapter 7 155
Clean and unclean (7:1-23) 155
The faith of the Syrophoenician woman (7:24-30)..162
Bringing people to Jesus (7:31-37)............................166
Chapter 8 172
Jesus feeds the four thousand (8:1-10).....................172
The yeast of the Pharisees and Herod (8:11-21)........177
The blind man at Bethsaida (8:22-26) 182
Peter confesses Jesus as the Christ (8:27-30) 188

    Jesus foretells his death and resurrection (8:31-38) .. 196

Chapter 9 201
    The transfiguration (9:1-13) 201
    Jesus heals a boy with an unclean spirit (9:14-32) 208
    Who is the greatest? (9:33-37) 213
    Anyone not against us is for us (9:38-41) 219
    Temptation to sin (9:42-48) 223
    Salt and fire (9:49-50) 229

Chapter 10 233
    Teaching about divorce (10:1-2) 233
    The Lord's answer (10:3-12) 235
    Children and the Kingdom of God (10:13-16) 243
    The rich young man (10:17-31) 248
    Jesus foretells his death a third time (10:32-34) 253
    The request of James and John (35-45) 254
    Jesus heals blind Bartimaeus (10:46-52) 258

Chapter 11 263
    The triumphal entry (11:1-11) 263
    Jesus curses the fig tree and the lesson thereof (11:12-14; 20-21) 270
    Remarks about faith and prayer (11:22-25) 275
    Jesus cleanses the temple (11:15-19) 276
    The authority of Jesus questioned (11:27-33) 281

Chapter 12 285
    Parable of the tenants (12:1-12) 285
    Paying taxes to Caesar (12:13-17) 288

The Sadducees ask about the resurrection (12:18-27) 292
The great commandment (12:28-34) 298
Whose son is the Christ? (12:35-37) 305
The widow's offering (12:41-44) 312

Chapter 13 322
The beginning of the end (13:1-8) 322
There will be false messiahs (v.6) 324
There will be wars (v.7) 325
There will be constant upheaval in the world (v.8) 326
There will be an increase in earthquakes (v.8) 326
There will be famines (v.8) 326
There will be troubles of every kind (v.8) 327
Persecution for the sake of the gospel (13:9-13) 328
The abomination of desolation (13:14-23) 335
The second coming of Christ (13:24-27; 32-37) 338
The lesson of the fig tree (13:28-31) 339

Chapter 14 342
The plot to kill Jesus (14:1-2) 342
Jesus anointed at Bethany (14:3-9) 342
Judas betrays Jesus (14:10-11; 17-21) 348
The last supper (14:12-26) 353
Jesus foretells Peter's denial (14:26-31) 359
A fraternity of failures 360
Gethsemane (14:32-52) 361
Jesus before the council (14:53-65) 365

The Sanhedrin 366
Function and procedures 367
Peter denies Jesus (14:66-72) 374

Chapter 15 377
Jesus before Pilate (15:1-20) 377
The crucifixion and death of Jesus (15:21-39) 383
Jesus is buried (15:42-47) 390

Chapter 16 397
The Resurrection (16:1-8) 397
Jesus appears to Mary Magdalene (16:9-20) 402
Parting words (16:15-18) 405
The significance of the ascension (16:19-20) 409

APPENDIX A 417
Who Killed Jesus? 417
Did the Jews kill Jesus? 417
Did Pontius Pilate kill Jesus? 420
Did Satan Kill Jesus? 421
Did the sins of the world kill Jesus? 423
The ultimate cause 423

APPENDIX B 425
Judas 425

APPENDIX C 428
Pontius Pilate 428

Bibliography 433

Foreword

Reading the writings of some outstanding biblical preachers had a marked influence on my life as a young person. I had several favourite authors; let me mention a few of them: F. B. Meyer, G. Campbell Morgan, A. T. Robertson, John Stott, Leon Morris, F. F. Bruce and H. L. Ellison. I valued their writings because they helped me to get into the Word, to get background information that I did not have access to which helped illumine the text, and to be nourished by scriptural truth. It was clear that these writers had studied and meditated on biblical passages carefully to see what the biblical author meant. They then attempted to apply what the passage said to the present-day hearers (some of these authors were more helpful, when it came to application, than others). These writings helped me realise the power of the Word to speak to us and transform our lives. As a young person, I determined that I too would study the Word with rigour.

So I still occasionally read such books as part of my devotions as a change from my normal routine of reading and studying the Bible inductively. I also sometimes go to the beach and spend time with such books while basking in the glory of God's creation. I read them on trains and planes and in airports. Such books must be read slowly, a few pages at a time, if we are to reap the maximum benefit from them. I take this as part of my pursuit of pleasure. There are few pleasures as rich and enjoyable as reflecting on the eternal truths of God. Nowadays I have added several other authors to my list of favourite biblically grounded devotional writers. Here are some of them, Don Carson, Robert Coleman, David Gooding, E. Stanley Jones, Dennis Kinlaw, Robert Murray M'Cheyne, J. A. Motyer, John Piper, A. T. Robertson, Tom Schreiner, Chris Wright, and Philip Yancey.

I do not always agree with the applications of the passages that these authors make (Actually, I do not fully agree with every little detail of application in this book too). That is one of the challenges of application. But because some people disagree with our applications we should not shy away from making such applications. The applications are not divinely inspired and inerrant like the Word of God. These expository writers open up the inerrant Word to me so that I could understand it and apply it to my personal life. They teach me that I must seek to engage the Scriptures in a thoroughgoing way to let it speak specifically to the issues we face today.

When I started reading Kieran Beville's book on Mark I planned to quickly skim through the book and get a sense of what it is saying to write a Foreword for it. However, I soon realised that this book would be a source of personal nourishment if I read it slowly, meditatively. That is what I have been doing for several days. I have been delighted to receive nourishment by being exposed to Mark through the writing of a careful student of the Word and a skilful expositor.

I recommend this book to anyone seeking nourishment through biblically informed reading. I also recommend it to anyone who wishes to study, or to teach or preach from the book of Mark. It is based on careful study, but it presents the results of scholarly study in a way that anyone could understand. That very good combination is not often found in expository books.

Ajith Fernando
Teaching Director, Youth for Christ, Sri Lanka

Introduction

Mark's Gospel is the shortest of the four Gospels but often the most detailed. It is a fast-paced, action-packed drama, rich in narrative and theology. As such, it is full of exciting stories, which have much truth to teach about Jesus and the gospel message. What Mark records was probably what Peter preached concerning Christ.[1]

Barnabas had brought the newly converted Saul to meet the saints in Jerusalem at a time when all the others were afraid to meet him (Acts 9:27). Mark was a cousin of Barnabas. Scripture records a sharp disagreement between Paul and Barnabas about Mark's usefulness in ministry (Acts 15). Paul wanted to revisit all the brothers in the towns where they had preached the gospel to see how they were doing. Barnabas wanted to take Mark, his cousin, (Colossians 4:10) with them but Paul thought this was unwise. When they had reached Perga, in Pamphylia, on the mainland of Asia Minor, Mark left them and returned to Jerusalem (Acts 13:13). Paul regarded this as desertion.

Thus, Scripture records that Paul and Silas had such a sharp disagreement about Mark's 'usefulness' or 'suitability' for ministry that they parted company (Acts 15:39). Barnabas

---

[1] Not that it is merely a verbatim transcript of Peter's words. God does not bypass individual personality. Mark processes the raw material under the influence of the Holy Spirit until it is refined and shaped in accordance with the conventions of the Gospel genre and his particular theological thrust.

took Mark and sailed for Cyprus, but Paul chose Silas and went through Syria and Cilicia. This issue was not an unholy dispute; instead, it was a matter of principle. This shows the consistently compassionate and courageous nature of Barnabas. This passage of Scripture shows that Christians will disagree on issues concerning the integrity, consistency, character, and usefulness of others. It is clear that there can be legitimate differences amongst believers on such matters. Paul rejected Mark but Barnabas, who was by name and nature an encourager, accepted him.

James Russell Lowell has said that 'Mishaps are like knives that either serve us or cut us, as we grasp them by the blade or the handle.'[2] Many believers bear the marks of mishaps, but these scars tell stories of God's gracious dealings with them. Many believers are also able to take these mishaps and use them as tools in God's work.

Mark was written about A.D. 55. It is the first of the Gospels.[3] When Luke was writing Acts (about A.D. 63), he was referring to the incident between Paul and Barnabas which had taken place fourteen or fifteen years earlier. Mark wrote the gospel six or seven years *after* Paul had rejected him. God had a future ministry for Mark and what an amazing task he entrusted to him!

---

[2] James Russell Lowell (1819–1891) was an American Romantic poet, critic, editor, and diplomat. He is associated with the Fireside Poets, a group of New England writers who were among the first American poets to rival the popularity of British poets. These poets usually used conventional forms and meters in their poetry, making them suitable for families entertaining at their fireside.

[3] Christian Publishing House would disagree with this date and would rather date the Gospel of Mark to about A.D. 60–65. In addition, Mark was not the first Gospel, it was the Gospel of Matthew, which was authored about A.D. 45-50. Therefore, the order of the Gospels first to last would be Matthew (45-50), Luke (56-58), Mark (60-65), and then John (98).

Later, Paul speaks of Mark as his companion in Rome and pays high tribute to his service. By the date of Colossians 4:10 Mark is in the company of Paul who was a prisoner (probably in Rome). Paul is apparently intending to send him on a mission to Colossae, so that he must have forgiven and forgotten the past. Paul also mentions Mark among the apostolic group in Philemon 24. Interestingly the theme of that brief epistle is 'love exemplified'.

Paul (author of the qualifications for office in the church; 1 Timothy 3) later requests the assistance of Mark and states that Mark is 'helpful to me in my ministry' (2 Timothy 4:11). It is clear from this that they were reconciled, as Paul sent Mark with Timothy on the mission to Asia Minor. If God used only perfect people to accomplish his purposes, there is much that would remain undone for lack of available and qualified candidates.

Mark is careful to explain Jewish customs to Romans readers. He is concerned to portray the deity of Jesus through his miracles. One-third of the book is given to Christ's last week on earth. The book opens with the statement, 'The beginning of the gospel of Jesus Christ, the Son of God' (1:1). This needs to be kept in mind. The gospel is all about Jesus! He is the Son of God. As the story unfolds it becomes clear that he is not just the Son of God but is, in fact, God the Son.

CHAPTER 1

John the Baptist prepares the way (1:1-8)

In verse two of chapter one Mark quotes the prophet Isaiah (700 BC): 'As it is written in Isaiah the prophet, "Behold, I send my messenger before your face, who will prepare your way, the voice of one crying in the wilderness: 'Prepare the way of the Lord, make his paths straight.'" That messenger was John the Baptist (a cousin of Jesus). This link with Isaiah shows that Jesus was the long awaited Messiah, the fulfillment of prophecy.

John the Baptist preached a baptism of repentance in the wilderness. Here is God's ordained means of communication. He was sustained by God's provision. He lived in the desert and wore clothing made of camel's hair with a leather belt around his waist. He ate locusts and wild honey (I recommend porridge for preachers today!). There is something strange and lonely about this figure. He is a little bit ascetic, a bit weird, like the prophets of the Old Testament. But he has been commissioned by God with a message of repentance. God's ways might appear strange and his servants might appear to be a bit peculiar. Some might want to change those ways and make the gospel more attractive. But the message is 'repent'. This calls people to acknowledge that they are sinful by nature and that they have sinned in thought, word and deed, by commission and omission. Sin is not just bad things that people do, it is also failing to do the good that ought to be done. James confirms this, 'whoever knows the right thing to do and fails to do it, for him it is sin.'–James 4:17

Repentance is about turning away from a selfish way of thinking and a lifestyle that is compatible with it and turning toward God, his will and ways, as understood through his Word. In this condition, quickened by the power of the Holy Spirit, the sinner must cry out to God for forgiveness and salvation and resolve by God's grace to forsake their sinful ways and turn to God in faith. The call to repentance holds forth the truth that there is a judgment and accountability.

Today this kind of message is not attractive and many will reject it. People do not want to be told that they are sinners. The Bible teaches that 'all have sinned and fall short of the glory of God.' (Romans 3:23) Paul, who wrote these words to the Roman believers, goes on to tell them that 'the wages of sin is death, but the free gift of God is eternal life in Christ Jesus our Lord.' (Romans 6:23) Therefore, sin is not just nasty things that other people do. However, many in John's day responded positively to the call to repentance. So verse 5 of chapter 1 says, 'And all the country of Judea and all Jerusalem were going out to him and were being baptized by him in the river Jordan, confessing their sins'. This is a way of speaking which is not meant to be taken absolutely literally. If it were taken completely literally, it would mean that everybody in the region repented and was baptized. That would not allow for any exceptions. Rather, it simply means that a great many were going out to hear him preach and were being baptized.

John was a great preacher but he was humble. He understood his relative insignificance in relation to Jesus: 'And he preached, saying, "After me comes he who is mightier than I, the strap of whose sandals I am not worthy to stoop down and untie"' (Mark 1:7). John proclaimed Christ. This is the central theme of all good gospel preaching. All preachers need to have this perspective. Jesus is the superior and the preacher is the subordinate. The preacher must be commissioned by God, conscious of his unworthiness, humble, preach repentance and be Christ-focused. But he must also be aware of the great power of God, as John was. Jesus is the golden thread in all the Scriptures, Old Testament and New Testament, in all genres (law, history, wisdom, poetry, prophecy, gospel, epistle and apocalyptic). Nobody is worthy to speak on behalf of Jesus but by God's grace some are chosen for this special task.

John does not promote himself; rather, he promotes Christ. He draws attention to the power of Jesus. He heralded the message that the Messiah was about to enter the scene. He created a sense of expectation and anticipation about Jesus so that there was a stir or a 'buzz' one might say today.

I once read a newspaper article about the death of Major Ronald Ferguson, the father of Queen Elizabeth's second daughter-in-law, Sarah, Duchess of York.[4] For several years he had a place in the queen's escort at the Trooping the Color ceremony. Apparently, he once earned a gentle rebuke from the queen for riding so close to her in a procession that he blocked out part of the public's view of its monarch!

The preacher must never earn a rebuke from his sovereign Lord that he eclipsed the people's view of their monarch! John's Gospel records the account of some Greeks who came to Philip with a request: '"Sir," they said, "we would like to see Jesus."' (John 12: 21) These words should be written on every pulpit to remind preachers of their sacred duty to present Jesus. The people have a desire and expectation to see him and the preacher has a duty to ensure that their hope will not be disappointed! It has been said of the preacher Joseph Parker (a contemporary of Charles Haddon Spurgeon) that when he preached people said: "Oh what a great preacher!" but when Spurgeon preached people

---

[4] Entitled 'Minor toff with connections to high society and low places', *The Irish Times*, Saturday, March 22, 2003, p.14.

said: "Oh what a great Savior!" It is the preacher's job to exalt the Savior.

What a great privilege John the Baptist had to be the forerunner of Christ. He followed in a long line of messengers of God who proclaimed the coming of the Messiah. It is a great privilege to speak *of* God and it is an even greater privilege to speak *for* God. This is a great privilege, which carries great responsibility and accountability. Ultimately, John's uncompromising commitment to preaching against sin cost him his life. He was imprisoned for challenging Herod about his sinful life and eventually beheaded. It is a high calling to preach the truth without fear or favor and it can cost a great deal.

If you were to rank the leaders of God's kingdom, whose lives and ministries are recorded in the Old Testament, who would you say was captain or chief amongst them? Perhaps you would say Abraham or Moses or David. Who would you say was the greatest? We would probably rule out some people (like Jonah) but what about Elijah, Elisha, Isaiah, Jeremiah, Ezra, Nehemiah or others? Well, Jesus answers this question: "Truly, I say to you, among those born of women there has arisen no one greater than John the Baptist" (John 11:11). This is high praise indeed from the lips of the Lord. He was fearless and focused on Christ. He was humble, conscious of his own littleness but aware of God's greatness. He preached against sin. He preached repentance and proclaimed Christ and Christ alone. He proclaimed the power of Christ. He created a sense of expectation and anticipation about Jesus that aroused people's curiosity about the Messiah. He belongs to a noble tradition of martyrs who died for speaking the truth. He knew that it was all about Jesus! As people looked to him he told them of one greater then himself. He pointed people to Christ. When people looked at John the baptizer, they saw a man who, in his outward appearance seemed peculiar. However, what they heard was wonderful. The gospel is wonderful because Jesus is wonderful.

The baptism and temptation of Jesus (1:9-12)

Why was Jesus baptized by John when John's baptism was one of repentance? Jesus had no sin so it was not a ritual cleansing or symbolic and public turning away from sin. Christ was publicly inaugurating his ministry. He participated in the religious rites and rituals of the time in Israel. He read and taught in the synagogue at Nazareth. He would have been circumcised. He was regularly in the temple. This baptism fits in with Jesus submitting himself to the order that God had put in place. He was fulfilling the old order and introducing the new order. The baptizing that John conducted was an outward sign of an inward faith. So Jesus was baptized by John in the Jordan: 'And when he came up out of the water, immediately he saw the heavens being torn open and the Spirit descending on him like a dove. And a voice came from heaven, "You are my beloved Son; with you I am well pleased."' (1:10-11) Here is evidence of the Trinity: Jesus, the Holy Spirit (in the form of a dove) and the voice of the Father. Matthew says, "This is my beloved Son, with whom I am well pleased." (Matthew 3:17) This was a public statement announcing Christ and affirming him in ministry.

It was a momentous occasion and a dramatic event. Christ was empowered by the Holy Spirit and approved by the Father. Now that Jesus is anointed and approved it might be expected that he would launch into a public ministry of preaching, teaching and performing miracles. But that is not what happens. Surprisingly, he is sent out to the desert. It is amazing how (in the experience of many believers) a public stand in baptism is followed by a wilderness experience. God does not tempt us but he does allow trials. It is clear from this passage of Scripture that Christ's experience in that wilderness was a time of testing and temptation. Satan did not drive him into the desert. It was the Holy Spirit who sent him there. Therefore, this was part of God's plan for his beloved son, that he be tested and strengthened for the divine mission entrusted to him.

Mark does not give any detail about the nature of the temptations Christ endured but Matthew does:

Matthew 4:1-11

¹ Then Jesus was led up by the Spirit into the wilderness to be tempted by the devil. ² And after fasting forty days and forty nights, he was hungry. ³ And the tempter came and said to him, "If you are the Son of God, command these stones to become loaves of bread." ⁴ But he answered, "It is written,

"'Man shall not live by bread alone,
but by every word that comes from the mouth of God.'"

⁵ Then the devil took him to the holy city and set him on the pinnacle of the temple ⁶ and said to him, "If you are the Son of God, throw yourself down, for it is written,

"'He will command his angels concerning you,'

and

"'On their hands they will bear you up,
lest you strike your foot against a stone.'"

⁷ Jesus said to him, "Again it is written, 'You shall not put the Lord your God to the test.'" ⁸ Again, the devil took him to a very high mountain and showed him all the kingdoms of the world and their glory. ⁹ And he said to him, "All these I will give you, if you will fall down and worship me." ¹⁰ Then Jesus said to him, "Be gone, Satan! For it is written,

"'You shall worship the Lord your God
and him only shall you serve.'"

¹¹ Then the devil left him, and behold, angels came and were ministering to him.

Christ was engaged in the serious spiritual exercise of fasting. Those who enter that world of prayer, fasting, getting alone with God and focusing on ministry soon find themselves in a spiritual battle. When Jesus was at his weakest (physically) and when he was most vulnerable Satan tempted him. He was hungry and the tempter said "if". This is not a temptation about breaking his fast. It is not just about the physical need. Satan questioned Christ's identity, ministry and power. Satan likes to sow doubt when we are vulnerable. We might be physically tired, but the temptation is not just about that. The struggle is spiritual.

Jesus answered: "It is written, "'Man shall not live by bread alone, but by every word that comes from the mouth of God.'" Here he quotes Deuteronomy 8:3. His answer shows that he is well aware that the temptation is spiritual, not physical. It also shows a familiarity with the Scriptures. Our temptations too have a very real spiritual dimension. However, Satan does not give up. He says two can play that game and he now quotes Scripture (Psalm 91:11-12) and the battle intensifies: 'Then the devil took him to the holy city and set him on the pinnacle of the temple and said to him, "If you are the Son of God, throw yourself down, for it is written, "'He will command his angels concerning you,' and "'On their hands they will bear you up, lest you strike your foot against a stone.'" First Satan tried to *distract*, then he tries to *destroy*. Notice how Satan questions Christ's divine nature, "If you are the Son of God". He wants to sow doubt and reap discouragement. The history of heresy shows Satan using Scripture.

Satan does this with believers too. "If you are a Christian why don't you behave like one?" Of course, the believer's behavior ought to be holy but when we fail, as we inevitably do, he is there to make insinuations and dishearten. The devil knows Scripture very well but he twists it for evil purposes. It is encouraging to know that the Lord himself was tempted and therefore understands when his followers go through this experience. The writer to the Hebrews says: 'For because he himself has suffered when tempted, he is able to help those who are being tempted' (Hebrews 2:18). Jesus defends himself with the sword of the Word, "Again it is written, 'You shall not put the Lord your God to the test.'" Here Jesus is quoting Deuteronomy 6:16. The battle is based on Scripture and its proper interpretation, as it often is! Was this not true at the time of the Reformation?

In the third and final temptation, Matthew records that: 'Again, the devil took him to a very high mountain and showed him all the kingdoms of the world and their glory. And he said to him, "All these I will give you, if you will fall down and worship me." Here Satan wants to *derail* Jesus from his mission. Many are derailed in the spiritual life by wealth and fame. Now Satan's bargaining becomes bolder. He sees this as a fair trade off and offers wealth, glory and worldly power if Jesus submits to him. This is less subtle. It is a crude offer. The mask is off and the gloves are off now. He does not question Christ's divine nature now. Rather he says, "I will give you all of this if you will yield to me." Satan can reward those who submit to him. Many find what he has to offer attractive and they enter into a pact with him, often unconsciously. However, this is a pact that will cost your very soul. Materialism, power, fame, wealth; how many have traded their faith for these baubles? Notice Christ's answer: 'For it is written, '"You shall worship the Lord your God and him only shall you serve."' Here he quotes 1 Chronicles 21:1; Deuteronomy 6:13.

Satan is a determined and persistent enemy. On three occasions, Christ uses Scripture to defend himself and defeat the attack of Satan. If Jesus, being as he was, the Son of God / God the Son, used Scripture to protect himself spiritually then so should we. David said, 'I have stored up your word in my heart, that I might not sin against you.' (Psalm 119:11) When did Jesus memorize those verses? Perhaps it was in childhood. Maybe it was from frequently reading Scripture as a young man. This is how we are to withstand the attacks of the enemy. Some people think that Satan is a myth. If you believe that, he has already won the battle for your soul.

The apostle Paul writing to the Ephesians said:

Ephesians 6:11-17

¹¹ Put on the whole armor of God, that you may be able to stand against the schemes of the devil. ¹² For we do not wrestle against flesh and blood, but against the rulers, against the authorities, against the cosmic powers over this present darkness, against the spiritual forces of evil in the heavenly places.¹³ Therefore take up the whole armor of God, that you may be able to withstand in the evil day, and having done all, to stand firm. ¹⁴ Stand therefore, having fastened on the belt of truth, and having put on the breastplate of righteousness, ¹⁵ and, as shoes for your feet, having put on the readiness given by the gospel of peace. ¹⁶ In all circumstances take up the shield of faith, with which you can extinguish all the flaming darts of the evil one; ¹⁷ and take the helmet of salvation, and the sword of the Spirit, which is the word of God,

Three times, it says to 'stand'. We are expected to stand our ground, to withstand the attacks. Commentators vary about whether there would have been armor for the back but I am inclined to think not, because Paul does not mention any in this list. In *flight* mode, we are vulnerable but in *fight* mode, we can be victorious if we put on the whole armor of God. Paul tells us that the sword is the Word of God. Would you face the enemy with all this armor but without a sword? The sword is both a defensive and offensive weapon. The Christian must model Christ in all things, especially in becoming familiar with Scripture and using it in the spiritual battle.

Satan desires to have you, as he desired to have Peter. Many Christians have been through great temptations. God has brought them through. People are sometimes severely tested because God has a special ministry for them.⁵ The devil wants to distract them, sow seeds of doubt, question their spiritual identity and rob them of assurance. If he can't distract he will try to derail or destroy. In the history of the church times of revival are always associated with a return to the Word of God. In the Reformation, the Word took center stage. In churches where preaching is prized as something of great value there is strength but in churches where it is marginalized or devalued there is shallowness.

---

⁵ "God does **not** tempt us, but he does allow us to go through temptations. As we know from Abraham, God can test us, but never tempt us with sin. God allows us to face the trials that the natural course of life takes within this imperfect age. He allows us to face the trials of our own free will decisions. Simply being steadfast to a Christian life that is counterintuitive to the wicked world that we live in can be a trial that God has allowed.

The [above] text [from Matthew] specifically states that the Spirit led Jesus into the wilderness "to be tempted." How do we reconcile that Jesus is being led by the Spirit "to be" tempted?

First, (*Peirazo*) can be rendered either as "tempted" (ESV, NIV, LEB) or "tested" (CEV, MSG), but seeing that Satan is carrying this out, it is best to be rendered "tempted." This is not a literal versus a dynamic equivalent issue, because almost all dynamic equivalents have "tempted."

Second, God would have foreknown that Satan was going to tempt Jesus and that he would wait until his weakest moment to do so. What Satan would see as an opportunity to tempt Jesus, God may very well see as an opportunity to allow Jesus to be tested as he did with Abraham, establishing his faithfulness. Therefore, God allowed Jesus "to be" tempted/tested, which he used as a test to confirm what he would already know to be true, an evident demonstration of Jesus' faith. Jesus' actions would establish or demonstrate the Father's confidence in him. Jesus clearly revealed that his faith was a living faith." (Andrews 2013, 92-93)

We must learn to wield the Word like a sword in battle. Soldiers were not just given swords and sent out to battle. They were taught skills in using the sword. A lot could be learned naturally from frequently handling a sword and much could be learned from watching others using it. However, training is essential for soldiers. That is why soldiers could easily defeat civilian resistance. It was the soldier's skill that enabled him to conquer and be victorious. Do you want to be among the vanquished or the victorious? It is important that we learn to handle the Word well.

The apostle Paul advised the younger Timothy, 'Study to shew thyself approved unto God, a workman that needeth not to be ashamed, rightly dividing the word of truth.' (2 Timothy 2:15 KJV) In fact, Timothy was taught the Word of God from childhood, as his mother and grandmother were believers. In times of trial let us remember that Jesus knows and cares and he invites us to draw near to him for strength: 'For we do not have a high priest who is unable to sympathize with our weaknesses, but one who in every respect has been tempted as we are, yet without sin. Let us then with confidence draw near to the throne of grace, that we may receive mercy and find grace to help in time of need.'–Hebrews 4: 15-16.

Spurgeon wrote eloquently of the temptation of Christ in the wilderness:

> **"Then was Jesus led up of the Spirit into the wilderness to be tempted of the devil."** A Holy character does not avert temptation—Jesus was tempted. When Satan tempts us, his sparks fall upon tinder; but in Christ's case, it was like striking sparks on water; yet the enemy continued his evil work. Now, if the devil goes on striking when there is no result, how much more will he do it when he knows what inflammable stuff our hearts are made of. Though you become greatly sanctified by the Holy

Ghost, expect that the great dog of hell will bark at you still. In the haunts of men, we expect to be tempted, but even seclusion will not guard us from the same trial. Jesus Christ was led away from human society into the wilderness and was tempted of the devil. Solitude has its charms and its benefits and may be useful in checking the lust of the eye and the pride of life; but the devil will follow us into the most lovely retreats. Do not suppose that it is only the worldly-minded who have dreadful thoughts and blasphemous temptations, for even spiritual-minded persons endure the same; and in the holiest position we may suffer the darkest temptation. The utmost consecration of spirit will not insure you against Satanic temptation. Christ was consecrated through and through. It was His meat and drink to do the will of Him that sent Him: and yet He was tempted! Your hearts may glow with a seraphic flame of love to Jesus, and yet the devil will try to bring you down to Laodicean lukewarmness. If you will tell me when God permits a Christian to lay aside his armor, I will tell you when Satan has left off temptation. Like the old knights in war time, we must sleep with helmet and breastplate buckled on, for the arch-deceiver will seize our first unguarded hour to make us his prey. The Lord keep us watchful in all seasons, and give us a final escape from the jaw of the lion and the paw of the bear.[6] (Spurgeon 1995, February 21 AM)

---

[6] C.H. Spurgeon's *Morning and Evening*, iphone app 20th February, evening reading.

The calling of the first disciples (1:14-20)

This passage begins by stating that John the Baptist had been arrested. Serving God can bring trouble into one's life. John the Baptist proclaimed the truth about sin and judgment, which Herod resented, and John was imprisoned. This indicates what was to come for Jesus. The gospel causes division. People who want to continue in their sinful ways despise the gospel and the people who proclaim it. I remember being in Bellevue Baptist Church in Tennessee some years ago when Adrian Rogers was senior pastor there.[7] His sermons were broadcast on radio and because he preached the truth about homosexual practice (that it is sinful) gay activists / lobbyists mounted a protest outside his church. In much the same way John the Baptist, attracted the attention of Herod who had a sexually immoral lifestyle.

John's incarceration did not stop the message of the gospel being proclaimed. God's plan continued and now Jesus emerges in ministry. The first thing we notice about Jesus is that he was a preacher. Many people have an unbiblical view of Jesus as meek and mild, a person who would not offend anybody. Jesus did identify himself in these terms, so certainly, he was humble and generally gentle as a lamb but he could be and frequently was as ferocious as a lion, notably with the Pharisees. He is both the Lamb of God and the Lion of Judah. Jesus, like John, proclaimed the truth without fear or favor. The text states that it was the gospel of God that he proclaimed. This was and still is a divine message for mankind. As such, it is revelation, not speculation. It was and still is good news. It is not a human message but a

---

[7] The late Adrian Rogers, formerly three-time president of the Southern Baptist Convention, was pastor of Bellevue Baptist Church (a congregation of more than 28,000 members) for thirty-two years. He is known as one of the fathers of the Conservative Resurgence movement that brought the Southern Baptist Convention back to its biblical roots.

message from God. It is not a new philosophy. This is the unfolding of God's eternal plan. Jesus himself was at the center of that plan as the promised Messiah.

What did Jesus preach? Verse 15 states clearly that he proclaimed: "The time is fulfilled, and the kingdom of God is at hand; repent and believe in the gospel" (1:15). He proclaimed that the fullness of time had come and that the promise was now fulfilled. He announced the kingdom of God. He told people to "repent" and "believe". This is a summary of his message. This was his theme. Considering that John had been imprisoned for this kind of preaching it is very courageous. So we see Jesus bravely proclaiming the truth in a land where the secular authority had the power to punish and imprison and even put to death those who did so. Such courage is still evident today amongst many who proclaim the gospel in lands where dictators and monarchs despise the gospel rule of morality.

As Jesus was 'Passing alongside the Sea of Galilee, he saw Simon and Andrew the brother of Simon casting a net into the sea, for they were fishermen. And Jesus said to them: "'Follow me, and I will make you become fishers of men.'" (16-17). It seems almost casual rather than intentional that these particular men were called. What would have happened if they were not there on that day or if two other people were there instead? However, there is nothing accidental about this encounter.

In Acts 9, we read how the Lord told Ananias that Paul was "a chosen instrument...to carry my name before the Gentiles and kings and the children of Israel". Throughout Scripture, believers are called God's chosen ones. God selects us individually. He calls and commissions us in his service. Already we see how clever Jesus is in the way he calls Simon and Andrew. Right from the start, we see that there is something very interesting in the way Jesus speaks as he addresses fishermen and invites them to join him as fishers of men.

It was no small thing that Jesus asked them to do; to leave their livelihood and follow him. The Lord still calls people to follow him. He calls people to leave their self-sufficient ways, commit to him, and trust him. Many disciples have left good careers behind in order to follow Jesus. This is a challenge. If the Lord calls a person to a new role, he will equip and provide all that is needed so that his plans and purposes will be fulfilled. Notice these men 'immediately ... left their nets and followed him.' Maybe fishing was bad. Maybe they were fed up with it and this new direction could not be as bad as fishing! There was no questioning. There was no contract (no paper or electronic one anyway). There was no discussion about terms and conditions, no job description, no salary. It does not seem very attractive. But it was the most meaningful event in their otherwise ordinary lives.

Without hesitation, they followed. There must have been something very attractive about Jesus. Did they realize what they were letting themselves in for? Many of us have set out on our spiritual journeys in response to the call of Jesus. When we began, we did not know where that road would lead. We simply believed and it was fun for a while; an adventure. However, the road led to the sorrow of separation from friends. There was a cost and perhaps initially we did not know it would be like this. Perhaps we thought this new beginning would be bliss all the way. Nevertheless, there is a forsaking involved in following Christ.

Notice also that the call Christ issued to these men is more like a command than an invitation. Jesus expected them to comply. God expects those whom he calls to accept the privilege unquestioningly. The life of true discipleship is not always a pleasure but it is always a privilege. The call from Christ gives huge significance to these ordinary men. If they had not been called, they would have been lost in obscurity. This is true, not just of Simon and Andrew but of James and John. If they said "no" they would have been shrouded in infamy. However, they accepted the call and followed. It was immediate and complete obedience.

Let the Christian bear in mind that Jesus is the leader and they are just followers. It is amazing that God involves us at all in his kingdom. Jesus could have done all this on his own but he chose to involve ordinary people to fulfill his mission. He still invites people to be partners in his great plans and to participate in the affairs of the kingdom. He does not need us and yet he wants us. It is a great privilege to be involved in this partnership in the gospel. Those of us who are involved in it should have that sense of gratitude to the Lord that swelled our hearts in the infancy of this spiritual life.

There is always a forsaking of something in order to follow Jesus. We are called not just *to* something but also *from* something. The Christian is called from a particular way of life. This is a high calling on our lives. We are called from darkness to light, from the secular to the sacred or perhaps from false religion to true spirituality. Peter, writing on the theme of suffering and glory says of the first-century believer who emerged from Judaism: '...you were ransomed from the futile ways inherited from your forefathers' (1 Peter1:18). The same can be said for all who come to Christ from any institutionalized and dead religious heritage.

Not everyone is called to leave their secular occupation but all disciples are called to follow. What does that mean? It means not going our own way. Jesus leads the way. He goes before us. It means going in a particular direction. It means walking *away* from certain things and *towards* God. It means imitating Christ. It means learning from him and walking in his ways. He determines the direction. He sets the pace. We do not know where it will lead but we know that Christ's life was a sacrificial life. He calls us to serve.

So now, at this stage Jesus had two disciples. They were what we might call rookies or raw recruits, who knew nothing. How many followers does Jesus have today? Even Jesus started with a few people and invested in them. He taught them for three years. Then Jesus repeats the same thing: 'And going on a little farther, he saw James the son of Zebedee and John his brother, who were in their boat mending the nets. And immediately he called them, and they left their father Zebedee in the boat with the hired servants and followed him.' (19-20) Here he calls James and John, both fishermen and brothers, like Simon and Andrew. Here we see something of the cost of discipleship as they leave their father Zebedee. Zebedee had hired servants but his sons left the family business. They were repairing broken things, now they would learn to minister to broken people.

Abraham was called by God to leave one way of life and find friendship with God. That is what a life of faith is. It involves following step-by-step, staying close to the Lord and walking in his ways. It is a new direction, a new destiny and our lives have meaning and purpose. There is nothing wrong with being a fisherman. My near ancestors (uncles and grandfather) were fishermen. However, these first disciples were called to lives of far greater significance. They heard the call and heeded it. Perhaps Jesus is calling you to follow him, to become his disciple. Maybe you are already a disciple but now he is calling you to full-time service with a specific commission to go and make disciples. Do you hear the voice of God? There is much to distract, not least by way of alternative occupation. Are we attentive, obedient to his call and commissioning?

Jesus took care of these men, all his disciples, and even the hungry crowds that followed him out of curiosity. He fed them and taught them. His disciples were under his care. They were close to him. It all seems so simple and carefree at this point in their journey, but it would be a road marked with agony and ecstasy. It might seem to be a life of freedom from the mundane toil of earning a living by fishing, with all its hardships and perils. Nevertheless, there were things they did not understand, their hopes and expectations were to become frustrated, and the journey took them down the road of disappointment and fear to Calvary.

In recruiting these four men (Simon, Andrew, James and John) Jesus had now recruited one-third of his team. It was not that they had unique or special gifts or qualities, which were useful to God. If we were starting a movement, we would probably choose people with other/better skills, qualifications and experience. Jesus had the power to multiply fish miraculously to feed thousands of people. He did not need fishermen. Later, when Christ was crucified, they became disillusioned and returned to their old way of life as fishermen. That is what people do when they experience trauma. They go back to the place where things were simpler and safer. Yet, God met them in their despair and restored them to the right path. Their lives were utterly changed as a result of knowing Jesus.

We can never go back. There is nothing back there. We are called to follow him and that means learning from him and living as he wants us to live. Jesus passes by and calls people. How very sad that many do not heed the call. He invites us to forsake the old life, to follow him in friendship and fellowship. It is an invitation to join his family of redeemed souls. May God enable us to hear and heed his call, not just for salvation as a once-off transaction, but also for service in the kingdom today!

Jesus drives out an evil spirit (1:21-29)

On our journey, so far, we have looked at John the Baptist preparing the way for Jesus, his fearless preaching and his imprisonment. We have witnessed the baptism and temptation of Jesus and the cosmic struggle between Christ and Satan in the wilderness. We noted how persistent the devil was and how Jesus resisted temptation by defending himself and defeating Satan with Scripture. We observed the summoning of the first disciples (Simon, Andrew, James and John) and what it means to follow Jesus.

Now we encounter the Lord driving out an evil spirit. Here we see Jesus once again opposing the powers of darkness. With his small group of disciples, he went to Capernaum and when the Sabbath came, he went into the synagogue to teach. We do not know what he taught on that occasion, but we do know that whatever it was it amazed his hearers. His style of teaching was different to that of the rabbis because he spoke with authority.

I remember when I first heard real teaching of Scripture; it was alive, not a dead letter. I recognized that it was different to the homilies I had heard before. The textbook (the Bible) was the same but the interpretation and application was different and so too was the conviction and passion of the person speaking. It came with force and power and appealed to my mind, heart and will. The preacher was an authentic believer and there was a note or tone in his voice that rang true, something about him that was quantitatively different. Many of the 'sermons' I had heard up to that point were dull and uninteresting. They seemed to be rattled off without any real understanding that this was the living Word of God, which could transform people's lives. However, the Holy Spirit quickened my heart and opened my mind to hear and understand the Scriptures.

It appears from the passage we are considering that the teachers of the law were not as interesting to listen to as Jesus. Even though it was the same law (Scripture) that Jesus used, there was something special in the way he handled it. He aroused and sustained the attention of his listeners and they were amazed. They recognized the difference between the dead letter and the living Word. Here is a cameo of Jesus the teacher, fascinating those who heard him with insight and authority. The Pharisees had power as establishment figures but Jesus had the authority of heaven. These are different things. The Pharisees were the religious elite. They had control but no influence. They drove the people but Jesus led them and they willingly followed the Good Shepherd. If you drive sheep, they will be afraid. However, they will follow the one who feeds them and tenderly cares for them. The Pharisees exerted force and they burdened the people with extra-biblical rules and regulations. They magnified the law and minimized grace. Therefore, here is Jesus teaching in the synagogue on the Sabbath 'as one who had authority'. Christ's power was different because he was the authorized one sent from heaven. He has that divine sanction and that was evident in his teaching.

There was an incident in the synagogue. A man who was possessed by an evil spirit cried out "What have you to do with us, Jesus of Nazareth? Have you come to destroy us? I know who you are---the Holy One of God." To possess means to own. Here is a man who was created by God but under the controlling power of evil. Christ came into the world to liberate those under the controlling influence of the devil and his demons. This wretched man is a miserable soul occupied, preoccupied and dominated by demonic power. His mind was enslaved to evil. Christ's teaching in the synagogue was not only effectively undermining the authority of the scribes and Pharisees but his very presence was a threat to the dominion of darkness and there was a disturbance in the spiritual realm.

If Mark had not told us that an evil spirit possessed this man, we might not know it from his words alone. He calls out: "What have you to do with us, Jesus of Nazareth? Have you come to destroy us? I know who you are---the Holy One of God." The "us" that he refers to might simply mean the

Jews in general or this particular religious community in Capernaum. So he might simply have been speaking as a Jew (in the synagogue on the Sabbath) asking Christ how his message fits in with Judaism. His question, "Have you come to destroy us?" might be taken to mean: "Is your teaching going to undermine our religion and draw people away from it to some new order?" However, we have Mark's comments and the wider context to show us the reality that this man was possessed by an evil spirit. This does not simply mean that he was a bad-minded sort of individual with a contrary personality. It means that he was in the grip of the powers of darkness!

In this opening chapter of Mark's Gospel, we see Satan and his servants interacting with Jesus. Satan tried to distract, derail and destroy Jesus. Now this demonic spirit clearly recognizes Christ. He refers to him by name as "Jesus of Nazareth". Not only that but he goes on to declare openly that he knows the true spiritual and divine nature of Christ. Thus he acknowledges that Jesus is "the Holy One of God." Even demons know the truth. But they do not submit to it and they are not controlled by it. What the man said was true but it was a reaction to the presence and teaching of Christ. A spontaneous outburst exposed his true spiritual condition. When preaching is Christ-centered and anointed by the Holy Spirit it can provoke hostile responses. Christ's teaching astonished the people who heard it but it disturbed demons. Then Jesus rebuked him saying, "Be silent, and come out of him!" Jesus spoke sternly, not to the man, but to the demon that possessed the man. Christ commanded him to be quiet and ordered the demon to come out of him. The exorcism was instant: 'And the unclean spirit, convulsing him and crying out with a loud voice, came out of him'.

The cynic might say this was all stage-managed like the healing marquis[8] shows and T.V. trick-pony events. They say

---

[8] Movie house

that physicians in medieval times used to advise people to open the windows of their houses and let the demons out and that the real efficacy of such action was in letting fresh air in. Others less skeptical but doubting the miraculous might say that this man was an epileptic. They would contend that this primitive society did not know what that condition was so they called it 'demon possession'. The implication is that they now know better. This might seem like a plausible argument because Scripture itself seems to mix up these two distinct things. For example, Matthew records an occasion when Jesus healed a boy with a demon:

Matthew 17:14-18

[14] And when they came to the crowd, a man came up to him and, kneeling before him, [15] said, "Lord, have mercy on my son, for he is an epileptic and he suffers terribly. For often he falls into the fire, and often into the water. [16] And I brought him to your disciples, and they could not heal him." [17] And Jesus answered, "O faithless and twisted generation, how long am I to be with you? How long am I to bear with you? Bring him here to me." [18] And Jesus rebuked the demon, and it came out of him, and the boy was healed instantly.

However, the boy's father misdiagnoses the problem. Scripture does not say he was an epileptic. Rather this man says it. Not everything in Scripture is to be taken at face value. There is a proper way of interpreting. The argument that epilepsy was misunderstood as demon possession (because of the similarity of symptoms, such as convulsions) does not hold up because Scripture recognizes epilepsy and the difference between it and demon possession.

Speaking of Jesus Matthew says, 'So his fame spread throughout all Syria, and they brought him all the sick, those afflicted with various diseases and pains, those oppressed by demons, epileptics, and paralytics, and he healed them' (Matthew 4:24). Both secularism and superstition have popularized false notions about demon possession. Christ performed exorcisms in his ministry, including this one recorded in the first chapter of Mark. Christ gave his disciples the power to expel demons through faith and prayer.

There are different kinds, causes and degrees of demonic influence. Spiritual discernment is needed in any such diagnosis. Primarily there are two kinds of demonic influence. First, there is indirect rule through sin whereby fallen man is self-centered rather than God centered. In this way, all of humanity is under the rule of Satan. Second, there is direct influence through sin (rebellion against God).

The causes of demonic influence are rebellion against God such as blasphemy against the divinity of Christ and atheism. False religions are idolatrous and pagan. Occult practices cause demonic influence. Dabbling in Ouija boards, séances, tarot cards, horoscopes, fortune telling, psychics and mediums is dicing with the devil. It does not matter that these things are commonly practiced or that they are indulged light-heartedly, naively or frivolously. They are dangerous.

Forms of Eastern mysticism such as transcendental meditation are dodgy. So too is indulging in drugs and pornography, as they involve the abandonment of self-control and often lead to addiction. Reiki and yoga are also dubious practices and often open the door to demonic activity. This may seem to be an extreme statement. It is not the physical exercise of yoga that is problematic but the mystical and meditational aspect, which can become a quasi-religious mental orientation. Beware of any alternative medicine that has its roots in eastern mysticism such as acupuncture. There are many things widely believed to be harmless. If they are harmless or ineffective, why waste time and money on such things. People might indulge in them innocently but that does not mean that they are harmless.

Some of these so-called panaceas are more the work of autosuggestion than the devil but they are not harmless.

Beware of the New Age Movement and new revelations of false Christs / prophets. Beware of the cults, which lead their adherents into a demonic bondage of conscience. Beware of pride and self-glorification. These were attributes of Lucifer. Historically the cult of emperor worship (Nero and Hitler) was demonic and this is evident in the profoundly evil acts they authorized.

Today this demonic activity is practiced in North Korea. Much of godless philosophy and psychology and their so-called non-judgmental approaches to counseling are questionable. Certain political ideologies can be anti-Christian and lead one into harmful ways of thinking (e.g., humanism, communism and fascism). These things can become a channel for the demonic. One wonders if groups such as the Taliban are ruled from the headquarters of Satan.

Perversion (homosexuality, heterosexual promiscuity and pedophilia) can open the door to demonic influence. Some kinds of violence (torture, rape and abortion) are manifestations of demonic activity. It is not always possible to say exactly where the dividing lines might be drawn between human depravity, diabolical activity and demonic possession.[9]

---

[9] **Genesis 6:5 The American Translation (AT)**
⁵ When the LORD saw that the wickedness of man on the earth was great, and that the **whole bent of his thinking was** never anything but **evil**, the LORD regretted that he had ever made man on the earth.

Genesis 8:21 The American Translation (AT)
²¹ I will never again curse the soil, though the **bent of man's mind** may be **evil from his very youth**; nor ever again will I ever again destroy all life creature as I have just done.

Jeremiah 17:9 English Standard Version (ESV) ⁹ The heart is deceitful above all things, and desperately sick; who can understand it?

Some are more mentally bent toward wickedness and evil than others are, namely, (serial murders, pedophiles, homosexuals, drug addicts, drunkards, extreme lust, and the like). However, this does not

Were the crimes of Moira Hindley and Ian Brady (the moors murders) that tortured, raped and killed several children in the 1960s in England, demonic? They enjoyed sadomasochistic sex (and made audio recordings of their victims suffering) which includes the aptly named practice of 'bondage' sex. What about people who make snuff movies[10] today? One wonders if some (if not all) of the priests, who were pedophiles in recent Irish history were under demonic influence. What about the evil actions of people like Marc Dutroux, the Belgian serial killer and child molester convicted of having kidnapped, tortured and sexually abused six girls during 1995 to 1996, four of whom he murdered? What about Josef Fritzl, the Austrian who for twenty-seven years imprisoned and raped his daughter Elisabeth thousands of times in his basement-dungeon, where she gave birth to a total of seven of his children? Are these shocking and depraved acts the outcome of human depravity or is there some kind of demonic influence? These are high profile cases, but such things go on all the time in this fallen world. It is sickening and heartbreaking.

In certain cultures, curses, spells and voodoo are dark spiritual arts connected to Satan. In our society, magic can have a dark side too. In western culture the recent obsession with angels and the inappropriate roles attributed to them, especially as spiritual mediators, is rather worrying. Even certain kinds of music can take people on a path to spiritual bondage.

---

give him an excuse to indulge in his leanings toward a particular direction. It simply means more effort on his part, i.e., putting on the new person (Eph. 4:20-24; Col. 3:9-10). One's leanings, desires may drive him toward gross sin, but his determination, Christian counseling, and the Holy Spirit can dominate where he ends up. Moreover, have no doubt, Satan and his demons play off our sinful inclinations.

[10] A snuff film is a pornographic movie or video that allegedly ends with the murder of one of the participants in a sex act (slang).—Encarta Dictionary

We do not want to be paranoid about such things, but we should not be naïve either. Many people today will deny the existence of evil, but the realities mentioned above (and we could cite volumes of such incidents) show that such denial is ludicrous. Temptation to sin comes to all, obsession to sin comes to many and possession comes to some. Christ can bring deliverance.

In the passage in Mark that we are considering, the response of those who witnessed the casting out of this demon is one of amazement. They were amazed with his teaching, both the content and style: 'And they were all amazed, so that they questioned among themselves, saying, "What is this? A new teaching with authority!' They were astonished that he had authority over demons: "He commands even the unclean spirits, and they obey him." The point is being made here in Mark's Gospel that Jesus has authority over the powers of darkness. This led to word about Jesus spreading, 'And at once his fame spread everywhere throughout all the surrounding region of Galilee'. Those who witnessed this incident in the synagogue might not have become disciples, but they certainly bore testimony about Jesus. They talked about him, his teaching and his power over unclean spirits.

Christ's disciples are his witnesses and must gossip the gospel. We must bear testimony to the one who has fought the spiritual battle on our behalf and liberated us from the powers of darkness. The good news of the gospel is that such redemption is available to all who trust call on Jesus' name!

Jesus heals many (1:29-34)

As we continue our journey with Jesus in this passage of Scripture, we see the Lord entering the home of two of his disciples. It is a natural outcome of true discipleship that Jesus should enter our homes. Presumably, Jesus went there for rest and refreshment. Here we see the disciples are serving Christ by opening up their home to him and the presence of Jesus in that home brought great blessing to that home and the wider community. The text tells us that 'Simon's mother-in-law lay ill with a fever, and immediately they told him about her'. The first thing we should notice here is that Simon Peter was married. He was not celibate. He had a mother-in-law and she was ill.

Simon and Andrew tell Jesus about the woman's condition. They had just witnessed the miracle in the synagogue where Jesus cast out a demon from a man possessed. I am sure that in telling Jesus about this woman they were hoping that he could help her and as such, this was a prayer of sorts. We do not know where Peter's wife was; possibly present but not mentioned, possibly away on that occasion (fetching water or buying food for the household). It is possible that she was deceased, but all of this is speculation. We are not told anything about Peter's wife. I suspect that she was not in the house at the time because if she was then she would have been the one expected to provide hospitality to Jesus.

Anyway, Simon and Andrew tell Jesus about Peter's mother-in-law in hope and expectation. We can talk *about* the sick and talk *to* the sick but we must tell Jesus about our loved ones. In prayer, we can come to him with hope and expectation. Moreover, Jesus does not disappoint. He took the woman by the hand and helped her up, 'and the fever left her, and she began to serve them'. He goes to her when she could not come to him. This is another miracle, but closer to home. Simon and Andrew had witnessed an amazing miracle in the synagogue. It was a spiritual happening in a spiritual place. It is one thing to observe the activity of Christ in the synagogue but another thing to witness the power of Christ demonstrated in our homes. Miracles are not just for others in the church (synagogue) but also for us, in answer to our requests, for those close to us. Somebody in the family receives the touch of the Lord. Does somebody in your family need the touch of the Lord today? She is made well, and her recovery is so complete and swift that she is able to serve them.

It might seem a little unfair to us that the woman is just out of her sick bed when she has duties to attend. It might seem inappropriate that Simon and Andrew should have brought Jesus there in the first place, as the woman was sick. It might seem peculiar to the modern mind that these men did not serve and allow the woman to rest! But she did not need to recuperate because she was completely better. I think it would have been humiliating for her if she could not offer hospitality to a guest, especially to one who functioned as a rabbi (teacher in the synagogue). Therefore, Jesus healed her and in doing so enabled her to do what she really would like to do. What a great privilege it is to serve Jesus. We too have been healed,

Isaiah 53:4-5

4 Surely he has borne our griefs
    and carried our sorrows;
yet we esteemed him stricken,
    smitten by God, and afflicted.
5 But he was pierced for our transgressions;
    he was crushed for our iniquities;
upon him was the chastisement that brought us peace,
    and with his wounds we are healed.

We are healed to serve, and it is a privilege we should enjoy.

Word got out somehow that Jesus was in that home and that he had brought healing and blessing to that home. Is that true of our homes? What word of Christ's power and blessing will be spread abroad about us? Many people came to that house because of Jesus. They brought the sick, the demon possessed, and Jesus healed many of various diseases and drove out evil spirits. There was a healing epidemic! Jesus still heals today in answer to prayer: 'Behold, the LORD's hand is not shortened, that it cannot save, or his ear dull, that it cannot hear' (Isaiah 59:1).[11] Scripture tells us that 'Jesus Christ is the same yesterday and today and forever' (Hebrews 13:8) and that he is consistent in character and power: "For I the LORD do not change" (Malachi 3:6). Let us offer service to the Lord, not in payment for his healing but in gratitude. Let us tell Jesus about the sick and tell the sick about the healer.

In this passage of Scripture, the power of God was made manifest. Heaven was declaring, "This is my beloved son in whom I am well pleased". It was not just a voice from heaven as happened at Christ's baptism. It was more than words. The kingdom was inaugurated with power and this is absolutely clear in the signs and wonders performed by Jesus. We need that today. We need vital encounters with God in our experience. We need the voice from heaven. We need the Scriptures to affirm who Jesus is. However, we should have more than that. We should be first-hand witnesses of the great power of God demonstrated in miraculous ways.

Simon and Andrew must have been so glad that they told Jesus about Simon's mother-in-law. They could have thought, "We should not bother Jesus now, he has been teaching in the synagogue and he performed a miracle there, but now we should just let him rest." Yet, they cared about this sick woman and felt compelled to tell Jesus. What an excellent outcome! The woman was made well, and the faith of these disciples must have been strengthened. They believed enough to ask and that faith was rewarded. Will we ask on behalf of

---

[11] In reference to modern day miraculous healings, Christian Publishing House would suggest the following article, so as to have a balanced view, **Does God Step in and Solve Our Every Problem Because We are Faithful?** http://www.christianpublishers.org/prayer-does-god-answer

others? The outcome can be the same for us. It might not be the Lord's will to heal in all circumstances but at least we should ask. Jesus had demonstrated his power over demons, now he displays his power over sickness. His activity authenticates his true identity as God the Son! People will come to the home where Jesus dwells. They will be drawn in hope of healing. In addition, those who come to him in faith must do so knowing that he has the power to heal today. Christ brings hope to needy homes and heals us for service in the kingdom.

Jesus prays in a solitary place (1:35-39)

Jesus rises before dawn and goes away to a solitary place where he can be alone in prayer. He had displayed tremendous power over demons and sickness. He had a busy day the day before where he taught in the synagogue and delivered a man from demon possession. Later that same day he restored Peter's mother-in law to health and healed many who came to Peter's home. There he also cast out many demons. Therefore, if anybody was entitled to a lie in, breakfast in bed or a day off it was Jesus. But we see him taking time before the busyness of the day to pray. This is an important pattern for all disciples of Jesus. In fact it is an essential element of the spiritual life. The Christian needs to spend time alone with God, the heavenly Father.

Jesus must have known that there would be many pressing demands on his time and attention during that day. So he prepared himself spiritually for whatever might lie ahead. Are we following the example of Christ in this matter or do we rush headlong into the day, unprepared? Jesus connected with heaven. This was the source of his strength and power. If we are weak and not experiencing a victorious life we should look to this matter and put things right. If Jesus felt the need to commune with heaven how much more, we need to do so! We need to charge our batteries regularly. Some Christians charge their mobile (cell) phones more often than their souls in prayer. If you were going to some important occasion (say a graduation/conferring ceremony or wedding) you would be sure to charge the battery in your camera. If you were going to be away from home you would be sure to have your laptop and mobile phone juiced up to the maximum. Yet, many neglect this discipline and then wonder why they are struggling to cope with the difficulties of life. We are all busy but we need to get alone with God and have that vital communion with him, so that we can face whatever lies ahead. There are quantitative and qualitative dimensions to prayer and so it ought to be both frequent and fervent.

The hymn by Joseph Scriven (1820-1886) identifies the great privilege of prayer:

> What a Friend we have in Jesus, all our sins and griefs to bear!
> What a privilege to carry everything to God in prayer!
> O what peace we often forfeit, O what needless pain we bear,
> All because we do not carry everything to God in prayer.
>
> Have we trials and temptations? Is there trouble anywhere?
> We should never be discouraged; take it to the Lord in prayer.
> Can we find a friend so faithful who will all our sorrows share?
> Jesus knows our every weakness; take it to the Lord in prayer.
>
> Are we weak and heavy laden, cumbered with a load of care?
> Precious Savior, still our refuge, take it to the Lord in prayer.
> Do your friends despise, forsake you? Take it to the Lord in prayer!
> In His arms He'll take and shield you; you will find a solace there.
>
> Blessed Savior, Thou hast promised Thou wilt all our burdens bear
> May we ever, Lord, be bringing all to Thee in earnest prayer.
> Soon in glory bright unclouded there will be no need for prayer
> Rapture, praise and endless worship will be our sweet portion there.[12]

---

[12] Words by Joseph Scriven, 1855. Scriven wrote this hymn to comfort his mother, who was across the sea from him in Ireland. It was originally published anonymously, and Scriven did not receive full credit for almost thirty years.

Jesus ensured that he could not be easily disturbed. We too need to get away from the distractions and have this daily retreat with God. God is always near and can be accessed any time in prayer. The almighty is available and accessible. Still, our relationship with God must be more than launching occasional prayer missiles and submitting shopping lists or wish lists. Any meaningful relationship is based on the quantity and quality of communication that exists. If we spend time in the presence of God, it will be of immense benefit to us as individuals. It will also enrich all our other human relationships with family, friends, colleagues, neighbors and casual acquaintances. All our daily encounters will be better if we spend time with God. Time spent in prayer is an investment in our own spiritual life. But it enhances all our other relationships because our attitudes are being conformed to the will of God. If our attitudes are right, then our actions and reactions will be more likely pleasing to God. Prayer paves the way for peace of mind in the stresses of life. Prayer is a vital part of the process of sanctification whereby we are being transformed into the likeness of Christ. The apostle Paul writing to Christians in Rome said:

Romans 12:1-2

[1] I appeal to you therefore, brothers, by the mercies of God, to present your bodies as a living sacrifice, holy and acceptable to God, which is your spiritual worship. [2] Do not be conformed to this world, but be transformed by the renewal of your mind, that by testing you may discern what is the will of God, what is good and acceptable and perfect.

Maybe your prayerlessness is not because you do not understand the importance, privilege, and value of this spiritual exercise. Maybe it has nothing to do with your business. It might be simply that you do not know what are proper matters about which you are to pray. If this is so then you can take the example of Christ from John 17 and pray for yourself (we know our issues best). We can pray for

Christians in our immediate circle, especially in our local church or fellowship as this promotes good relations and nurtures harmony. We can pray for all believers, especially those in the persecuted church. If we do not know, let Jesus teach us how we ought to pray.

Luke 11:2-4 New King James Version (NKJV)

² So He said to them, "When you pray, say:

Our Father in heaven,
Hallowed be Your name.
Your kingdom come.
Your will be done
On earth as *it is* in heaven.
³ Give us day by day our daily bread.
⁴ And forgive us our sins,
For we also forgive everyone who is indebted to us.
And do not lead us into temptation,
But deliver us from the evil one."[13]

This prayer teaches us that we have unrestricted access to our heavenly Father. It teaches us that we belong to his family and that we can have a dynamic, living relationship with him. It invites us to approach God with confidence in the knowledge that he desires fellowship with us. We should delight in such communion.

Not only are we his children but we are part of the universal family of those who call God their Father through faith in Jesus Christ. Our God is the majestic deity who rules from heaven. We should pray that our lives as Christians will reflect well on the great name of Jesus. We can pray that his name will be honored in our lives, homes and churches, in other words, for our testimony. Let us pray that God's

---

[13] Note that this is a model, or a basic pattern of the way we are to pray, not that it should be repeated over and over again, from memory, or some prayer book. The above prayer gives us some examples of what to pray about and prioritizes them as to importance.

kingdom will come in our hearts so that he not only resides there but reigns there also. We can pray that the kingdom of God would be established and strengthened in places where Christianity is repressed. We can pray that the revealed redemptive will of God (in his Word), be disseminated, read, preached, taught, understood and accepted. There may be times when we wonder about God's will in our own circumstances. We may be perplexed and confused and wonder what is happening. At such times, and indeed at all times let us pray that his will be done. This prayer tells us to pray for our physical needs. We should not take them or anything else for granted. There are many in today's world, including Christians, who lack the basic necessities of life such as food, shelter and clothing. Let us pray for them and give to them from the abundance with which the Lord has blessed us. Let us pray especially for those who are imprisoned for their faith. In many cases, the person imprisoned is the breadwinner and the family is left without any means of support. Pray that God's grace will be made increasingly manifest in the hearts of his people, so that we will be known for our capacity and willingness to forgive others. Pray that no root of bitterness takes hold in our lives (resentments, grievances). This prayer teaches us that we can pray for deliverance from the assaults of the evil one. The persecuted church today needs us to join with them in this prayer that they will be delivered from the attacks of the evil one. The Lord's Prayer teaches us to pray. Therefore, we are without excuse. Let us not neglect this great privilege.

Simon and his companions go looking for Jesus and find him in prayer in a quiet place. They reproach the Lord for not meeting their expectations: "Everyone is looking for you," they said. How like them we are in this regard. Sometimes we go searching for Jesus with that attitude, where were you? They did not realize the importance of prayer and needed to learn from the Master. They wanted Jesus to do their bidding. They were no longer glad witnesses to the power of God. They wanted to control it.

However, Jesus had other plans. He was not going to return to that place. Jesus wanted to go to the nearby villages to preach. He told the disciples that was why he had come into the world. Today some Christians want to move away from preaching and yet they claim to be followers of Jesus. They think it is old fashioned and irrelevant and their gatherings will not have any preaching. Jesus was a preacher! He came into the world to preach the gospel. We learn from this passage that he was an itinerant preacher. He travelled throughout Galilee preaching in their synagogues and driving out demons. He was a man with a mission and a message. He was immersed in the Word of God and in prayer. He had power and authority and he exercised it against the powers of darkness. Christ's ministry was focused on spreading the message of the gospel. He wanted to reach those who had not heard. He walked away from communities who had heard enough and seen enough to believe but had no faith.

When Simon and those who were with him found Jesus they said, "Everyone is looking for you." There is a tone of disapproval in the accusatory way they say this. It is as if they are saying, "We have better things for you to do". They seem to think there are more pressing practical needs and prayer is hindering Christ from fulfilling duties that are more important. If we set aside time for prayer, we need not be surprised if others (people close to us who should know better) become resentful. They have other expectations. There are duties to attend to (even spiritual duties). But we must not be distracted from prayer or undervalue the importance of prayer. People recognized Christ's authority in preaching because his mind was saturated in the Scriptures and his heart was bathed in prayer. Spiritual power is obtained through prayer. Our service too must be saturated in prayer if it is to be effective.

Jesus cleanses a leper (1: 40-45)

Here is the story of a leprous man who met the Lord and Master of mankind. He was a man with a serious and contagious disease of the skin that at its worst damaged nerves and caused disfigurement. The word 'leprosy' in the Bible refers to various dermatological disorders. I do not want to get hung up on technicalities, so suffice to say that whatever condition this man was in it caused him to come to Christ and plead for cleansing. We do not know the full extent of the problem. He may have been hideously disfigured or not but we do know that as a leper he was deemed to be unclean and as such he was an untouchable outcast from society.

This incident reveals the compassionate character of Christ. By focusing on it we see what Jesus did for that man and it stimulates us to think of what he has done for us. May it also inspire us to believe that he can radically transform the lives of others, especially those that are rejected by society! Compassion is more than sorrow or pity. The Pocket Oxford Dictionary defines compassion as 'pity inclining one to help or be merciful'. Christ-like compassion brings to fruition that inclination to help.

This leprous man met the Lord and Master in his wretched and pitiful condition and begged him on his knees. Another gospel account (Luke) tells us he 'fell on his face and begged him.' (5:12) The posture this man assumes and the compassionate response of Jesus indicate that the skin-disorder was nothing less than what we know as leprosy. The context makes it difficult to think of it as anything less and it is certainly not some kind of rash! It is reasonable to assume, therefore, that his condition was chronic. In fact, Luke tells us that he was 'a man full of leprosy' (5:12). It is worth bearing in mind that Luke was a physician, who would have observed the detail very keenly indeed.

Leviticus 13 outlines regulations concerning infectious skin diseases. Chapter 14 of Leviticus outlines the detailed regulations to be observed in relation to cleansing from infectious skin diseases. They relate to ceremonial cleansing after the priest has examined the person and after healing has taken place. In other words, they were not a ritual cure! The Judaic law clearly stated, "The leprous person who has the disease shall wear torn clothes and let the hair of his head hang loose, and he shall cover his upper lip and cry out, 'Unclean, unclean.' He shall remain unclean as long as he has the disease. He is unclean. He shall live alone. His dwelling shall be outside the camp" (Leviticus 13:45-46). Yet this man came into the middle of a crowd and within arms-length of Jesus.

Here is a man who was shunned. Can you imagine the loneliness? Can you imagine the pain of separation; perhaps even from loved ones? There may very well have been a loss of livelihood. Imagine the awfulness of the absence of intimacy. Consider the damage to his self-esteem and confidence. Imagine the shame, the stigma, and the rejection. He lived either alone or with other lepers. It was a bleak situation. We do not know how long he was in that condition. He was obviously aware that his condition was beyond his control. It was bad enough for him to take desperate measures. That is what his coming to Christ is, an act of desperation conceived in hope.

To whom could he turn? There was no cure for leprosy. No physician could help him. To affect a cure was a task beyond all human power. Lepers were quarantined from the community and so he was separated and segregated irrespective of family ties or occupational considerations. I wonder if he had heard of Jesus or perhaps seen him from a distance. Maybe the miracles of Jesus were a topic of conversation in the leper colony. Were they saddened that Jesus had not yet cured a leper? Nobody had cured a leper since the days of Elisha when Naaman was cured. That story would have been part of his traditional religious lore and perhaps it permitted this nameless man to allow hope to enter and grow in his heart. Although his identity is not known to us, he is a real person and not a type invented for moral instruction. This is not a parable. He nurtured and cherished that hope until it grew into faith. So by the time we meet him he is publicly acknowledging his faith in Christ with these words, "If you will, you can make me clean." He does not doubt that Christ *could* cure him, but he cannot be certain if Christ *would* cure him.

Maybe he thought that Jesus would not even look upon him because he was loathsome. It is possible that many doctors, priests and teachers of the law had brushed him aside. We must remember that there is no record that this man had witnessed any miracle of the Master firsthand. There must have been rumors. We have the benefit of hindsight through the gospel accounts. He hadn't yet seen that divine compassion for himself. But he was about to experience the grace of God in his life. Jesus would look at him with eyes full of compassion and speak to him in a compassionate tone.

He did not doubt that Jesus could help him, but it remained to be seen if Jesus would help him. He could at least try; he had nothing to lose and everything to gain. However, there was one remaining difficulty; how could he gain access to Jesus? He could not go into the town to seek him. As a leper, he was forbidden to enter the crowd that usually surrounded Jesus. However, he could wait on the road to Capernaum. Imagine him waiting there alone and then the moment arrives. He hears the noise of a crowd and his heart pounds as Jesus approaches. The one who could deliver him from this horrible bondage is approaching. This leprous man comes up close to Jesus and drops on his knees and cries out "If you will, you can make me clean." He had done it. How would Jesus respond? It probably felt as if the clock had stopped as he waited to hear from Jesus. But that agonizing moment of suspense was very brief. There was no protracted delay. Our text says, 'Moved with pity, he stretched out his hand and touched him and said to him, "I will; be clean." And immediately the leprosy left him, and he was made clean.' He was instantly cured.

This man had acknowledged his own miserable condition. In coming to Christ, he declared that he was ready to receive mercy and that Jesus was able to dispense it. He made a passionate appeal. There were no preliminaries, no introduction, customary salutation or greeting. He came very directly to the point. He had one opportunity and he was determined not to miss it. I wonder if you have ever noticed that he does not actually ask Jesus, directly, to heal him. Is that not extraordinary? Rather he makes a very profound statement of faith. This man had grasped the very important truth that Jesus had the power and authority to make him well. In short, he was saying you can do it: will you?

Look at the response of Christ. He did not say, "I want you to learn from your suffering." He did not say, "Curing one leper won't make much difference in a suffering world." He did not say, "My mission is spiritual, not physical. Go to a physician". He healed him. The master could have healed him with a word, but he went beyond words and touched him! This is not an insignificant detail. Here is a man who had not been touched for some time: a man whose presence was detested by others. However, Christ was filled with compassion. Whichever way we look at it, he had compassion and used it powerfully or he had power and used it compassionately. Jesus was overwhelmed (moved) and issued a command that had all the force and authority of heaven. This miracle, like all miracles, demonstrates the power of God but it is also an important insight into the compassionate nature of God. The miracles authenticate his authority and validate his divine identity. Nevertheless, Jesus was not trying to prove his true identity by demonstrating his power. This was no public relations exercise designed to attract a greater following. In fact, we learn from the rest of the account that Jesus wanted it hushed up. It is not that Christ had an ulterior motive in ministering to this man, rather it is simply that he was moved. He healed out of love for the sufferer.

Jesus touching this man would have shocked onlookers who knew of the ritual uncleanness of lepers. Jesus set him free out of love. It was a compassion that expressed itself in gracious deed. Although this is a story about physical healing there is a spiritual parallel in that this is what Christ has done for all sinners "He took our illnesses and bore our diseases." (Matthew 8:17; Isaiah 53:4) What a beautiful story it is: such a tender outpouring of God's heart.

Imagine what it must have been like for this miserable man to look into the face of Jesus. Imagine what it must have been like for him to see such tenderness in those eyes. Can we even begin to understand the emotions he experienced when he felt the touch of Jesus' hand? He heard the words he desperately desired to hear and he must have heard them in a tone of voice saturated in love. It is ironic but it is enough to make us envy this leper! He had a hideous disease and was transformed in an instant because he threw himself upon the goodwill of Jesus and did not find him begrudging in dispensing bountiful grace. It is very unsatisfactory in life to depend on the goodwill of others for our happiness or wellbeing. People are fickle, frail and flawed. Perhaps you are conscious of your own great need and aware that only Jesus offers hope. Will you put yourself on the road where you can meet with Jesus and have that vital life-transforming encounter with him? Will you humble yourself before him and call out for help? Will you look into the face of Jesus to behold the tender compassion of his eyes upon you? Will you come so close to him that you may feel his touch? Come and hear the loving voice of the Savior.

This man deeply touched the sympathies of Jesus. The incident shows Jesus acting in character. The direct appeal of the leper's question cut a passage to the heart of Christ because it petitioned his true nature. That nature has not changed. 'Jesus Christ is the same yesterday, and today, and forever' (Hebrews 13:8). He is sympathetic to our situation, 'For we do not have a high priest who is unable to sympathize with our weaknesses.' (Hebrews 4:15) Do we really understand the heart of Jesus? Is this the picture we have of Christ? Do we have problems or needs? In human relationships, we sometimes share a problem knowing that the listener does not have the power to change anything. Nevertheless, we value their sympathy. However, Jesus has both the sympathy and the power if only we will believe!

We are made in the image of God and our capacity for love (frail and flawed as it is) is merely a faint trace of that residual image. What is imperfect in us is perfect in God. In this miracle, we get a glimpse of that loving nature and it warms our hearts to him.

Let us return for a moment to this leper. Imagine how night after night he lay down burdened with disease and without hope. Think of what it was like morning after morning to wake to the realization of his misery. Are you living a burdened life? Jesus said, "Come to me, all who labor and are heavy laden, and I will give you rest" (Matthew11:28). It is very unlikely that your problem is leprosy but perhaps you are emotionally afflicted with depression, anxiety or stress. Maybe you have never come to Christ to be released from the disease of sin that afflicts every life. Come and cast yourself upon him and he will graciously pardon. He can sympathize because he knows what it is like to be afflicted. In the Garden of Gethsemane, Jesus was deeply distressed and troubled: "My soul is very sorrowful, even to death."—Mark 14:34.

This poor man must have felt miserable. He had to contend with the corroding influence of leprosy as it ate into his flesh. Perhaps you have seen cancer debilitate a loved one? Were you moved to compassion? Of course, you were! But that compassion is only a diluted attribute of what is undiluted in Christ. Sometimes all that we can bring to Jesus is our need. This man was a leper and he is so associated with the disease that he is nameless. That is what he is and that is who he is. In our society, we tend to identify people by their professions (doctors, teachers etc.). That practice was familiar at the time of Christ. Jesus himself was known as a carpenter, "Is not this the carpenter...?" (Mark 6:3) It must have been devastating to be cast aside, not only to be redundant but also to take on the identity of an outcast. He could not shake off the affliction or the consciousness of it. It pervaded the physical and the psychological. He was a leper; that was his identity.

Have you ever been conscious of your true identity before God? Have you come to that point in your life where you can say with David, 'For I know my transgressions, and my sin is ever before me.' (Psalm 51:3) It must have been emotionally painful to present himself to Jesus. As he came within close proximity to that crowd that always attended the Master, would he have seen disapproval and disgust registering on the faces of others. What a marked contrast when he beheld the face of Jesus! It was different in the company of fellow lepers. However, even there he always saw others as a loathsome reflection of what he was himself.

We must come with our sins in our woeful condition or we cannot come at all. This man begged Jesus on his knees. Have you ever been driven to your knees in this way? Those who are conscious of their unclean condition before a holy God may cast themselves on the compassion of Christ and hear those liberating words "be clean". We must realize that we cannot help ourselves and overcome our condition. This man's life was radically transformed. In this story, we see the power, the love and the will of God working in harmony. May we have that approach of deep faith in our on-going relationship with God! It is the word and touch of the Master that makes the difference.

CHAPTER 2

Authority to forgive sin (2:1-12)

Jesus healed people of various diseases. In this passage of Scripture, we see Jesus healing a man who was paralyzed. Four men carried him on a stretcher. However, there may have been more than four in their company. They were concerned about him out of compassion, so they brought him to Jesus. He could not go to Christ himself. He needed others who were concerned enough and compassionate enough to help. Clearly then this man had to be brought to Jesus. Here we find Jesus preaching to a crowd in Capernaum. His fame was spreading about his words and works.

There were obstacles in the way of getting this man to Jesus. The house was full and the overflow blocked the entrance. The crowd surrounding Jesus was a barrier. Can we, as believers, sometimes be a barrier to other people coming to Christ? I sometimes think it is possibly more daunting than we realize for some people to come among us.

Everybody in that crowd was there for their own reasons, either to hear Jesus preaching, to be healed of some infirmity, to witness another miracle or just out of curiosity. It's understandable but it resulted in almost preventing this paralytic from coming to Christ. It was meant to be that he should have this encounter with Jesus. It was what we might call a divine appointment. The crowd at the house made it impossible for them to gain entry through the door. But the flat roof (typical of houses in that region at that time and still so today) could be accessed by means of an outside stairway. A typical peasant's home would be comprised of just one room.

These four men were determined to get this paralytic close to the Lord. This shows two things: firstly, their affection for the paralyzed man and secondly, their faith in Jesus. These men dug a hole in the roof of this house (probably consisting of straw, compacted earth and tiles). I wonder what the owner of the house thought of that! This was possibly the home of Simon and Andrew, though we cannot be sure about that. Not only is their determination remarkable but so too is their ingenuity. Their determination and ingenuity are really outward signs of their faith in Jesus. And this faith was obvious to Jesus and he healed this man because of them. These men are an example to us because they had enough compassion to cause them to do something. They could have gone to hear Jesus on their own but instead they went out of their way and made the effort to bring this needy person to Christ. This is possibly, why they were late arriving to a packed house. Do we have enough compassion to cause us to bring others to Jesus?

It took four men to carry him. Here is a good example of team effort. They worked together. They had the will and they found a way. We need to have that kind of compassion, determination, co-operation and ingenuity in bringing people to Jesus. Their courage, resourcefulness and trust in Christ are noteworthy. One commentator refers to these four men as "'friends in need" who were proving to be "friends indeed"'.[14] They did not talk but trusted and that confidence in Christ was all that mattered. Crucially in this section, we see Jesus not only the physician of the body but also the physician of the soul. The way the Lord healed him (i.e. the words he said) are peculiar. He said, "Son, your sins are forgiven." The word "Son" is endearing, not condescending. On the surface forgiveness does not appear to be what the man wanted or

---

[14] William Hendriksen, *Mark, New Testament Commentary*, Banner of Truth, 1975, p.88.

needed. However, his greatest need (which is the same for the healthy and the ill, then and still) is for forgiveness.

The passage does not say that the man repented of his sins but in looking to Christ for help there must have been a repentant attitude. We know from this passage that Jesus could read people's minds and knew what was in their hearts:

Mark 2:6-8

⁶ Now some of the scribes were sitting there, questioning in their hearts, ⁷ "Why does this man speak like that? He is blaspheming! Who can forgive sins but God alone?" ⁸ And immediately Jesus, perceiving in his spirit that they thus questioned within themselves, said to them, "Why do you question these things in your hearts?"

We are left wondering if there was some connection between this man's spiritual and physical condition. There seems to be some relationship between the two. This does not mean that there is necessarily a *specific* connection between illness and sin. There is always a *general* connection between illness and sin because we live in a fallen world where illness and suffering were not part of the original created order. Illness and suffering will not be part of heaven (the new order for the redeemed). In the previous section of the gospel (the healing of the leper), the compassionate character of Christ is demonstrated. However, Christ's compassion is not the emphasis here. This is not about Jesus taking pity on a cripple. Rather the emphasis here is that Jesus has the authority to forgive sins.

It is this issue, which brings him into conflict with the religious leaders. This is the first of several incidents recorded by Mark, which identify this tension between Jesus and the religious leaders. They were traditionalists and opposed to Christ because his teaching ran counter to their cherished religious views. Some people prefer their traditions to Jesus. They might not necessarily openly express their opinion but

Jesus reads their thoughts. The reasoning of the Pharisees was flawless. Only God can forgive sins and so it was blasphemous for anyone else to claim to do this. Christ's claim to forgive this man's sins was, therefore, in their thinking, blasphemous. Clearly, they did not realize who Jesus was. They were so close to the truth and yet so far away, like others today who even study the Bible.

In the light of this claim to forgive sins, the question arises: Is Jesus a liar, a lunatic or is he the Lord? The scribes and Pharisees might have tolerated Jesus if he was just a teacher. They might have grumbled about his unorthodox views but put up with it. They might have even been prepared to believe that Jesus was a prophet with a message from God. However, the idea that he was God was just too much for them. This was, in their thinking, heresy and blasphemy. So the point of conflict here was a theological one for these religious people. Sound theology helps us understand more about God but theology can also be an obstacle to faith if it is merely blind adherence to unexamined dogma. We must be very careful that our theology does not hinder us from recognizing God's activity.

The reason Jesus said to the paralytic "Son, your sins are forgiven" was so that they (the Pharisees, scribes and all present) would hear the claim and the man's healing would verify his claim to have the authority to forgive sins. The healing was instantaneous and obvious, as the man walked out of the house in full view of everybody. I can imagine the crowd parting (like the Red Sea) wide-eyed faces of astonished men and women and maybe even wet-eyed joy for the former paralytic. The people were understandably amazed and praised God. It is interesting that God is glorified through this activity. This will be the outcome of a genuine miracle. It is the hallmark of a true work of God. In fact, if God is not glorified and the work is attributed to somebody else it is unlikely that it was a genuine work of the Lord. However, sadly, sometimes others will steal God's glory.

The fact that the people were praising God is a stark contrast to the attitude of the teachers of the law. They did not share in the joy of the occasion. This should have pleased the teachers of the law but it did not. This reminds me of the time when others and I came to know Christ as our Savior and Lord, in Ireland in the 1970s. The religious establishment was furious with what was going on. One might have expected that, at a time when teenagers were indulging in recreational drug use and promiscuous lifestyles that they would be pleased to hear of young men and women coming to faith in Christ, but they were not. The status quo was threatened and they got a glimpse of a new day dawning when their power would be diminished. That is similar to what is going on in these verses. It was spiritual activity that did not fit in with their preconceived notions. These establishment figures lacked faith. They had knowledge and even expertise in the Scriptures. However, they could not (would not) recognize the activity of God right under their noses. Sadly, there is much religion like this, where all i's are dotted and all the t's are crossed but it is a dead thing and it blinds people to the truth. These faultfinding teachers of the law were hostile to Jesus and became increasingly hardened to the truth. As we journey with Jesus through the message of Mark, we will see their animosity grow.

The people who praised God were part of the same religious tradition but they responded differently to what they had witnessed. Matthew says the crowd was 'awestruck'. Luke says they were 'seized with astonishment...and filled with awe'. All of these gospel writers make it clear that 'all' (except the Scribes and Pharisees) the people praised and glorified God. This is the only appropriate response to God's gracious activity, as he is the great physician who healed body and soul that day, and has continued to do so up unto this day! Jesus has the authority to forgive sins. Let us give praise and glory to God!

Jesus calls Levi (2:13-17)

Jesus called Levi, a tax collector and Levi followed the Lord. This man belonged to a profession that was despised because they collected tax for the occupying Roman authorities. They had contact with Gentiles and for this reason; the Jewish religious leaders shunned them. If you were starting an organization, would you choose the despised and rejected? I think we would be concerned about public relations. We would want the most competent, qualified and most influential people. Nevertheless, Jesus chose the most peculiar people (four fishermen and a tax collector). The gospel is not just for a religious elite and the calling of Levi indicates this.

First-century tax collectors in Palestine were generally ruthless, as one would have to be to collect tax for the Roman occupying power. Their work involved other unpleasant duties such as repossessions, evictions and imprisoning poor defaulters. Many of them were extortionists who demanded more than was due, thus making their living by keeping the surplus. Many of them sub-contracted their responsibilities to others and became rich by getting a percentage from each of their sub-contractors. So unfortunate debtors often had to pay exorbitant additions to what they owed. Contractors would frequently engage sub-contractors from the localities where debtors lived and this local information enhanced their effectiveness and efficiency. However, it made the tax collector a hated figure. Tax collectors in first-century Palestine were generally perceived as informers, traitors and instrument of oppression. Pharisees taught their students not to associate with tax collectors because they were often in contact with Gentiles and worked on the Sabbath. This made them ritually unclean. This is one reason why the Pharisees despised Jesus. However, our journey with Jesus shows us that he met with 'undesirables' and ate with them. The Lord was frequently found in the company of outcasts and the untouchables. In doing this, he incurred the resentment of the Pharisees.

Sadly, there is a form of Christianity today that is nothing more than holy huddles (i.e., like-minded Christians). Some churches are like private clubs, which are no-go zones for the unsaved and un-churched. Such private enclaves seem to prefer their traditions to anything else.

Jesus went to the home of Levi and ate a meal there in the company of many other tax collectors. The Scribes and Pharisees were disturbed that Jesus associated with 'tax collectors and sinners' and they asked his disciples "Why does he eat with tax collectors and sinners?" When Jesus heard it, he said to them, "Those who are well have no need of a physician, but those who are sick. I came not to call the righteous, but sinners."

We live in a health conscious age but many people today do not feel good. People (young and old) are bored with life. Depression, anxiety, stress and suicide are all too common. Many people are restless, and unhappy. There is a soul sickness. Therapists surround us, so why are people unhappy? Jesus compared himself to a doctor. What does he mean? Why visit a doctor? A person does not go because he feels a little bit ill. If you had a headache, indigestion, or tummy upset you would not phone the doctor. If it is not serious enough and you can avoid going to the doctor you will probably treat yourself with painkillers or something over the counter from the pharmacy. However, if the pain or the problem is persistent and it does not go away, then we get worried and make an appointment to see the doctor.

Is this not true spiritually as well? You get up most days and do not have a care in the world. Then there are other days when life is a bit hard and you feel a bit down, a little uneasy, bored, frustrated or just empty. So what do you do? You treat yourself. You go shopping, buy something nice to wear, have a night out (go to a film, a restaurant) or book a holiday. Still, there are other days when these problems become more pressing. The sense of boredom becomes unbearable, frustration builds up; depression deepens and seems to know no end. You feel empty. There is an aching vacuum in your heart and life seems meaningless. You are restless and sleepless, fearful and anxious. It is time to go to Jesus, the great physician of the soul.

Are you anxious or depressed? Perhaps there is something eating away at your soul. Deep down you know that shopping therapy, a night out or a holiday will not solve the problem. You know that the problem will still be there the next day. It is at that point that the soul begins to cry out for help. You know you need a doctor. If you are in this unhappy condition, you need to go to Jesus, the great physician of the soul. Maybe you can successfully hide your true condition from your husband, your wife and your children. Yet, deep down in your soul there is something not right. If you are at this point of crisis and you are wondering what the next step is, you have to make an appointment to see the doctor.

The soul doctor is Jesus. His surgery is always open. He is never booked up or away on holidays. Come to the Christ to be examined and diagnosed. If you go to your doctor with a physical complaint, he will ask you some questions, maybe take your temperature, check your blood pressure, and listen to the rhythm of your heartbeat with his stethoscope. He then makes a diagnosis. When you go to Christ, the great physician of the soul, he conducts a thorough examination of your life. He will look at your thoughts, words and deeds. Nothing will escape his attention as he gives you a thorough examination. Every word, every lie, every half-truth, every curse, every blasphemy, every hard word that hurt others will come to light. His diagnosis is that you are suffering from the disease of sin and he prescribes the remedy. Jesus can treat your condition and bring healing to your soul.[15]

Just as your doctor might look into your ears with a scope and light, so Jesus will delve into the innermost being of your soul if you allow him to examine you. He will look into the dark recesses of your mind and there he will search with his light all your emotions. He will see your feelings, passions, greed, lust, hatred, envy and pride. It will all be open to his discerning eye. When Jesus looks at your soul in this way, he makes a diagnosis. He looks at your unhappiness, frustration, boredom, and emptiness of life and the guilt that eats away at your soul. He sees your fears and anxieties and his diagnosis is that you are suffering from the disease called sin. You are at dis-ease with God, alienated from him and unable to find true purpose and fulfillment.

Sometimes when the doctor tells you what is wrong you do not always immediately understand. However, a good doctor explains how the healthy body ought to work and how the illness you have affects that part of the body and why it is not working properly. And so it is with Jesus. The way you were intended to work was this. You were created in the image of God, to be in relationship with him, to worship him and enjoy blessing. However, God has been displaced from the center of your life. You have put yourself first. You have said, "I'm going to do my own thing; I'm going to make my own decisions." Therefore, the commandments of God have been ignored, belittled and violated. That is why you are frustrated and bored and you find life empty and unfulfilling, because of sin.

---

[15] Here we offer a disclaimer, in that, if you are suffering from depression, you need to see a Christian counselor as soon as possible. The above is dealing with spiritual sickness not mental or physical illnesses.

You must allow Jesus to treat your condition. He can cure you, today. Are you familiar with the idea of 'referred pain'? That is pain that appears in one place but the cause is somewhere else. The same is true of spiritual sickness. The cause of spiritual sickness is that you are not in right relationship with God. However, the pain appears elsewhere and we do not always make the connection. That is the brilliance of Jesus the doctor, who makes the connection. He says the reason you feel like that is because of this. Sometimes the doctor asks questions and you know he has put his finger on it. The root of your problem is the absence of God from your life. You have edged him out. Sin (which is essentially selfishness) has taken over. You might not like to hear it but you know that Christ's diagnosis is correct. Your condition is serious.

The doctor does not send you away after he has made a diagnosis. First, he writes a prescription. The cure for your condition is to have your sins forgiven. When you are physically ill, the tablets you collect from the pharmacy are often very expensive. That is because research chemists have spent time working out what combination of chemicals will deal with that virus or bacteria. Then there is the factory where they are made with the machinery and workers to make them. Then there is the transport cost to get them to the chemist, who is also highly trained. This is what Jesus prescribes and the good news is that there is no fee for you to visit him and there is no charge for the medicine, which he prescribes. It is free to you but it has cost a great deal to produce this cure. Jesus freely prescribes forgiveness of sins.

The first great medical counsel that was convened to produce a remedy for the condition of people's souls took place way back in eternity. That was when God the Father, God the Son and God the Holy Spirit produced a cure for sin. It was decided amongst them that one of them would come to earth to redeem people from that fatal disease of the soul called 'sin'. That decision led to Christ's crucifixion. That and the resurrection were the climactic events of God's plan to save people from their sins. The cross is the cure. The cost is inestimable. To God the cost was great. He gave his only Son that we might be set free from the bondage of sin. To us it is offered as a free gift. The price has been paid in full. The cure is available.

One step remains to be taken. You have gone to the doctor. You have been examined and diagnosed. You have received the necessary prescription. You have gone to the pharmacy and collected the medication. Now you must take the medicine if you are to get well. Jesus invites you to believe in him and accept the abundant life he offers. Jesus is the doctor of the soul. He came into this world to call sinners to repentance. He calls you now to follow him. His prescription for your condition is that you come to the foot of the cross, yield your life to him, and seek forgiveness. Do not reject his invitation to spiritual wellbeing.

Jesus questioned about fasting (2:18-22)

When I was a child, Friday was a fast day for the Roman Catholic Church in Ireland and it was observed in my parent's household. It meant that one was not allowed to eat meat and so fish was eaten instead. However, in a previous generation, Wednesdays and Fridays were fast days and I believe Ash Wednesday is still a fast day in the Roman Catholic Church today. We were also obliged to fast before mass/communion on Sunday mornings. It was a penance, a sacrifice offered to God to gain his favor. Fasting is part of some religions today. Lent is a time set aside for fasting in the Roman Catholic Church tradition. There is a place for fasting in the Christian church as a time of reflection, abstinence and generosity towards the poor. The historic Protestant position contends that any approach to God, which includes fasting, offered up, as meritorious work toward salvation is inappropriate. This is based on the understanding that the Bible clearly teaches that salvation is by grace, through faith and that it is a gift of God.–Ephesians 2:8-9.[16]

For most people it was/is merely a cultural practice that has little or no religious meaning. Fish is still very common on Fridays, as fasting did not mean not eating but rather abstaining from meat. Some charities (especially during Lent) organize fasts in solidarity with the hungry of this world as a means of raising funds. This is a good thing (well-motivated with a good outcome). However, it is essentially a humanitarian exercise even though some people may be motivated by their religious faith to participate in this. In the passage under consideration, people were observing what was going on and they noticed differences between the teaching of John the Baptist and Jesus. They were looking for continuity but Jesus emphasizes discontinuity between the old order and the new. Jesus fasted for forty days in the wilderness (Luke 4:1-2) but fasting was not part of Christ's teaching and some people wondered why he was not instructing his disciples to fast.

For the followers of Jesus there was an obvious discontinuity with some aspects of Jewish piety, custom and practices. In the setting and circumstance in which Christ taught his disciples to pray the Lord's Prayer (Matthew 6) Jesus talks about hypocrisy and he instructs his hearers about proper ways of charitable giving, praying and fasting. In doing this, he condemns those who engage in these activities in a wrong manner. Christ emphasizes the importance of a person's motives. He teaches that credible spiritual activity emerges from authentic attitudes. It is clear from the context that the practice of engaging in these activities is of no

---

[16] Are Christians required to fast? Christian Publishing House would suggest the following article, so as to have a balanced view, **The Meaning of Laws** http://www.christianpublishers.org/mosaic-law-christians

spiritual value if they are motivated by the desire to gain honor and respect in the community. The important principle, which the Lord emphasizes, is that true heart religion has spiritual value but mere external observance of religious rituals is worse than worthless; it is an offence to God.

In the Islamic religion Ramadan is a month set aside for Muslims to abstain from food, drink, smoking and sex during the hours of daylight.[17] I am involved in training Arab leaders for Christian ministry in the Arab world. This work takes me to the Middle East where I teach hermeneutics (the principles of biblical interpretation). I have been there during Ramadan. In the country where I work it is illegal to eat, drink or smoke in public during the hours of daylight during Ramadan. One is also expected to refrain from indulging in sex during the hours of daylight. Even chewing gum is considered *haram* (an Arabic term meaning 'sinful'). Many Muslims do not conform to these injunctions to the letter but most conform to some extent and all conform in public. Once when I was in the Middle East during Ramadan it was July and in the intense heat, it is easy to become dehydrated. Those who observe Ramadan gorge themselves on a large pre-dawn breakfast called *suhur* and eagerly await *iftar, which* is breaking the fast at dusk. This is a celebration meal, which usually includes extra and special dainties only available during Ramadan. For example, *qatayef* is a special dessert, commonly served during Ramadan. Sometimes called 'Arabic pancakes', *qatayef* is filled with either sweet cheese or nuts (often almonds) and then fried. They are absolutely delicious! More food is sold during Ramadan than at any other time of year. The supermarkets offer special deals. Even McDonald's has a 'McRamadan' meal. Ironically, many people who observe the fast put on weight during this religious festival. Undoubtedly, many

---

[17] The date of Ramadan varies from year to year (always twenty days before the previous year) and lasts for a month.

Muslims observe Ramadan out of a sense of genuine religious conviction but there is also a great deal of hypocrisy about observing this fast. It seems to make people more cantankerous than pious. There is intimidation and coercion surrounding observance of Ramadan. Many Muslims are simply afraid either because they deem it to be sinful and fear the angel at their left shoulder recording their deeds, which according to Islam will be weighed on scales in judgment, or they are afraid to express dissent because of the legal and social ramifications. It is imposed on them and because it is not voluntary, many of them eat in secret.

Fasting is about abstaining and feasting is about indulging. However, the feasting Jesus is talking about is not a hedonistic, 'eat, drink and be merry, for tomorrow we die' kind of philosophy. Jesus wants us to enjoy spiritual life not to just endure it (John 10:10). In the parable of 'The Pharisee and the Publican' (Luke 18:9-14) we see two different kinds of men, two different approaches to God and two different outcomes. This parable tells us something about the right and wrong way to approach God. The Pharisee in this parable belonged to an elitist group of experts in Judaic law. They were the theologians of their day. As custodians of truth, they corrupted it by adding man-made regulations which became burdensome traditions imposed on people. Pharisees were the strictest sect of the day. They took pride in their piety and privileged position. Furthermore, they were petty in their practice of observing man-made regulations.

The Pharisee in the parable (presented as typical of this group) focused on the 'dos' and 'don'ts' of religion (including fasting). He prays about himself in what is essentially an exercise in public self-congratulation. This man recited the good things he does and the bad things he abstains from doing. His is a misplaced confidence in self-righteousness. He says that he fasts twice a week. However, this sacrifice is offered to God in order to gain merit and so his approach is wrong! What the Pharisee did and abstained from doing was appropriate but not as a package offered to God to earn merit toward justification. Isaiah says, 'all our righteousness acts are like filthy rags' (Isaiah 64:6). Fasting will not get us any brownie points or credit on a loyalty card (in terms of justification or sanctification). In other words, we are neither saved nor sanctified by fasting.

In a passage about true and false fasting Isaiah says that fasting ought not to be merely an occasional thing. Rather it is a lifestyle of servant-living for God and others.

Isaiah 58:2-12

2 Yet they seek me daily
   and delight to know my ways,
as if they were a nation that did righteousness
   and did not forsake the judgment of their God;
they ask of me righteous judgments;
   they delight to draw near to God.
3 'Why have we fasted, and you see it not?
   Why have we humbled ourselves, and you take no knowledge of it?'
Behold, in the day of your fast you seek your own pleasure,
   and oppress all your workers.
4 Behold, you fast only to quarrel and to fight
   and to hit with a wicked fist.
Fasting like yours this day
   will not make your voice to be heard on high.
5 Is such the fast that I choose,
   a day for a person to humble himself?
Is it to bow down his head like a reed,
   and to spread sackcloth and ashes under him?
Will you call this a fast,
   and a day acceptable to the Lord?

   6 "Is not this the fast that I choose:
   to loose the bonds of wickedness,

> to undo the straps of the yoke,
> to let the oppressed go free,
>   and to break every yoke?
> ⁷ Is it not to share your bread with the hungry
>   and bring the homeless poor into your house;
> when you see the naked, to cover him,
>   and not to hide yourself from your own flesh?
> ⁸ Then shall your light break forth like the dawn,
>   and your healing shall spring up speedily;
> your righteousness shall go before you;
>   the glory of the Lord shall be your rear guard.
> ⁹ Then you shall call, and the Lord will answer;
>   you shall cry, and he will say, 'Here I am.'
> If you take away the yoke from your midst,
>   the pointing of the finger, and speaking wickedness,
> ¹⁰ if you pour yourself out for the hungry
>   and satisfy the desire of the afflicted,
> then shall your light rise in the darkness
>   and your gloom be as the noonday.
> ¹¹ And the Lord will guide you continually
>   and satisfy your desire in scorched places
>   and make your bones strong;
> and you shall be like a watered garden,
>   like a spring of water,
>   whose waters do not fail.
> ¹² And your ancient ruins shall be rebuilt;
>   you shall raise up the foundations of many generations;
> you shall be called the repairer of the breach,
>   the restorer of streets to dwell in.

Should Christians fast today? If Christians fast at all, it is usually about something important. It is a way of showing God you mean business. What is Christian fasting? Biblically, fasting is abstaining from food, drink, sleep or sex to focus on a period of spiritual growth. Specifically, we humbly deny something of the flesh to glorify God, enhance our spirit, and go deeper in our prayer life. Christian fasting is not some kind of a 'work' that is commanded by Christ or required by Scripture. If we do not fast, we are not sinning.

However, that does not mean that fasting is not recommended as a part of our spiritual growth. The Book of Acts records believers fasting before they made important decisions: 'While they were worshiping the Lord and fasting, the Holy Spirit said, "Set apart for me Barnabas and Saul for the work to which I have called them." Then after fasting and praying they laid their hands on them and sent them off' (Acts 13:2-3). Fasting and prayer are often linked together. Too often, the focus of fasting is on the lack of food. However, the purpose of fasting is to take our eyes off the things of this world and instead focus on God. Fasting is a way to demonstrate to God and to ourselves that we are serious about our relationship with him.

Although fasting in Scripture is almost always a fasting from food, there are other ways to fast. Anything you can temporarily give up in order to focus better on God can be considered a fast. The apostle Paul advised believers at Corinth, 'Do not deprive one another, except perhaps by agreement for a limited time, that you may devote yourselves to prayer' (1 Corinthians 7:5). This speaks of fasting from sex, within marriage. Fasting should be limited to a set time, especially when the fasting is from food. Extended periods of time without eating are harmful to the body. Fasting is not intended to punish the flesh, but to focus on God.

Fasting should not be considered a 'dieting method' either. We shouldn't fast to lose weight, but rather to gain deeper fellowship with God. Some people may not be able to fast from food (diabetics, for example) but everyone can temporarily give up something in order to focus on God. Even unplugging the television for a period of time can be an effective fast.

Although it is a good idea for believers to fast from time to time, fasting is not required in Scripture. The primary Biblical reason to fast is to develop a closer walk with God. By taking our eyes off the things of this world, we can focus better on Christ. We should pay attention to the words of Jesus on this matter,

Matthew 6:16-18

[16] "And when you fast, do not look gloomy like the hypocrites, for they disfigure their faces that their fasting may be seen by others. Truly, I say to you, they have received their reward. [17] But when you fast, anoint your head and wash your face, [18] that your fasting may not be seen by others but by your Father who is in secret. And your Father who sees in secret will reward you.

Christian fasting is more than denying ourselves food or something else of the flesh. It is a sacrificial lifestyle before God. It is not just a one-time act of humility and denial before God; it is a lifestyle of servant ministry to others. At first glance, the passage in Mark's Gospel under consideration may appear as if it is about fasting but it is not. This is about Christ's authority to overturn the prevailing practices of piety. Jesus turned the sorrow of fasting into the joy of feasting.

Along with prayer and almsgiving, fasting was one of the three main pillars of Jewish society. The Mosaic Law requires fasting only once a year, on the Day of Atonement (Leviticus 16:1-34; 23:26-32; Numbers 29:7-11) and Pharisees fast weekly (Mondays and Thursdays, see Luke 18:12). People were being called, not to a new Judaism, but to a new order. There is both continuity and discontinuity between Old Testament and New Testament. Christianity is a deep-seated departure. Some people wanted familiarity. This is a passage about the power of the new where Jesus emphasizes the incompatibility of the old and new.

Jesus uses three pictures: a wedding, a patch and new wine. It is interesting to note that this question about fasting follows a story about eating (2:13-17). We may presume that in failing to fast the disciples of Jesus are following the Lord's example. Just as the fasting of John's disciples, reflect a practice of his. This passage is not about fasting *per se*. Rather it is about the relative authority of John the Baptist, the Pharisees and Jesus. Does Jesus have authority to suspend fasting? Yes. Jesus refers to himself as a kind of bridegroom, whose presence makes imposed religious fasting inappropriate because he is the cause of celebration.

Lord of the Sabbath (2:23-28)

The Pharisees were constantly watching Jesus to see if he broke the law. It seems as if they followed Jesus around, especially on the Sabbath. They waited for him to make a mistake. They listened carefully to what he said and watched everything he did. They wanted to find something that they could construe as a violation of the commandment concerning the Sabbath. On this occasion, they criticized Christ when his disciples picked heads of grain in a field on the Sabbath. They seemed to be always lurking in the shadows ready to pounce. They were eager to find fault.

It is clear from Christ's answer that he understood this commandment correctly. A cluster of beliefs, rules and traditions had grown around this commandment, which amounted to legalism. It had become a question of what can I do and what can't I do? The Pharisees formulated a whole list of things that were legitimate and other things that were not permitted. Their interpretation of this commandment was wrong. They missed the heart and purpose of it.

They became very ingenious at working out how far you could go and what you could do and still keep this commandment. The phrase, 'a Sabbath day's journey', is used in the Bible. Luke uses it for example, '...they returned to Jerusalem from the mount called Olivet, which is near Jerusalem, a Sabbath day's journey.' (Acts 1:12) This refers to the number of steps that were permitted on the Sabbath. The teachers of the law referred to the Pentateuch (books of the law), specifically Exodus and Numbers and fitted two verses together. They came up with the idea that two-thousand paces was the maximum permitted for a Sabbath day's journey. So the law was observed if you walked two-thousand paces but it was broken if you took an extra step. This distance is approximately three-quarters of a mile (1.2 kilometers). This was their typical way of thinking. Judaism had become legalistic.

Legalism is a certain kind of mindset and it is still around today. Sadly, it exists within the church. There are people that constantly watch for any deviation from the established order. These people are unnerving. They are suspicious of everything. When they are around you have to watch your Ps and Qs. I believe they are in most Christian churches. We need overseers and defenders of the faith and people who are careful and vigilant. However, the legalist has a certain kind of spirit that is in love with tradition and anything new is suspect. They remind me of the gargoyles on some church buildings.[18] They are the ogres of the church. Basically they want things done their way. They major on orthodoxy. They are heresy hunters who are set in their ways with a formula to which they expect everybody to conform.

They are invariably pious people. They are nearly always leaders in positions of authority in the church. They obstruct and hinder. They are nitpickers. They crack the whip and everybody has to fit in with their agenda. They are control

---

[18] Gargoyles are the ugly / comical faces carved on a building, often church buildings. They are usually part of the waterspout. The word is French for 'throat' because the water passes through the throat of the figure.

freaks who abuse their authority and in their company, you will never feel comfortable and secure. Today's Pharisees would tax smiling if they could. They seem to be experts at frowning. Sadly, many people are afraid of them and want their approval. They are bullies who coerce people into conformity, often in subtle ways and always with an air of superiority that is mistaken for spirituality. They are code-keepers and ritual observers. Even though they are involved in ministry, they are fakes. They do not know that and many others do not seem to know it either. If you want to be in their favor, you have to tick all their boxes. They often pray publicly. They are eloquent and articulate in prayer. But Jesus despises them because they burden the people. They are grace-killers. You will have gathered by now that I have met a few Pharisees in my time and that I do not have much time for them. God is open-handed. They are tight-fisted. They appear good from the outside but they are rigid as a corpse and stink like one that has been dead for a month! But let us beware of the potential for pharisaic attitudes within ourselves.

Christ's comment on the Sabbath is most interesting, "The Sabbath was made for man, not man for the Sabbath." Here Jesus is saying people need the Sabbath. It was given out of the kindness of God for the benefit of all, including animals, the land and the poor. In this sense, it was effectively a constitutional right to a day off. We should have a positive attitude to the Sabbath. Legalism ruined the whole concept of the Sabbath in Christ's day and maybe in our history and experience it spoiled our appreciation of the Lord's Day.

The Pharisees made Sabbath observance doable. In other words, they qualified and quantified every detail of what was allowed and what was disallowed. As such, Sabbath observance became measurable. If you measured up you could say you kept the Sabbath and feel proud and pious.

They externalized it. This is an attitude of mind that still exists today.

There are people who observe the Sabbath in a superficial manner. Religious people are prone to it. Therefore, even if we do observe the Lord's Day we should be careful not to become unduly proud of our piety. After all, let us remind ourselves, we are not justified by the keeping of the law. However, the law is, nevertheless a standard to which we ought to aspire. It is something to aim for. We have noted how the religious leaders waited to pounce on Jesus about any perceived breach of the Sabbath. They were wrong in their attitudes but it must be noted that they placed great emphasis on Sabbath observance. They rightly understood that it was important but wrongly made it a burdensome religious duty.

We should look positively on Sunday and see it as an opportunity to be grasped. It is an opportunity to begin the week with God and we should guard the day and make it different. The profanity of the world pollutes. There is much emphasis today on healthy living; eating the right foods, taking exercise and detoxifying the body. Nevertheless, Sunday is a day for detoxifying the soul. The Lord's Day can be an oasis where we can take spiritual refreshment and fortify ourselves for the week ahead. The Lord's Day is not something to be anticipated with misery and foreboding rather it is something to be looked forward to. Normal duties during the rest of the week prevent us from giving God our undivided attention. Our occupational responsibilities inhibit us to a certain extent. Therefore, when it comes around in the cycle of the week we should squeeze out of it all the blessing we can get. In addition, we should give to God all that we can give.

Scripture records what Jesus did on the Sabbath. He exercised mercy in healing the sick. What the disciples were doing was perfectly legitimate, 'If you go into your neighbor's standing grain, you may pluck the ears with your hand, but you shall not put a sickle to your neighbor's standing grain' (Deuteronomy 23:25). The Pharisees were shocked that they were doing this on the Sabbath and immediately expressed their disapproval. The question to Christ is not simply a question; it is a charge, an accusation. The way the Pharisees reasoned was that work was forbidden on the Sabbath and what the disciples were doing was reaping (work). The rabbis drew up a catalogue of thirty-nine principal works and each of these categories had six subdivisions, which were all forbidden on the Sabbath. The law did not forbid what they were doing but their traditions did!

Jesus answers them, "Have you never read what David did...?" He confronted those who were proud of upholding the law and teaching it to others. He points out that they seem to be unfamiliar with the fact that the ceremonial law allowed its restrictions to be relaxed when there was real need. The showbread was for the priests only and yet David and all his company ate it. The point Christ is making is that if David had the right to ignore a divinely appointed ceremony as necessity demanded then Jesus had a greater right to set aside a man-made Sabbath regulation. By forbidding the disciples to pick grain when they were hungry, the Pharisees were changing the concept of the Sabbath into something it was never intended to be. The Sabbath serves our good and we were never meant to be slaves to it.

God made the Sabbath and Jesus reminds these tyrants of that. Jesus was deeply distressed at their stubborn hearts. Jesus claims authority over the Sabbath and in so doing makes it clear that nobody has any right to find fault. Therefore, Jesus asserts his authority over the Sabbath. The action of David was contrary to the law but he was not condemned for it. Jesus does not argue that the Sabbath was not broken rather he suggests that such a violation, under certain conditions, could be allowed. The Sabbath is a gift from God to provide rest from work and opportunity for worship. Jesus makes it clear that it was not created for its own sake but the Pharisees had made a kind of moral straightjacket out of it. Jesus set people free, not from proper Sabbath observance, but from slavish adherence to a man-made code. We should exercise our freedom and enjoy the Lord's Day because it if both for God's glory and our good.[19]

---

[19] Are Christians required to keep a weekly Sabbath day? Christian Publishing House would suggest the following article, so as to have a balanced view, **The Meaning of Laws**
http://www.christianpublishers.org/mosaic-law-christians

CHAPTER 3

The man with the shriveled hand (3:1-6)

The Pharisees questioned Jesus about Sabbath observance when his disciples picked heads of grain. Now we meet them again. Richard Baxter said, 'The hypocrite's bellows blow out the candle under the pretense of kindling the fire.' The Pharisees have the external appearance of spirituality but their hypocrisy quenches the Spirit. This incident of the man with the shriveled hand fits in with the previous section because in both passages Jesus demonstrates that he is Lord of the Sabbath.

Here is a man who has a paralysis in his hand, which would have made life difficult for him. The occupations of the time focused around building and agriculture, primarily physical work (e.g., stonemason or plowman). This was an age before computers. It was a time when a man's worth was measured by his physical prowess. His earning potential (and indeed his masculinity) related to muscle. There was no disabled person's welfare. There was no equal opportunity legislation for people with a disability. There were no access and empowerment programs for the disadvantaged. It was a world where the strong survived and the weak went to the wall. Most likely he was not self-sufficient and probably relied on others (depended on almsgiving).

It is not made known if his condition is a congenital birth deformity or an injury from accident or some kind of disease. Whatever the cause his condition must have had an emotional as well as a physical dimension and I suspect that he was psychologically scarred. He probably had feelings of self-consciousness and inferiority because of his ugly and embarrassing limb. I wonder if he was envious of able-bodied men. This possibly affected his dignity, self-esteem and relationships. If he was not already married before an accident which caused this situation then who would marry him? His earning potential would have been restricted. He probably felt cut off, as much social interaction formed around work. This could give rise to loneliness.

Whatever about the physical and psychological there may have been a spiritual dimension to the issue. Maybe his affliction brought him close to God. We notice that he was in the synagogue on the Sabbath. It seems that he was a religious man. It is reasonable to assume that he went there to pray. I wonder what he prayed. Maybe he prayed for work, for money, food, for friendship, for healing.

He met Jesus! How often we find Jesus in the synagogue on the Sabbath. There is a power struggle between the Pharisees and Jesus. Someone has said 'Dead devotion is a living mockery' (Anon). How true this was of the Pharisees. The tension comes to the surface in hostile questions. The Pharisees were among God's chosen people. They were the most religious, in the synagogue, on the Sabbath, with Jesus. Yet they missed what was really going on! Augustine said, 'It is no advantage to be near the light if the eyes are closed.' The tension grows and ends in confrontation and it becomes quite sinister as they plot to kill Jesus.

However, Jesus was well able to handle them. A. W. Tozer said, 'When hypocrites ran up against Jesus it was like a cat running into a mowing machine.' It is possible to attend to religious duties (go to church) and not see Jesus for who he really is. We need to watch out for our own tendency to hypocrisy. George Bernard Shaw said, 'The English churchgoer prefers a severe preacher because he thinks a few home truths will do his neighbour no harm.' Our text tells us that the

Pharisees watched Jesus. It was the kind of close scrutiny given to a potential wrongdoer.

I once took a group of disadvantaged youth to a historical site and when we had finished our tour, we passed through the shop on our way out. I remember well the way the security guard watched these young people. He was not just looking at them; rather he was scrutinizing them suspiciously. That is how the Pharisees looked at the Lord.

This man with the shriveled hand shows courage in obedience despite the intimidating atmosphere. The Pharisees saw it (as one commentator put it) that Jesus was 'unnecessarily practicing medicinal therapy on that day.' Think of what the Pharisees witnessed. Jesus performed this miracle before their eyes and their religion (its man-made rules) hindered them from appreciating it and glorifying God. These enemies of Christ were blind, stubborn and legalistic. Their silence shows that they were not really interested in seeing the law observed. They did not argue their case. Ironically, they wanted Jesus to break the law so that they could feel justified in conspiring with the Herodians to kill him.

Jesus was doing good deeds on the Sabbath and the Pharisees were plotting murder. How absurd and evil their position was. They were listening to Jesus (not to seek spiritual enlightenment) but to trap him. Jesus read their minds and asked them, "Is it lawful on the Sabbath to do good or to do harm, to save life or to kill?" Jesus was angered and grieved at their hardness of heart. Opposition (religious or otherwise) will not prevent God's will from being done. Jesus healed this man. The Pharisees, though in the presence of the Lord, would not acknowledge God's activity.

Herodians were supporters of Herod Antipas (Tetrarch of Galilee) ruler of a quarter of Galilee. The Pharisees formed an alliance with them. Herodians thought that Christ's following were potential political rebels. Both groups were interested in preserving the status quo (political/religious). So perhaps their alliance was not so strange. The religious establishment and the political powers united in opposition to Christ because he threatened to undermine their power. Theirs was a political alliance based on self-interest.

Many people have been intimidated by religious leaders (watching in the wings) and have capitulated out of fear. Jesus commanded this man to stretch out his hand. We like to present our best aspect. However, Jesus wants us to present that deformed, dysfunctional, and ugly part of ourselves so that he can deal with it. We need to present our weaknesses to him. Is there something in your life that you keep hidden? Is there something in your life that makes you feel ashamed or inferior, some embarrassing problem? You might not have a shriveled hand but maybe you have an untamed temper, an untamed tongue or an uncontrolled passion. Present yourself today to Jesus. Stretch out that hand. Pews and even pulpits are full of critics and faultfinders. Forget them. Spiritual healing is found in Christ not in dead religion. Religion failed this man as it does many today.

Jesus condemned the hypocrisy of the Pharisees (as a class). It is interesting to note what the problem of the Pharisees was. Jesus described hypocrites as those who are blind to their own faults and prone to judge others, "You hypocrite, first take the log out of your own eye, and then you will see clearly to take the speck out of your brother's eye." (Matthew 7:5) He described them as blind to the workings of God: "You hypocrites! You know how to interpret the appearance of earth and sky, but why do you not know how to interpret the present time?" (Luke 12:56) He described them as blind to a true sense of values. There was a woman who was bent over for eighteen years. She could not fully straighten herself and Jesus freed her from her disability. The Lord put his hands on her, immediately she was made straight, and she glorified God. Nevertheless, the ruler of the synagogue was indignant because Jesus had healed on the Sabbath and he said, "There are six days in which work ought to be done. Come on those days and be healed, and not on the Sabbath day." Then the Lord answered him, "You hypocrites! Does not each of you on the Sabbath untie his ox or his donkey from the manger and lead it away to water it? And ought not this woman, a daughter of Abraham whom Satan bound for eighteen years, be loosed from this bond on the Sabbath day?" (Luke 13:14-16) Jesus described Pharisees as those who overvalue human tradition:

Mark 7:6-8

⁶ And he said to them, "Well did Isaiah prophesy of you hypocrites, as it is written,

"'This people honors me with their lips,
   but their heart is far from me;
⁷ in vain do they worship me,
   teaching as doctrines the commandments of men.'

⁸ You leave the commandment of God and hold to the tradition of men."

Jesus described Pharisees as those who paid attention to external rituals while neglecting inner spirituality. See Matthew 23 (seven woes to the Pharisees). According to Christ Pharisees are those who love public displays: "Thus, when you give to the needy, sound no trumpet before you, as the hypocrites do in the synagogues and in the streets, that they may be praised by others."–Matthew 6:2.

Therefore, if we are to avoid hypocrisy we need to be aware of our own faults and frailties and less prone to judging others. We need to be open to the activity of God and have a proper sense of values by understanding what is right and wrong as well as what is important and unimportant. We must avoid allowing traditions to supersede the Word of God and be truly concerned about our inner spirituality and standing before God. Examining ourselves in the light of this standard is certainly an exercise in humility.

There can be no doubt that Jesus despised the Pharisees because they did not practice what they preached. They burdened the people. Everything they did was for others to see. They were full of their own self-importance. They shut the door to the kingdom of heaven in people's faces. They were blind guides who neglected justice and mercy. They were greedy and self-indulgent. Jesus described them as snakes, desolate, corrupt, hypocritical, and on the road to hell.[20]

A great crowd follows Jesus (3:7-12)

Christ's popularity was increasing. His reputation as a healer and miracle worker was spreading to regions that are more distant. The sick came to him in such numbers that it became dangerous with such large crowds pressing around him. Evil spirits publicly acknowledged his divinity. The people came to be healed. Jesus has not lost his power to attract those who are ill. Many people today come to Christ for help when they are diagnosed with serious illness. Religious people and people who are not religious will come to Christ if they are suffering from some physical or psychological health issues, financial pressure and/or trouble in relationships.

Jesus was beginning to be popular but things would change in the future, to such an extent that there were just a few people with Jesus when he was crucified. The crowd called out for Barabbas to be set free when they could have demanded the release of Jesus. In addition, it seems that it all changed very rapidly. Later on in chapter 11 of Mark, we read that many people spread their cloaks on the road when Jesus

---

[20] Christian Publishing House would suggest the following articles, so as to have a balanced view, **(1) Hellfire - Eternal Torment?** http://www.christianpublishers.org/hellfire-eternal-torment **(2) Hellfire - Is It Just?** http://www.christianpublishers.org/hellfire-is-it-just

made that triumphal entry into Jerusalem. Others spread leafy branches that they had cut from the fields. There was a procession of people who were shouting "Hosanna! Blessed is he who comes in the name of the Lord! Blessed is the coming kingdom of our father David! Hosanna in the highest!"–Mark 11:9-10.

I think there are a number of reasons for the sudden disappearance of the people who were healed and those who witnessed miracles: fear of the Pharisees, love of their religious traditions, pride in their culture, peer pressure. Many fall away. There are all kinds of pressures to go back or not follow any further. In the end people turned against Jesus, bore false testimony against him, and acquiesced in perverting justice. The law clearly forbade such activity: "You shall not join hands with a wicked man to be a malicious witness. You shall not fall in with the many to do evil, nor shall you bear witness in a lawsuit, siding with the many, so as to pervert justice."–Exodus 23:1-2.

They had heard the teaching of Jesus...they must have been impressed with his wisdom. Many people who are attracted to Jesus do not become disciples. These people did not take Jesus as a guide or leader. They went to Christ for what they could get from him. They did not conform to his teaching. They were not in any sense devotees of Christ.

What does it mean to follow Jesus? Jesus said, "If anyone would come after me, let him deny himself and take up his cross and follow me." (Matthew 16:24) So following Jesus is about allowing him to lead. It is about self-denial and the way of the cross. The Lord also said, "If anyone serves me, he must follow me; and where I am, there will my servant be also." (John 12:26) There is a cost in following Jesus. In a passage about the cost of following Jesus we read:

Matthew 8:18-22

¹⁸ Now when Jesus saw a crowd around him, he gave orders to go over to the other side. ¹⁹ And a scribe came up and said to him, "Teacher, I will follow you wherever you go." ²⁰ And Jesus said to him, "Foxes have holes, and birds of the air have nests, but the Son of Man has nowhere to lay his head." ²¹ Another of the disciples said to him, "Lord, let me first go and bury my father." ²² And Jesus said to him, "Follow me, and leave the dead to bury their own dead."

Many in the 1970s were just caught up with the novelty of Jesus and the Jesus movement flourished for a time. Then when people counted the cost, many fell away. In one of the saddest passages of Scripture, we read about Solomon turning from the Lord:

1 Kings 11:1-8

¹ Now King Solomon loved many foreign women, along with the daughter of Pharaoh: Moabite, Ammonite, Edomite, Sidonian, and Hittite women, ² from the nations concerning which the Lord had said to the people of Israel, "You shall not enter into marriage with them, neither shall they with you, for surely they will turn away your heart after their gods." Solomon clung to these in love. ³ He had 700 wives, who were princesses, and 300 concubines. And his wives turned away his heart. ⁴ For when Solomon was old his wives turned away his heart after other gods, and his heart was not wholly true to the Lord his God, as was the heart of David his father. ⁵ For Solomon went after Ashtoreth the goddess of the Sidonians, and after Milcom the abomination of the Ammonites. ⁶ So Solomon did what was evil in the sight of the Lord and did not wholly follow the Lord, as David his father had done. ⁷ Then Solomon built a high place for Chemosh the abomination of Moab, and for Molech the abomination of the Ammonites, on the mountain east of

Jerusalem. ⁸And so he did for all his foreign wives, who made offerings and sacrificed to their gods.

Solomon wrote three books of the Bible (Song of Solomon, Ecclesiastes and Proverbs). Such apostasy in one so wise is very sad indeed. Peter declared that he would follow the Lord wherever he went and whatever the cost but he deserted Jesus and so too did the other disciples.

Therefore, there are spectators and players. Many were being blessed by Christ's healing power and many who 'followed' were just interested in Jesus the miracle worker. This begs the question: What kind of followers are we? Do we come to Jesus for what he can do for us? Are we devoted to him? The good news was spreading and people were coming to Jesus from places that are more distant. I suppose many were seeking healing for themselves or for their relatives and friends. The size of the crowd caused a problem. The fact that these people wanted to touch Jesus was also a problem. They were not content to wait in hope that Jesus might touch them.

I saw news footage of the Glastonbury Music festival recently where one of the stage performers (a lead singer from a band) walked down by the barrier between the stage and the crowd, who were watching and obviously enjoying the performance. He reached out his hand and as he walked along everybody in that front row touched him in response to his outstretched hand. However, with Jesus there was no barrier, no stewards and no police, just a few disciples. The use of the boat shows how Jesus prepared in advance for this possibility of being mobbed.

Why did Jesus silence the unclean spirits? He did so because they were an unsuitable means of spreading the message of the gospel. A proper understanding of the messiah had not yet been disclosed in Christ's teaching and so the time was not right. Jesus had yet to make it clear what exactly was the nature of the messianic role; that he had to suffer and die for the sins of the people. The scribes were telling people that Jesus and the demonic powers were allies (3:22) so if Jesus allowed himself to be advertised by demons it would make their case seem more credible.

The choosing of the twelve apostles (3:13-21)

Here Jesus goes for higher ground and this elevation gives him an advantage with the crowds so that he can be seen by all. Jesus takes control of the situation and he decided who could come to him. Jesus still calls people to him. He takes the initiative in salvation. He now puts in place a structure of leadership. This is not a call to discipleship but a commissioning to duty. These people were appointed to preach and to cast out demons. They would be in the front line of the spiritual battle.

Jesus still chooses people to come to him and he gives them meaningful roles in the kingdom of God. God entrusts his work to human hands. Like the first disciples, they might not be the people we would choose. We might look for better qualifications and experience, a better psychological profile or more influential people. However, the Lord selects ordinary people to do extraordinary things. God does not choose us because of our talents, skills and abilities. Rather he chooses us and then equips us for the tasks he entrusts to us.

Jesus went home and the crowds gathered again. It is interesting that even Jesus' family did not understand him. They were not ready and they did not understand. How often Christ was misunderstood and opposed, even from the most unlikely source. I know a man who (in the 1970s) was beginning to develop a drinking habit. However, he gave his life to the Lord and was delivered from potential alcoholism. When his mother learned about this, she told him that she would prefer if he was an alcoholic rather than become a "born-again" Christian. A friend of mine, when he gave his life to Christ, heard bitter words from his mother. His brother (her son) had died a few years before. When he told her of his faith in Christ, she said that she wished he had died instead. In the context of the time, there were few evangelical Christians and those who professed to be "born-again" were perceived as having joined a cult. Opposition at home hurts.

Jesus' family went out to seize him because they thought he was out of his mind. Sometimes even people in our own families might think we are fanatics. I heard about a young woman who was converted to Christ in Ireland in the early 1970s and her family committed her to a psychiatric institution. There may be those even in our families who will try to force their will upon us, especially if there is opposition from the religious authorities.

Sadly, all these men chosen by Jesus to establish and lead the church deserted Jesus when he was arrested. I think in their hearts they did not forsake Jesus but they were afraid and confused and they abandoned him to his captors and tormentors. One of them even betrayed the Lord. It is not that Jesus was a poor judge of character. All his work has a purpose. God works to an eternal plan, one that will not be thwarted. He will never be outsmarted or outmaneuvered. God knows what he is doing and his choices are sovereign. He makes no mistakes or bad decisions. We might wonder why God chose him or her rather than another more competent person or a person with a more pleasant personality. However, what we should be wondering is why God chose us! We should understand that we are chosen by God. We are commissioned by Christ and entrusted with sacred duties. He has a special role for us, even though from a worldly point of view there are people who are more competent and influential. We should not expect our families to always understand the activity of God (the Lord's family thought he was out of his mind). Sometimes we are weak, afraid, confused and we fail Jesus but he never forsakes us. We are called to follow where he leads. The way of the cross is to serve the Lord and obey his Word.

Family opposition (3:20-21)

Sometimes even people in our own families might think we are fanatics. The disciple of Jesus must realize that the world will not understand his/her faith. They will not accept his/her faith. There can be indifference, hostility, sneering, ridicule, bullying. The new Christian who has not been raised in a Christian home might expect more understanding and support from his family but should not be surprised if that support is not forthcoming. The believer who is converted from false or nominal religion can expect resistance and opposition from community and family. Your big sister might come to you and say, "Believe it privately but don't upset your parents". She might say, "You don't even have to go to mass, just pretend. Tell mum and dad you are going and come to the pub with us."

Still, what about the disciple from a Christian home where the parents and siblings are genuine believers? Can they expect more encouragement when they go into public ministry? Often they do receive the support one might expect. However, sadly, sometimes, they do not. Parents tend to be ambitious for their children. They want them to do better in life than they have done themselves. They want them to have good careers (medicine, law, teaching, business etc.). Some Christian parents will actively steer their children away from 'full-time' ministry. This is especially true if the person has some kind of professional degree in a secular sphere (medicine, law, teaching, commerce etc.). These parents (whose responsibility it is to give spiritual guidance) would prefer their children to have more lucrative or prestigious occupations. Why? Perhaps it is because they have a low view of the ministry. Maybe it is because they feel anybody can be a pastor, missionary, or preacher. Maybe they know (as elders, deacons and even pastors) that the pay is not good. Is it because they know that the job is difficult? They see it as unrewarding; a job that brings lots of stress and where the people they serve can be thankless.

I wonder how Jesus felt when his family tried to intervene in his public ministry. I am sure they were concerned for his safety and welfare. They wanted to protect him from danger. If your son told you he wanted to be a pastor would you be overjoyed? If your daughter said she was going to be a missionary to the Muslims would you rejoice? Would that paternal instinct override the spiritual? There is the temptation for the family member (brother, sister, mother, father) to try to persuade the young zealot to desist from this fanaticism. Well-meaning people who love us can seek to hinder us in our spiritual lives, thinking they are doing us good.

The unpardonable sin (3:22-30)

The section about Jesus and Beelzebub is about blasphemy against the Holy Spirit. We have seen the antagonism of the Pharisees towards Jesus. They felt power was being taken from them as they witnessed people following. He was drawing large crowds and influencing them by his teaching. The old order was beginning to unravel. The Pharisees were now plotting to kill Jesus. The religious and political leaders saw him and his teaching as a threat to the established order. They now accused Jesus of being in league with the devil. Yet, Jesus refuted this and exposed the absurdity of their argument: "How can Satan cast out Satan? If a kingdom is divided against itself, that kingdom cannot stand. And if a house is divided against itself, that house will not be able to stand."

Those who refer to the activity of the Holy Spirit as the work of Satan should be warned that this is dangerous. Those who refer to the truth as a lie should be advised of the danger of persisting in that position. Jesus said, "But no one can enter a strong man's house and plunder his goods, unless he first binds the strong man. Then indeed he may plunder his house." This is exactly what Jesus was doing in setting people free from the controlling power of Satan. It is clear (as we saw earlier) that the religious leaders colluded with the political powers to kill Christ. To call light darkness or good evil or Jesus' work Satanic is a very serious matter. But what is clear now is that they were in cahoots with Satan. The teachers of the law attributed Jesus' healing to Satan's power rather than to the Holy Spirit. This was blasphemous and Jesus warns that such things will not be forgiven. Blasphemy against the Holy Spirit is an unpardonable sin. This sin involves attributing the work of the Holy Spirit to the devil.

The Bible teaches that God forgives sin ... that is why Jesus came into the world. The Spirit gives life and teaches us about Christ. The sin against the Holy Spirit means consciously, willfully and persistently resisting his attempts to draw us to Christ. God eventually gives up on those who resist his call. It is not so much that God refuses to forgive rather it is the sinner who refuses to allow God to forgive. Scripture tells us that 'The Lord is not slow to fulfill his promise as some count slowness, but is patient toward you, not wishing that any should perish, but that all should reach repentance' (2 Peter 3:9). Nonetheless, it also informs us that 'the wrath of God is revealed from heaven against all ungodliness and unrighteousness of men, who by their unrighteousness suppress the truth.'–Romans 1:18.

Some have wondered if they have committed the 'unpardonable sin'. What Jesus is speaking of here is not an isolated act but a settled conviction and attitudes that reveal the true condition of the soul; those who continually harden their hearts to God. It is likely that those who are worried that they might have committed this sin have not actually done so. Their very sensitivity to the issue is evidence of this.

Christ's disciples (Christians) follow the truth of Scripture. Others have departed from this and adhere to man-made rules and regulations and human traditions. These traditions are deemed to be sacred but in reality many such traditions contradict the clear teaching of the Bible. We have seen how the crowds that followed Jesus disappeared. One day they were shouting "Hosanna" and shortly afterwards they were saying, "crucify him!" The religious leaders intimidated them. They loved their traditions more than the Word of God. They yielded to the peer pressure of the religious community. People are still like that today. However, one day the sheep will be separated from the goats. A day of reckoning is coming. In addition, the cowards who would not follow Jesus and the critics of Christ will be judged.

Jesus' mother and brothers (3:31-36)

Jesus brothers did not at this point believe. The fact that they were not disciples is borne out by John's Gospel 'For not even his brothers believed in him.' (John 7:5) In my own spiritual journey, the verses under consideration referring to Christ's siblings played a significant part in my conversion. I had been raised to believe that Mary, the mother of Jesus, was assumed into heaven still in a state of chastity with her virginity intact. The Bible teaches that she was a virgin when she conceived Jesus by the power of the Holy Spirit. However, she did have other children afterwards. The obvious meaning here has been avoided and twisted by those who want to protect their own false theology. It has been argued that these 'brothers and sisters' were sons and daughters of Joseph by a previous marriage. This cannot be inferred because Scripture makes no mention whatsoever of any such previous marriage, whether he was widowed or divorced or polygamous. We meet Mary and Joseph on a number of occasions in the Gospels, prior to Christ's birth and after it and no mention is made of these so-called half-brothers and sisters.

Apart from the fact that there is no Scriptural warrant at all for believing, they were half-brothers and half-sisters or 'cousins' it is a very unsound hermeneutical principle to make inferences from the silence of Scripture. It is all right to have a sanctified imagination and to speculate about the lives of biblical characters in order to animate the text and make vivid the possible feelings and thoughts of characters, so long as everybody knows it is merely speculation, within the bounds of revelation and reason. However, it is not all right to build doctrine where there is no foundation. Even to build doctrine where there is slender foundation is inappropriate. The notion that Mary never had sexual relations with Joseph needs to be knocked on the head for the absurd and frankly, twisted, theory that it is. It is rooted in the idea that sex is sinful. Sex was invented by God, is intended by God for married people, and is not, therefore, bad. Only those with weird attitudes to sex, such as celibate hierarchy could think like this. They have made a deity out of Mary without any Scriptural warrant and fly in the face of clear and abundant teaching to the contrary. This is heretical. It might be dear to the hearts of millions of people but it is a lie. To distort God's Word like this is grievously offensive to God and those responsible will be held accountable to the Lord.

The proper interpretation is that they were sons of Joseph and Mary, younger half-brothers and sisters of Jesus. There is no other valid interpretation. In fact, this is not an interpretation; it is merely a reading of what the text says. Four of these brothers are named later in this Gospel.

He went away from there and came to his hometown, and his disciples followed him. In addition, on the Sabbath, he began to teach in the synagogue, and many who heard him were astonished, saying, "Where did this man get these things? What is the wisdom given to him? How do his hands do such mighty works? Is not this the carpenter, the son of Mary and brother of James and Joses and Judas and Simon? And are not his sisters here with us?"—Mark 6:1-4.

However, in the passage we are considering Jesus says something very important concerning relationships:

Mark 3:31-35

³¹ And his mother and his brothers came, and standing outside they sent to him and called him. ³² And a crowd was sitting around him, and they said to him, "Your mother and your brothers are outside, seeking you." ³³ And he answered them, "Who are my mother and my brothers?" ³⁴ And looking about at those who sat around him, he said, "Here are my mother and my brothers! ³⁵ For whoever does the will of God, he is my brother and sister and mother."

Jesus makes it clear that there is a spiritual family and that membership of this family is evidenced by obedience to his teaching. He makes it clear that membership of this spiritual family is more important than our human families. To be related by blood is the closest biological relationship. However, to be related through the redeeming blood of Jesus is the most important spiritual relationship. Are you a member of that family of Christ?

CHAPTER 4

The parable of the sower (4:1-20)

Jesus regularly preached in the synagogue on the Sabbath and in the temple (Mark 1:29, 39; 3:1; 6:2). Here his pulpit is a boat. Imagine that scene. Jesus spoke to the people from a mountain (Matthew 5:1 ff.); a house (Mark 2:1 ff.); in a cemetery (John 11:38 ff.); in the desert (Mark 8:1-4). Jesus spoke wherever he could and to whomsoever would listen; Jews, non-Jews, rich, poor, men, women, children. His teaching was rich with illustrations from everyday life.

Here we see the Master teaching through a parable. Mark uses only a small selection of the parables, which Jesus taught. Parables have been described as 'earthly stories with heavenly meanings'. A parable is a story (not necessarily about real people and events) that illustrates some truth. Jesus used this valuable method of instruction and aroused and sustained people's interest. Truth embodied in a story is accessible to all people irrespective of their level of education or intellectual ability. Parables enlighten and persuade in a unique and compelling way. They use familiar imagery in such a way that it brings new and unfamiliar insights. In this way, it is an engaging form of communication. Essentially a parable is a story designed to illustrate a moral or spiritual lesson; a narrative that is constructed for the sake of conveying important truth. Parables are an interesting way of presenting important principles. The parable, therefore, has its place in Scripture and functions perfectly well, wherever it is used. Inherently figurative language draws an illustration from life.

Sometimes Jesus explained the parables and other times he did not. Christ interpreted this parable for us and that prevents us from allegorizing wildly. One well-known example of violating this principle is Augustine's allegorizing of the parable of the Good Samaritan (Luke 10:25-37):

The man who fell into the hands of robbers is Adam. Jerusalem is heaven, and Jericho signifies man's mortality. The robbers are the Devil and his angels who stripped man of his immortality. In beating him, they persuaded him to sin, and in leaving him half dead the Devil and his angels have left man in a condition in which he has some knowledge of God but is yet oppressed by sin. The priest represents the Law, and the Levite represents the Prophets. The Good Samaritan is Christ who, in bandaging the man's wounds, seeks to restrain sin. Oil is hope and wine is a fervent spirit. The man's donkey is Jesus' incarnation, and the man being placed on a donkey pictures his belief in the incarnation of Christ. The inn is the church. The next day pictures the Lord's resurrection, the two coins represent either the two precepts of love or this life and the life to come. The innkeeper is the Apostle Paul.[21]

Perhaps we find this amusing and suppose we would never be guilty of such interpretations. How about the hymn:

> He poured in the oil and the wine,
> The kind that restoreth my soul
> He found me bleeding and dying on the Jericho Road
> And he poured in the oil and the wine.

The parable of the Good Samaritan is about loving your neighbor or even your enemy and showing kindness and mercy.

---

[21] Augustine, *Quaestiones Evangeliorum 2*, p.19

At the time of Christ, seed was broadcast (scattered) by hand and some seed fell on unproductive ground. The 'secrets' of the kingdom are those things God has revealed to his people. The truth is proclaimed to all but only those who have ears to hear will understand. Jesus compares his preaching to the ministry of Isaiah. Isaiah gained some disciples (Isaiah 8:16) but his preaching also exposed the hardheartedness of many who resisted his message from God. Prosperity gives a false sense of self-sufficiency, security and well-being. In a passage that speaks of the vanity of self-indulgence, Solomon says:

Ecclesiastes 2:4-11

⁴ I made great works. I built houses and planted vineyards for myself. ⁵ I made myself gardens and parks, and planted in them all kinds of fruit trees. ⁶ I made myself pools from which to water the forest of growing trees. ⁷ I bought male and female slaves, and had slaves who were born in my house. I had also great possessions of herds and flocks, more than any who had been before me in Jerusalem. ⁸ I also gathered for myself silver and gold and the treasure of kings and provinces. I got singers, both men and women, and many concubines, the delight of the sons of man.

⁹ So I became great and surpassed all who were before me in Jerusalem. Also my wisdom remained with me. ¹⁰ And whatever my eyes desired I did not keep from them. I kept my heart from no pleasure, for my heart found pleasure in all my toil, and this was my reward for all my toil. ¹¹ Then I considered all that my hands had done and the toil I had expended in doing it, and behold, all was vanity and a striving after wind, and there was nothing to be gained under the sun.

The parable of the sower begins and ends with a call for careful attention. This suggests that its meaning may not be self-evident. It is not so much that alert minds are needed to comprehend the truth. Rather truth is spiritually discerned as the Holy Spirit illuminates it.[22] The point of the parable is that the kingdom of God will produce much fruit. The 'secret' is that the kingdom of God has drawn near in the person of Christ. It is a secret because it was previously unknown. It is not something reserved for the close associates of Christ. It is proclaimed to all but, only those who have faith can understand.

However, Christ's parables were not always clear (the disciples themselves had difficulty understanding them 7:17). Jesus challenges us to penetrate beneath the surface meaning and to discern the deeper truth(s). There is a tone of rebuke in Christ's statement that the disciples should have been able to interpret this parable because the meaning is clear. But what we notice is that they receive an answer. Jesus helps them understand. If we ask, the Lord will make his Word clear to us.

The farmer is Jesus and the seed is the Word of God. Jesus is talking about the spread of the gospel and the kind of reception it receives. We have seen how Jesus received negative responses to his preaching. The seed that falls on the hardened path refers to those who have no reception to the Word. Satan snatches it from them before it has opportunity to take root. The seed sown on stony soil represents another hindrance to the proper reception of the Word. Persecution and trials were very real in the first-century Roman church (this Gospel was written with the Roman Christian in mind). This is a reality in the experience of many who hear the Word in various parts of the world today. Some will defect or recant because they are not deeply rooted and established

---

[22] Christian Publishing House would suggest the following articles, so as to have a balanced view,

(1) The Work of the Holy Spirit (esp. Biblical Interpretation) http://www.christianpublishers.org/holy-spirit-the-work-of (2) How Are We to Understand the Indwelling of the Holy Spirit? http://www.christianpublishers.org/holy-spirit-indwelling

in their faith. The third group of people responds well initially and seems to be progressing well in their faith but they become distracted by the cares of this world. Worries or wealth choke the spiritual life so that growth is inhibited and they are unproductive. James warns of the deceitfulness of riches:

James 5:1-5

¹ Come now, you rich, weep and howl for the miseries that are coming upon you. ² Your riches have rotted and your garments are moth-eaten. ³ Your gold and silver have corroded, and their corrosion will be evidence against you and will eat your flesh like fire. You have laid up treasure in the last days. ⁴ Behold, the wages of the laborers who mowed your fields, which you kept back by fraud, are crying out against you, and the cries of the harvesters have reached the ears of the Lord of hosts. ⁵ You have lived on the earth in luxury and in self-indulgence. You have fattened your hearts in a day of slaughter.

However, some seed falls on good soil. Such people are open and receptive to the gospel and respond to it positively. Their hearts are cultivated to receive the Word. These people become what they were intended to be. Beautiful lilies can emerge from dung heaps! "Consider the lilies, how they grow: they neither toil nor spin, yet I tell you, even Solomon in all his glory was not arrayed like one of these." (Luke 12:27) How many times have we seen broken people from dysfunctional homes being transformed by the power of the gospel? The question is which category do we fit into? Are you someone who hears the Word but immediately it is snatched away? Perhaps you are someone who once heard the Word and joyfully and positively responded to it but maybe that initial positive response has changed because of circumstances in your life. Maybe you never developed to the point where spiritual roots took hold in the soil of your heart. Maybe you went along fine for a while but when you encountered opposition, (ridicule, rejection) you withered away. Maybe you welcomed the Word of God once but then you decided to pursue your career and get the nice car and lovely house. None of those things are bad in themselves but have they choked your spiritual life?

Notice how Jesus refers to the "deceitfulness of riches". Materialistic desires and selfish ambitions can lead away from the spiritual path. What have you got that will be an enduring legacy? Jesus said: "Do not lay up for yourselves treasures on earth, where moth and rust destroy and where thieves break in and steal, but lay up for yourselves treasures in heaven, where neither moth nor rust destroys and where thieves do not break in and steal." (Matthew 6:19-20) Are you or will you be numbered among those who hear the Word of God and accept it?

This parable calls us to hear and heed the Word of God and to receive it and respond to it positively. God longs to make something beautiful from our lives. He longs to bless abundantly. May that seed take root, germinate, blossom and bear fruit in our lives and in the lives of others for the glory of God!

A lamp under a basket or on a stand (4:21-25)

Putting a lamp in such a place seems ridiculous and even dangerous. It serves no purpose if it is hidden. The purpose of the lamp is to shine so that its light might be evident and dispel the darkness. Christ's true identity is still concealed at this point. However, it will not always be so as subsequent history has shown. Nevertheless, even now Jesus has not yet been manifest in all his glory. That day is yet to come. Jesus is the light of the world. He is to be elevated in our lives so that people have the advantage of the light. We are to bring that Christian perspective to bear in our conversations and in all situations.

The parable of the measure (4:21-25)

This parable is incorporated under the heading of the parable of a lamp under a basket or on a stand. But Jesus is saying something different here: "Pay attention to what you hear: with the measure you use, it will be measured to you, and still more will be added to you. For to the one who has, more will be given, and from the one who has not, even what he has will be taken away." He starts with a clear call for attention. There is a summons to listen carefully. This may (at a casual glance) seem to be teaching a kind of Karma. That is, if you do good things then good things will happen to you but if you do bad things then bad things will happen to you. This is the philosophy of the Buddhist, Hindu and Sikh religions in relation to one's destiny or fate. But this Parable of the Measure is about spiritual perception. The more one hears and heeds the teaching of Jesus the more will be revealed and the greater the blessing will be. However, if one ignores the truth or fails to apply it then the little perception they have will be taken away.

The parable of the seed growing (4:26-29)

This parable emphasizes the mysterious power of the seed to produce a crop. All that the farmer can do is plant the seed on suitable ground. He cannot make it grow. Nor do we fully understand how it grows. Agricultural science can explain it in scientific terms but it still remains a mysterious process. The kingdom, though hidden at this point will come to fruition. That time of Judgment is coming when God will put the sickle to the crop.

The parable of the mustard seed (4:30-34)

In this parable, the mustard seed is very small but it produces a treelike shrub. The emphasis here is that the kingdom of God has apparently weak and insignificant beginnings but a day will come when it will be great and powerful. We should not judge a work of God by its apparently insignificant beginnings. God entered this world as a baby with all the weakness, vulnerability, and dependency of such an entity. Thus, we see the humble beginning of the kingdom in the incarnation. The great and mighty nation of Israel began with God's dealings with just one man.

Jesus calms a storm (4:35-41)

Jesus invites his disciples to travel with him "Let us go across to the other side." One day when Jesus was preaching a large crowd gathered. He got into a boat and sat in it on the sea, and the crowd was on shore listening to his every word. Imagine them gathered along the beach: some sitting on the sand as close to the water as possible, maybe letting the waves creep over their feet to get relief from the heat of the day. I imagine some sitting on driftwood and rocks listening intently. They hear several parables. Eventually Jesus is alone with his disciples. The public ministry ended and the private ministry began. Jesus invites his disciples to be alone with him. He invites us to come away from the crowd, sit at his feet, and listen to him. How special they must have felt to have the privilege of drawing near to him. Do we, as his disciples, feel special to have been called apart to be tutored by him? The spiritual life is a journey that begins with an invitation from the Lord to come out of the crowd and share intimacy with him. For the disciples on that day the adventure began with an invitation. However, as they traveled with Jesus a storm occurred and they became afraid. Jesus calmed that storm and the disciples were amazed. The drama ends with a very important question: "who then is this?"

We have accepted Christ's invitation to follow him, be near him, rest in him, and learn from him. The adventure has begun. Storms will come but Jesus is with us. We are on a journey with Jesus at his invitation. We are on our way to another shore. He says to us, as he said to them on that day, "Let us go across to the other side." What a traveling companion! His presence guarantees safe passage.

There is a purpose in the storms of life. The disciples were traveling with Jesus. How like the Christian life this is. Here is an invitation to all disciples, which is loaded with promise. It is an invitation that has eternal significance. We have the presence, provision, power and protection of Christ along the way. It is a cameo of our journey through this life to that other shore that awaits us. There we will have uninterrupted fellowship with our Lord. Surely, it thrills our souls to have the fellowship and friendship of Jesus as we go. It is a picture of security and safety. Here on this shore we are often weary. We are pilgrims picking our way through life. When we respond to the invitation (get in the boat) we will have the companionship of Christ on the journey and ultimately we will reach that other shore, despite storms along the way.

The storm they experienced was a furious tempest. The waves beat into the ship and they were afraid they would drown. There is a lesson here: storms come to disciples! They were traveling with Jesus, at his invitation. They had obeyed Jesus, yet the storm came. You may be passing through a storm even though you are an obedient disciple. You may be wondering, how this can be. However, there is purpose in the storms we experience. The storm, which Jonah experienced, brought him back from backsliding. Paul was shipwrecked but it opened new doors of witness. This storm that the disciples experienced tested their faith and led them to a point where they recognized the power of God at work in their experience. We may feel frightened by the circumstance we find ourselves in but just as Jesus was with them in the storm so too he will be with us in our storms.

The disciples were in a boat with Jesus going to a quiet place to be alone with their master when a great storm arose and they were afraid of losing their lives. They did not fully understand who Christ was. Only God could command the winds and the sea to obey him. It was a moment of realization for them. They may not have come to understand fully the deity of Jesus but they had a brief glimpse of that possibility and it frightened them more than the storm.

In verse 40, the Greek word *deilia* (δειλία) is used for 'afraid' as it is translated in the ESV. This word refers to a spirit of fearfulness, which is not from God: 'for God gave us a spirit not of fear but of power and love and self-control.' (2 Timothy 1:7) It means cowardice or timidity and is never used in a good sense. But in verse 41 the Greek word *phobos* (φόβος) is used for 'great fear' as it is translated in the ESV. This word refers to fear, dread, panic, alarm, terror. It is always used with this significance in the four Gospels. It can be a fear caused by the intimidation of adversaries or a reverential fear of God. This latter sense is not merely a fear of God's power of righteous retribution but a wholesome dread of displeasing the Lord.

In Mark 4:40-41 it is clear that the disciples were afraid before and after the miracle (during the storm and after it had been stilled). They were frightened by the storm but terrified by its quelling.[23] Jesus asks them why they *are* afraid, not why *were* they afraid. He is asking why they *still* have no faith even after he calmed the storm. The miracle should have taught them that he does care, that he is powerful and loving.

---

[23] For similar instances of awe induced by being in the presence of the Almighty see Isaiah 6:5 and Luke 5:8.

This should have given them comfort and confidence derived from his presence and power. The experiences of life are sent for a purpose and may sanctify us if we respond rightly to them. The fear that the disciples experienced as a result of Christ's miracle is a mixture of dread, astonishment and reverence. The disciples began to realize that Jesus is far more powerful than they had imagined. The disciples seem to have been impressed at this point with the power, majesty and glory of Christ and vocalize this in the question: "What kind of person is this?"

Do we fully understand the unrestricted power of God that is at work in our lives? Jesus was asleep in the boat, after a long day of preaching, and the disciples waken him and say, "Teacher, do you not care that we are perishing?" They rightly understand him to be a wonderful spiritual teacher but their understanding is limited for they do not realize the divine nature of the one to whom they speak.

There is a tone of accusation in their question. We should not judge them too harshly. They were terrified. In certain situations, our faith is stretched and our understanding is limited. Yet their terror is mixed with trust. These experienced sailors turn to Jesus (a carpenter) for help. That makes no sense without faith. Their faith was far from perfect. But even little faith is faith and there is the hope that our faith will be strengthened. They felt that Jesus was not attentive enough to their immediate crisis. Do we ever feel like that? Christ commanded the winds to cease. I imagine the only sounds they heard at that moment were the gentle lapping of the water against the boat and the pounding of their hearts. They ask, "...who then is this?" This is an important question. May we answer, as Thomas did on another occasion: "My Lord and my God!"

CHAPTER 5

Jesus heals a man with a demon (5:1-20)

This man is a demoniac not a maniac! Here Jesus demonstrates his power over the forces of evil by casting out demons from a possessed man. Like the calming of the storm, it proves the divine nature and power of Jesus. The wild sea and the wild man were both, from a human point of view, untamable. However, Jesus subdued both.

Jesus and the disciples went across the lake where the population was largely Gentile. In that place, there is a large herd of pigs (considered to be unclean by Jews). The setting is interesting. There is a cemetery with tombs. It is a place of the dead. The man is at home there. The image conveyed is one of death, disorder, decay, and destruction. Often in Palestine people were buried in open caves hewn from the limestone rock. This would be an appropriate location for a horror movie. Since it was already evening when they started to cross the lake (4:35) it was probably dark by the time they arrived on the far shore.

The possessed man lived in tombs, screaming night and day and cutting himself with stones. How very destructive these demons were, causing this man to self-harm! The commentator, William Hendriksen points out that this is a sad picture of '...demonic malevolence coupled with human indifference and impotence.'[24] He goes on to say however, 'But in the end divine omnipotence and benevolence come to

---

[24] Hendriksen, William. *Mark* (New Testament Commentary), Banner of Truth, 1975, p.189.

the rescue and triumph.'[25] The helpfulness of Jesus and the helplessness of this man are contrasted. But Hendriksen also points out that Christ's helpfulness and the people's heartlessness are strikingly contrasted.[26]

It would seem that the people who lived in the area were primarily concerned for their own safety and protection. However, all their efforts to restrain this man were unsuccessful. No human power can contain the work of the devil and his servants. No matter how powerful the means used (chains) they cannot produce the desired result. So it seems some effort had been made to control this man but without success.

The man fell on his knees in front of Jesus. This may be understood as an act of homage rather than an act of worship. In other words, it is an acknowledgement of Christ's identity. He is not necessarily regarding Jesus with reverence and adoration. The demons showed respect because they recognized that one far superior to them had confronted them. This is an acknowledgement of their inferiority. They feared exorcism and pleaded not to be tortured. Perhaps this means that they did not want to be sent to that final destination of eternal torment.

There was more than one demon occupying and controlling this man. The word 'legion' refers to a division of three-thousand to six-thousand men in the ancient Roman army. It may not mean that there were that exact number of demons but it does mean that they were great in number. He was totally under the controlling influence of these demonic powers. His life was miserable. He was chained like an animal. His strength was greater than all who had attempted to restrain him.

---

[25] Hendriksen, William. *Mark* (New Testament Commentary), Banner of Truth, 1975, p.189.
[26] Hendriksen, William. *Mark* (New Testament Commentary), Banner of Truth, 1975, p.189.

We see the destructive force of the demonic powers in the killing of the herd of swine. There were two-thousand pigs in this herd, which is a great number by any standard and very valuable in monetary terms. Failing to destroy the man these demons destroyed the pigs. Demons are the devils workers and he is the destroyer.

Why Jesus allowed the demons to enter this herd of swine is not clear. Maybe he wanted all to see that they had left the man and to have tangible evidence of this fact. Or perhaps he wanted them to see how destructive they were. Where they went after the pigs were killed is not known. The herdsmen immediately ran to tell everyone what had happened. The response is surprising.

Mark 5:14-17

14 The herdsmen fled and told it in the city and in the country. And people came to see what it was that had happened. 15 And they came to Jesus and saw the demon-possessed man, the one who had had the legion, sitting there, clothed and in his right mind, and they were afraid. 16 And those who had seen it described to them what had happened to the demon-possessed man and to the pigs. 17 And they began to beg Jesus to depart from their region.

Here is an amazing picture of order restored and a picture of what Jesus has done for the Christian. We too were spiritually naked but he clothed us and brought peace to our souls. The troubled man was now clothed and in his right mind. Yet the people were afraid of this new situation. It is amazing what people will get used to. Even though the power that was at work in this man was evil and destructive they seemed to prefer it to the new order. Rather than honoring Jesus and pleading with him to stay in their area and perform other great deeds they pleaded with Jesus to leave. Only God the Son can deliver people from the tyranny of evil. Instead of rejoicing and celebrating this as good news they are afraid (in the presence of one who is so powerful) and they asked Jesus to leave their region. They must have seen the incident as well-intended but very destructive. They probably feared that such power could be used again with unforeseen and unwanted results. Jesus did as they wished. He does not remain where he is not wanted.

Jesus decided to return to the west side of the lake and the man who had been delivered from demon possession wanted to go with him (naturally). However, Jesus would not allow this. This man had been the beneficiary of great mercy and grace. Jesus had shown him compassion and liberated him. Others had tried to restrain him and failed. They could not even contemplate delivering him. Instead Jesus told him to return to his family and bear testimony to the power and grace of God. This is a more difficult task. Many people want to be where the buzz is happening. They want to be in the seminary with Jesus teaching them and explaining the meaning of the parables. It is difficult to go home and bear witness through words and holy living. But this is what Christ required of this man. This is what he also asks us to do. To bear witness to what he has done for us.

We might think our liberation from the powers of darkness is a lesser miracle than the one we read about in the life of this man but the devil does not easily let his captives go. Therefore, Christ laid down his life to set us free. We are branches plucked from the fire of hell. We too were under the controlling influence of the powers of darkness but Christ has set us free. People in our community may not be pleased about it. They might prefer things the way they were. This man was entrusted with a great task; to bear witness to the truth of what Jesus had done for him. Christ wants us to do the same. The man obeyed Jesus and bore testimony to what Jesus had done for him. He went to the Decapolis (a league of ten cities, where all but one was located east of the Jordan River). There the people heard his testimony and marveled.

What about the destruction of the pigs? They were the property of somebody. The people of this community were selfish. Their possessions and prosperity were of greater value than the liberation and restoration of this wretched man. He was enslaved, abandoned, and merely restrained by them. Christ granted the request of the demons to allow them to enter the herd of pigs. He also acceded to the people's request that he leave town. But he refused the earnest request of the newly liberated man to go with him. When God refuses to grant his followers, what they ask it is not necessarily a sign of his disfavor. Missionary activity begins at home but it does not necessarily end there. He is to return to the community that had neglected him. They had asked Jesus to leave so he sends them a missionary who can bear testimony from personal experience and that is a powerful witness. That is what we are called to do, to bear witness from our personal experience of deliverance, to testify in our own homes and in our communities and to obey Jesus in this regard. Even if we will not be well received and if nobody is converted, Jesus wants others to hear the message and so he sends us to speak of him. We have been delivered from the great power of darkness by the greater power of God. We might not have manifested the symptoms of our condition as this man did. However, we too were under the controlling influence of the powers of darkness.

Many African-American slaves when liberated after the American Civil War stayed on the plantations. It was what they were used to. They had made a home of their place of enslavement. Many people today are so institutionalized that they are afraid to leave their place of captivity. Those who have been liberated by Jesus belong to God's marvelous kingdom of light and should avail of that freedom.

Jairus' daughter (5:21-24; 35-43)

Visit any good bookshop and you will find a section displaying the biographies and autobiographies of men that the world regards as great. There are shelves hosting an array of life stories. Presidents and prime ministers peer majestically from the dust covers of hefty tomes. These are the familiar faces of famous men, who have proved themselves in positions of leadership. There you will see the accounts of the achievements of emperors and kings, great generals and military men who have established notoriety. Then there are the books with front cover photographs of media personalities, celebrities with charming and charismatic smiles. These include picture books of film stars and pop idols. In the bargain bin you might find the biography of some athlete who thrilled spectators in a previous generation. There you may find big discount stickers partially covering the faces of former sporting giants. This is the world's view of greatness but what is the heavenly perspective?

When God looks at men, he sees either men, who have come to faith in Christ or men who have not. Let us consider a man who has been made famous in the Gospels of Matthew, Mark and Luke. His name is Jairus. Is there any reason why he should be regarded as a great father? In answer to that, it can be said that Jairus did the greatest thing a father can ever do. Here was a man with a certain position and reputation in the community. He was a ruler in the synagogue, a leader among his people. He did not come to Christ conscious of his reputation. Rather he approached with an awareness of his great need.

It is instructive to observe how he came in humility. He assumed the posture and attitude of a beggar by falling at the feet of Jesus. He implored Christ to come to his house. Jairus came to Christ with a troubled heart. Christ welcomes those who are conscious of their great need and come in humility.

Listen to his gracious invitation: "Come to me, all who labor and are heavy laden, and I will give you rest" (Matthew 11: 28). What was it that compelled this man to come to Christ? There was a difficulty in his home that upset him. His little girl was dying. It was a problem that he could not solve and he realized that there was one who could make a difference. He had the affection of a loving father and it caused him to cast himself upon the compassion of Christ, not for himself but for his only daughter, twelve years old. How he must have loved her, his precious princess! He needed the touch of Jesus on the one he loved. The greatest thing any father can do is to come to Jesus as Jairus did on behalf of his beloved child.

As a father, his love was exemplary. He came into the presence Christ, the one whose pity and power worked in harmony to produce the promise, "Do not fear, only believe." It is an astonishing pledge considering that Jairus had just been informed of his daughter's death. His appeal to Jesus is based on the hope that the heart of Christ is compassionate. It is like David's plea to God, 'Have mercy on me, O God, according to your steadfast love; according to your abundant mercy' (Psalm 51:1). Desperation gave birth to faith, a faith that dared to believe that "nothing will be impossible with God."–Luke 1:37.

He came to communicate with Jesus about his child's condition. Was she not privileged to have such a father? Surely, the most privileged children in the world are those who have such a father to intercede on their behalf. Those children, whose names are frequently found on the lips of their fathers in prayer, are privileged indeed. Here is a man, a father in the presence of Christ, before the throne of grace, interceding for a loved one. The most underprivileged children are the ones whose parents do not pray for them. This story gives hope to fathers, especially those who are conscious of their own inadequacies in the face of great difficulty. There is one to whom we may come on behalf of our children. He is the one who says, "Do not fear, only believe."

What a challenge that was to Jairus' faith and it is no less a challenge to ours! Jairus faced a tremendous test of a father's faith. News arrived that his daughter was dead. Jesus spoke words of encouragement, "Do not fear, only believe." Who would Jairus believe? Would he accept the report of her death? Would he trust in the promise of Jesus? There are times in a father's life when all the hopes he cherished for his loved one seem to be displaced by doubt and even despair. Oh the heartache of a father when all seems lost! But Jairus had just witnessed the healing of the woman who had an issue of blood for twelve years. Perhaps this incident had strengthened his faith. When we walk with the Master there are incidents that we encounter along the way that strengthen our faith. Jesus speaks: "The child is not dead but sleeping."

These words have a special significance in my spiritual life. When I was a child, my mother encouraged me to visit the cemetery to pray for her parents who were buried there.[27] It was on one of these visits I had my first memorable encounter with Scripture. We did not have a Bible at home and the reading of Scripture at Mass never affected me. There, in that cemetery, not far from my ancestors' grave was a headstone on the grave of a two year old girl which bore the inscription, "She is not dead but sleepeth". I do not know exactly what age I was but I think I was about ten years old. I

---

[27] They are buried in the grounds of St. Mary's Cathedral (Church of Ireland) in Limerick city. My maternal ancestors have had that plot since before the Reformation and it is one of the few Roman Catholic plots there. This use of prayer is widely practiced by people of various religions. It is my understanding now that one ought to pray for the living because when they are dead their destiny is already determined and that depends entirely on whether or not they are trusting in Jesus' finished work at Calvary as atonement for their sins.

remember reading it and being fascinated with these words and what they conveyed. I believe it was the first time I ever contemplated the immortality of the soul. I would not have put it like that at that time but I definitely thought of the possibility that there was life after death. This idea must have been conveyed to me by my mother but there was something qualitatively different about the words of Jesus which penetrated my heart. Two thousand years after they were spoken in a distant land these words, written in stone, still had the power to communicate the truth. I did not come to Christ in faith until several years later, at the age of fifteen, when I heard the gospel explained by a stranger whom I met in a park. Nevertheless, these words spoken by Jesus to Jairus touched me in a special way. I remember thinking of the sorrow of a child dying and contemplating the possibility and the hope that death was only temporary. God's Word has power; let us never forget that.

The daughter of this great father was restored to health. What ecstatic joy that must have instilled in the man's heart. He was astonished. May every father be like Jairus and recognize the terrible condition of their children and how they need the touch of the Savior! Mark's account informs us that he specifically requested that Jesus would touch her: "My little daughter is at the point of death. Come and lay your hands on her, so that she may be made well and live." (5:23) May every father believe that Christ is approachable and able! May every father come in humility as Jairus did, helpless but hopeful! May Christ visit our homes and put out unbelief. May each father know the great joy of this great father, Jairus. He saw the one he loved given new life by Jesus.

The Lord's Table is a celebration of the newness of life that is ours as a result of the touch of the Master's hand. In our journey in life, we have had an encounter with him. His promise required faith. Perhaps we saw others being transformed (as Jairus did that day) and this gave us hope to believe. We had to come in humility, recognizing our own helplessness. The Lord welcomes those who intercede on behalf of others. Christ cares for our concerns. When he intervenes everything is different. There were those who laughed at Jesus but they witnessed the power of God in this miracle. He was mocked at his death on the cross too. There will always be those who sneer at Jesus and those who put their faith in him. It seems from this story that Jesus was delayed, interrupted and/or distracted. It seems that events just occurred in a way that was unfortunate for Jairus. The worst had happened and it seemed to others that this situation was beyond the power of Jesus. They thought it was too late. There are situations that seem impossible where we might think that even the Lord cannot put this right. But there is nothing beyond the power of God. God's power was made even more evident in raising a dead girl than it would have been in healing a sick girl.

The crucifixion of Jesus seemed like that to the disciples. It seemed that the worst had happened and that it was too late now. Their hopes were dashed. It seemed that events had unfolded in a way that was unexpected and unforeseen and that things had gone terribly wrong. They had witnessed much, even Jesus raising others, like Jairus' daughter, from the dead. How easily the candle of hope is snuffed out by the winds of circumstances in those of little faith. Come to the feet of Jesus and intercede on behalf of your loved ones who are afflicted with the disease of sin. Come on behalf of those who are dead in their sins and dare to believe that the touch of those nail-pierced hands can bring newness of life. Don't let the scoffing of others discourage you, "Do not fear, only believe."

Jesus heals a woman with an issue of blood (Mark 5:25-34)

This woman had a problem. She had an issue of blood for twelve years. This we understand as continuous menstrual bleeding or some such form of hemorrhaging. Religion had failed her. Doctors had failed to cure her. It is an astonishing incident which is communicated in parenthesis almost as an aside or interruption to the story about Jairus' daughter. It seems that the continuous progress of Jesus was obstructed in the situation of Jairus. How quick the disciples were to believe it was too late, to limit the power of the Master and to resign themselves to the idea that nothing could be done now. How wrong they were. But are we not like that? Do we always believe, always hope, always pray?

Faith brought this unnamed woman to Jesus. He speaks tenderly to her and addresses her as "Daughter". This suggests that she belongs and that he does not see her as an outcast. She was transformed by her encounter with Christ and her life from that day forward would have been so much better. She wanted to slip away quietly but Jesus confronted her gently. Jesus wants her to bear public testimony to his transforming power.

This story presents Jesus as the hope of the hopeless. Nobody could tame the demoniac or help him. Nobody could raise somebody from the dead. Nobody could cure this woman. But Jesus triumphs over this human hopelessness in a majestic display of his divine power. Not only did Jesus heal this woman but he perfected her faith. The power and pity of Jesus work together in harmony to bring great changes in people's lives.

A large crowd was pressing around Jesus. This seemed to be the usual situation wherever he went. The woman in the crowd thought she could take the blessing and leave unnoticed. She had suffered with her apparently incurable condition for twelve years. Jesus was on his way to the home of Jairus but he was delayed by the crowd. The Lord was frequently interrupted in his ministry as in this episode. He was interrupted while praying (Mark 1:35ff), speaking to a crowd (Mark 2:1ff), sleeping (Mark 4:38-39), conversing with his disciples (Mark 8:31ff) and travelling (Mark 10:46). Yet Jesus is not frustrated or defeated by any of these interruptions.

Here was a woman who was sick. She must have been physically weakened by this continuous and excessive loss of blood. She must have been psychologically impacted by her predicament. In such an unhealthy condition, she could not have felt strong. The strongest thing about this woman is her faith. Her condition got worse from the unsuccessful and unhelpful interventions of physicians. So in this terrible and deteriorating state she came to Jesus, a broke and broken woman. She spent all she had in search of a cure but actually got worse. She had lost her health, wealth and dignity. Her condition made her ceremonially unclean (Leviticus 15:19ff). Jairus and this woman would have been at opposite ends of the social order. He was a prominent person and she was an impoverished outcast. It seems that people from all classes in society turned to Christ for help. She certainly had faith, though her faith was not perfect.

It is not necessary to touch the physical Jesus or artifacts that belonged to him (clothing) in order to be healed. What counts is a person's faith in the power, mercy and grace of the Lord. She thought Jesus would not even notice her touching his garment (or tassel) but he did. Even though her faith was far from perfect, the Lord nevertheless rewarded it by restoring her to health. She wants to remain anonymous but he forces her gently out into the open. Instantly her affliction was ended. It was an encounter that impacted on her physically and spiritually. The power within Christ responded to the faith of the woman. But he wanted her to glorify him. The words of the psalmist seem apt: '...call upon me in the day of trouble; I will deliver you, and you shall glorify me' (Psalm 50:15). Whatever blessings are bestowed from heaven must be acknowledged in thanksgiving that glorifies the Lord. The woman had reached out to Jesus and was delivered from her predicament but she had not, as yet, glorified him. Up to now, she was like one of the nine cleansed lepers who neither acknowledged nor thanked the Lord for the healing he had wrought:

Luke 17:11-19

11 On the way to Jerusalem he was passing along between Samaria and Galilee. 12 And as he entered a village, he was met by ten lepers, who stood at a distance 13 and lifted up their voices, saying, "Jesus, Master, have mercy on us." 14 When he saw them he said to them, "Go and show yourselves to the priests." And as they went they were cleansed. 15 Then one of them, when he saw that he was healed, turned back, praising God with a loud voice; 16 and he fell on his face at Jesus' feet, giving him thanks. Now he was a Samaritan. 17 Then Jesus answered, "Were not ten cleansed? Where are the nine? 18 Was no one found to return and give praise to God except this foreigner?" 19 And he said to him, "Rise and go your way; your faith has made you well."

The woman had believed with her heart but had not yet confessed with her mouth (Romans 10:9). Jesus asked who touched him and the disciples interpret his words in a literal sense. Jesus is asking who had touched him in this meaningful way, not just the physical touch. Of course, this woman touched Jesus physically and Jesus is not denying that but there is more to it. The response of the disciples showed a lack of insight and seems even to have a disrespectful tone. Jesus ignored them and looked around until his gaze rested on this woman. She responded to Christ's question and accepted the invitation to step forward and acknowledge what Jesus had done for her.

She was afraid. For a woman to speak in public was considered improper. She was ashamed because of the nature of her condition and to have to speak publicly about it would be embarrassing. The impropriety of her actions would come to light because she was deemed to be ceremonially unclean and yet she had touched the Master. This would be considered inappropriate by bystanders. She could not be sure how Jesus would respond to her sneaky way of stealing the blessing. This explains why she was so afraid.

However, Jesus does not rebuke her rather he addresses her as "Daughter" which is an inclusive term, a family term and an intimate word. This is a word that would reassure her that she belongs to the community of faith from which she had been quarantined. It restores her dignity. How lovely the Savior is! He speaks lovingly to her as a father to a child. He praises her for her faith. It was not her faith that cured her but faith was the channel through which the cure had been brought about. When Jesus says, "your faith has made you well," he is saying that it was his response to her faith that cured her. In saying this, he leaves no room for the superstitious view that his clothes had in any way contributed to the healing.

Jesus pronounced her cured. These words paved the way for the woman's complete reinstatement in the religious and social order. He bestows the blessing of peace upon her. It is possible to come into the presence of the Lord afflicted with some condition and to press through and reach out and touch the Master. Those who reach out in faith can touch the great physician of body and soul who has the power to make them whole. Those who have been made whole by the Master must confess (publicly acknowledge) his power at work in transforming their lives. God wants to be glorified by such testimony to his transforming power.

The word in the Old Testament book of Numbers for the 'corner' (which can be translated as 'hem' or 'fringe') of the garment (where the tassels would be) is the same as the word in Malachi for 'wings':

Numbers 15:37-39

37 The Lord said to Moses, **38** "Speak to the people of Israel, and tell them to make tassels on the corners of their garments throughout their generations, and to put a cord of blue on the tassel of each corner. **39** And it shall be a tassel for you to look at and remember all the commandments of the Lord, to do them, not to follow after your own heart and your own eyes, which you are inclined to whore after.

Malachi says 'the sun of righteousness shall rise with healing in its wings' (Malachi 4:2). Is this a prophetic image made vivid in this incident? In the beautiful story of Ruth and Boaz, her kinsman redeemer, we see the significance and symbolism of the corner of one's garment.

Wash therefore and anoint yourself, and put on your cloak and go down to the threshing floor, but do not make yourself known to the man until he has finished eating and drinking. However, when he lies down, observe the place where he lies. Then go and uncover his feet and lie down, and he will tell you what to do." And she replied, "All that you say I will do." Therefore, she went down to the threshing floor and did just as her mother-in-law had commanded her. And when Boaz had eaten and drunk, and his heart was merry, he went to lie down at the end of the heap of grain. Then she came softly, uncovered his feet, and lay down. At midnight the man was startled and turned over, and behold, a woman lay at his feet! He said, "Who are you?" And she answered, "I am Ruth, your servant. Spread your wings over your servant, for you are a redeemer." And he said, "May you be blessed by the LORD, my daughter."—Ruth 3:3-10.

Christians can say with certainty that their kinsman redeemer has taken them under the shadow of his wings and he has spread his cloak over them. He has healed all our diseases and taken away our infirmities. He has arrayed us in robes of righteousness.

The disciples failed to understand the question the Lord asked, "Who touched me?" How often disciples fail to understand the Lord? They were probably concerned with getting Jesus to the home of Jairus in order that he could minister to Jairus' daughter. They were well motivated but they had their own agenda. Do we ever have a 'Jim-will-fix-it' Jesus? How often do we feel that the interruptions to our plans are a nuisance rather than divine appointments? How slow we are to understand that Jesus is at work in the delays, the interruptions and the apparent disasters. We want Jesus to minister into a situation, in a certain way, at a specific time and in a particular place. However, Jesus will fulfill his purposes in his own way and work to his own sovereign agenda.

Mary and Martha, the sisters of Lazarus and the friends of Jesus were disappointed with his delayed arrival. However, they were to witness the amazing power of God at work in their situation. Maybe you are in the waiting room of the great physician's surgery and feeling anxious and the Bible (in your present experience) is about as interesting as the outdated and irrelevant magazines you find in the doctor's waiting room. Reach out that finger of faith. Here was a hopeful woman in a desperate situation. She dared to believe and God rewarded that faith. God was glorified then and he will be glorified in your situation. Have faith, press through to Jesus, and publicly glorify the Lord.

CHAPTER 6

Jesus rejected at Nazareth (6:1-6)

Jesus goes to his hometown, Nazareth, where the people were astonished at his wisdom and his works. We learn a few things from this passage of Scripture. First, that Jesus was a carpenter. Second, that Jesus had four brothers and an unspecified number of sisters (which must mean at least two as it is plural). Therefore, there were at least seven children (5 boys and not less than two girls) in the family of Mary and Joseph. The Lord's brothers were James, Joses, Judas and Simon. The sisters are not named but there is reference made to them: "are not his sisters here with us?" Mary's conception of Jesus was miraculous but thereafter she had several through the normal process of sexual intimacy. The notion that Mary was a virgin all her life needs to be seen for what it is: a human fabrication that is not supported by Scripture.

This passage states that they took offence at him. The people acknowledge his wisdom and witness his miracles but stop short of acknowledging his divinity. And Jesus said to them, "A prophet is not without honor, except in his hometown". This is a bit of the Bible that is often quoted. It is a common proverb because the phenomenon is common enough. It is hard to impress those who know you best. To them he was just the local lad. The passage points out that Jesus could 'do no mighty work there, except that he laid his hands on a few sick people and healed them. And he marveled because of their unbelief. And he went about among the villages teaching.' (5-6)

Jesus probably had a special affection for the place where he grew up (Nazareth) as we all tend to do. His foster father Joseph was from Nazareth but Jesus was born in Bethlehem. Mary and Joseph had to go to Bethlehem to register in a Roman census and their first child, Jesus, was born there. We know they did not return directly to Nazareth because Joseph was warned in a dream. They went to Egypt. We do not know how long they stayed in Egypt. Perhaps when Herod died and the threat against the child's life was lifted they returned. From that time on, Nazareth was Jesus' hometown.

Nazareth was a relatively unimportant and obscure place. It is not mentioned at all in the Old Testament. There is no mention of Nazareth in the writings of Josephus, the Jewish historian. The rabbinical writings (the *Talmud* and the *Mishnah*) do not have a single reference to Nazareth. It was a town of less than five hundred people situated on approximately sixty acres of rocky, hilly land. There are farms in Ireland that are fifty times bigger than this and ranches in Texas that are hundreds, perhaps even thousands of times bigger. For urban dwellers that might not be familiar with rural land measures let me say there are bigger shopping complexes (malls and their parking lots) in many cities! It was not a place of influence. It was not a center of education. It was not a strategic location in terms of commerce. Yet Jesus lived there for most of his earthly life.

In his father's workshop plows would be repaired, maybe boats built, furniture made. Jesus in his pre-incarnate existence dwelt in heaven where he was worshipped by hosts of angels who did his bidding. But when he came to earth he lived in a community of about five hundred sinners (including his mother, Mary, his foster-father, Joseph and his brothers and sisters) in Nazareth. The one who created the universe was now making doors, plowshares, window frames, chairs, wheels and carts. It was ordinary work. He humbled himself and lived among ordinary people. However, the community to which he belonged did not appreciate him. Jesus can empathize with those who are unappreciated.

Jesus' public ministry involved preaching to growing crowds of people and performing miracles. He healed a leper, a paralytic, a man with a shriveled hand, calmed the storm at sea, freed a demoniac from the powers of darkness, raised a twelve-year-old girl from the dead and cured a woman who had suffered greatly from an issue of blood for twelve years. His fame was spreading and his following was growing.

Jesus and his disciples travelled throughout Galilee but they were based in Capernaum. Now he comes to Nazareth, twenty-five miles from Capernaum. It is not clear what expectations Jesus might have had for this homecoming (of sorts) but what he experienced was rejection. Their attitude disappointed and amazed the Lord. It hurts when expectations are disappointed. These were people who knew Jesus quite well. They had seen him grow up. His parents were part of that community. His family still lived there. One might reasonably expect these people of Nazareth to be proud of Jesus. But they are not. There was no bunting, no balloons, no brass band, no reception committee, no honorary doctorate, no 'freedom of the city', no knighthood, and no civic reception. It has already been noted that at one point even his own family thought he was out of his mind (3:21). They thought he was delusional. So Jesus was unappreciated in his hometown by people who had a 'who does he think he is?' attitude.

Being amazed by Christ's preaching is not, in itself, a godly response. They did not recognize him for who he really was. They were bothered and bewildered that a Nazareth boy could speak to them in this way. They wondered where he had got his wisdom. It was a mystery to them and they were suspicious. They exhibited a sort of low-key hostility.

He had not gone to rabbinical school. They do not refer to him as 'Jesus'. However, one day every knee shall bow and every tongue confess that Jesus Christ is Lord (Philippians 2:10). They name all his brothers, but they refer to Jesus as "this man" (v.2). They refer to him as "the carpenter" (v.3) not as a prophet or a teacher. They refer to him as "the son of Mary and brother of James and Joses and Judas and Simon". They could not conceal their contempt. Then they also refer to Jesus as "the son of Mary". In Jewish society it was the name of the father which was attached to the male child, such as, Simon son of Jonah or James and John the sons of Zebedee. But Jesus is called the son of Mary. Maybe it means Joseph was already dead. Nevertheless, it is unusual and disrespectful and may even insinuate illegitimacy. They hardened their hearts. They had a "how dare you suggest that you know better" sort of attitude. His teaching (**to them** not necessarily a good thing) amazed them but he was amazed by their unbelief (lack of faith).

The world does not appreciate true spirituality because it exposes darkness. They say, "Who are you to speak of the truth?" "You are not a priest!" "You are a carpenter, not a theologian!" It can be demoralizing when people in your own circle reject you, at work when your colleagues despise you, in school when your fellow students treat you with contempt, at home when unconverted members of your family are unsupportive. Many people are cynical about faith or the evangelical brand of faith. People think believers are arrogant if they speak of Jesus as "THE way, THE truth and THE Life". God sees a godly woman walking with Christ year after year and her husband defiantly refusing to believe.

Without believing expectancy in Christ, nothing will come of planning and programs. Without believing expectancy in Christ, nothing will come of the most orthodox sermons. It was prophesied that Jesus would be despised and rejected: 'a man of sorrows acquainted with grief' (Isaiah 53).

Our fellowship with Jesus involves sharing in his sufferings: '...that I may know him and the power of his resurrection, and may share his sufferings' (Philippians 3:10). The KJV speaks of 'the fellowship of his suffering'. When we think of fellowship with Jesus we tend not to think of that kind of fellowship.

Jesus said, "A prophet is not without honor, except in his hometown and among his relatives and in his own household" (v.4). Notice the concentric circles here. A prophet is one who speaks for God! I'm not saying our evangelistic endeavors are on a par with prophecy! However, consider how Jesus was not respected: in his hometown of Nazareth, among his relatives (cousins), in his own household. We may encounter a similar kind of cynical attitude in our hometown, among our relatives and even in our own homes. Earlier in this Gospel, it was evident that Christ's family thought he was insane: 'Then he went home, and the crowd gathered again, so that they could not even eat. And when his family heard it, they went out to seize him, for they were saying: "He is out of his mind" (3:20-21).

Jesus was not appreciated in his own home. We might expect to be understood, admired, respected and accepted. It is difficult to do any kind of work that is not appreciated. But it is extremely difficult to do spiritual work that is viewed with contempt. Jesus turned his face steadfastly toward the cross with all its shame, agony and stigma. He faced his mission with an unshakable resolve because he had an unshakable love for the lost. Will we willingly partake of the fellowship of his suffering? Will we love the lost as he did? Will we endure ridicule and rejection for the gospel in our communities and families? Jesus shows the way, so let us follow him.

Jesus sends out the twelve apostles (6:7-13)

The Lord commissions the twelve apostles with a special task. They are given special power for this work. Jesus delegates the work of spreading the gospel. He entrusted this hugely important task to men who were less than perfect. Their faith was limited as was their understanding of who Jesus was. Yet he gives them this special work to do. Perhaps there is some significance in the number twelve. Twelve patriarchs had represented the old Israel and now Jesus was establishing a new order. The apostle John, in the book of Revelation, speaking of the New Jerusalem, says:

Revelation 21:12, 14

[12] It had a great, high wall, with twelve gates, and at the gates twelve angels, and on the gates the names of the twelve tribes of the sons of Israel were inscribed ... [14] And the wall of the city had twelve foundations, and on them were the twelve names of the twelve apostles of the Lamb.

They were clothed with a special authority. The Lord divided the twelve into groups of two. It seems sensible and practical to have two people work together. They provide a safeguard for each other against false accusations. They provide company and encouragement for each other.

The apostles obeyed Jesus. He sent; they went. They went out and preached repentance. They cast out demons. They anointed the sick with oil and healed many. In the ancient world oil was used widely for its medicinal properties, as in the parable of the Good Samaritan, who poured oil in the wounds of the man who was a victim of a violent mugging. However, it is unlikely that the disciples used oil as medicine. If it was used for its healing properties that would encourage the sick to look to the apostles for healing and this would have been perceived merely as a human thing. It was more likely symbolic of the presence of grace and the power of the Holy Spirit. In this way, they would be encouraging people to look to God for healing of body and soul. The healings were always miraculous and instantaneous and oil (usually olive oil) did not work in that way. The healings were supernatural.

Do we believe in the amazing power of God or are we skeptical and cynical? God's unlimited power can be made manifest in every generation and every geographical location. In times of revival, God does extraordinary things and I hope and pray that I will see such things in my day and in my land. We should all long to see a mighty outpouring of the Holy Spirit and pray and believe! The Lord's arm is not shortened. We should pray the prayer of Habakkuk, "Lord, I have heard of your fame; I stand in awe of your deeds, O Lord. Renew them in our day; in our time make them known..." (Habakkuk 3:2, NIV) Our God is a mighty God, active and alert to the prayers of the saints.

Christian leaders need to follow the example of Jesus in delegating to others the work of the kingdom. Sometimes, as a leader, it is easier to do things yourself. It is quicker, less complicated, and you can be sure it will be done exactly how you want it to be done. It is like teaching children to tie their shoelaces. Some days, when you are in a hurry, you might be tempted just to tie them yourself as that ensures that the job is done properly. Ultimately, it inhibits the development of the child. Getting others to do things in the church is like that, (I hope you will not find this patronizing or condescending). You know when you delegate that things are not going to be perfect. However, it is preferable to allow others the opportunity to explore, test and develop their gifting. Sometimes the person to whom a task is entrusted is just better at it than the leader. What is required in that situation is humility and a readiness to acknowledge the gifting of others. To use the analogy of the child again, that is the reverse situation where the father goes to the child for help, perhaps with computers, mobile phone settings and other electronic gadgets.

Jesus was part of a team, a motley crew of individuals. He invested in them. He entrusted vital work to them. When he started with them, they were rednecks or greenhorns who did not have a whole lot of theology but he taught them consistently and they grew in understanding. They were human, carnal, frail, feeble, flawed but they were instruments in God's hands and God crafted something special out of that raw material. Eventually he left them to carry on this work. But the Holy Spirit came in his place to provide counsel and comfort and challenge, as needed. God is the great finisher. The work he has commenced in us he will continue until it is complete, 'He who began a good work in you will bring it to completion' (Philippians 1:6). Jesus was a great team builder. He had a meaningful relationship with his disciples and he gave them a role in the kingdom and responsibility. When God gives us a work to do, he will enable us to do it. We need to listen to his voice, follow his instructions, be obedient and faithful and exercise faith. We need to believe our beliefs. We need to be diligent in doing what the Lord has asked us to do. We might be fearful. We might feel we have failed when we do not see results but we are called to faithfulness and there might be no apparent 'success'. Success in the spiritual realm is difficult to quantify and measure. What criteria will we apply? Faithfulness is the key. It is what God desires in his disciples.

There are instances recorded in the gospels about the disciples being unable to cast out demons (Matthew 17:19; Mark 9:28; Luke 9:40). But the Lord did not exclude them. He gave them further opportunity. If God were purely task-focused, he would not involve us in the work of the kingdom. However, God is concerned with the process of our development and so he allows us to do things and mess them up and try again. From the outset, Jesus was preparing his disciples for this mission and when he called the first disciples he promised to make them "fishers of men." (1:17)

Jesus withdrew from the crowd on several occasions to give the disciples his undivided attention. They had witnessed his wonderful works and heard his wise words. Now it was time for them to be sent out. Their apprenticeship was entering the practical phase. They would now be the official representatives of Jesus. That is what the Greek word for 'sent', in this context, means. So their words and works were to be an extension of his mission. Jesus sent them out two-by-two, which was, apparently, a Jewish custom. (Mark 11:1; Mark 14:13) The Lord called for the setting apart of Paul and Barnabas: 'While they were worshiping the Lord and fasting, the Holy Spirit said, "Set apart for me Barnabas and Saul for the work to which I have called them" (Acts13:2). This was so that the truthfulness of their testimony about Jesus could be established "On the evidence of two witnesses", a requirement in Judaic law. Later Paul and Silas (Acts 15:40) and Barnabas and Mark (15:39) went their separate ways, in pairs.

The power of the kingdom resides in Christ and in those whom he commissions to the work of the kingdom. God does not share his glory but he does share his work and it is a tremendous privilege to be involved in it. Those sent are called to trust the Lord to supply all their needs, spiritual and physical. They were to take just one tunic. This was to encourage them to accept hospitality. An extra tunic was used as a blanket in the outdoors at night. Jesus entrusted them with the same message that he preached:

Mark 1:14-15

[14] Now after John was arrested, Jesus came into Galilee, proclaiming the gospel of God, [15] and saying, "The time is fulfilled, and the kingdom of God is at hand; repent and believe in the gospel."

Jesus clearly anticipated the reality that the message of the gospel would not always be accepted. Just before a Jew entered (or re-entered) Jewish territory he shook the dust (from Gentile places) off his sandals. He would not carry even the dust of Gentile soil into the Holy Land. Jesus encouraged the twelve to engage in this symbolic act to show divine displeasure wherever the gospel was rejected, including Jewish territory. I suspect that the sight of such action would have shocked Jewish onlookers. The point here is that those who hear the gospel message are accountable for how they respond. Wherever the gospel is preached it brings judgment as well as salvation.

These disciples were Christ's ambassadors. Those who reject them and their message are effectively also rejecting Jesus and the gospel message. The mission of the twelve obviously reflected Christ's mission and the miracles they were empowered to perform was Christ's calling card. They authenticated or validated their mission as a divine mission. They preached repentance, cast out demons and healed the sick. This pattern of activity showed they belonged to Jesus and that the kingdom of God had come in power. So it is with the mission of the church today, it is patterned after the ministry of Jesus and involves proclaiming the Word of God, opposing the controlling influence of darkness and ministering to those who are in need. The gospel empowers. It brings salvation and security. It offers those who trust in Christ purpose, significance and hope.

The death of John the Baptist (6:14-29)

This passage presents us with some popular views of Jesus' identity. The mighty works of Jesus and his commissioned apostles are gaining traction. Some people thought he was a reincarnation of John the Baptist. This shows that they knew nothing about Jesus before his ministry in Galilee where we see Jesus and John together. There is no record of John the Baptist performing miracles during his lifetime and ministry. However, some thought that his resurrection status gave him that power. John had announced Jesus as the one to come. Others thought of Jesus as a manifestation of Elijah. Malachi had predicted Elijah's return as the Messiah's forerunner. One verse in that Old Testament prophetic book simply predicts that Jesus would have a forerunner: "Behold, I send my messenger, and he will prepare the way before me. And the Lord whom you seek will suddenly come to his temple; and the messenger of the covenant in whom you delight, behold, he is coming, says the LORD of hosts." (Malachi 3:1) However, another verse in Malachi suggests the return of Elijah: "Behold, I will send you Elijah the prophet before the great and awesome day of the LORD comes. And he will turn the hearts of fathers to their children and the hearts of children to their fathers, lest I come and strike the land with a decree of utter destruction." (Malachi 4:5) Some people regarded Jesus as a prophet, like the prophets of the Old Testament. Herod (who had executed John seemed to believe that Jesus was John the Baptist returned from the dead. No doubt, this was because of the similarity in the message calling for repentance and faith but also probably stimulated by a guilty conscience.

Mark devotes fourteen verses to the death of John but only five to his ministry (1:4-8). John had been arrested and imprisoned by Herod because he denounced Herod's adulterous relationship with Herodias. Herod had a brother named Philip and Herodias was Philip's wife. It is also believed possible that he was having an adulterous / incestuous relationship with his niece, Salome. The Mosaic Law prohibited marriage to one's brother's wife while the brother was still alive. In Leviticus chapter 18 there is a section about unlawful sexual relations. There it says, 'You shall not uncover the nakedness of your brother's wife.' (Leviticus 18:16) John had been courageous in denouncing Herod. John infuriated Herodias but initially Herod protected him. Herod seemed to recognize John's holy character. The daughter of Herodias (Salome) danced (probably a lewd dance) and Herod foolishly offered her anything she wanted, up to half his kingdom! The girl conferred with her mother and Herodias immediately replied that she should ask for the head of John the Baptist.

This reveals two things. First, the immediacy of the reply indicates the premeditated intention of Herodias. Second, the intense nature of her mother's hatred for John is evident in the fact that she counsels her daughter to decline a fortune in favor of her mother's murderous desire. This did not seem to bother Salome at all. In fact she adds two details. She wants the head immediately and she wants it on a platter. The whole incident shows the deeply depraved lives these people lived. It shows their contempt for human life. It demonstrates their utter corruption, that a man's life should be a pawn is such a sordid affair. John had been imprisoned, not for any wrongdoing but merely because Herod had the power to do so.

Herod was a wicked ruler. He had power and he used it inappropriately. He threw lavish birthday parties and thought nothing of justice, a fair trial and proportionate punishment. This was a high-society banquet attended by important, influential guests. Yet nobody objects. They were either afraid or they were people like Herod and Herodias, people who just did not care. On the other hand, maybe they disliked John because of his message of repentance. Perhaps they saw John as a thorn in the flesh that was spoiling their immoral way of life.

Many believers today are falsely imprisoned on trumped up charges or because they are a nuisance to the dictatorial power of corrupt political leaders. Such believers are often imprisoned because of their faith in Jesus in a culture, which is hostile to that. Some are imprisoned because they have advocated for justice, others for preaching the gospel. Some people really hate the moral stance of Christians. Their own consciences have become calloused and the moral integrity of the messengers of God is despised. They say, "How dare you point the finger at me!" "Away with your antiquated morality, outmoded values and old fashioned virtues!" When people want to sin the last thing they want to hear is any criticism or condemnation of their actions. Today many people are living immoral lives without restraint and this is mistaken for 'freedom'. There are many euphemisms for adultery. A euphemism is a mild or vague expression substituted for a harsher or more direct one. In the case of adultery, it is called 'an affair' or 'a fling'. In today's world there is much pornography, there are orgies, open marriages and all sorts of immorality.

Herod was a weak character and his perplexity of mind was probably related to a suppressed conscience. He had opportunity to repent with John the Baptist. Later he had opportunity with Jesus. However, he makes bad moral choices. The Old Testament King David, who had committed adultery with Bathsheba talks about that state of mind before confession of sin: 'For when I kept silent, my bones wasted away through my groaning all day long. For day and night your hand was heavy upon me; my strength was dried up as by the heat of summer.' (Psalm 32:3-4) The power of guilt can be very damaging. Psychiatric hospitals have many patients who have suffered from depression and psychotic episodes because they have ignored their consciences. If we are to be healthy and happy we must avoid sin. If we sin we should repent. That means resolving not to do it again and seeking forgiveness. If we continue to ignore our God-given conscience and if we ignore the moral law then we will become spiritually sick, psychologically unstable and even physically unwell.

Herod was curious about Jesus as a miracle worker and desired to see him. However, when that opportunity came he mocked Jesus:

Luke 23:6-12

⁶ When Pilate heard this, he asked whether the man was a Galilean. ⁷ And when he learned that he belonged to Herod's jurisdiction, he sent him over to Herod, who was himself in Jerusalem at that time. ⁸ When Herod saw Jesus, he was very glad, for he had long desired to see him, because he had heard about him, and he was hoping to see some sign done by him. ⁹ So he questioned him at some length, but he made no answer. ¹⁰ The chief priests and the scribes stood by, vehemently accusing him. ¹¹ And Herod with his soldiers treated him with contempt and mocked him. Then, arraying him in splendid clothing, he sent him back to Pilate. ¹² And Herod and Pilate became friends with each other that very day, for before this they had been at enmity with each other.

Herod and the guests were enchanted by the dance of Salome. They were united in politics, power, and wickedness. He was distressed by Salome's request. He had a kind of admiration for John but he did not have the moral fiber to do the right thing. Herod was a political person and he knew John was popular and was possibly concerned about the reaction of the people to John's execution (actually it was murder). He probably realized that this was his wife's plan all along and now she was having her own way and settling an old score. He had made a rash promise and in his perverse mind keeping that promise was more important than avoiding a grave injustice. He might have felt that not keeping his promise would have made him look foolish in the eyes of others. He could have declined by saying that he promised a gift but that what she requested would be criminal. It was into this man's hands that Jesus would later be put for a trial. In the case of John the Baptist, as in the case of Jesus, there was never going to be a judicious outcome. Pride caused Herod to murder rather than lose face among his invited guests. He ignored his conscience and he ignored the law he was empowered to uphold. Herod had rejected his own wife, married Herodias (his brother's wife) and now murdered John.

In addition to the absolute moral law of God (i.e. the Ten Commandments), people have God-given consciences so that they can hear and heed the little voice guiding them away from wrongdoing. It is God's microchip in the human heart and the default mode is designed to deter breaches in the moral code. The Commandments tell us clearly, what we already know: that we should not commit adultery and that we should not murder. Herod broke both of those God-given rules. When the warning light comes on in your car telling you that you need to put oil in the engine it ought not to be ignored. If it is ignored it will be at great cost. It is there for a good reason. Suppose the warning light was on and you decided rather than putting in oil you would take out the bulb or the fuse, which powers it. Would that be a sensible solution? People understand the sense of following the manufacturer's handbook. The Bible is the creator's handbook for us but many people ignore it. If you do not adhere to the manufacturer's handbook for some product or appliance, you effectively invalidate your warranty. The manufacturer's manual tells you how often you need to get your car serviced. We need to be tuned up regularly so that we are operating as we were designed. In Romans chapter 1, Paul speaks of unrighteous people suppressing the truth. He says such people will incur the wrath of God because they are without excuse.

Herod stood in judgment over Jesus. But that role will be reversed when Jesus stands in judgment over him. The same applies to all who reject Jesus. It applies to all who refuse to give Jesus a fair hearing. Those who scoff and mock now will face the terrors of judgment. Scripture warns, 'It is a fearful thing to fall into the hands of the living God.' (Hebrews 10:31) The secular rulers of this world are accountable to God for how they exercise their power.

A day of reckoning is coming for many such rulers who imprison God's servants without a fair trial. They will be judged for their callous cruelty. To persecute Christians is to persecute Jesus! When Saul (who later became the apostle Paul) encountered Jesus on the road to Damascus, the Lord said to him, "Saul, Saul, why are you persecuting me?"

Herod is an example of where a godless life can lead. He had material things but he lost his soul. Let us beware not to suppress our consciences or accept the godless values of this world. Let us who know the truth uphold it in the way we live and the words we speak.

The feeding of the five thousand (6:30-44)

Jesus is compassionate, considerate and caring. Mark shows us this in two ways, in Jesus' relationship with his own intimate band of twelve disciples and then with the people of the world. The twelve disciples have returned from weeks of ministry.[28] They now return and report to Jesus all they had done and taught. However, because of the crowds it was not easy for them to get time alone with the Lord. That day the twelve were hungry, but they could not sit down to eat because of the crowds. Jesus said, "Come away by yourselves to a desolate place and rest a while" (v.31). They probably had many stories to tell about people they led to faith, the casting out of demons, healing the sick, preaching and the many signs and wonders they performed. However, Jesus recognized their tiredness and understood that they needed rest and food. How very caring and kind the Master is.

---

[28] This period of time could have been as long as nine months.

Now consider Christ's circumstances. His cousin John the Baptist had been brutally killed for preaching. John had done what the Lord wanted him to do. The Lord's heart must have been aching and yet as he mourned he still cared for others. Many people were pressing in around him. The Lord was wounded and the disciples were weary from working for Jesus. The Lord's words: "Come away by yourselves to a desolate place and rest a while" may not be a message that all of us need to hear. It may be a message very few Christians need. J. C. Ryle said,

> There are only a few in danger of overworking themselves, and injuring their own bodies and souls by excessive attention to others. The vast majority of professing Christians are indolent and slothful, and do nothing for the world around them. There are comparatively few who need the bridle nearly so much as the spur.[29]

How committed are we to the Lord's work? How faithful are we in lovingly serving the church? How much time do we spend laboring for the kingdom of God? We have a compassionate Savior, not a hard task master who cracks the whip. We have a good shepherd who leads us. The Lord has given us work to do but he also calls us to rest. We all need times of retreat when we can go to the quiet place and rest with the Lord. But many Christians today are not doing that. We should have hobbies and leisure interests that would have the approval of the Lord. Is your television viewing and leisure reading and internet surfing suitable for a believer in Jesus? Our leisure should renew our spiritual vigor not weaken us. C.S. Lewis said:

> Our leisure, even our play, is a matter of serious concern. There is no neutral ground in the universe;

---

[29] J. C. Ryle, *Expository Thoughts on Mark*, Banner of Truth, 1857 (reprint) p.124.

every square inch, every split second, is claimed by God and counterclaimed by Satan . . . It is a serious matter to choose wholesome recreations.[30]

Jesus and the disciples get into a boat. It was approximately four miles across the lake and about a ten mile walk round to where Jesus was heading. There were at least thirteen men in that boat. On a calm day or on a day when the winds were unfavorable it would take as long to sail to that point as to walk to it. Mark tells us that the people 'ran there on foot'. I have this image in my head of thousands of people in a sort of mini marathon! Such was their eagerness to meet Jesus. They got to the other side before Jesus and the disciples: 'When he went ashore he saw a great crowd, and he had compassion on them, because they were like sheep without a shepherd. And he began to teach them many things' (v.34). Jesus and his disciples had gone there for some peace and quiet, to get away from the crowds. But the Lord was now at the height of his popularity. They dogged Jesus everywhere he went. However, the Lord was not angry with them, rather he felt sorry for them. They were hungry, physically and spiritually.

The Pharisees and Herod were their leaders and so it is no wonder he felt compassion for them. Have you ever seen what sheep do when they see the shepherd approaching? They run toward him because he brings them food. Sheep without a shepherd are lost and undernourished. They need to be led to green pastures. Sheep without a shepherd have no defense against wolves or thieves, they are vulnerable. Where would we be if the Lord had not taken pity upon us? As J. C. Ryle states:

> High in heaven, at God's right hand, he still looks with compassion on the children of men. He still

---

[30] C. S. Lewis, *Christian Reflections*, Collins Fount Paperbacks, 1967, p.52.

pities the ignorant, and them that are out of the way. He is still willing to teach them many things. Special as his love is towards his own sheep who hear his voice, he still has a mighty general love towards all mankind - a love of real pity, a love of compassion. We must not overlook this. It is a poor theology which teaches that Christ cares for none except believers. There is warrant in Scripture for telling the chief of sinners that Jesus pities them, and cares for their souls, that Jesus is willing to save them, and invites them to believe and be saved.[31]

The text in Mark's Gospel says of Jesus: 'And he began to teach them many things' (v.34). Thousands of people have hurried ten miles. They are hungry and far from home. Jesus has compassion for them. So what does he do? He preaches to them! Preachers should look to the example of Jesus. They should search their hearts to see if they, like the Master, are tenderly concerned about the unconverted? All believers should feel compassion for sheep without a shepherd? Do we care?

Consider the Lord's limitless power: 'And when it grew late, his disciples came to him and said, "This is a desolate place, and the hour is now late. Send them away to go into the surrounding countryside and villages and buy themselves something to eat." (vs.35-36) The disciples remind Jesus. Prayer can be just like that. Sometimes we go to the Lord with preconceptions about how certain situations should be resolved. We make suggestions to God as to how people could be helped. Our prayers are not perfect. We tend to give the Lord a bit of direction. The disciples too had pity for the people and in this they were like their Master. They were concerned and were being practical.

---

[31] Op cit., p.125.

Imagine a boy going out into the garden and picking a bunch of flowers for his mother, but in the process he picks weeds along with some beautiful flowers. He comes into the house smiling and proud of himself and shows his father the flowers, proudly declaring "for mummy!" His father says "let me rearrange them" and tenderly and unobtrusively he takes away the weeds. He arranges them in an attractive posy, puts them back in the little hands that picked them, and opens the door of the kitchen for his son to go to his mother with a toothless grin and the flowers in his hand! Jesus our mediator does something like this with our prayers. He takes our prayers, he removes all that is unacceptable, and then he presents our petitions to the Father.

The disciples wanted Jesus to send the people away so that they could feed themselves. But the Lord said something which is very typical of the way he deals with us: "You give them something to eat." (v.37) Here is the Bible's teaching on human responsibility. When we go to the Lord in prayer for the hungry (spiritually and physically hungry) he will instruct us to feed them. They protested that it would be a huge expense (eight months of a man's wages). They probably did not even carry that much money with them. The disciples protest that they do not have that much money. But we get the impression that even if they had they would not want to use it in this way. The Lord asks, "How many loaves do you have? Go and see." (v.38) The Lord is the provider but the believer is a crucially important channel for that provision. God generally does not use angels to do the work of the kingdom. He does not use angels to take the gospel to people. He uses saved sinners.

This event where Jesus fed five thousand people is a supernatural occurrence. Do we believe in the supernatural? There are churches (people who profess to be Christians) who teach that the parting of the Red Sea can be explained by freak tides. They say it was a natural phenomenon. There are teachers of religion in schools who teach that the story of the loaves and fishes really taught how Jesus set an example by sharing his disciples' picnic, so everybody else shared theirs. If the church does not believe in the supernatural, it is spiritually impoverished. Jesus without the miracles is just a teacher. A church divested of faith in the miraculous is just a religious club or moral society.

So what happened on this occasion? It was something so important that all four Gospel writers give an account of it. Did everybody take out their picnics, convicted by the example of the little boy? If that were the case many people who were still alive, when these Gospels appeared could have protested if there was simply a naturalistic explanation for what happened. In fact Jesus repeated this miracle a little later and Mark records that in chapter 8 of his Gospel, the feeding of four thousand. This was a miracle of multiplication. Verse 42 records that 'they all ate and were satisfied'. Jesus satisfies. As believers, we can say that we have tasted for ourselves the Bread from Heaven, and we are satisfied. Let us tell others that there is satisfaction in Christ. He provides for us:

    O Christ, in Thee my soul hath found,
  And found in Thee alone,
The peace, the joy I sought so long,
  The bliss till now unknown.

    Now none but Christ can satisfy,
  None other name for me;
There's love and life and lasting joy,
  Lord Jesus, found in Thee.

    I sighed for rest and happiness,
  I yearned for them, not Thee;
But, while I passed my Savior by,
  His love laid hold on me.

I tried the broken cisterns, Lord,
  But, ah, the waters failed!
E'en as I stooped to drink they fled,
  And mocked me as I wailed.

The pleasures lost I sadly mourned,
  But never wept for Thee,
Till grace the sightless eyes received,
  Thy loveliness to see.[32]

Jesus walks on water (6:45-56)

Here is an astonishing act, which defies the natural laws of the universe. It is impossible to walk on water. It contradicts the laws of physics. Some people find it easy to believe in the miraculous but others find it difficult. It takes faith to believe. Some people have more faith than others do. This is not just a symbolic story. It is an accurate historical account of a true incident. At least twelve men witnessed it. The disciples are going in a certain direction as instructed by their Master. It was late and dark and the wind was against them. Here the disciples were obeying Jesus but it was a struggle.

Maybe you find yourself in a situation where you seem to be making little, if any, headway. Progress is slow and painful and you are expending a lot of energy and getting nowhere. Along our journey in the spiritual life, we encounter forces that are stronger than us. We encounter things that slow us down and inhibit our progress. We might find ourselves in a situation where we are doing the best we can. However, in spite of our best efforts we are at sea, in a manner of speaking! The prevailing wind in this world is often against the disciples of Jesus. The moral wind blows in our faces and the currents, tides are not in our favor, and

---

[32] Anonymous.

sometimes we find ourselves growing weary with the struggle.

Would it not be easier just to go in the direction of the wind? Would it not be easier to say homosexuality is okay?[33] Would it not be easier to say abortion on demand is a human right? It is legal anyway, so what is all the fuss about? Would it not be easier to say unmarried people cohabiting is okay, if they love each other what harm can it do? Would it not be easier to say there is no hell?[34] Would it not be easier just to go with the flow? However, the master had sent them in a particular direction and to a particular destination where there they would rendezvous with Jesus.

If the disciples had decided to follow the way of least resistance they would not have been in this situation, struggling to go in the direction instructed. If they had followed such a course, Jesus would not have come to them in the way he did. Once again, the Lord is found in prayer, at the end of the day. We have seen Jesus before at the beginning of the day in prayer early in the morning. Jesus went up a mountain to pray. He was fit, physically and spiritually. From this elevated location, he sees the disciples in trouble. Here is a picture of how watchful the Savior is. From his lofty vantage point in heaven, he is ever vigilant in looking out for his disciples. We are not told what the Lord was praying about but I am inclined to think that he prayed for his disciples. No matter how dark or difficult our situation or how distant we are from our Lord he sees and he cares. Moreover, he intercedes and he intervenes for us according to the will and purposes of the Father.

---

[33] See the article, The Bible's Viewpoint of Homosexuality http://www.christianpublishers.org/homosexuality-bible-s-view
[34] Christian Publishing House Article: Hellfire - Eternal Torment? http://www.christianpublishers.org/hellfire-eternal-torment
Christian Publishing House Article: Hellfire - Is It Just? http://www.christianpublishers.org/hellfire-is-it-just

The Lord does not send us off on our own and leave us to accomplish the task in our own strength. Jesus looked out on that lake, he saw his disciples in distress, and he went to them. In the midst of that dark and dangerous situation Jesus appeared. He appeared at a time when he was least expected. When we are too weary to go any further Jesus appears. In the midst of this storm, the presence of Jesus brings peace. When he gets into the boat, the winds die down and the seas become calm. How true that is in our experience. When Jesus appears, the situation is different. Jesus says he will never leave us nor forsake us. He promises to be with his disciples always. The Lord got into the boat with his disciples and he gets into our situation too as he draws alongside. They are terrified because they think he is a ghost but he speaks to them. His words are words of peace and encouragement.

They had witnessed many miracles, most recently the miracle of the loaves and fishes. In that situation, the Lord did not merely add to the existing meager and very inadequate resources. Rather he multiplied what was offered to him. This shows us something of the bountiful blessing of the Lord. Yet they did not understand that miracle. Their hearts were hardened. How sad that they, having witnessed so much, had so little faith. How sad that we who profess so much and have experienced so much are sometimes like them!

They eventually arrive safely on the far shore and the record states:

Mark 6:54-56

[54] And when they got out of the boat, the people immediately recognized him [55] and ran about the whole region and began to bring the sick people on their beds to wherever they heard he was. [56] And wherever he came, in villages, cities, or countryside, they laid the sick in the marketplaces and implored him that they might touch

even the fringe of his garment. And as many as touched it were made well.

Where were all these people when Jesus was arrested, falsely tried and crucified? Mark does not record Peter's response in this situation but Matthew does.

Matthew 14:26-33

26 But when the disciples saw him walking on the sea, they were terrified, and said, "It is a ghost!" and they cried out in fear. 27 But immediately Jesus spoke to them, saying, "Take heart; it is I. Do not be afraid."

28 And Peter answered him, "Lord, if it is you, command me to come to you on the water." 29 He said, "Come." So Peter got out of the boat and walked on the water and came to Jesus. 30 But when he saw the wind, he was afraid, and beginning to sink he cried out, "Lord, save me." 31 Jesus immediately reached out his hand and took hold of him, saying to him, "O you of little faith, why did you doubt?" 32 And when they got into the boat, the wind ceased. 33 And those in the boat worshiped him, saying, "Truly you are the Son of God."

The unconverted mind is inclined toward unbelief. Even believers experience doubt. People have tried to explain this story by saying that Jesus walked on a sandbank with a shallow covering of water. However, Peter got out of the boat and for a moment, while his eyes were fixed on Jesus he walked on water too. Then he took his eyes off Jesus. He saw the waves and he became fearful, began to sink, and was rescued by the Lord. None of us is better than Peter. How true it is that when we are focused on Jesus and acting in accordance with the will of his Father, we can go beyond the ordinary. However, when we take our eyes off the Lord and begin to see the difficult circumstances that we are in then we begin to sink. The one who exercised most faith was criticized for the littleness of his faith. None of us has sufficient faith.

We become afraid in certain situations and forget that God is sovereign. We do not always recognize the Lord when he appears because we are not expecting him. We are doing something in our own strength and getting nowhere.

Matthew records a significant detail: 'And those in the boat worshiped him, saying, "Truly you are the Son of God."' This is where all miracles should lead: to the glory of God and the worship of him alone. This miracle affected the disciples in a way that the previous signs and wonders had not. They recognize the deity of Jesus and respond appropriately to that awareness. We too must acknowledge Jesus in this way. Let us expect him to see us in our struggle. Let us expect him to intercede and intervene. Jesus identified himself: "Take heart; it is I. Do not be afraid." Knowledge of Christ's true identity should dispel doubt, instill peace and inspire hope. Let us listen in the dark, when the forces that oppose us are stronger than us. Let us hear his voice. Let Jesus minister peace to our troubled hearts in anxious moments.

In this incident, it does not seem that the lives of the disciples are in danger. Rather it is clear that they were tired and frustrated and not making progress. Are you tired, frustrated and not advancing in the spiritual life? Are you worn out on this journey, wondering if it is worth the effort? When we get tired, we become discouraged and disillusioned. However, Jesus approaches and he brings the encouraging word and his presence changes everything. We will not always have favorable winds to carry us along. In fact if the disciples had a favorable wind that night they never would have experienced such a dramatic intervention in their situation. It is in the times of darkness and struggle, when we feel we can't go on any further that Jesus appears. We want our spiritual life to be plain sailing but it is not. We like sunny weather and a gentle breeze, blowing in the right direction. But often we face harsh gales and storms with the wind, not at our backs, but in our faces. We try our best but it seems that our best is not good enough. We cannot trust the vessel we are in. We cannot trust only in our own strength, resources, skills and experience. We cannot expect a favorable wind to carry us along in a pleasure craft. There is purpose in pain. The spiritual life is tough. The opposing forces are strong. But the power of the Lord is stronger!

There is no record that the disciples had called out to Jesus on that occasion. They were going it alone. It was their best individual and coordinated effort and it was failing miserably. They were right to use all their experience, skill and strength, as we should too. Nevertheless, we must realize that sometimes that is not enough. We need divine intervention. Nothing less will make a difference.

I imagine the disciples with their muscles aching, their lungs gasping for air, sweat pouring down their faces. I imagine Peter thinking if John were pulling his weight, we would be making more progress. I imagine Andrew thinking if we were all fishermen it would make a difference, but some of these guys are tax collectors. If mark was in the boat I imagine others thinking if Mark was bigger and stronger we would have a better chance. Are you in such a condition? Are you looking around at others and seeing their deficiencies? Are you wishing for a better team? Are you thinking if only we had an experienced (a fisher of men/evangelist) on board? If only he had more stamina and strength. In the middle of all of those thoughts of confusion and anxiety, the Lord appears and everything changes. Jesus is always near.

Chapter 7

Clean and unclean (7:1-23)

Once again, the Pharisees and teachers of the law (scribes) are gathering around Jesus. The scribes were the theologians of the day and they specialized in the law. They studied, interpreted and taught the Old Testament. They preserved and perpetuated the teachings of venerable rabbis of previous generations. The Pharisees were separatists trying to adhere to scribal teaching in how they lived their lives. There was an overlap inasmuch as many scribes would also have been Pharisees. In this passage, they try to find fault and make accusations. Therefore, there is another confrontation.

Many sharp clashes revealed their hostility to Jesus. These critics seem to be always waiting, ready to attack. The Pharisees and scribes hated Jesus for several reasons. First, he claimed divine authority. Second, he did not respect their traditions with respect to the Sabbath, fasts and ablutions. Third, he associated with publicans and sinners. Fourth, he was popular and exercised an unwelcome (unhealthy and unhelpful in their understanding) influence on the people. Fifth, he was completely unlike them. His humility contrasted with their pride, pettiness and false piety. His sincerity contrasted with their hypocrisy. He had a heart for sinners and those who were sick. They excluded sinners and were heartless about the sick (did not want Jesus to heal on the Sabbath). The way they practiced their religion was based on self-interest. Christ's ministry was selfless and sacrificial.

The Pharisees were local (from Galilee) but the scribes would have come from Jerusalem, the headquarters of Jewish orthodoxy. The Sanhedrin probably invited them, which was the highest court of justice and the supreme council in ancient Jerusalem (from the Greek *sunedrion*, meaning council). Their intention was to discover grounds for pressing charges against Jesus. They observe a breach of the law with regard to ceremonial washing by 'some' of the disciples. Their tradition demanded strict compliance in this matter as if salvation itself depended on such observance. They are devoted to their empty rituals. They were legalists. They present themselves as very concerned that the divine law is being broken but they are frauds, wearing masks of virtue to hide their real murderous intentions. The rabbis had divided the Mosaic Law into 613 separate decrees (365 prohibitions and 248 positive directions). They spelled out what was permitted and what was not permitted. They attempted to regulate every detail of the conduct of the Jewish people and it was oppressive, not liberating. We find the same kind of Jesuitical hair-splitting in many dead religions.

Here we see Christ the controversialist, not an establishment figure at all. But he was not some kind of fanatical revolutionary who just wanted to overthrow tradition. Jesus was not opposed to all things old in favor of the new. Jesus went beyond tradition to the original revelation. Their traditions had been superimposed on the Word of God. It seems that their traditions superseded the Word of God. This was two thousand years ago. However, that kind of religion still persists today and is not confined to Judaism. Jesus is saying that the kinds of things that the Pharisees are talking about, such as ritual washing, are unimportant. Jesus emphasized the importance of true heart religion rather than the observance of rites and rituals. Christ's emphasis was that the heart should be cleansed. This is consistent with the way he defined adultery as looking lustfully at a woman and murder as harboring hatred in the heart.

There are many people who call themselves Christian today who have a religion that consists of man-made rules and regulations. The authority of Scripture is not respected as the only or even the ultimate means of determining all matters of faith and practice. The Constitution of Lee Valley Bible Church (LVBC), where I am the pastor, states:

All Scripture of the Old and New Testament (66 books) as originally given is inspired by God and is historically accurate, entirely trustworthy, inerrant and infallible as the final authority for all matters of faith and conduct. Alive and active it is used by the Spirit of God to do the work of God in our lives.

This is not an opinion plucked from the air. The Constitution goes on to cite Scripture in support of this statement. Here are some of these verses: 'All Scripture is breathed out by God and profitable for teaching, for reproof, for correction, and for training in righteousness' (2 Timothy 3:16). 'For we did not follow cleverly devised myths...no prophecy of Scripture comes from someone's own interpretation. For no prophecy was ever produced by the will of man, but men spoke from God as they were carried along by the Holy Spirit' (2 Peter 1:16-21). 'For truly, I say to you, until heaven and earth pass away, not an iota, not a dot, will pass from the Law until all is accomplished' (Matthew 5:18). '...your word is truth.' (John 17:17) 'And beginning with Moses and all the Prophets, he interpreted to them in all the Scriptures the things concerning himself' (Luke 24:27). 'Your word is a lamp to my feet and a light to my path' (Psalm 119:105). 'And we impart this in words not taught by human wisdom but taught by the Spirit, interpreting spiritual truths to those who are spiritual.'–1 Corinthians 2:13.

All that we believe has and must have a foundation in Scripture, properly understood. Our interpretation must be based on sound principles of biblical interpretation. We do not have the liberty to add to or take away from the Scripture. Great truths, lost for centuries, buried under the worthless heap of human tradition, were rediscovered in the Reformation, so that salvation by grace alone, through faith alone, in Christ alone was once again restored to its rightful place as central to the gospel. It is vitally important to hold to the inspiration, authority, inerrancy/infallibility, and canonicity of Scripture in order to safeguard the apostolic doctrine entrusted to us. We are to be guardians of truth.

The Word of God is a dynamic living thing: 'For the word of God is living and active, sharper than any two-edged sword, piercing to the division of soul and of spirit, of joints and of marrow, and discerning the thoughts and intentions of the heart' (Hebrews 4:12). Illuminated by the Holy Spirit it convinces of truth, convicts of sin and calls us to Christ. It is an instrument in God's hands to bring about conversion. The Lord uses Scripture to commission us in our mission to this world. All the doctrines that we as a church subscribe to are contained in the Bible. In relation to Scripture, the trinity (Father, Son, Holy Spirit), Satan, man (origin, purpose, destiny), sin, salvation, sanctification, the church, end times, the ordinances (baptism and the Lord's supper), church government, the qualifications and roles of leaders and discipline.

In the passage under consideration, Jesus makes the general statement that these people (Pharisees and teachers of the law) were holding on to the false teachings of men. Then he identifies a specific issue and cites it in defense of his case. We could identify many issues where so called 'Christian' churches have departed from the truth of Scripture.

Here we see the extension of Christ's ministry to the Gentiles. These theologians were concerned with the issue of ceremonial purity and defilement. They were custodians of tradition and their instinct was to preserve and protect their traditions. They did not recognize divine activity under their noses. A great amount of oral tradition had developed around the law. It was passed on from one generation to the next. These were understood as binding regulations. Essentially the Pharisees were more concerned with the outward appearance than the condition of their hearts before God. Jesus pointed out that Isaiah's denunciation of the religious leaders of his day was an apt description of the religious leaders who stood before him. He calls them "hypocrites" A hypocrite is one who makes a false claim to virtue. Therefore, they are not merely people trying to adhere to scribal teaching. Hypocrisy involves insincerity and pretense. It comes from the Greek and means acting or feigning. A hypocrite is someone whose worship is merely outward and not from the heart. They appeared pious but that was a sham. They were not really devoted to God. They were members of an elite club.

Many people today would not forsake their traditions either even if they discovered the truth of Scripture because they are cowards or because they love their traditions more than the truth. Christ condemned such people. He despised them and there can be no getting away from that or downplaying it. Ordinary people were being misled and this grieved Jesus.

Some people, believers and non-believers, find it difficult to accept that Jesus despised anybody whether they were Pharisees, scribes, or any other person. They argue that he may have despised their attitudes, hypocrisy, and/or the sin that entangled them but he loved everyone. They would contend that the point is to hate the sin, but love the sinner and subscribe to the notion that this is what Jesus did and we should follow his example. Wrong! This is unbiblical. Jesus called the Pharisees a brood of vipers and described them as stinking like the inside of a tomb. He said they were of their father the Devil. He despised them as a group of people. Hypocrisy will not go to hell; it is the unrepentant hypocrite who will go there. Jesus did not love everyone! Syrupy religion might teach that but the Bible certainly does not! The Christian cliché, 'God loves the sinner but hates the sin' is not actually rooted in biblical theology.

One might wonder how that relates to the fact that Jesus asked for forgiveness for the same hypocrites that nailed him to the cross. Jesus certainly desires that all sinners (Pharisees included) should come to faith in him through repentance. This involves realizing their sinfulness, asking for forgiveness and resolving with God's help to live a transformed life in the power of the Holy Spirit. The Pharisees were despised by Jesus because they distorted the truth and were an obstacle to true spirituality. They burdened the people. They were not just corrupt but they were a corrupting influence. Nevertheless, he was willing to guide any genuine Pharisee who would listen (such as Nicodemus). Jesus did not absolve those who crucified him of the evil they had done but expressed his heart's desire that the Father would lead them to realize their wrongdoing and they would be sorry for what they had done. Such Godly sorrow leads to repentance. It is rather obvious from reading the Gospels that Jesus despised the Pharisees as a group of hypocrites and clearly expressed his contempt for them on several occasions. To deny that is absurd. The Lord desires that all will repent but those who do not he will send to Hell (a place of conscious and eternal torment) for all eternity. There is no contradiction in Jesus *desiring* repentance and *detesting* those who refuse to repent.

Christ's disciples clearly did not submit to these human rabbinic traditions. This body of tradition was meant to promote observance of the law. But in reality it distorted the law and even circumvented it. Jesus cites a specific example of this. The seriousness of the fifth commandment, to honor your father and mother, is emphasized by the penalty for a breach of this---the death penalty! Honor is different to obedience. Honor is inward, obedience can be merely outward. Obedience can be motivated by fear. Honor is inspired by love. The Pharisees' traditions provided a way around the law and assisted people in avoiding it and breaking it by looking for loopholes. Traditions took on a kind of sanctity of their own, God was displaced, and his Word eclipsed.

The Bible is the only authority in all matters of faith and practice. Ecclesiastical tradition cannot be allowed to have such authority. We must be careful that our interpretations (and selection) of Scripture are not merely subjective and biased. We are called to careful exegesis and exposition of the Word and a man who is lazy in that regard has no place in the pulpit. Some people declared that what they had intended to give their parents would now be devoted to God. Such promises were not necessarily fulfilled by giving money to the temple. However, by making such a promise the person was now exempt from his proper obligation under the law. Thus, parents could be excluded from benefiting from the gift, which should rightfully have been designated for them. Thus, the law was effectively nullified and the very purpose for which the law was given was set aside. Jesus exposes them.

Jesus effectively declared the kosher food laws null and void. He pointed out that all our actions and words emerge from our attitudes, thoughts and desires. So we must give attention in the spiritual life to the heart and we must be vigilant because, 'The heart is deceitful above all things, and desperately sick; who can understand it? "I the LORD search the heart and test the mind' (Jeremiah 17:9-10a). The heart is to be understood as the center of human personality that determines a person's actions and inactions. Jesus lists vices that emerge from unregenerate and carnal hearts (see verses 20-23). None of the other gospel writers were moved by Holy Spirit to address this list. However, it has New

Testament parallels in the writings of Paul (e.g. Romans 1:29-31; Galatians 5:16-22a). We are not obliged to observe ceremonial rituals as a means of pleasing God. Nevertheless, we must guard our hearts: 'Keep your heart with all vigilance, for from it flow the springs of life' (Proverbs 4:23). May The Lord help us as we seek to do this!

The faith of the Syrophoenician woman (7:24-30)

Christ's ministry is now being extended to the Gentiles (outsiders). The word 'Gentile' was a synonym for 'unclean' and 'foreigner'. The incident recorded here follows naturally from that which has just gone before where issues of ceremonial uncleanness emerge. Jews did not usually associate with Gentiles because such relationships would have made them ritually unclean. The writer, Mark, wants to emphasize that Christ's mission was also to the Gentiles. He stresses that the gospel is not restricted to Israel, even though historically it came to her first. Jesus went to Phoenicia (now Lebanon) where the city of Tyre was located. In those days, Phoenicia belonged to Syria. The Jews were God's chosen people and were meant to be a light to the world but they had come to think of themselves as God's privileged elite. God never intended that his mercy would be confined exclusively to Israel. The Hebrew nation was to play a strategic role in the unfolding of redemptive history. The story of the God reaches out to the unqualified and unworthy and embraces them. The Jews thought that the privileges of God's grace were the sole prerogative of Israel but Jesus said, "I have other sheep that are not of this fold, I must bring them also." (John10:16) These words were spoken to Jewish religious leaders about non-Jews who would be included in God's kingdom.

Here is a woman who is desperate and determined. She is an outsider. She comes from a different country, different race/ethnicity and has a different religion. An unclean spirit possesses her daughter. The woman comes to Jesus even though she is a Gentile, a foreigner, an outsider. She needs help and she is determined to get it. Jesus alludes to this woman as a dog. He does not explicitly call her a dog but it is implied in his words. She asks Jesus to heal her daughter, and Jesus calls her an undeserving dog! The Jews believed that this woman did not belong at the table with Jews. The word Jesus uses, however, refers to little dogs that were kept as household pets. He is saying that the Jews are the privileged children of the household but that the Gentiles are less privileged puppies. Nevertheless, it is used as a metaphor for people who are ceremonially unclean.

This woman was desperate. Perhaps as you read this you too have a great need. What are you desperate for? What do you want? She is desperate because of her relationship with someone else who is in pain. Of course, if the daughter's problem is solved then her own life will be better too. Jesus does not deny that she is unworthy but he accepts her in spite of her spiritual status. We are all unworthy.

This Syrophoenician Woman (she was of Greek origin) heard of his power and came him. Jesus intentionally tested her faith and found her to be persistent. The account in Matthew reveals that Jesus initially ignored her. It also says that the disciples begged Jesus to send her away because she was persistently crying out to the Lord. However, this woman persevered and in this regard she is to be emulated. We need to persist if we want to encounter God's power in our situations. Sometimes we let the disappointments of apparently unanswered prayer overcome our faith.

The Syrophoenician woman was humble in her asking. In the first century, Greeks had been recognized as the most intellectual nation on earth. They were renowned for their philosophy and literature. Philosophers like Socrates and Plato and mathematicians like Pythagoras were Greeks. There was much for which they could be proud. She could have taken Jesus' reply as an insult, taken offense, and left in a huff. After all Jesus was from Nazareth, an insignificant little town of no renown. However, in humility she said, "Yes, Lord, yet even the dogs eat the crumbs that fall from their masters' table." (v.27) Her response was not only clever but it showed a gritty determination to believe and hope. Obstacles do not daunt her.

We do not deserve anything from God but we can go to him with a humble attitude. So, whatever our need, let us go to Jesus in humility, be persistent and believe. Do we have needs in our lives? Most, if not all, people do. Some have greater and more urgent needs than others. Perhaps you are having difficulty seeing how those needs can be met. Do you have difficult family or financial problems? Is there a problem with a loved one? Is there some obstacle to happiness?

What remarkable faith this woman had. She believes that even a crumb from Christ will be enough! A woman who is in a desperate situation approaches Jesus. In our journey with Jesus through the message of Mark, we see desperate people coming to Christ. He never disappoints. We are told in verse 24 that 'he could not be hidden'. That is always the case! The presence of Jesus can never be kept secret. She faces several challenges, but she persists. She came to Jesus because faith and hope had been aroused in her heart. She was desperate and she saw Jesus as her hope. Perhaps you are at your wits end over some situation in your life and you need help. If so you should follow this woman's example. Maybe what you need is restoration and forgiveness.

This woman comes to Jesus for help and gets a response she might not have expected but she overcame the obstacles. Her heart must have been fearful, as it seemed she met resistance to her request. What obstacles did she overcome? There is the obstacle of race and religion. When the disciples see and hear this Gentile calling out to their Messiah, they react by telling Jesus to send her away. There is the obstacle of rejection. As Jesus speaks to this woman, his words appear harsh to our ears. Undaunted she continues to make her case. First, Jesus simply ignores her. It is as if he is indifferent to her cries for help. The disciples rejected her and now it appears that Jesus is rejecting her too. Then there is the obstacle of 'reality'. The realities of this situation are harsh. Her daughter was possessed by a demon. She was a foreigner who was not a Jew. These followers of Christ did not seem to care about her or her situation at all. It appears that her situation is hopeless.

Maybe you have cried out to Jesus and there has been no answer. Maybe you feel like giving up. Let me encourage you today. God's silence is not an indication of his unwillingness to meet your need. God's silences ought to serve to strengthen our resolve and our faith. What obstacles are you facing today? Be encouraged by this woman's story and be persistent in seeking the Lord. Obstacles can be opportunities for faith. The obstacles this woman faced might have discouraged her but they did not defeat her, rather they drew out her faith. Jesus took this woman and her small faith, led her along, and helped grow her faith? The obstacles of faith usually turn out to be opportunities in disguise. Plead in prayer, remonstrate reverently with the Lord and claim the promises of Scripture. When we continue to seek the Lord in spite of hindrances, we will eventually break through.

Faith also has obligations. Many people would have given up. Jesus ignored her, the disciples played the race card, Jesus even compared her to a dog and yet she persisted. Many would have thrown up their hands in frustration and stormed off in anger. She kept going in spite of everything that was thrown into her pathway. Why? She persisted because too much was at stake. Her little daughter needed to be delivered from bondage. How much does your problem mean to you? Have you encountered some obstacles along the way that have made you throw up your hands and quit seeking God? Keep bringing that need to Jesus until he answers! God invites us to come to him in prayer "Call to me and I will answer you." (Jeremiah 33:3) Jesus said "Come to me, all who labor and are heavy laden, and I will give you rest." (Matthew 11:28) Keep seeking his face until he responds. Keep asking, keep seeking, keep knocking and in his time, he will hand you down a morsel of answered prayer!

Jesus had tested her faith with hard words and her faith had risen to the challenge. Jesus commended two people for their great faith, a Roman centurion and this woman, both Gentiles. Here was a Gentile that had more faith than the Jewish scribes did and the Pharisees. Jesus rewarded her faith. She took Jesus at his word and went home and there she found her daughter healed. Perhaps you are in a situation every bit as hard and as painful as that faced by this woman. Maybe you have prayed about your situation and things remain the same. Maybe you feel it is never going to change. Perhaps you are discouraged and defeated. Take heart today. There is hope! Today might be the day when the Master responds to your cries. Today might be the day when you see that mountain moved in your life. Today might be the day when his peace replaces your pain. Peace comes from 'casting all your anxieties on him, because he cares for you.' (1 Peter 5:7) Consider the exhortation from the writer to the Hebrews: 'Let us then with confidence draw near to the throne of grace, that we may receive mercy and find grace to help in time of need.'—Hebrews 4:16.

Bringing people to Jesus (7:31-37)

Jesus healed people of various diseases and afflictions. In this passage of Scripture, we see the unique encounter of Jesus with a man who was deaf and dumb. We who are not deaf and dumb can never fully enter into what that means.

We may sympathize but we cannot really empathize. Unless we have experienced the problems inherent to and associated with this condition, we cannot fully understand.

Consider this man's predicament. Some might even say that deafness is worse than blindness. Imagine what life might be like if you could not express your feelings with words. He could not communicate effectively. There were no hearing aids. Sign language had not been invented; there were no computers, so no email, nor cell phones and text messages. He would have had chalk and slate to write a message, if he was literate. He could not hear the pleasant sounds around him, such as the singing of the birds or music being played. Neither could he hear the sounds that alert to danger. He could not engage in the pleasantries of conversation. He could not enjoy the interaction that is such a vital part of human intimacy and socialization.

This man's friends were concerned about him, so out of compassion, they brought him to Jesus. Why could he not come to Christ himself, unaided? He would not have been able to hear people talk about Jesus and his whereabouts. He could not ask others where he might be likely to meet Christ. He could not call out to Jesus like the blind man ("Jesus Son of David, have mercy on me!") or the leper (Mark 2:40-45). Clearly then this man had to be *brought* to Jesus. Therefore, we read that some people brought this man to Jesus.

We live in an age where church going is not the norm. Many things prevent people from attending religious services. It seems that some Christians feel that gospel preaching no longer works and they are, therefore, reluctant to invite friends, relatives, colleagues and others to church services. People need to be brought to Jesus today. Christ in one of his parables said that we are to compel people to come into the kingdom of God, to go out to the highways and byways (i.e., out into our communities, to our friends, family, coworkers, and the like).[35]

When we consider this deaf and dumb man, it is clear that he was in great need because he could not connect in a social way. However, many people in our society today are in even greater need because they cannot connect in a spiritual way. Surely, we too should be engaged in bringing people to Jesus. Jehovah's Witnesses and Mormons unashamedly invite people to their meetings.

The people who brought this deaf and dumb man to Jesus prayed. One might well ask, "Where in the text does it say that they prayed?" The Authorized Version of the Scriptures (AV) says 'they beseech' and the New International Version (NIV) says they 'begged him to place his hand on the man'. In one sense, this is just communication at a human level, where some people ask Jesus for help. Yet at another level, by way of implication, which may be drawn from Scripture, requests made to Jesus are prayers. Even unspoken yearnings in the hearts can be prayers. This appeal to Jesus is not prayer in the conventional sense but imploring and begging Jesus or simply asking him for aid is a kind of prayer, even if those making such requests are not aware of that. The fact that they implore Jesus reveals more than the nature of their petition - it reveals something about the quality (intensity) of their 'prayer'. They went to Jesus, the living God incarnate, interceding for this man who could not intercede for himself. We need to bring people to Jesus and to pray for them.

Jesus did not just simply touch the man as he was asked to do. Rather he put his fingers in his ears, spat on his finger and put it on his tongue. When we pray, we should ask God to do his will, whatever that may be. We should not instruct God. We must be prepared to accept that he will answer our

---

[35] Not to coerce but rather to coax and plead with people.

prayers his way. It is interesting that Jesus took this man aside from the crowd. He was not interested in conducting a public relations exercise. He was interested in meeting this individual and needy person.

This man had faith. Obviously, he did not and could not profess that faith orally. However, we can be sure he had faith. This is evident in the way he allows Jesus to put spit on his hand and touch his tongue. He knew Jesus could free him.

Jesus had a bad reputation in the eyes of some because of the obvious sinners he associated with. That was simply because Jesus touched the 'untouchable'. He touched the leper Mark 2:40-45. He let the immoral woman wash his feet with her tears and dry them with her hair, much to the consternation of some. Now he touched this deaf and dumb man.

Do we touch sinners? Men like General Booth touched sinners and a generation was revolutionized because of it. Charles and John Wesley touched a generation for Christ. They knew that the power of the gospel of Jesus could change lives.

Jesus looked to heaven. (v.34) The Son of God incarnate looked to heaven to source the power to heal this man. The person, who was perfect, sinless, unselfish, undefiled, separate from sinners, looked to heaven. Where do we look? Do we look to confidence; our abilities, our education and training (theological or otherwise), i.e., ourselves, or do we look to heaven for the power of God? If Jesus needed to look to heaven to obtain strength from the Father and pray, if Jesus needed to pray in solitude early in the morning and even throughout the night, how much more do we need to do it?

Duncan Campbell, a humble man of God, arrived one day to a packed church on the Isle of Lewis in Scotland during a move of God (1940s and 1950s). As he stood in the pulpit he realized he couldn't say anything. There was a young man sitting in the congregation whom he knew was a man of God. Duncan asked him to stand to, "lead the congregation in prayer, because you are nearer God than I am." Witnesses testify that he 'looked to heaven and prayed: "Father, I can see your throne. I know that your throne is there, and at your right hand there is the Lord Jesus Christ and there's power there, let a bit of that power go and bless us!" People started falling down around him in conviction of sin and in tears. John Wesley on his 80th birthday felt he had backslidden because he could no longer get up at 4.30 in the morning to meet God in prayer. He was dismayed that he had to lie in until 5am. Martin Luther, who shook the whole of Europe for Christ said he had so much to do some days that he had to pray for two hours.

This is an age of prayerlessness. We pray little. E. M. Bounds in *Power through Prayer* discusses the idea that praying little is like a salve to our conscience. We think we have dealt with God and it makes us feel all right the rest of the day and we pray no more. A visiting preacher was asked to "give a little word" so he stood in the pulpit and said, "Look at your Sunday morning, and see how popular the church is. Look at your Sunday evening and see how popular the pastor is. Look at your prayer meeting and see how popular God is."

When Jesus looked to heaven, he sighed. This was a prayer that had no words from the very depths of his being. It was a prayer of compassion. There are times when we cannot put into words the inexpressible feeling welling up within our souls and all we can do is groan to God (Romans 8). Jesus looked at this poor, pitiful man, and he said: *"Ephphatha"*, meaning, "be opened". Literally, it means "the string of his tongue was loosed". The chord that bound him to silence was loosed and that aural capacity began to detect sound.

Hear Him ye deaf, His praise ye dumb,

Your loosened tongues employ.
Ye blind, behold your Savior come,
And leap, ye lame, for joy!
My chains fell off! My heart was free!
I rose, went forth, and followed Thee.[36]

This man went about declaring what Jesus had done, although instructed by Jesus not to. It is peculiar that many today behave in an opposite way because we have been instructed to go and tell and we remain dumb! The change in this man's life was so great he could not keep his mouth shut! People were overwhelmed with amazement saying "He has done everything well" (v.37). Today Jesus still does all things well. Go and tell somebody what he has done for you.

---

[36] Charles Wesley (1707-1788), *O For A Thousand Tongues to Sing*, 1739, *Christian Hymns*, Evangelical Movement of Wales, 1977.

Chapter 8

Jesus feeds the four thousand (8:1-10)

This passage is similar to the earlier miracle recorded in Mark 6:30-44 where Jesus feeds five thousand people with five loaves and two fish. We noted then that all ate and were satisfied and that there were twelve baskets full of leftovers. We commented on the fact that Jesus supplies and satisfies. In the earlier passage, Jesus instructed the disciples to feed the people. They said they did not have the food on hand nor the resources (perhaps the willingness to spend what they had on this). We saw how Jesus was motivated by compassion and that clearly the disciples were not as compassionate as Christ was. On that occasion, Jesus took what was offered to him and he blessed it abundantly as he always does with what little we have. He asked that the people be seated and organized into groups of hundreds and groups of fifties. The disciples wanted the people sent away. It was clear that the disciples did not expect such a miracle.

So now, we come to the passage in Mark 8:1-10. This passage is about spiritual understanding or lack of it. The disciples fail to understand. They had recently witnessed the opening of the ears of the deaf man (which we have looked at in chapter seven). They will later see Jesus opening of the eyes of a blind man. These are gracious interventions in the lives of real people. However, they are also preparing the way for the opening of the spiritual understanding of the disciples.

There is a striking similarity between the two accounts of the feeding of a crowd, in chapter 6 and here in chapter 8.

Was there one feeding which was recorded twice or was it two separate feedings? Many people, especially biblical scholars, have asked this question. Most scholars believe that there was only one and take this passage (8:1-10) as a duplicate recording of the same event. However, we need to be wary of believing something merely because it has the credibility of scholarship. In other words, the majority does not automatically equal right. Apart from the fact that scholars differ, it is often the case that scholarship stands in authority over Scripture when it should stand in humility before it. There is a difference between studying the text of Scripture to find truth and imposing one's views upon it. This is the difference between *exegesis* and *eisegesis*.

One important principle of biblical interpretation is to accept that the Bible is right in its historical accuracy. It is about believing that the events recorded there are true. Many will scoff at such a 'simplistic' approach but we will endure such scorn for the sake of Christ. There is a theological thrust in the Gospels as a genre of literature. We accept its literary style but this does not invalidate its historical accuracy. There is a difference between meditating on the Scriptures as a subordinate and scrutinizing them as a scholar. I believe in scholarship. I dislike the anti-intellectual attitude of some Christians. We need people involved at the intellectual level as well as at the operational level. Many scholars are not believers. However, spiritual things are spiritually discerned: 'The natural person does not accept the things of the Spirit of God, for they are folly to him, and he is not able to understand them because they are spiritually discerned' (1 Corinthians 2:14). Thus, a person who is not born again has no right to speak authoritatively about the meaning of Scripture. In fact, such a person has no ability to do so. But there are some scholars who claim to be believers and one would have to wonder about their approach to Scripture. The believer starts with the view that the Bible (the text of Scripture) is the infallible Word of God and proceeds from there. We need to be alert when reading commentaries, Christian books, and not swallow everything the author tells us, completely. We should pray for believers who are in the cut and thrust of the world of scholarship. Pray that they will be protected and produce not just technically accurate material but inspirational and devotional material that will be for the glory of God and the good of God's people.

Is this a cut and paste job? Is it just poor editing of the Gospel? Should this section be deleted? This raises important issues about scholarship, which need to be addressed. It raises questions about the inspiration, authority, canonicity and inerrancy of Scripture. Is this passage inspired by God and in the Bible for a purpose? Is it just a repetition for emphasis, just to stress things already presented? Does this passage (if it is merely a duplicate of a previous passage) have no authority? Does it not rightfully belong in the canon of Scripture? Are the differences in detail errors based on poor memory or bad writing? Alternatively, is this passage unique in some way?

There are good reasons to support the view that two separate events are recorded. Once again, we see Jesus meeting the needs of hungry people in a desolate place but there are significant differences in detail. This time there are seven loaves (as distinct from five in the event recorded in chapter 6). They also had a few (unspecified number) small fish. This time there were seven baskets full of leftovers (as distinct from the 12 full baskets recorded in the previous incident). Is this because details like that are deemed unimportant or that Mark could not remember the detail. Detail is an important element in the authenticity of a story. If we introduce doubt about detail then the whole structure is in danger of collapsing.

In principle we believe that 'All Scripture is breathed out by God and profitable for teaching, for reproof, for correction, and for training in righteousness' (2 Timothy

3:16). Scripture does repeat many of its teachings (e.g. in the letters of Paul and Peter). Therefore, repetition is not a problem to the authenticity and authority of the Word. Scripture repeats things that are very important because we are slow to learn and we need to be told repeatedly.

Verse 4 records, 'And his disciples answered him, "How can one feed these people with bread here in this desolate place?" Does this present a problem? If the disciples had already witnessed such a miracle, why would they ask such a question? I think the answer to that is that although the two events happen in quick succession as we read this fast-paced and action-packed Gospel there would have been some length of time between the two events (I don't know exactly how long). The disciples were frequently slow to understand the power of Jesus. They did not always expect Jesus to meet a crisis situation by performing a miracle. How very like them we are.

However, in this passage Jesus himself clearly refers to two feedings:

Mark 8:18-21

[18] Having eyes do you not see, and having ears do you not hear? And do you not remember? [19] When I broke the five loaves for the five thousand, how many baskets full of broken pieces did you take up?" They said to him, "Twelve." [20] "And the seven for the four thousand, how many baskets full of broken pieces did you take up?" And they said to him, "Seven." [21] And he said to them, "Do you not yet understand?"

The obvious must also be stated; that Mark clearly thought of these miracles as two separate events. In the story (true account) in chapter 8, it is Jesus who recognized the physical needs of the crowd. Whereas in the story (true account) in chapter 6 it was the disciples (6:35-36) who raised the issue of such needs (asking Jesus to send the people away to cater for themselves). The disciples' reply (here in chapter 8) shows that they had completely forgotten the earlier event when the 5,000 were fed. This is perhaps the strongest argument against the view that there were two separate events. Could they possibly have forgotten such an amazing miracle? However, as already mentioned, a considerable period might have elapsed since the feeding of the 5,000. Even mature believers who have experienced God's power and provision have subsequently acted in unbelief. The disciples were not mature! They frequently lacked understanding and were often reprimanded by Jesus for this. Jesus was sometimes reluctant to perform miracles and so the disciples did not expect him to meet every crisis in that way.

Here in this passage the people were not organized into groups. Jesus gave thanks separately for the bread and after each prayer the disciples distributed the food. In both cases, Jesus' provision was sufficient. However, it was not merely sufficient it was abundant. Seven basketsful of fragments were left over. The Lord's provision is more than adequate for the situation. If we yield what we have to him he will abundantly bless.

The following hymn sums up the idea of God's gracious and abundant provision:

He giveth more grace as our burdens grow greater,

He sendeth more strength as our labors increase;
To added afflictions He addeth His mercy,
To multiplied trials He multiplies peace.

When we have exhausted our store of endurance,
When our strength has failed ere the day is half done,
When we reach the end of our hoarded resources
Our Father's full giving is only begun.

Fear not that thy need shall exceed His provision,
Our God ever yearns His resources to share;
Lean hard on the arm everlasting, availing;
The Father both thee and thy load will upbear.

His love has no limits, His grace has no measure,
His power no boundary known unto men;
For out of His infinite riches in Jesus
He giveth, and giveth, and giveth again.[37]

The yeast of the Pharisees and Herod (8:11-21)

The disciples are again to be found in a needy situation. We have already looked at two recorded incidents where they were unable or unwilling to provide for crowds of hungry people. Now they do not have bread for themselves. All they had between them was one loaf. Jesus warned them to watch out for the yeast of the Pharisees and Herod. Perhaps Jesus is saying that religion and politics corrupt the purity of the gospel. If so, he is surely speaking about the false

---

[37] Annie Flint (1866-1932), *Christian Hymns*, Evangelical Movement of Wales, 1977.

religion of man-made rules, rites and rituals rather than true religion with its biblical imperatives.

Many people have tried to use the gospel as a tool to achieve social justice and they have lost their way. Certainly Christian mission ought to be concerned about social justice. Certainly Christian mission should address poverty, human rights and environmental issues and so on. However, the gospel is to be distinguished from the political and social agenda by its spiritual message. Religion and politics can become corrupting influences on the purity of the gospel. We must not become so concerned about establishing the kingdom of God here on earth that we neglect to proclaim the message of the gospel: that people are sinners who need to repent and believe in the Lord Jesus Christ and his completed work on the cross for salvation.

Jesus sternly rebukes the disciples for their lack of understanding, hardness of heart, failure to believe what they have heard, failure to believe what they have seen and their failure to remember what they have experienced. It is astonishing that they are still so immature. What about us? Do we understand, as we ought to? Do we have believing hearts? Do we accept what we have heard? Do we cherish what we have seen? Do we remember what we have experienced? Do these things in our relationship with the Lord strengthen us? Do they inspire confidence and hope?

Jesus started to talk about the yeast of the Pharisees and Herod. The disciples took what he was saying about yeast to be a reference to the fact that they had very little bread; just one loaf which was insufficient to feed themselves. They got it wrong. They were very literal in their interpretation. But Jesus was speaking about yeast as a corrupting influence and the danger of that. In Scripture, yeast is a symbol of evil. Just as a small amount of it can leaven an entire loaf, so too evil has a permeating power. Its corrupting influence cannot be contained.

The Pharisees had demanded a sign. (11-12)They wanted Jesus to prove his credentials but God requires faith. The disciples started a discussion about the fact that they had just one loaf of bread. Perhaps they were trying to find out who was to blame for this. They were so engrossed in their own conversation that they did not pay heed to what Jesus was saying. There are many discussions among the disciples of Jesus that exclude Jesus. Sometimes we become so engrossed in our dialogues that we do not heed the voice of the Lord. We should always be attentive to the voice of Jesus. We should always try to understand what he is saying. We should not allow what the Lord is saying to become garbled or distorted through the filter of our immediate concerns. They should not have been so concerned with their immediate material needs. They should have remembered how abundantly the Lord had provided for them and for others. We too should have confidence in God's providential care. He is the provider and he supplies all that we need.

The poet William Cowper (1731-1800) wrote the hymn 'God Moves in a Mysterious Way'. It is one of the best hymns ever written on the theme of God's providence. It was the last hymn he ever wrote, with a fascinating story behind it. He spent eighteen months in a lunatic asylum and attempted suicide several times. During his stay in the asylum, he began reading the Bible and had a genuine conversion experience. He was periodically haunted with deep depressions. However, between these periods of melancholia he was a gifted writer. One night he decided to commit suicide by drowning himself. He called a taxicab (horse-drawn carriage) and told the driver to take him to the Thames River, London. Fog descended that was so thick it prevented him from reaching his destination. After driving around for a while, the cab stopped and let Cowper out. To Cowper's surprise, he found himself on his own doorstep! There were other failed attempts at suicide. On that evening, he tried to hang himself but the rope snapped. Even in our blackest moments, God watches over us!

God moves in a mysterious way

His wonders to perform;
He plants His footsteps in the sea
And rides upon the storm.

Deep in unfathomable mines
Of never failing skill
He treasures up His bright designs
And works His sovereign will.

Ye fearful saints, fresh courage take;
The clouds ye so much dread
Are big with mercy and shall break
In blessings on your head.

Judge not the Lord by feeble sense,
But trust Him for His grace;
Behind a frowning providence
He hides a smiling face.

His purposes will ripen fast,
Unfolding every hour;
The bud may have a bitter taste,
But sweet will be the flower.

Blind unbelief is sure to err
And scan His work in vain;
God is His own interpreter,
And He will make it plain.[38]

Jesus is asked for a sign to show that he is the real thing and he refuses to give a sign. Is this the Lord's way of showing us that faith is about believing in spite of lack of evidence? Human nature wants proof before they commitment. When

---

[38] William Cowper (1731-1800), *Christian Hymns*, Evangelical Movement of Wales, 1977.

we go to buy a new car, we take it for a test drive. When we buy clothes, we try them on first or make sure we can exchange them if they do not fit. We like to try before we buy. Jesus performed many miracles but the Pharisees wanted incontrovertible proof. They had no faith and the disciples seemed to suffer from spiritual amnesia.

Jesus got into a boat and headed across the lake. The Pharisees came out to argue with him. They did not come out of genuine spiritual curiosity. They did not come for a friendly chat or a theological discussion, but for a dispute. So they began to question him and they asked him for a sign from heaven. That seems rather innocuous. They are not asking Jesus for something he has not already done. They are not asking Jesus for something that he cannot do. So why does Jesus refuse them? This whole encounter with the Pharisees is about faith and what faith really is. The Pharisees seek a sign, but Jesus had already given many signs. These men had been present at many of the healings and other miracles that Jesus had performed. They have seen Jesus in action repeatedly. So why do they ask for another sign?

The request for a sign is not a request for a miracle they have seen that before. They have seen the power of Jesus. They do not deny the power of Jesus. They just do not believe it is from God. Their request is a demand that he demonstrate the legitimacy of his actions. Why did not Jesus try to convince them? By approaching Jesus in this way, the Pharisees are in essence asking the Lord to remove the need for faith. Jesus refuses to comply. Their question for a sign is not a question of faith, but a question of unbelief. I cannot say to the Lord "I will believe if you fulfill certain conditions".

Jesus gets back in the boat and as they head out Jesus warns them to be careful and watch out for the yeast of the Pharisees and of Herod. The disciples think that Jesus is upset with them because they only brought one loaf of bread. Jesus speaks of the yeast in the sense of corruption. The corruption in the lives of these Pharisees has worked though their whole person to the point where it has affected their judgment in matters of faith. Jesus is exasperated by the immaturity of the disciples. He gets them to remember what has happened in the past. He goes through the details of their experience: the feeding of the five thousand and the parallel feeding of the four thousand. Notice the disciples get all the facts right, but they cannot interpret them. They did not join up the dots. The writer to the Hebrews defines faith like this: 'Now faith is the assurance of things hoped for, the conviction of things not seen.' (Hebrews 11:1) This is the kind of faith to which we are called.

The blind man at Bethsaida (8:22-26)

Among the many people Jesus healed some were blind. At the outset of Christ's ministry he publicly read a passage from Isaiah which outlined his manifesto: "The Spirit of the Lord is upon me, because he has anointed me to proclaim good news to the poor. He has sent me to proclaim liberty to the captives and recovering of sight to the blind, to set at liberty those who are oppressed, to proclaim the year of the Lord's favor."–Luke 4:18

John the Baptist was imprisoned by Herod and unsure if Jesus was the Messiah. He sent some disciples to get clarity on this. Jesus said, "Go and tell John what you have seen and heard: the blind receive their sight, the lame walk, lepers are cleansed, and the deaf hear, the dead are raised up, the poor have good news preached to them." (Luke 7:22) These things were offered as evidence.

The healing of this blind man is unique as the only miracle that occurs in two stages. Jesus arrives at Bethsaida and a blind man is brought to him. Those who bring him to the Lord beg Jesus to touch him (v.22). They intercede on his behalf. Concerned friends, similar to those who brought the paralytic, bring him. (See Mark 2:3) Jesus takes this blind man out of the town, leading him by the hand. This is similar to what he did with the deaf mute.–see Mark 7:33.

Jesus heals him in two stages. In stage one (vs.23-24), Jesus spat on his eyes and then touched him. When asked if he saw anything, he looked up and said, "I see men like trees, walking." In stage two (v.25), Jesus put his hands on his eyes again. His sight was completely restored and he saw everyone clearly. We do not know why Jesus did it this way. Why take the blind man out of the town of Bethsaida? Was it to avoid publicity? Was it to establish a one-to-one relationship with the man? Why did not the man receive perfect sight immediately? Was it the spiritual condition of the man himself (no faith or weak faith)? Any explanation is speculation at best. The Lord does not always do things the same way!

Jesus healed at least eight blind men, using a variety of approaches. Two men were healed by a simple touch of their eyes. (Matthew 9:27-31) A blind and mute man was simply healed. (Matthew 12:22) Two more blind men were healed by a simple touch of the eyes (Matthew 20:30-34). Blind Bartimaeus was healed with a simple word (Mark 10:46-52). A blind man was healed with the anointment of his eyes with clay and spittle, followed by washing in the pool of Siloam.– John 9:1-7.

Similarly, prayer is not always answered the same way. The Lord may say "yes" and the prayer is answered immediately. The Lord may say "yes, but wait awhile". The Lord may say "yes, but not in the way you expect". Spiritual growth occurs in stages, similar to how this particular miracle occurred. Therefore, we should expect our spiritual growth to take time. The apostle Paul addressed the Corinthian believers like this: "But I, brothers, could not address you as spiritual people, but as people of the flesh, as infants in Christ. I fed you with milk, not solid food, for you were not ready for it. And even now you are not yet ready." (1 Corinthians 3:1-2) Peter says, "Grow in the grace and knowledge of our Lord and Savior Jesus Christ."–2 Peter 3:18

We are spiritually blinded by sin and in need of healing. We need the special attention of Jesus to be healed. When Jesus heals us of spiritual blindness it may take a while to see clearly. People who cared enough about him brought this man to Jesus. They had confidence in the power and compassion of Christ. This story is about having eyes to see, but not really seeing. It reminds me of how a seascape painting by the artist Henri Matisse was once hung upside down in the Museum of Modern Art in New York, being left that way for about six weeks! One hundred and sixteen thousand viewers strolled past *Le Bateau* admiring it but unaware it was upside-down.

This healing takes place in the city of Bethsaida, on the north shore of the Sea of Galilee. A city named after the daughter of Caesar Augustus. Up to now, Mark has presented the reader with a collage of stories about spiritual blindness and misunderstanding on the part of both Jesus' disciples and the religious leaders of his day. From this point forward, the disciples seem to see more and more of the picture, of who Jesus really is and the focus is instead on the sharpening of their spiritual vision. In a sense, this story pictures the spiritual journey in which we all find ourselves. Mark places this miracle after several stories that emphasize the disciples' spiritual blindness. Jesus said, "Do you not yet perceive or understand ... Having eyes do you not see ... Do you not yet understand?" (Mark 8:17-21) Mark places this miracle story just before Peter proclaims Christ as the Messiah. This is followed by the transfiguration where the disciples seem to enter a spiritual dimension as never before. By putting together the story of the blind man receiving his sight and of the disciples, gaining spiritual insight Mark is emphasizing here the importance of spiritual sight.

The blind man's sight comes in stages. Jesus gradually gives him sight. It is the only miracle story in the Gospels to speak of Jesus' healing as proceeding in stages. Jesus puts his hands on his eyes, the man first sees people that he says look like trees. Then with a second touch from Jesus, he sees clearly. Elsewhere, in all Jesus' other miracles the Lord heals completely and instantaneously. Mark intends us to understand this healing in stages as a process like that of spiritual illumination. We gradually gain spiritual sight. By the gradual healing of the blind man, Jesus is showing how spiritual sight develops, from lack of sight, to partial or blurred sight, to our spiritual sight ever increasing until that day when we will see God 'face to face.' Then we will see all things clearly. So much of our experience of seeing God in the present is but a poor reflection. The journey of faith is a gradual spiritual illumination of seeing God more and more clearly. We are told that the blind man eventually 'saw everything clearly.' (v.25) This is a double entendre, as in the Greek it literally means 'to see into.' Therefore, it is inferring spiritual perception. In other words, it is about opening the eyes of the soul. It is not just about looking. Behind the looking there needs to be the perspective of faith. Paul speaks of 'having the eyes of your hearts enlightened.' (Ephesians 1:18) Many of us will be familiar with the hymn sung prayerfully in church:

Open The Eyes Of My Heart

Open the eyes of my heart, Lord
Open the eyes of my heart
I want to see You
I want to see You.

To see You high and lifted up
Shining in the light of Your glory

Pour out Your power and love
As we sing holy, holy, holy.[39]

We have started a spiritual journey that is all about seeing into the mysteries of God. The journey of faith is a gradual process of illumination. Our disposition needs to be like the people in this story who beg Jesus to give this man sight. We should have that deep desire that others would see God in clearer and clearer ways. The spiritual life is ultimately about learning how to see into the deepest dimension.

God is a God of, redemption, restoration, hope and of new beginnings. Those who are redeemed can say: "I was blind but now I see." In some ways, it is the most curious of all Jesus' miraculous signs. The story is simply told, but not as easily understood. This is the only instance of healing in which Jesus asked if the person was healed. The man replied that he could see people and that they look like trees moving. In other words, he could see, but not clearly. Then Jesus again placed his hands on the man's eyes. Then his eyes were opened, his sight was restored, and he saw everything clearly. Why did he do it like that?

Chrysostom said that this miracle occurred in stages because of the imperfect faith of the man.[40] He did not seek healing from Jesus; others brought him to Jesus. The first glimmer of sight caused him to believe, and Jesus went on to heal him completely. That may be so. We simply do not know why this miracle was performed this way. The question Jesus asked seems to indicate that the method was intentional. It seems that the man had not been born blind, but had lost his sight. He knew the appearance of trees and

---

[39] Paul Baloche, *Mission Praise*, Marshall Pickering, 1999.

[40] Chrysostom was bishop at Antioch in the late 4th century and in his later days the much admired archbishop of Constantinople who left voluminous writings. He was such an articulate and eloquent preacher that he was given the Greek epithet, *chrysostomos*, meaning 'golden mouthed' in English and Anglicized to Chrysostom.

men. The fact that it is a progressive healing dramatically emphasizes the immediacy of Jesus' other miracles. R. C. Foster comments on this matter:

> We cannot tell why the miracle was performed in two steps. The question Jesus asked seems to indicate that the method was His deliberate plan. The man had not been born blind, but had lost his sight, for he knew the appearance of trees and men. McGarvey holds that the miracle was not gradual, but consisted of two instantaneous miracles, each of which accomplished exactly what Jesus intended; and that Jesus used this different method to reveal that He could heal in part and by progressive steps. It certainly did dramatically emphasize the immediacy of Jesus' other miracles.[41]

To see the full picture the context must be kept in view. This miracle was also a parable-in-action designed to teach that full sight of the riches of God in Christ does not come at once. We should never assume that, because we can see some truth, we know all truth. We should realize that seeing a little does not mean we see everything clearly. Peter (in Mark 8:27-29) confessed Jesus as the Christ. Yet, in the verses immediately following (31-32) when Jesus began to talk about going to Jerusalem to die before being raised from the dead Peter took him aside and began to rebuke him! Peter understood Jesus was the Messiah but he did not understand fully what that meant.

Redemption is the beginning of the road not the end of the journey. William Barclay says:

> Usually Jesus' miracles happened suddenly and completely. In this miracle the blind man's sight came back in stages. There is symbolic truth here. No man

---

[41] R. C. Foster, *Studies in the Life of Christ.* Grand Rapids: Baker Book House, Reprinted 1971, p. 696.

sees all God's truth all at once. One of the dangers of a certain type of evangelism is that it encourages the idea that when a man has taken his decision for Christ he is a full-grown Christian. One of the dangers of Church membership is that it can be presented in such a way as to imply that when a person becomes a pledged member of the Church he has come to the end of the road. So far from that being the case the decision and the pledge of membership are the beginning of the road. They are the discovery of the riches of Christ which are inexhaustible, and if a man lived a hundred, or a thousand, or a million years, he would still have to go on growing in grace, and learning more and more about the infinite wonder and beauty of Jesus Christ.[42]

It is my hope and prayer that in our journey with Jesus through the message of Mark our understanding of Jesus and our appreciation for him will grow as we gain more spiritual insight through the illuminating ministry of the Holy Spirit.

Peter confesses Jesus as the Christ (8:27-30)

Here the spiritual enlightenment of the disciples enters a new phase. Jesus had opened the eyes of the blind man at Bethsaida. Now the eyes of the disciples are opened and they begin to see Jesus for who he really is. Jesus asked his disciples a question: "Who do people say that I am?" Perhaps the limitations of his humanity meant that he simply did not know what people were saying. On the other hand, more likely he wanted to test them and draw them out in conversation. There were a number of ideas circulating about

---

[42] William Barclay, *The Gospel of Mark*, *The Daily Study Bible Series*, Vol.3, Philadelphia: Westminster Press, 2nd edition, 1956, p. 194-195.

who Jesus was. They were mostly based on the idea of reincarnation, which is not taught anywhere in Scripture.

Some thought he was John the Baptist. Some thought he was Elijah (who had been taken to heaven alive in a chariot of fire). Others thought he was one of the prophets. John the Baptist was recently deceased as Herod had beheaded him. He was a preacher who proclaimed Christ and called for repentance. He had been imprisoned for his fearless stand on moral issues, which incurred the displeasure of Herod. He baptized Jesus at what could be seen as an inaugural ceremony in the earthly ministry of Christ at which God the Father spoke from heaven and said he was well pleased with Jesus. The Holy Spirit descended on Jesus in the form of a dove, the symbol of peace. Thus, Jesus was publicly anointed for ministry on earth.

Elijah was a prophet in the Kingdom of Samaria during the reign of Ahab (9th century BC). He defended the worship of *Yahweh* over that of the more popular Baal, notably on Mount Carmel. His prophetic ministry as spokesman for God in his day involved a demonstration of extraordinary power which involved raising a boy from the dead and bringing fire down from the sky. Instead of death, he was taken up in a chariot of fire. In the book of Malachi Elijah's return is prophesied "before the coming of the great and terrible day of the Lord", making him a harbinger of the Messiah. In Islam, the *Qur'an* describes Elijah as a great and righteous prophet of God. He is noted for his powerful preaching against the worship of Baal.

Two thousand years ago, the Jewish people were expecting to see Elijah literally return from heaven to announce the appearance of the Messiah. They had been promised that this was going to happen by the Old Testament Prophet Malachi: "Behold, I send my messenger, and he will prepare the way before me" (Malachi 3:1). This prophecy need not necessarily refer to Elijah, as it could be understood to refer to John the Baptist. Then Malachi goes on to say:

Malachi 4:1-5

¹ "For behold, the day is coming, burning like an oven, when all the arrogant and all evildoers will be stubble. The day that is coming shall set them ablaze, says the Lord of hosts, so that it will leave them neither root nor branch. ² But for you who fear my name, the sun of righteousness shall rise with healing in its wings. You shall go out leaping like calves from the stall. ³ And you shall tread down the wicked, for they will be ashes under the soles of your feet, on the day when I act, says the Lord of hosts.

⁴ "Remember the law of my servant Moses, the statutes and rules that I commanded him at Horeb for all Israel.

⁵ "Behold, I will send you Elijah the prophet before the great and awesome day of the Lord comes.

Elijah ascended into heaven in a chariot of fire (2 Kings 2).[43] This spectacular event happened about 850 years BC. Later, in about 450 BC, Malachi prophesied that Elijah would return from heaven to herald the coming of the Messiah. The return of Elijah prophecy is important is because it became one of the primary reasons why the Jewish people rejected Jesus' claim to be the Messiah. They concluded that Jesus' claim to be the Messiah could not be true because Elijah had not returned. Therefore, they believed he was an imposter.

Justin Martyr (circa 100 AD) was a very prominent Christian at a time when Christianity was still in its infancy. He has been described as 'the most notable of the second

---

[43] Christian Publishing House would recommend the reading of the article, Did Enoch and Elijah Go to Heaven?
http://www.christianpublishers.org/enoch-and-elijah-heaven

century [Christian] apologists.'[44] He wrote a book called *The Dialogue with Trypho the Jew*, which is a record of a discussion between Justin Martyr and Trypho, a Jewish rabbi. Before Justin became a Christian, he was a follower of the Greek philosophers and he still wore the characteristic flowing robes of a Roman philosopher. This dialogue begins with Justin telling the rabbi that he believes that Jesus was the long awaited Messiah. The following excerpt contains this rabbi's response.

> When I (Justin) had said this, [the students who were with the rabbi] laughed; but he smiling, says, 'I approve of your other remarks, and admire the eagerness with which you study divine things; but it were better for you abide in the philosophy of Plato. It were better for you abide in the philosophy of Plato rather than be deceived by false words, and follow the opinions of people of no reputation... for when you have forsaken God, and reposed confidence in man, what safety still awaits you?" But Christ - if he has indeed been born, and exists anywhere... has no power until Elijah comes to anoint him, and make him manifest to all. And you, having accepted a groundless report, invent a Christ for yourselves, and for his sake are inconsiderately perishing.[45]

This rabbi reveals exactly what the Jewish religious leaders and the Jewish people of two thousand years ago were expecting to see before the Messiah appeared. Furthermore, they also expected the Messiah was going to

---

[44] Tim Dowley, *Handbook to the History of Christianity*, Eerdman's, 1977, p. 108.

[45] *Ante Nicene Fathers, Vol. 1, The Apostolic Fathers*, Edited by Rev. Alexander Roberts, Sir James Donaldson and Arthur Cleveland Coxe, (first published 1885) republished New York: Cosimo Classics 2007, p. 198.

free them from Roman domination and exalt Israel over all the nations of the earth.

Jesus explains how the prophecies from Malachi were actually fulfilled,

Mark 9:11-13

¹¹ And they asked him, "Why do the scribes say that first Elijah must come?" ¹² And he said to them, "Elijah does come first to restore all things. And how is it written of the Son of Man that he should suffer many things and be treated with contempt? ¹³ But I tell you that Elijah has come, and they did to him whatever they pleased, as it is written of him."

In Matthew's account of the Transfiguration when Jesus and the disciples were returning from the mountain the statement is clearer:

Matthew 17:10-13

¹⁰ And the disciples asked him, "Then why do the scribes say that first Elijah must come?" ¹¹ He answered, "Elijah does come, and he will restore all things. ¹² But I tell you that Elijah has already come, and they did not recognize him, but did to him whatever they pleased. So also the Son of Man will certainly suffer at their hands." ¹³ Then the disciples understood that he was speaking to them of John the Baptist.

Clearly, Jesus taught that this was a true prophecy. Jesus agreed that Elijah indeed must return before the Messiah comes. But then, to the surprise of everyone there, Jesus claimed that John the Baptist was the fulfillment of this prophecy and the disciples clearly understood what he said.

How could John possibly have been the return of Elijah? The rabbis might have also pointed out that even John himself had said that he was not Elijah. At one point, early in his ministry, John the Baptist was asked whether he was Elijah. He answered that he was not. (John 1:21) He was not literally, Elijah returned. A statement made at the beginning of the Gospel of Luke where the birth of John the Baptist is foretold can resolve what might seem like a contradiction. The angel of the Lord, speaking to Zechariah says: "...for he will be great before the Lord...he will be filled with the Holy Spirit ...And he will turn many of the children of Israel to the Lord their God, and he will go before him in the spirit and power of Elijah...to make ready for the Lord a people prepared" (Luke 1:15-17). So Elijah had returned from heaven in the "spirit". John went, "on before the Lord, in the spirit and power of Elijah." Viewed this way, both John and Jesus were right. The same "spirit and power" of God that had animated Elijah eight hundred years earlier had returned to animate John the Baptist.

Elijah was a man of much energy, determination and dynamism in his zealous service toward God, and Elisha sought a two-part share of Elijah's spirit as his successor. (2 Ki 2:9, 15) John the Baptizer revealed the same dynamic drive and spirited zeal that Elijah had possessed, which gave rise to John having a powerful effect on those who listened to him. Therefore, he could be said 'to go in the spirit and power of Elijah.' (Lu 1:17) In other words, John the Baptist did not have some spirit of Elijah, such as an essence or entity that had dwelled in Elijah and was then in John. Rather, the "spirit," was a mental disposition toward his service to God.

Even today, two thousand years later, the Jewish religious experts still await the second coming of Elijah. Every year at the Passover meal (in time honored tradition) an extra place at the table is still set for Elijah, hoping that this will be the year when he finally returns to join them.

What does the Bible mean when it speaks of Elijah coming again? Was this a literal prophecy, or did John the Baptist fulfill the prophecy in spirit? Alternatively, is it that the prophecy has a double-fulfillment: one of John the Baptist, and one of Elijah? Jesus told the multitudes concerning John the Baptist that he was the messenger of Malachi 3:1 and the Elijah of Malachi 4:5:-

Matthew 11:11-15

¹¹ Truly, I say to you, among those born of women there has arisen no one greater than John the Baptist. Yet the one who is least in the kingdom of heaven is greater than he. ¹² From the days of John the Baptist until now the kingdom of heaven has suffered violence, and the violent take it by force. ¹³ For all the Prophets and the Law prophesied until John, ¹⁴ and if you are willing to accept it, he is Elijah who is to come. ¹⁵ He who has ears to hear, let him hear.

Understanding John as Elijah makes sense when we look at what the angel of the Lord spoke to Zechariah concerning John's ministry before he was ever born. This does not deny that Elijah himself will actually come again in his physical presence before Jesus returns to the earth. It is not that John the Baptist partially fulfilled the prophecies of Malachi rather there is a double fulfillment. Scripture declares many prophecies to have dual references or partial fulfillment. In hermeneutics, this is called the 'double reference principle'. Many of the prophecies concerning Jesus were double reference prophecies. This means that they had an immediate fulfillment, and a future fulfillment.

For example, Stephen claimed that the prophet, which Moses spoke of in Deuteronomy 18:15-19 was Jesus Christ. However, the context of Deuteronomy 18 is about Moses speaking of Joshua who was to be the next leader of Israel. Also, Matthew claimed the statement in Hosea 11:1 which says: "...out of Egypt I called my son..." (Hosea 11:1) was fulfilled when Jesus lived in Egypt until the death of Herod (Matthew 2:14-15). This verse in the context of Hosea, however, is about God speaking of the Israelite's exodus from

Egypt. Furthermore, consider the prophecy from Jeremiah and how it is used by Matthew: 'Thus says the LORD: "A voice is heard in Ramah, lamentation and bitter weeping. Rachel is weeping for her children; she refuses to be comforted for her children, because they are no more" (Jeremiah 31:15). Matthew attributed the prophecy of Jeremiah to the slaughter of the male children in Bethlehem (Matthew 2:16-18). But in the context of Jeremiah 31, however, this prophecy was given by Jeremiah to the Jewish captives in Babylon promising them that their children would once again inhabit the land of Canaan.–Jeremiah 31:16-17.

John the Baptist fulfilled the prophecies in spirit at Jesus' first coming but Elijah himself will fulfill the prophecies at Jesus' second coming. Elijah will come back again in his physical body to prepare the way for Jesus' return. The context of the two prophecies in Malachi indicate that Elijah was going to come back to turn the hearts of Israel to the Lord before the Messiah came to set up his earthly kingdom, so that the Lord's fury would not rest upon them when he came himself.–Malachi 3:1-3; 4:1-6.

Jesus asks the disciples an important question in this passage of Scripture: "But who do you say that I am?" Peter answered him, "You are the Christ". Everyone must answer this question. Even those who profess to be disciples of Jesus must confess this with their lips and hold it to be true in their hearts. To the Muslims Jesus was a prophet. This is also the understanding of other faiths concerning Jesus. To the Jews he was an imposter. In the opinion of many today he was a good man, a teacher. Some say Jesus never existed, that he was just a religious concept, that the Gospels are a fairytale or a composite accumulation of myths that teach moral truths in narrative form. Jesus moves from the general question, "Who do people say that I am?" to the more specific question, "But who do you say that I am?" To deny that Jesus is the Messiah is to reject his person and work. People will be held accountable for what they believe and profess about Jesus.

Jesus foretells his death and resurrection (8:31-38)

Jesus now begins to teach his disciples that he must suffer, be rejected by the religious leaders and be killed. He tells them that he will rise again from the dead. This is a new phase in the ministry of Jesus. He is preparing those closest to him for what was about to happen. The Lord could see into the future and he was building the disciples up for what lay ahead. The Lord always does this. He strengthens his disciples through his Word for the road ahead. Jesus knew that the eternal plan of salvation was on time and on target.

This passage of Scripture shows that he taught them plainly. He wanted them to be in no doubt that the traumatic events that were about to unfold were part of God's intentional plan of redemption. When we look back at how the disciples reacted when Jesus was arrested and crucified, it is extraordinary that they still did not understand. He had not spoken to them in parables about this. He was an excellent teacher and he made his meaning clear. However, it is amazing what people do not want to hear. When people have certain expectations and things do not work out as they had hoped they get disappointed. They might have plans for our lives and they might be working to a certain agenda but God may have other plans. This passage shows that the disciples of Jesus can be astonishingly slow to understand what God is doing.

Nevertheless, it is clear that Peter (at least) understood what Jesus was saying, because Peter took the Lord aside and rebuked him. Imagine that! To rebuke means to express sharp disapproval. It is a form of hostile criticism. We rebuke others when we think they are wrong. Therefore, Peter criticized the Lord harshly and expressed his disapproval of the plan that

Jesus had just explained. There is none as blind as those who do not want to see! Here the pupil thought that he was above the master (as pupils sometimes tend to do). In fact the better, the pupil, the more likely this is to happen.

Jesus must have had his back to the disciples because he turned around and looked at them. Why is that detail included? Perhaps Peter was representing the group in what he said. Maybe the disciples asked Peter or agreed that Peter should try to talk Jesus out of this daft plan (as they saw it). Alternatively, it might be that Jesus wanted to make it clear that he (not Peter) was their leader. Jesus had often rebuked the disciples for being slow to understand. However, here his rebuke is different. After all it was not that Peter misunderstood, rather it was that he thought he knew better! Peter (and probably all the disciples) wanted Jesus to be the great emancipator of Israel. They wanted Jesus to free their nation from Roman occupation. They expected the Messiah to be a secular deliverer who would empower the Jewish people. They were wrong. Many people since have tried to squeeze Jesus into their mold. When Jesus rebuked Peter he said, "Get behind me, Satan!" Jesus put Peter in his place. Peter was actually being used by the devil to try to deter Jesus from fulfilling his divine mission. Spiritual opposition might come from those closest to us. Sometimes Satan is pulling the strings.

Remember how Satan tempted Jesus in the wilderness and tried to get the Lord to abandon his mission? Well Jesus identifies these words from Peter as a satanic attempt to obstruct or dissuade him from doing what he came to earth to do. He told Peter in the plainest possible way that he was not in tune with the eternal (heavenly) plan of God. He told Peter that he was looking at this from a human point of view and that he did not have a spiritual (heavenly) perspective. Now Jesus calls the disciples to him and explains that not only is he going to the cross but that he expects his disciples to follow him all the way even unto death. Jesus explains what following him really means: "If anyone would come after me, let him deny himself and take up his cross and follow me" (v.34). This is about living for the kingdom.

The world of the disciples must have seemed like it was spinning out of control when Jesus was arrested and brought before the religious leaders. However, God is sovereign. There are things that are out of our control but they are not outside the control of God. Jesus seemed powerless and even pitiable but things are not always, what they seem. Christ could have stopped those who mocked and tormented him but he was focused on the bigger picture and so submitted silently to their taunts. When we feel we are being treated unfairly we should remember Jesus was treated unjustly. He has walked this road ahead of us. He does not drive his sheep rather he gently leads them. Jesus carried his cross through the crowded streets. Along the way he met Simon who helped to carry his cross and he also met the women who were weeping. He could have cursed the whole world for the way he was being treated but he did not. We must not become bitter and curse the world. Is our cross too heavy? God will send help to bear the load. Even in the midst of great trouble we will find the loving faces of those who weep for us. God sent his only Son to bear our burdens on that tree at Calvary. Do we really understand the way of the cross?

If Jesus wanted to, he could have had the last word. Many of us like to have the last word! He could have justified himself and proven to everyone that he was the Messiah. He could have proven that this was his mission and not a terrible mistake. It is difficult for us not to have the last word, especially when we are right! The truth will come out in the end as it did with Jesus. The restraint of the Jesus is exemplary. Justifying ourselves is not what really matters. What is important is that we are in right relationship with God and with others. In his dying moments, Jesus reached out to the repentant thief. Jesus did not reject this man. Christ could have said: "You are a law-breaker and you are getting what you deserve." But he didn't. Nobody would have had a better claim to self-righteousness than Jesus. But Christ's words were words of reconciliation and love. This is the way of the cross. Jesus was completely selfless. He was kind and compassionate to a distressed soul and spoke words of comfort and reassurance, hope and significance.

May we be less self-absorbed and more like Jesus. Jesus has much to teach us about acceptance and belonging. That thief was rejected by society. He was deemed unfit to live in the Roman Empire but God accepted him and promised him an immediate place in his kingdom. Everybody who reaches out to the Lord will find forgiveness and friendship. This dying man recognized something in Jesus that led him to hope and believe. Believers must be people that distressed souls will look to for help.

Jesus explained that his followers should not be too fond of this world because this temporal world is temporary. We are pilgrims, as the hymn reminds us:

This world is not my home, I'm just a passing thru,
My treasures are laid up somewhere beyond the blue;
The angels beckon me from Heaven's open door,
And I can't feel at home in this world anymore.[46]

The Lord said, "For whoever would save his life will lose it, but whoever loses his life for my sake and the gospel's will save it" (v.36). Jesus was a master of rhetoric. In our understanding rhetoric might be a bad thing. We might tend to think of it as manipulative words used persuade us to give our allegiance (or money) to some political or ideological cause, or to buy a product etc. Jesus did not manipulate people but he was a superb communicator. He could capture and sustain people's attention and captivate their hearts and

---

[46] Albert E Brumley, 1937, public domain.

minds. He spoke the truth but he spoke in an interesting way, a way that distilled the essence of truth into pearls of wisdom. That is why his words are so memorable and engaging even after two thousand years.

"For whoever would save his life will lose it, but whoever loses his life for my sake and the gospel's will save it" (v.36). These words are not just surprising they are subversive, because they overthrow expectations. They turn our understanding upside down. Those who invest everything in this life will lose everything. Those who invest in eternity will have riches beyond measure. "For what does it profit a man to gain the whole world and forfeit his soul?" (v. 36) Many people have lost their souls by investing everything (time, talent, money) in things that ultimately do not matter. Whatever projects we are committed to, whatever plans we have are not just meaningless if they distract our attention from God: they are dangerous! The devil wants to deceive us. He will offer us opportunities that will take our thoughts and time away from God, opportunities that we will find tempting and hard to resist. Jesus is teaching us that nothing is more important than the spiritual life. He is inviting us to adopt this perspective in all aspects of our lives. Our spirituality should not be merely compartmentalized in such a way that it touches some areas of our lives but not others.

There is a stern warning at the end of this passage. There Jesus tells us that those who are ashamed of him in this world will incur his displeasure. Will Jesus be ashamed of us or pleased with how we lived our lives? The way of the cross is selfless, not selfish. May God help us to live in a way that is pleasing to him by following his example!

Chapter 9

The transfiguration (9:1-13)

In the opening verse of this ninth chapter of Mark's Gospel Christ promises that some of his disciples will live to see the power of God made manifest in an awesome way. This indeed happened on the Day of Pentecost and the book of Acts records the fact that many signs and wonders accompanied the activity of the church in its early days.

In the event of the transfiguration, the disciples got a brief glimpse of the glory of God. Jesus declared himself the light of the world, which means that he exposed the works of darkness and illuminated the path of righteousness. But in the transfiguration he was radiant in a different way and there was an evident luminosity.

There is a beautiful prayer in the Old Testament book of Habakkuk, which says, "O LORD, I have heard the report of you, and your work, O LORD, do I fear. In the midst of the years revive it; in the midst of the years make it known; in wrath remember mercy" (Habakkuk 3:2). Here is a prayer that expresses a heartfelt desire to see the power of God manifest in his day! It is a prayer of all the saints who long to see God's power made manifest in their generation. It ought to be our prayer today. God's power was made manifest throughout the ages, through the ministry of the prophets. It was made manifest in the incarnation and the resurrection. But it was also made visible in the transfiguration. Here we see something of his divine nature, which is incorporeal and intangible. It is a mystical and mysterious thing.

The transfiguration is a momentary manifestation of the glory and power of the kingdom. Jesus tells those listening to him that they will "not taste death until they see the kingdom of God after it has come with power" (v.1). This could refer to death in general terms or it could refer to experiencing death for the sake of Jesus. In either case before their death (whatever might be the circumstances of their deaths) they will witness the coming of the kingdom of God in power. This refers to the *Parousia* (the coming of the Holy Spirit). Only Peter, James and John witness the transfiguration. These three were also present at the healing Jairus' daughter (5:37) and later on in the Garden of Gethsemane (14:33). They seem to be Christ's closest disciples.

The transfiguration occurred six days after Jesus foretold his death and resurrection. That is less than a week after Peter tried to talk Jesus out of his stated aim of going to the cross. This privileged revelation was given to Peter, James and John, the inner circle of disciples. The high mountain on which this event took place is most likely Mount Hermon about forty miles northeast of the Sea of Galilee but some say this incident might have occurred on Mount Tabor which is the highest mountain in that area of the world (9,000 feet above sea level). In winter, it is often snow-capped. It is located near Caesarea Philippi where the previous events at the end of chapter eight had taken place. (8:27)

The word transfigured means that Jesus was changed into another form. The word used is the Greek word from which we get our English word metamorphosis. This word is used elsewhere in Scripture to describe progressive change into the moral likeness of Christ. The apostle Paul, writing to the Romans said: "Do not be conformed to this world, but be transformed by the renewal of your mind, that by testing you may discern what is the will of God, what is good and acceptable and perfect" (Romans 12:2). To the Colossians he expressed a similar idea: "And we all, with unveiled face, beholding the glory of the Lord, are being transformed into the same image from one degree of glory to another. For this comes from the Lord who is the Spirit" (2 Corinthians 3:18). Both thoughts contain the idea that the believer is involved in a process of sanctification, which is transformative.

Jesus clothes became radiant (dazzling white). He seems to have been changed temporarily into a heavenly being. The apostle John later wrote the book of Revelation where he says: "...and in the midst of the lampstands one like a son of man, clothed with a long robe and with a golden sash around his chest. The hairs of his head were white, like white wool, like snow. His eyes were like a flame of fire..." (Revelation 1:13-14). The transfiguration seems to give us a preview of the exalted Christ. The appearance of Elijah fits in with the Jewish expectation that his presence would announce end times. Both Moses and Elijah were there as representatives of the Law and the prophets because the Old Testament was being fulfilled in Jesus.

True to form Peter responded impulsively. His words show that although he was greatly moved by the experience he did not fully understand it. How often that is true of our encounters with God. Peter wanted to prolong this moment, as we all would like to do when we experience a foretaste of heaven. But before Jesus could enter permanently into his glory and eternal rest he had to suffer and die. Peter seemed to have great difficulty accepting the idea of a suffering Messiah. Mark is sensitive to Peter in the way he records Peter's confusion and senseless comments.

Clouds may symbolize God's presence: 'And as soon as Aaron spoke to the whole congregation of the people of Israel, they looked toward the wilderness, and behold, the glory of the LORD appeared in the cloud' (Exodus 16:10). God spoke at the baptism of Jesus from a cloud (Mark 1:1). At the transfiguration God told the disciples that he loved his son and endorsed his mission, which would involve suffering and death. The voice of God from the cloud said: "This is my beloved Son; listen to him." Here the word listen means obey. This is what God expects of all disciples.

The disciples were puzzled about what Jesus said about the resurrection. Jesus says that it is "...written of the Son of Man that he should suffer many things and be treated with contempt." This is possibly a reference to Isaiah:

Isaiah 53:3-12

³ He was despised and rejected by men;
   a man of sorrows, and acquainted with grief;
and as one from whom men hide their faces
   he was despised, and we esteemed him not.

⁴ Surely he has borne our griefs
   and carried our sorrows;
yet we esteemed him stricken,
   smitten by God, and afflicted.
⁵ But he was pierced for our transgressions;
   he was crushed for our iniquities;
upon him was the chastisement that brought us peace,
   and with his wounds we are healed.
⁶ All we like sheep have gone astray;
   we have turned—every one—to his own way;
and the Lord has laid on him
   the iniquity of us all.

⁷ He was oppressed, and he was afflicted,
   yet he opened not his mouth;
like a lamb that is led to the slaughter,
   and like a sheep that before its shearers is silent,
   so he opened not his mouth.
⁸ By oppression and judgment he was taken away;
   and as for his generation, who considered
that he was cut off out of the land of the living,
   stricken for the transgression of my people?
⁹ And they made his grave with the wicked

and with a rich man in his death,
although he had done no violence,
   and there was no deceit in his mouth.
¹⁰ Yet it was the will of the Lord to crush him;
   he has put him to grief;
when his soul makes an offering for guilt,
   he shall see his offspring; he shall prolong his days;
the will of the Lord shall prosper in his hand.
¹¹ Out of the anguish of his soul he shall see and be satisfied;
by his knowledge shall the righteous one, my servant,
   make many to be accounted righteous,
   and he shall bear their iniquities.
¹² Therefore I will divide him a portion with the many,
   and he shall divide the spoil with the strong,
because he poured out his soul to death
   and was numbered with the transgressors;
yet he bore the sin of many,
   and makes intercession for the transgressors.

I believe the purpose of the disciples witnessing the transfiguration was so that they might behold something of the glory of Christ before his humiliation on the cross. As such, it was intended to strengthen their faith. Jesus was transfigured to show his disciples his power and glory.

How can we make sense of that mountaintop episode in the lives of the disciples? Both Moses and Elijah experienced God's presence on a mountaintop experience. In Exodus when Moses came down after his mountaintop experience with God, his face was radiant. In their accounts of the transfiguration Matthew and Luke add that, not only were Jesus' clothes shining (as in Mark), but also that his face was shining. When we read the crucifixion story in light of the transfiguration, we see some striking contrasts. Mark's story of Jesus moves from the blinding light of the transfiguration to a shocking darkness as Jesus is crucified. From clothes dazzling white to clothes stripped from Jesus' body, from two saints flanking Jesus on the mountain to two criminals flanking him at the cross. From the disciples wanting to stay on the mountain with Jesus forever to the disciples fleeing arrest and denying any knowledge of Jesus, from God reiterating that Jesus is his "Beloved" to Jesus calling to God: "Why have you forsaken me?" The transfiguration shows us that following Jesus can take us to the peak experiences of the mountaintop but also to the valley of struggle, persecution, and even martyrdom.

Moses, Elijah, and Jesus all experienced God on a mountaintop. Our highest, most profound, most enlightening experiences happen when we are close to the God. So we pray and gather together to worship and these acts are potentially transforming. These contemplative practices are ways of letting go of our ego, the masks we wear, our busyness, and our distractions. These practices of prayer and presence open us from our isolation to connect us to God and to one another. An experience of transfiguration is no guarantee that the darkness will stay away. Moses had to go back down the mountain to continue wandering in the wilderness. Jesus' transfiguration happens as he turns his face toward the cross. This is both literally and figuratively a mountain-top experience. A cloud overshadows the mountain and the voice of God speaks: "This is my beloved Son; listen to him." This would be a memorable moment for the disciples who witnessed it. Certain moments in God's presence are a foretaste of heaven.

The concluding remarks in Martin Luther King's last sermon offer a glimpse of the heaven he anticipated:

> I don't know what will happen now. We've got some difficult days ahead. But it doesn't matter with me now. Because I've been to the mountain top. And I don't mind. Like anybody, I would like to live a long life. Longevity has its place. But I'm not concerned about that now. I just want to do God's

will. And He's allowed me to go up to the mountain. And I've looked over. And I've seen the promised land. I may not get there with you. But I want you to know tonight, that we, as a people will get to the promised land. And I'm happy, tonight. I'm not worried about anything. I'm not fearing any man. Mine eyes have seen the glory of the coming of the Lord.[47]

Although he was speaking about civil rights for African-Americans, his words have a spiritual parallel and resonance.

Peter, James and John (up on that mountain) had been given nothing less than glimpse into the future. They saw past the suffering and death of Jesus, which the Master had predicted a few days before. For one brief shining moment, they glimpsed the glory of the Lord. We all experience those energizing, even life-changing, mountaintop experiences during the course of our pilgrimage. If we want to have a mountaintop experience and get a glimpse of heaven, we must make ourselves available. Peter, James, and John were invited up the slope because they were already in the company of Jesus. We must listen to Jesus ("This is my beloved Son; listen to him"). We hear him as we worship and as we study Scripture. It is easy to let other voices drown out the voice of the Lord and so we must be attentive to the Master.

Our work is in the valley. The church is the only institution that exists primarily for the sake of those outside it. If we listen to Jesus, we hear him say, "Go therefore and make disciples" (Matthew 28:18) and "If anyone would come

---

[47] This was delivered on April 3, 1968 on the eve of his assassination. He preached at Mason Temple in Memphis, Tennessee, the headquarters of the Church of God in Christ, the largest African American Pentecostal denomination in the United States. Quoted by Clyde Fant and William Pinson (eds.) *20 Centuries of Great Preaching*, Vol. XII, Waco, TX: Word Books, 1971, pp. 352-353.

after me, let him deny himself and take up his cross and follow me."—Mark 8:34.

Jesus heals a boy with an unclean spirit (9:14-32)

This is the last exorcism story in Mark. Jesus comes down from the mountain with Peter, James and John. They go from the sublime experience of the mountaintop to this satanic encounter. Here is another passage that demonstrates the compassion and power of Jesus. It is about belief, unbelief and prayer. The disciples had failed to cast out this evil spirit. Jesus suggests that their failure was related to unbelief. Was it unbelief on the part of the disciples, the father (though the mother might be there too) who brought the boy or the crowd? Hardly the crowd as they would merely have been witnesses rather than participants.

Jesus seems to be frustrated or exasperated with their faithlessness. Therefore, it is clear that faithlessness is not pleasing to the Lord. The father (probably) appealed to Jesus for help. He brought his son to Jesus. He addresses Jesus as "Teacher" and this might reveal something of his limited understanding of the true nature of the Lord. He says: "Teacher, I brought my son to you, for he has a spirit that makes him mute. And whenever it seizes him, it throws him down, and he foams and grinds his teeth and becomes rigid." He describes the awful symptoms of the boy's condition. Here we see the great physician at work. Jesus asks the father of the boy how long his son has been in this condition. The boy had been in this pitiful condition for a long time ("from childhood") which implies that he was beyond childhood but still not a man.

We see how destructive this malevolent spirit is. It had often cast him into fire and water to destroy him. The devil is described in Scripture as a roaring lion who goes about seeking whom he may devour and destroy. Jesus, by stark contrast, says that he came to give life so that people might experience life to the full. The father's appeal to Jesus shows that he has hope rather than strong faith: "But if you can do anything, have compassion on us and help us." The man's approach to Jesus was a shot in the dark, a vague hope without much confidence and Jesus picks him up on this, "'If you can'! All things are possible for one who believes. "The man immediately shouts out: "I believe; help my unbelief!" It is a very interesting and honest thing to say. It is paradoxical and even funny! He immediately made up his mind that he believed but recognized how feeble that belief was. How often we are like this. We believe but our faith is frail. When the angel Gabriel appeared to Mary and told her that she (a virgin) would conceive she asked how this could be. The angel told her that it would happen by the power of the Holy Ghost and said, "For nothing will be impossible with God."

Later the disciples asked Jesus privately, "Why could we not cast it out?" And he told them, "This kind cannot be driven out by anything but prayer." While Peter, James and John were with Jesus on the Mount of Transfiguration, the other disciples had a different kind of encounter. They could not heal a young boy and the teachers of the law probably seized on this opportunity to question their authority. These disciples had an important lesson to learn about faith. Sometimes we learn best through our failures instead of our successes. Christ returns to his disciples and finds them in a bit of a pickle. He laid aside his robes of glory and returned to the work of his ministry in opposing the powers of darkness. Matthew Henry said, "Christ's glory above does not make him forget the concerns of his church below, which he visits in great humility. And he came very seasonably, when the disciples were embarrassed and run a-ground...."[48]

When we come to the end of ourselves, it is often in that place that we experience the power of God. The disciples and perhaps others are rebuked for their lack of faith. The father's approach to Jesus was more an act of desperation than an act of faith. Jesus shifted the man's attention from the failed efforts of the disciples to the power of God. Throughout the Bible, we are taught the importance of faith. The writer to the Hebrews says that without faith it is impossible to please God (Hebrews 11:6). Jesus makes a remarkable statement here - everything is possible for him who believes. Our faith is not in our faith, but rather our faith is in the character of God and the promises in his Word. The father of this boy is like many people who profess faith. They believe and yet they have doubts. This father's reply is an honest admission of the condition of his heart. He is like many believers who want to believe but have doubts. So the man cries out in faith, "I do believe" but he realized he needs help with his doubts. When we come to God, we will not only be given faith but we will also receive help to overcome our unbelief.

Evil is at work in the world but Jesus has overcome the powers of darkness. Do you believe Jesus can heal the same way today? Notice three things. First, Jesus said all things are possible to those who believe. Second, the father said he believed but asked for help with his unbelief. Third, the boy was healed, which indicates the father's faith, even with some of his doubts, was enough. When our faith wavers, we need to go to God and ask for help to believe and for help to overcome doubts.

---

[48] Matthew Henry, *Matthew Henry's Commentary on the Whole Bible, complete and unabridged in one volume*, Peabody: Massachusetts, Hendrickson, 1991, p.1797.

The disciples wanted to learn what they did wrong. This indicates they were genuinely interested in doing whatever it takes to be a servant. This is the right attitude to have before the Lord. However, Jesus indicates that faith only comes through prayer. As we maintain a regular prayer life, our faith grows. In prayer, we learn more about the character and attributes of God. The disciples ask why they could not cast out this evil spirit. The Lord's reply indicates that we need to spend time in prayer for others who are under the controlling and destructive influence of the powers of darkness. Prayer really does change things. So let us be willing to spend time each week to pray for the needs of others. Certain miracles require prayer and fasting. We all experience times of frustration and defeat in our Christian lives. Even though we labor tirelessly and conscientiously in our service to the Lord there might be no evidence of the Spirit of God working in power. But power comes through prayer. The Savior's words remind us of the necessity of prayer.

Jesus had commissioned his disciples to preach and cast out demons: 'And he appointed twelve (whom he also named apostles) so that they might be with him and he might send them out to preach and have authority to cast out demons' (Mark 3:14-15). And they were already successful at it: 'And they cast out many demons and anointed with oil many who were sick and healed them' (Mark 6:13). In the absence of Jesus, the disciples had a crisis of faith and failed in their ministry. Jesus was weary with the spiritual slowness of the disciples but he did not give up on them. It is comforting to know that even though we weary the Lord with our lack of faith he does not write us off. He persists in instructing us.

Maybe this boy's father had set out to find Jesus believing and hopeful but now (because of the failure of the disciples) he is not so sure. Sadly, the failures of the followers of Christ can hinder the faith of others so that they are not so sure about Jesus. Jesus zooms in on the father's "If" clause like a barrister. The question was not whether Jesus had the power to heal the boy but whether the father had the faith to believe that Jesus could do it. This man's declaration of faith acknowledged that his faith was far from perfect. It was still mixed with unbelief. However, he is honest and asks Jesus to help him. Faith is like gold, which is refined in the cauldron of experience.

Perhaps the disciples failed to exorcise this demon because they had taken for granted the power given to them. Perhaps they had come to believe that such power was inherent within them. This would explain why they no longer depended prayerfully on God for it and their failure showed this lack of prayer. Let us beware lest our success in ministry, service or any sphere leads us to have this kind of misplaced confidence in ourselves. We depend utterly on God: "Not by might, nor by power, but by my Spirit, says the LORD of hosts" (Zechariah 4:6). When we begin to function in our own strength the power of the Lord departs. Service for the Lord must be offered in a spirit of humble dependence on '...him who is able to do far more abundantly than all that we ask or think, according to the power at work within us, to him be glory in the church and in Christ Jesus throughout all generations, forever and ever. Amen.'–Ephesians 3:21

At the end of this section, there is a shift in thought so that in verses 30-32 we see Jesus focusing his teaching ministry on the twelve. He sought a secluded place where he could do this undisturbed and free from distraction. Once again, he predicts his death. They had not understood the first time. Now he introduces more detail, specifically that he would be betrayed or delivered up. The New International Version (NIV) translates the Greek verb as 'betrayed' and this points to Judas. But the word literally means 'to be delivered up' or 'handed over'. A better understanding is that Jesus was 'delivered up by God'.[49] God took the initiative in providing salvation. The delivering up of Jesus was part of his plan of redemption. This is made clear by the apostle Paul in his letter to the Roman believers: '...who was delivered up for our trespasses and raised for our justification.' (Romans 4:25) Later he says: 'He who did not spare his own Son but gave him up for us all, how will he not also with him graciously give us all things?' (Romans 8:32) As early as Origen (185-232) it was interpreted to mean 'delivered up by God'.

Who is the greatest? (9:33-37)

The disciples are not able to understand the truth that the Messiah must give his life. They cannot comprehend the idea that Jesus came to this world not to be served, but to serve. They do not fully understand it until after Jesus dies on the cross and rises from the dead. Then all the pieces of the jigsaw fit together and they will preach his death and resurrection in power and the world would be turned upside down. They thought Jesus would establish his kingdom on earth and reign in power. They thought he would defeat Israel's enemies and restore the ancient glory to Israel. However, Jesus came to die and rise again so that all who receive him might have everlasting life. That is the truth Jesus, which tried to teach his disciples. Moreover, that is what he wants us to know as well.

In complete contrast to Jesus selfless love, the disciples are preoccupied with prestige, power and status. They talk about who will be the greatest in the kingdom of God. Jesus uses these events to teach his people then, and now, that true greatness come from humble service to others. By examining this passage, we are reminded that those who think they are

---

[49] This begs the question 'who killed Jesus?' For a fuller treatment of this important question see 'Appendix A'.

the greatest among might not be great at all. However, the path to true greatness is available to all who would walk it.

A discussion was in progress among the disciples so that when they reached the end of their journey, Jesus asked them what they were talking about. His question is met with an embarrassing silence. Peter, James and John had been chosen to witness something very special (the transfiguration). That sense of privilege led to arrogance. They had just had the most amazing spiritual experience. They glimpsed the glory of God, saw Elijah and Moses and heard the voice of God in the hovering cloud. They are elated (understandably) but they begin to feel superior to the others. Now there is a power struggle between Peter, James and John. They want recognition and the adulation of others. When they were talking among themselves, the issue seemed important. But we can see how silly, immature, and self-centered they were. The same group dynamics operate today where there is much pettiness, power-struggling, attention seeking, jealousy and rivalry among not only church members but also among Christian leaders.

Jesus was talking about matters of eternity but they could only focus on their own self-interests. Look at the context: Jesus has just revealed his glory, proven his power over demons, and reminded them the he is going to die and rise again from the dead and they are squabbling about who should be first. In every church, there are those who want a title or power. They want to be recognized as the greatest and the best. Interestingly John later in life criticized a man by the name of Diotrephes as one who 'likes to put himself first' (3 John 9). Some people love the preeminence. Pride and selfish ambition was the sin of the angel Lucifer. Some people want to control the church, to be the boss. However, Christ is the head of the church and he will not share his glory with anybody. Diotrephes is the kind of person we should strive not to be!

There are no masters in the church that must be served! But there are plenty of people in the church who need to learn to serve others. We serve each other but Christ alone is our master. There is a hierarchy inasmuch as there has to be a structure of authority and accountability. It is a chain of command not to be understood as a validation of superiority.

The question Jesus asked those disciples went straight to what was in their hearts. What is in our hearts is often on our lips. We might feel we deserve better recognition, more respect and so on but let us remember that when this life is over we will stand before the Lord either in embarrassment because we wanted to be first or we will hear him say: "Well done."

In order to correct the immature and foolish thinking of his disciples, Jesus sat down to teach them. When a rabbi sat, in those days, he demonstrated authority over his students. Jesus speaks of a great paradox. He tells them that the way to greatness is through serving others. He tells them that the door to the first place is located in the servant's quarters. The word 'servant' in verse 35 is the same word translated 'deacon' elsewhere in the New Testament. The word refers to those who wait tables. The literal meaning of the word is 'to kick up dust'. It is the image of a servant kicking up little puffs of dust as he moves from one duty to another. Jesus is teaching that true greatness is achieved through the humble service of others.

Some people think they deserve respect and preferential treatment just because they occupy a certain position. They are bosses in the world of work and they expect to have the same role in the church. The church treasurer should have more than good accounting/book-keeping skills. The church secretary should have more than good administration skills. The preacher should be more than a good communicator. Every role requires humility and a selfless attitude. I would prefer to have an uneducated elder who was humble than a theologian who was not. I would prefer a deacon who was teachable to a biblical scholar who thinks he has nothing to learn. Moreover, it is not about what I would prefer but what the Lord looks for. Some preachers strut about like peacocks expecting to be admired and praised. There are celebrity pastors and guru preachers who readily accept the homage of others.

If you really want others to respect you, serve them. Put them before yourself and meet their needs without wanting anything in return. When we humble ourselves, the Lord will exalt us in due time. Jesus said, 'Whoever exalts himself will be humbled, and whoever humbles himself will be exalted' (Matthew 23:12). Peter who on this occasion wanted to take that place of pride on the podium later said: 'Clothe yourselves, all of you, with humility toward one another, for "God opposes the proud but gives grace to the humble."–1 Peter 5:5.

Jesus demonstrates the principle by placing a child before the disciples as a kind of object lesson. He tells them that if those who receive a child in his name are in fact receiving both the Son and the Father who sent him. Children tend to be overlooked because they are not deemed important enough. Some people do not mind serving important people but don't want to serve those without power or status. The word 'receive' carries the idea of displaying hospitality. In those days, hospitality was very important and still is very important in many cultures, particularly the Middle East today. When a person showed up at your house, you were expected to 'receive' them and serve them, meeting their needs in terms of food and drink and the opportunity to freshen up by washing. Jesus is telling us that when we serve the least among us, we are in reality serving him. By serving the least important and even the least deserving, we are honoring the Lord. Jesus could have just told them this but he illustrates his point by using a child.

Children (then especially but even now) are at the bottom of the social ladder. They were/are largely ignored by most adults. Jesus used a child to teach the disciples about service because children really cannot do anything for adults. A child cannot enhance a person's position in society. A child cannot add to our success. A child cannot make us more important in the eyes of the world. However, a child can teach us much about ministry! Every parent knows what happens when a baby comes along. That child demands everything. From day one it must be served, an adult must meet every need. Children need constant care and attention. If they are ignored, they let us know. Parents give and give and give again. I am not sure if it ever ends!

Jesus used a child because children need to be served, but they cannot really serve us in return. That is a lesson we all need to take to heart. Too often, we only serve those who can do something in return for us. The Lord would have us reach out to those who are the neediest. He would have us serve those who cannot or will not serve us in return. He desires that we do as he did and give all for those who may break our hearts in return. When we as a church reach out do we look for people like ourselves? Do we look for those we think will be a blessing to the church? Do we want people with education, money, talent and potential? Do we look for people who can help us become a success? Jesus had a habit of reaching out to people who could do nothing for him in return: the leper, the prostitute, the social outcast, the marginalized and excluded. He reached out to the paralytic, Jairus' daughter, the widow of Nain, the Gaderene demoniac, blind Bartimaeus and the dying thief at Calvary amongst others.

The night he was arrested, when he and the disciples finished their meal in the upper room, Jesus washed his disciple's feet. (John 13:1-17) He took the place of a slave and washed the dirty feet of men who would run away before dawn. He washed the feet of Peter who would deny him three times before daybreak. He even washed the feet of Judas Iscariot who would betray him into the hands of his enemies that very night. This event has been sanitized into a pompous ceremonial annual Easter ritual by some people who profess to be Christians. It needs to be taken out of the realm of symbolism and brought in to the daily reality of life. Too many people are fighting for the top and too few are fighting for the towel. Jesus freely served those who would break his heart. When the next day dawned, Jesus performed the greatest service of all. He went to Calvary to die on the cross for sinners like us. Jesus set the example for us. He was a servant of the neediest people of all, those who could never repay him. He was a servant to those who would betray him, desert him, fail him, deny him, and dishonor him. He was a servant to you and me when he died on the cross. Later in this Gospel Mark records the words of Jesus: "For even the Son of Man came not to be served but to serve, and to give his life as a ransom for many." (Mark 10:45) He is the exemplar *par excellence*. We are to serve without regard to a person's position in society, their ability to help us, or their power and influence. We need a heart that is willing to serve the least among us for the glory of God alone.

During the American Revolution a man on horseback came upon a group of soldiers who were trying to pull down a tree. They were almost able to get the job done, but they lacked just a little strength. It appeared that the help of just one more man would be sufficient to get the job done. This man noticed their commanding officer standing off to the side, shouting orders. "Why don't you help them?" the man asked. The officer responded indignantly, "Sir, I am their commander! I give the orders and they do the work!" Hearing that the man got off his horse, took off his coat, rolled up his sleeves and gave the tired men the help they needed to complete their task. When they were finished, the man looked at the officer and said, "Sir, if your men need any further assistance please call on me at any time." The officer replied, "Thank you friend, who are you and where may I call for you if needed?" The man answered: "I am General George Washington and you can find me in the commanding General's tent." With that, he rode off leaving the officer standing there astonished and embarrassed.

We need to get off our high horses, roll up our sleeves and serve wherever needed without regard for our status. The Lord condescended to serve. Our God is a servant king and he calls us to follow his example.

Anyone not against us is for us (9:38-41)

John refers to an earlier incident where the disciples had encountered somebody not from within their circle of fellowship who was casting out demons in the name of Jesus. Whoever it was appeared to be successful because the gospel records John saying that he witnessed it. The disciples tried to stop him because he did not belong to their group. But Jesus corrects their understanding and attitude to such things. Jesus responds by telling them to let people like that alone. If they are doing good works in the name of Jesus, they are not against him. Rather they are working for him. Jesus goes on to tell his disciples that even if someone just gave a disciple a cup of water in the name of the Lord, that person would surely be rewarded for their service.

There are several lessons here for the church today if we are willing to receive them. Sometimes we can be as the Lord's disciples were on this occasion. If a church, a ministry or an individual does not do everything, just as we do things we are quick to criticize or even condemn them. We are prone to judge them. Our instinct might be to shun them or even silence them. Certain evangelical churches have this tendency. They can be exclusive to the point where one needs a letter of recommendation to be allowed inside the door of the building. They are critical of those who are different to them. If we have that kind of spirit then we need to hear what Jesus has to say here. We need to be reminded of a few truths. No church, no preacher and no ministry have an exclusive hold on the truth. Truth is always much bigger than our grasp of it. I'm not saying doctrine is unimportant. We are custodians and guardians of truth. The primary thing is whether the Lord is being glorified. Issues over which evangelicals are in disagreement in their interpretation of Scripture should be treated with integrity and charity. Such matters should be treated with an earnest desire to be faithful in all things to the Scriptures.

Christians can be quite territorial about ministries. Some people have a 'this is my turf' kind of mentality. They can engage in power struggles and even character assassination. These petty rivalries are often motivated by jealousy. Jealousy over the things of God is nothing new. When it comes to faith, one size does not fit all. Church, of course, should be based on more than the shared experience of like-minded people who enjoy mutual camaraderie. There is a body of apostolic truth that must rule and regulate the faith and practice of any particular local church. Nevertheless some believers will feel uncomfortable or unfulfilled in a church where others feel at home. Some will have different expectations about how things ought to be done. Some will want to do evangelism in a way that others might feel is potentially risky or compromising. But we should not condemn them. We need to be very careful not to be critical of any activity that might be the work of the Holy Spirit. The way certain groups do things may irritate or even infuriate us but God works in mysterious ways. Jesus was unconventional, radical and surprising. We need to be careful that we do not judge a church, a ministry or a preacher just because they are different than we are. Somebody once criticized Moody for the way he conducted evangelism. He responded with an open mind and asked the person who criticized him how he did it. The man said, "I don't evangelize" Moody's response was, "I like my way better."

There are things that go on in other churches that one might dislike. There are theological views that one might dislike. You might dislike extra-biblical standards such as forbidding the drinking of alcohol, imposing dress codes (hats and frocks for women). Another person might dislike vestments and clerical collars. Some Christians dislike the insistence on using A.V. (Authorized Version) only. Others believe that forbidding rock music is secondary, cultural and counter-productive. However, this passage helps us attain perspective. Even if I may not like this or that about a church or a ministry, if they love Jesus and preach the gospel we are on the same side. Our methods may be different. Our theology in non-essential matters might be different. We might not see eye-to-eye on all things even within a church. I am not condoning what others do but I am not condemning other genuine Christian groups who do things differently. Their leaders will give an account to God.

The exorcist that John refers to in this text was casting out demons in Jesus name. That means that he was doing it by Christ's authority. Clearly, he was successful at it. John seems to be speaking on behalf of the disciples. No doubt, they remembered their own failure to drive a demon out of the boy mentioned earlier in this chapter. This exorcist must have been a disciple but not part of the exclusive twelve who were constantly with Jesus. We must be wary of exclusivity. Jesus did not have as restrictive a view as his disciples regarding who could legitimately participate in ministry in Christ's name.[50]

---

[50] See Numbers 11:16-30 for an interesting narrative which serves as a commentary on what ought to be the right attitude of God's people to unauthorized and unorthodox ministries.

God can and does use the most unlikely people in the most unconventional ways. This text is not an excuse for accommodating heresy or for forging compromising relationships. It does not legitimize ecumenism, pluralism, liberalism or an inter-faith agenda. It is no excuse for diluting or distorting the truth in order to fit in with the prevailing culture. This text does not validate the notion that it does not matter what people believe so long as they believe in Jesus. But what it does tell us is that the Holy Spirit is not a genie in a bottle that we alone have in our possession. The Spirit of God will rest wherever he chooses and we might be surprised at how he operates.

How does this text, "For the one who is not against us is for us" (v.40) relate to the words of Christ recorded elsewhere, "Whoever is not with me is against me." (Matthew 12:30) The context of this latter verse also relates to the casting out of demons. When Jesus cast out a demon (on the Sabbath), the people began to wonder if he was the promised Messiah. When the Pharisees heard this, they said: "It is only by Beelzebul, the prince of demons, that this man casts out demons." Jesus points out the absurdity of this. It is clear that in our relationship to Jesus there can be no neutrality. Therefore, agnosticism is unbelief in the same way as atheism. There is a cosmic struggle between the powers of darkness and believers and we are either for the Lord or not.

The giving of a cup of water (mentioned in text under consideration) is an act of hospitality. If it is given to a disciple of Christ, it is sanctified by the Lord and will be rewarded in some unspecified way. But this does not endorse the philosophy of karma or a theology of salvation by good deeds, both of these are heretical notions with no warrant in Scripture. Scripture is clear on this matter. There is only one way to heaven but there are many ways to Christ. Let us be careful not to develop a critical spirit that condemns others who do things differently. The Pharisees were nitpickers and faultfinders. If God waited for us to be perfect before he used us, none of us would be useful instruments. However, in spite of our imperfections, lack of understanding, foolishness, and sinfulness he does use us to accomplish his purposes. We are merely the tools he uses with his divine skill to craft something which glorifies God. The church is constantly fragmenting in schismatic squabbles but the gospel unites believers of all cultures.

Temptation to sin (9:42-48)

This is a passage about the demanding requirements of discipleship. It presents a true spiritual perspective that teaches something of the seriousness of sin and the wrath of God. The Bible talks about hell as a place of conscious and eternal torment. There is a stern warning about not causing others to sin. There is a clear caution about ensuring that we do not commit sin. Certainly if we sin (and we all do), there is forgiveness, grace and mercy for the penitent (1 John 1:9). However, this is not an excuse for a casual attitude to sin. Because certain activities and lifestyles are deemed normal (or are legal) that does not mean they are acceptable in God's eyes. There is a difference between law and morality.

This passage calls for purity and piety in actions and attitudes. We are so prone to sin in thought, word and deed. We sin by doing wrong and by failing to do good as opportunity allows. Jesus has something to say to us about all this. It has to be made perfectly clear that once a person is saved he cannot lose his salvation. But habitual sin and unrepented sin is serious. The world might take it lightly and perhaps some Christians might take it lightly but God does not. Where do you stand on this matter right now in your personal walk with the Lord? The Word of God must shape our opinions and values, not by society's norms. Just because everybody is doing, it does not make it right. Just because it is legal does not make it right.

This passage teaches us that true spiritual perspective is about understanding the importance of entering eternal life. We cannot attain it by sinless perfection. That is impossible (1 John 1:8). The law is a signpost to the cross! We enter the kingdom of God by being born again. The Christian is saved and sustained by grace.

This passage is not to be taken literally. It is not about cutting off limbs and gouging out eyes. But we must understand that sin is serious and take radical means to prevent it. That means avoiding certain situations that may cause you to sin. The parts of the body mentioned (hand, foot and eye) speak of the reality that these are the means of sin. Where do our feet take us? What do we set our hands to do? What is the focus of our eyes?

The word translated 'hell' is *gehenna*. This is a Greek form of the Hebrew words *ge hinnom* (Valley of Hinnom). This was the valley along the south side of Jerusalem used in Old Testament times for human sacrifices to the pagan god Molech.[51] King Josiah put a stop to this dreadful practice (2 Kings 23:10). The Valley of Hinnom came to be used as a place where human excrement and rubbish was disposed of and burned. The fire of *gehenna* never went out and the worms never died. It is a symbolic image of divine punishment.[52]

This passage teaches that whatever causes you to sin or be a stumbling block to others, thereby causing them to sin,

---

[51] See Jeremiah 7:31; 19:5-6; 32:35.
[52] Christian Publishing House suggests the following articles be read:
Hellfire - Eternal Torment?
http://www.christianpublishers.org/hellfire-eternal-torment
Hellfire - Is It Just?
http://www.christianpublishers.org/hellfire-is-it-just

must be dealt with swiftly and severely. Sin must be stamped out. This is a call to holiness in living both as a testimony before the watching world and as the only acceptable lifestyle to the Lord. Jesus issues a series of stern warnings to his disciples. He uses vivid language that cautions us to be careful how we live our lives. His words move us out of our comfort zone. The Word of God will comfort the afflicted, but it will also afflict the comfortable and smug. Like the disciples, the modern church has become far too comfortable in this world. He shocked his listeners. We too need this kind of shock treatment. These verses shake us up and get our attention.

We are commanded to protect the least among us from sin. Jesus says that one would be better off having a millstone tied around one's neck and being cast into the sea than to cause others to stumble. The word translated 'millstone' literally means 'a donkey stone'. It refers to a stone used as a mill to grind grain. It was so heavy a donkey was tied to it to turn it. If such a stone was tied around the neck of an individual and that person was thrown into the sea, that person would be pulled to the bottom and drown. It is a graphic image describing a horrible death. Yet Jesus says it would be preferable for a person to die this way than for them to cause one of his little one to fall into sin.

Jesus says being a cause of stumbling to one of his disciples grieves God and it will not go unpunished. Those who persecute believers will experience the wrath of God. The writer to the Hebrews says, 'It is a fearful thing to fall into the hands of the living God' (Hebrews 10:31). How do believers cause others to stumble? There are many ways. It could be by directly tempting others to sin. This kind of behavior is seen throughout the Bible beginning with Eve. The brother of Moses, Aaron, led others into an orgy of sin. From the time of the fall in Eden, men and women have been seducing each other, including Christians as well. People can also be led into sin indirectly. When we treat others in insensitive, unloving and unkind ways, we can cause them to sin. We can spark an angry reaction. People can be led into sin by a bad example. Paul's advice to Timothy is clear and it applies to all of us: '...set the believers an example in speech, in conduct, in love, in faith, in purity.' (1 Timothy 4:12) People can be led away through false doctrine.

People may be willing to forgive a wrong against them but if you harm one of their children you are in big trouble. God says that the person who offends one of his little ones is in big trouble. Jesus refers to the "hand", the "foot" and the "eye" because these are three problem areas when it comes to dealing with sin. The hand refers to the things we do. The foot refers to the places we go. The eye refers to the things we see or desire to have. Thus, these three words describe areas where we are tempted to sin. Consider the following verses:

Genesis 3:6

⁶ So when the woman saw that the tree was good for food, and that it was a delight to the eyes, and that the tree was to be desired to make one wise, she took of its fruit and ate, and she also gave some to her husband who was with her, and he ate.

1 John 2:16-17

¹⁶ For all that is in the world—the desires of the flesh and the desires of the eyes and pride of life—is not from the Father but is from the world. ¹⁷ And the world is passing away along with its desires, but whoever does the will of God abides forever.

Jesus is saying that we need to take drastic action against whatever causes us to sin. He is speaking figuratively in a way that emphasizes the horrible nature of sin. He is not commanding us to mutilate our bodies. In the early days of the church, some men took these words literally. One of the more notable examples was Origen of Alexandria. He had such a problem with sexual lust that he had himself emasculated to get rid of that temptation. Surgery on the outside will not cure the problem on the inside. All sin proceeds from the heart. (Mark 7:18-23) What Jesus is talking about in these verses is how we are to deal with our sins in a proactive and preventative manner.

When temptation to sin comes into our lives, we must deal with it immediately, harshly, ruthlessly, consistently and decisively. Jesus warns people that nothing in this world is so valuable that it is worth going to hell over. Yes, Jesus believed in hell and if you do not believe in hell, you do not believe in Jesus.[53] Jesus says that hell will be characterized by terrible realities. He quotes Isaiah 66:24 and says that people in hell will suffer in terrible ways: "where their worm does not die and the fire is not quenched." He is speaking about the internal torments people will suffer in hell. The story Jesus told about the rich man who died and went to hell shows that he had an active and accurate memory (Luke 16:25). Those in hell will remember every opportunity they had to be saved. They will be reminded for all eternity that they did not have to be in that horrible place and those thoughts will torment them. So according to Jesus the agonies of hell are real, unceasing and unimaginably horrible. Above all, they are avoidable. Hell is a place of punishment (Matthew 25:41); fire (Luke 16:24; Mark 9:43-44) thirst (Luke 16:24-25); pain (Luke 16:24, 25, 28; Revelation14:10-11), divine wrath (2 Thessalonians 1:8-9); frustration and anger (Matthew13:42; Matthew 24:51); eternal separation from God. (2 Thessalonians 1:8-9) Hell is real. Sin is not something to be toyed with. Many who think they are the masters of their sin are actually its slaves.

---

[53] The desire of God is that all should be saved but whoever rejects his gift of salvation through unbelief or indifference will be separated from God and cast into hell, a place of conscious and eternal torment (Luke:16:19-31; Revelation 20:15)

There are many places in the world that I would like to go. I would love to go to Israel some day and Canada. I am sure you have a list of your own. Of course, there are some places I do not want to go. I do not care anything about going to North Korea or Afghanistan. I do not want to go to prison, the dentist or the hospital either. There are some places people do not want to go. There is one place where no one wants to go and that place is the subject of Christ's teaching in these verses. The place no one wants to go to is called 'hell.' Yet it is a place to which everyone is headed unless they are trusting Jesus for salvation. The Lord Jesus has something to say about that horrible place called hell. What he has to say needs to be heard today. Jesus wants us to know that hell is real and terrible beyond description and that no one ever has to go there!

Jesus only spoke about heaven once, while he spoke of hell eleven times! Today many, both in the world and in the church, have rejected the notion of hell altogether. There are huge numbers of Christians even in evangelical Protestant denominations who do not believe in a literal hell. This is true of many faculty and students in leading seminaries in the United States and the UK who do not believe in hell.

That might be man's view of the subject but what does the Word of God say about hell? The Bible clearly teaches that there is a literal place called hell. (Psalm 9:17; Luke 12:5; Luke 16:19-31) If hell is real (and it is) then who will be there? Jesus tells us very plainly, why hell was created. It was designed as a place of eternal punishment for Satan and his demonic followers. (Matthew 25:41) At the end of time Satan, along with the Antichrist and the false prophets will be cast into hell (Revelation 20:10). However, there are others in hell. Jude speaks of certain fallen angels being in hell (Jude 6). Is hell then just a place for spiritual beings, like angels/demons that have rebelled against God? No! In a passage about the final judgment Matthew records Jesus' words which say a day is coming when people will be sent to hell: "Depart from me, you cursed, into the eternal fire prepared for the devil and his angels."—Matthew 25:41

The Bible is clear about who will be in hell. Psalm 9:17 tells us that the 'wicked will be turned into hell.' The bottom line is this: everyone who rejects God's plan of salvation through Jesus Christ will go to hell (John 8:24; 2 Thessalonians 1:9-10). What this means is that anyone who has not trusted Jesus Christ by faith is headed to hell. Religious people, moral people, decent people, friends, relatives, family members, anyone who is not saved is surely headed for the destruction and torment of hell. It is not that they will be lost someday, the fact is, they are lost this day (Ephesians 2:1-3; 12) and the wrath of God already dwells on them (John 3:18, 36). They already have their ticket to hell and the only thing that will save them is coming to Christ for salvation (John 3:16). Spread the good news that Jesus came into the world to save sinners. What does he want to save them from? He wants to save them *from* the fires of hell[54] and save them *to* the fellowship of heaven.

Salt and fire (9:49-50)

The last two verses in this section (49-50) are a challenge to interpret. Verse 49 says, "For everyone will be salted with fire" and verse 50 says, "Salt is good, but if the salt has lost its saltiness, how will you make it salty again? Have salt in yourselves, and be at peace with one another." There is a verse in the Old Testament which helps cast some light on how to interpret these words of Jesus: "...with all your

---

[54] Christian Publishing House suggests the following articles be read:
Hellfire - Eternal Torment?
http://www.christianpublishers.org/hellfire-eternal-torment
Hellfire - Is It Just?
http://www.christianpublishers.org/hellfire-is-it-just

offerings you shall offer salt." (Leviticus 2:13) Every believer is to be a sacrifice to God. The apostle Paul corroborates this idea: 'I appeal to you therefore, brothers, by the mercies of God, to present your bodies as a living sacrifice, holy and acceptable to God, which is your spiritual worship.' (Romans 12:1) Just as salt always accompanied the temple sacrifices, so fire (persecution, trials and suffering) will accompany the true disciple's sacrifices. As Peter said: 'In this you rejoice, though now for a little while, if necessary, you have been grieved by various trials, so that the tested genuineness of your faith—more precious than gold that perishes though it is tested by fire—may be found to result in praise and glory and honor at the revelation of Jesus Christ.' (1 Peter 1:6-7) He went on to say: 'Beloved, do not be surprised at the fiery trial when it comes upon you to test you, as though something strange were happening to you.' (1 Peter 4:12) The words in Mark must have had a very special meaning to the church in Rome. These words must have helped them understand the purifying fires of persecution.

Salt was very important in the ancient world. It was used as a preservative to prevent food from spoiling. However, salt could lose its saltiness. Jesus is warning his disciples not to lose that characteristic which prevents decay. We are not to lose our spirit of devotion and self-sacrifice to Jesus and the gospel. Christ's disciples can only be at peace with one another where that kind of devotion prevails. In the context of this passage, Jesus warns against offending weaker believers. He cautions people to avoid the terrible and tragic consequences of sin. He is saying that sin is a destroyer and that it must be handled ruthlessly. And now (in these closing verses) Jesus warns that serving him will require sacrifice and purity: "For everyone will be salted with fire." Jesus is telling his disciples they can expect to be cleansed through refining fire. God allows us to go through persecution and trials in an effort to make us more like Jesus. (2 Timothy 3:12; 1 Thessalonians 3:3-4; Acts 14:22; 1 Peter 4:12-13) Jesus says,

"Salt is good!" and so it is. Salt was a valuable commodity in that day. The word 'salary' comes from the Latin word *salarium*. It referred to the fact that often, Roman soldiers were paid their wages in salt, which could be traded in a barter system for other goods and services.

Salt was necessary in the days before refrigeration. Meat and fish would quickly spoil, but if meat was pickled in a brine solution it would keep for long periods of time, even in a warm climate. Salt was also good because it made the unpalatable tasty. Some foods just need a little salt to make them edible. Salt was often placed into wounds to help them heal and stop the spread of infection. So salt was a preservative, a flavoring, an antiseptic, and a currency. Salt is good, but if the salt loses its saltiness what good is it? Salt in our day is pure and it does not lose its flavor. In that day, it could be contaminated with other minerals and after a time would develop a bad flavor. Salt in that condition was good for nothing and had to be to be thrown away.

Jesus then says: "Have salt in yourselves..." In other words be useful and effective and something good. How do we do that? By not causing others to stumble and fall into sin, by avoiding sin at all costs in our own lives, by willingly embracing the salt of a sacrificial life and the persecution that comes with it. When we do this, we will demonstrate another quality of salt. Salt creates thirst. When believers are salty (walking as Jesus would have them walk) they create a thirst for the things of God in the lives of the lost around them. The best witness for Jesus Christ is a salty Christian who lives like Jesus. (1 John 2:6) Like salt, we are to be a preserving agent in the world. Our very presence should raise the moral standard. We are to promote honesty, stir the conscience and make people want to live a little cleaner. Our lives should make a difference in the world around us. We are to make this world thirsty for Jesus. We are to make this world a better, more appetizing place to live. We are to help stop the spread of corruption in the world. Jesus is telling his followers, that if they are going to be his servants, they can expect trials to purify them.

Jesus closes this chapter by saying: "be at peace with one another." Remember the disciples had been arguing about who was the greatest among them. They had rebuked a man who was working in Jesus' name because he was not one of their inner-circle. The Lord is saying we should not be worried about who is the greatest and we should not be rebuking others. Rather we should be in the business of examining our own hearts. We should salt ourselves and judge our own faults. Are you struggling to live the right kind of life and having trouble? Is the Lord purifying you through trials? Are you leading people to the Lord, or away from him? The Lord can help us in whatever condition we are right now if we come to him.

Chapter 10

Teaching about divorce (10:1-2)

This is not the first time these people confronted Jesus and it will not be the last. In every encounter Jesus outsmarted his pharisaical adversaries and this humiliation probably infuriated them all the more. Now they come to Jesus with an argument they think is unanswerable. We are told in verse 2 that they came 'tempting' him. This word carries the idea of testing in a malicious sense. They are attempting to trap Jesus in a theological controversy. They are trying to undermine his credibility in the eyes of the people. Verse one reveals that a great crowd had gathered to hear Jesus teach. The Pharisees were probably jealous of Christ's popularity and fearful about his potential influence.

To understand this confrontation we need first to comprehend the context. What was the state of marriage in Israel in that day? Marriages in ancient Israel were arranged and were not usually based on love. The notion of romantic love being the basis for a marriage would have been peculiar to that culture, which had more pragmatic and political criteria for such unions. Men took wives for convenience. Marriage was the only lawful way for a man to satisfy his sexual appetite though prostitution was not uncommon. When a man married a woman, he got a sexual partner, and as a bonus, he got someone to clean his house, cook his meals, wash his clothes and give birth to his children. Women were viewed as possessions that could be acquired and abandoned as the needs and desires of the husband changed.

The question the Pharisees ask is very straightforward: "Is it lawful for a man to put away his wife?" The phrase "put away" means to divorce. They want to know if a man is permitted to divorce his wife based on the Law of Moses. There were two basic schools of thought about this in Israel. Two famous rabbis had handed down their teaching on the matter and most people in Israel followed one of these two rabbis. One of these rabbis was a man named Shammai. He taught that the only lawful reason a divorce could be granted was for adultery. The Law commanded that adulterers were to be put to death by stoning. (Leviticus 20:10) By the New Testament time period, however, stoning for that reason had fallen into abeyance and divorce became the remedy for adultery in the marriage.

Only the man was allowed to seek a divorce. Women could not divorce their husbands regardless of their reasons. A small minority of the population and the religious leaders followed the teachings of Shammai. The other rabbi was a man named Hillel. Hillel had a liberal view of divorce. He taught that a man could divorce his wife for any reason at all. For example, if she took down her hair in public or if she was seen talking to another man. He could divorce her for the most trivial reason such as, if she ruined a meal by burning the food or by putting too much salt into it. He could put her away if she spoke evil of her mother-in-law or if she was infertile. Even if her husband saw a woman he thought was prettier, she could be divorced.

Most of the Pharisees followed the teachings of Hillel. This is clear in Matthew's account of this same encounter. In Matthew 19:3, they asked, "Is it lawful for a man to put away his wife for every cause?" It seems odd that the Pharisees, who were so strict in every other area, were so liberal in this area. Most of the Pharisees married and divorced as it pleased them. Of course, this is the way of a legalist. They always find loopholes to allow the flesh to be gratified. If Jesus sided with the view taught by Shammai, he would alienate many of the people who came to hear him speak. Most of the men in his audiences would have embraced the teachings of Hillel. It is likely the Pharisees were hoping that Jesus would contradict the Law of Moses and they could accuse him of heresy. He did attack their interpretation of the Law. This confrontation took place in the jurisdiction of Herod Antipas. He was a regional King who married his brother's (Philip's) wife. John the Baptist had condemned this marriage and Herod would eventually execute John. (Matthew 14:4) The Pharisees possibly hoped that Jesus would be arrested and executed for preaching against the marriage of Herod and his wife. Whatever their motives were for coming to Jesus, they were not interested in the truth. They were only interested in justifying their own sinfulness in their own eyes.

That is still the way people are today. Many people do not care about the truth. They want to justify their sins, or cling to their traditions and beliefs. Our opinions will die when we do, but the Word of God will endure forever.– Psalm 119:89; 1 Peter 1:25; Matthew 24:35

The Lord's answer (10:3-12)

Jesus turns the question back to them (v.3). He asks them, "What did Moses command you?" In other words, Jesus asks. "What does the Word of God say about this matter?" Jesus knows what these men believe about this issue. He knows that most of them have been married and divorced many times. He knows they are guilty in the eyes of God. He knows they follow the teachings of the rabbi Hillel. He also knows that the opinions of men are irrelevant. Therefore, Jesus focuses the issue on the Word of God. That is always a good tactic to use when someone tries to draw you into a theological argument. Just look at them, hand them a Bible and say, "show me".

Their answer (v. 4) proves their ignorance of both the Word of God in relation to divorce: "Moses allowed a man to write a certificate of divorce and to send her away" (v. 4). Their response in Matthew 19:7 says, "Why then did Moses command one to give a certificate of divorce and to send her away?" The word "command" is used. These men believed divorce was not just a right, but also an obligation to be followed. The Pharisees base their argument on Deuteronomy.

Deuteronomy 24:1-4

¹ "When a man takes a wife and marries her, if then she finds no favor in his eyes because he has found some indecency in her, and he writes her a certificate of divorce and puts it in her hand and sends her out of his house, and she departs out of his house, ² and if she goes and becomes another man's wife, ³ and the latter man hates her and writes her a certificate of divorce and puts it in her hand and sends her out of his house, or if the latter man dies, who took her to be his wife, ⁴ then her former husband, who sent her away, may not take her again to be his wife, after she has been defiled, for that is an abomination before the Lord. And you shall not bring sin upon the land that the Lord your God is giving you for an inheritance.

Most Jews interpreted this passage to teach that divorce was an obligation. However, these verses do not command, recommend, or even suggest divorce. These verses were given to regulate a situation that had gotten out of hand. Men were divorcing their wives and sending them out of their homes with a certificate of divorce. It is said that the husband had found some 'indecency' in his wife. This word does not refer to adultery or fornication. Both of these offenses were punishable by death. (Deuteronomy 22:20-22) This refers to an immodest act that falls short of the legal definition of adultery. She might have been caught flirting with other men or uncovering herself in public. This was often subjective and open to abuse and in many instances just an excuse for the man to get rid of the woman. Rather than commanding or condoning divorce, Deuteronomy 24:1-4 was given to control divorce, which was rampant in that society.

The Pharisees and others who advocated easy divorce were guilty of misinterpreting and misapplying the Word of God. Jesus reminds them that the only reason Moses permitted divorce was for "hardness of heart" (v. 5). Divorce is the result of sinful attitudes such as hardness of heart.

Jesus is moving closer to the cross and his enemies increase their attacks in frequency and ferocity. Those who hate him grow bolder and nastier in their attempts to discredit Jesus in the eyes of the people and of the ruling authorities. The Pharisees and the scribes have already tried to undermine the Lord's authority on several occasions. They come to him seeking his opinion on one of the most hotly debated issues of that day. They are not really interested in Christ's opinion on divorce. They were trying to trip him up.

Divorce was as common in that society as it is in ours today. It was common for a Roman man to have as many as fifteen to twenty wives in his lifetime. Divorce rates among the Jewish people were not that drastic, but divorce was a real problem in that culture too. It continues to be a problem in ours as well. What is needed is teaching that is biblical, contextual, clear and compassionate. Jesus is calling for fidelity in marriage.

Divorce is complex and controversial. It is a subject that is highly charged with emotion. Marriage as God intended is for love and fulfillment and it is tragic when it degenerates into discord and bitterness.[55] We must hold to a biblical position

---

[55] The Lord must be honored by presenting the biblical truth on this issue in a sensitive but uncompromising manner. It might be an

because that is ultimately best for all: "I am convinced that the teaching of Jesus on this and every subject is good --- intrinsically good, good for individuals, good for society..."[56]

So far, we have made only preliminary remarks by way of introduction to the context, background and principles in relation to the issue of divorce. The question was asked in the context of a socio-religious culture where there were two rival rabbinic schools, that of Shammai and that of Hillel. Shammai took a legalist position and Hillel took a lax position. The word "unseemly" which refers to marital unfaithfulness or un-chastity was interpreted in the broadest manner to include the trivial and frivolous so that a woman could be divorced for basically any reason whatsoever, so if she was an incompetent cook or if he just fancied somebody else he could put her aside. The Pharisees want to know whose side Jesus was on (legalist or lax) and what rabbinical school he would endorse.

The Pharisees were preoccupied with the grounds for divorce but Jesus emphasized the institution of marriage. They wanted Jesus to spell out the legitimate reasons for divorce but Jesus did not answer them in the way they wanted. Instead, he poses a counter-question about their interpretation of Scripture. He refers them back to Genesis; to the creation of mankind as male and female (chapter 1) and the institution of marriage. (chapter 2) These passages emphasize that marriage is both exclusive and permanent (leaving and cleaving). Marriage is a divine institution where two people become one. The Pharisees called Moses' provision for divorce a *command* but Jesus identified it as a *concession* to the hardness of human hearts. They had a garbled version of Scripture and little regard for its true

---

unintended outcome that such teaching adds to the pain and distress of those whose marriages have failed.

[56] John Stott, *The Message of the Sermon on the Mount*, Bible Speaks Today Series, IVP, 1998 P.92.

teaching. There is neither command nor encouragement to divorce contained in the passage in Deuteronomy 24:1-4. These verses refer to certain procedures if a divorce takes place and then (at the most) permission is implied reluctantly and divorce is tolerated. Jesus implied that it was not a divine instruction but only a divine concession to human weakness. The Pharisees took divorce very lightly but Jesus took it very seriously. Seen in this way it is clear that Jesus liberated women from grave injustice. His position was very much in their favor though it may not be generally understood in that way now. So much so, that with only one exception Jesus called all remarriage after divorce adultery.

A separation without divorce in legal terms is a modern arrangement unknown in the ancient world. God instituted marriage as an exclusive and permanent union (between a man and a woman) which must not be broken. Thus to divorce one's spouse and marry another or to marry a divorced person is to enter an adulterous relationship and this is forbidden. It has already been stated that there is a difference between law and morality and in this situation, it needs to be stated again. Marital unfaithfulness (adultery) constituted grounds for divorce. Even the rival rabbis Shammai and Hillel were agreed on that. Some have argued that the exceptive clause permits divorce if some premarital sexual sin is later discovered.[57] The world says divorce is permissible if the marriage is irretrievably broken down. But this is not actually compatible with the teaching of Jesus. This reluctant permission of Jesus must be seen for what it is: an accommodation to the hardness of human hearts. It must be understood in the immediate context where Jesus emphatically endorses the permanence of marriage in God's

---

[57] "And I say to you: whoever divorces his wife, except for sexual immorality, and marries another, commits adultery" (Matthew 19:9).

purpose and in the wider context of biblical teaching on reconciliation.[58]

The discussion should never be focused on the legitimacy of divorce. To be preoccupied with this is to be guilty of the Pharisaical attitudes that Jesus condemned. Jesus emphasized the exclusive and permanent nature of marriage as a divine institution. Divorce is a tragic departure from God's will. Divorce should be examined in the light of what Scripture has to say, not only about marriage, but also about reconciliation. It is important for Christians to understand and accept God's view of marriage. We are not to be *a la carte* Christians where we choose to accept certain teachings and decline to accept other truths because they are not to our liking. The Christian is to accept the whole counsel of God.

The human tragedy that arises out of divorce is immeasurable. For every thousand marriages that end in divorce there are at least two thousand adults and (probably) several thousand children that are affected. Add to that the devastation that divorce brings into the extended families (particularly grandparents) and the number of those impacted by divorce increases vastly. Nobody involved in divorce escapes totally undamaged. It happens in evangelical Christian churches and it affects all members, adherents and friends of those congregations. People take sides with the man or the woman and the couples' children take sides with mum or dad. Divorce brings pain into a home, a church and a community.

However, we live in an age when many families have been touched by divorce. Many marriages fail. People who have been through divorce know the pain, the shame and the turmoil it brings with it. Nobody really wants divorce. Traditionally when a man and woman got married, they

---

[58] God was willing to forgive his adulterous wife Israel. This is illustrated in the narrative about by Hosea and Gomer.

hoped it would last forever. Nevertheless, divorce has come to be understood as an 'opt out' clause in what is meant to be a binding contract. People have strong opinions on this issue. True Christians profess that the Bible is the ultimate authority in all matters of faith and practice. Therefore, when it comes to this topic we need to be clear about what the Bible teaches and to submit to that. We must have a biblical standard not some other measure of right and wrong. The church should be busy teaching about marriage and reconciliation. We want to stem the tide of divorce, and uphold the sanctity of marriage. We cannot dilute what Scripture says just so people will feel better about themselves. To do that would not be an act of love but an act of deception. A human standard may be more lenient than the Bible or it may be stricter than the Bible but it will never be better than the Bible.

What does God think of divorce? Divorce occurs because there is sin in the hearts of one or both of the parties involved. Regardless of the reasons for a divorce, there is always sin at the heart of it. One or both of the parties involved is guilty of some hardness of heart. One or both parties will not repent of their sins or forgive the other. That is why the Lord says he hates divorce. (Malachi 2:16 NKJV) This clear statement in Malachi was made at a time when the men of Israel were forsaking the wives of their youth and marrying foreign women who were outside covenant relationship with the Lord. In ancient Israel, divorce was out of control. Men were divorcing their wives for all kinds of frivolous reasons. All a man had to do was to say to his wife three times, "I divorce you!", and in the eyes of man, they were divorced. Wives were being sent out of their homes by their husbands. A certificate of divorce told society that the woman was not a harlot, but that she was free to remarry. The law was given to control a system that arose out of their refusal to honor God's ideal for marriage. Such a situation should never have existed in the first place. But because of the sinfulness of the human heart it did and it needed to be controlled.

It should be borne in mind that divorce is never commanded in any situation. Even in cases of adultery, no one is ordered to get a divorce. Reconciliation should always be the first option. I believe the Lord would not have a woman continue to live in a situation where she is abused physically, psychologically or sexually and fearful. As a pastor, I would advise a woman in such a situation that she should not stay in such a damaging and dangerous environment and that she should not keep her children in such an environment. There are situations where the physical and emotional abuse is so strong that the couple cannot continue to live under the same roof.

In the Old Testament period the Law did not make provision for divorce and remarriage in cases of adultery because adultery was punished by stoning the adulterers to death. (Deuteronomy 22:22) This was the requirement of the judicial law. Adultery brought about the end of a marriage by death, and the innocent party was free to remarry.

Divorce is neither commanded nor commended in Scripture. It was merely permitted as a gracious concession to human weakness. In our society, some people are married on a whim and divorced at their convenience. That is not God's will for marriage. Marriage is a solemn and binding union. Unfortunately, sin has ruined everything God created, even the institution of marriage. The sad truth is that people get divorced. Many families have been shattered by divorce. Many thought it could never happen to them. The disciples learn that God has a higher view of marriage than society. Jesus upholds the view of marriage as a lifelong covenant. Divorce violates God's original ideal of marriage.

Christ's relationship with the church (Ephesians 5:21-33) is described as a marriage where the church is his bride. Marriages should be based on mutual, sacrificial love and faithfulness. Jesus says when either a man or a woman divorces and marries another person; they are guilty of adultery in the eyes of the Lord: "And I say to you: whoever divorces his wife, except for sexual immorality, and marries another, commits adultery." (Matthew 19:9; Matthew 5:32) This does not mean that a person should divorce their spouse for committing adultery. There is always repentance, reconciliation, and restoration. The innocent party is free to remarry and in doing so, they are not guilty of adultery.[59] The teaching of Scripture on this issue is good for individuals, families and society.

Children and the Kingdom of God (10:13-16)

It was a common practice for Jewish parents to bring children to the rabbi so that he could bless them and pray for them. Parents would take their children to the synagogue, where the elders would pray for the life of the child. This is similar to the way we dedicate a child and parents to the Lord. The Lord's disciples rebuke these parents. The disciples see the children as a nuisance, a hindrance to his real ministry. They seemed to think that the Master's time was too precious to spend on children. However, Jesus was outraged by this attitude and he rebuked them severely. Jesus made it clear that children must not be hindered in coming to him.

Children can be noisy in church. They require special attention such as crèche and junior Sunday school classes appropriate to their age. We are constantly trying to find material and activities suited to their needs, aptitudes and abilities. Children cannot contribute financially to the church. Generally, children are challenging but they are not a

---

[59] 1 Corinthians 7:10-16 is complex passage that has a bearing on this issue but I am teaching on Mark's Gospel with a more focused lens. There are many good books on this topic for those who want to pursue the matter further.

nuisance to be endured; they are a blessing to be enjoyed. Psalm 127:3 says, '...children are a heritage from the LORD'. This verse is often understood to refer to families but it could just as easily refer to the family of the church. We are blessed by the children among us. Parents and the church have special responsibilities towards children. We have a responsibility to lead them to faith, wholeness and maturity in Christ.

The parents in this passage cared about the spiritual welfare of their children. They brought their children to Jesus so that they might be blessed. This is what all parents should do for their children. The Bible calls believing parents to teach their children about God and right and wrong.

You shall love the LORD your God with all your heart and with all your soul and with all your might. And these words that I command you today shall be on your heart. You shall teach them diligently to your children, and shall talk of them when you sit in your house, and when you walk by the way, and when you lie down, and when you rise.– Deuteronomy 6:5-7

The New Testament renews that challenge to parents: 'Fathers, do not provoke your children to anger, but bring them up in the discipline and instruction of the Lord.' (Ephesians 6:4) Parents have an obligation to ensure that their children are spiritually instructed. That means bringing them to church consistently. It means sending them to the Sunday school class where the instruction is suited to their age and understanding. Parents have a duty to read the Bible with their children and to pray with them and for them, not just in church but at home, every day. It means praying for them and with them and opening the Bible with them at home.

However, the responsibility is not just about the words we speak. It should be natural to discuss spiritual things at home with our children. Children learn by observing and imitating so we need to be good role models. Are we walking consistently with integrity before the Lord? Parents are called to instill virtue in their children. They are obliged to train their children in righteousness. This means teaching them spiritual values. Most importantly of all it means teaching them the way of salvation, by grace alone, through faith alone in Christ alone. Christian parents have the great privilege of bringing their children to Jesus.

Christian parents are called upon to shape the spiritual perspective of their children. This means teaching them that the Bible is an incomparable treasure as a manual for living. The pastor, elders, deacons and every member of the church has a responsibility to the children of the church.[60] We must never obstruct them from coming to Jesus. Rather we must assist them to come to Christ, for salvation and sanctification. We must remove obstacles from their path, such as doubt. But the primary responsibility for the spiritual welfare of children of all ages rests with the parents and that means both mother and father. It is not just a maternal duty it is also a paternal responsibility. We should be like the parents in this passage who want to bring their children into contact with Christ. This is the best thing we can ever do for our children. We might not have much by way of material possessions to offer them but if we bring them to Jesus he can bless them abundantly.

Christian parents have the responsibility of modeling their faith in Jesus. If our faith has no transforming power to make us better people (not perfect people) our children will perceive that. We can talk about our faith, but if we do not live out our faith, it translates into hypocrisy in the eyes of our children. We are to stimulate a spiritual hunger in our

---

[60] Due account of this must be evident in the church's health and safety statement which is designed to minimize risks to their welfare and offer the best protection possible.

children and satisfy it with the things of God. We are to nurture our children in the things of God, not brainwashing them. They should be guided but not coerced. They should always have the freedom be honest with you about faith. We can encourage them to seek the kingdom of God. If you are in love with Jesus, your children will be attracted to him too.

D. L. Moody once returned from a meeting and reported two and a half conversions, "two adults and a child, I suppose?" asked his host. "No" said Moody, "two children and an adult. The children gave their whole lives. The adult had only half of his left to give." Children are sinners who need the Savior. The psalms say, "I was brought forth in iniquity, and in sin did my mother conceive me" (Psalm 51:5) and "The wicked are estranged from the womb; they go astray from birth, speaking lies" (Psalm 58:3). Paul says that we are "by nature children of wrath." (Ephesians 2:3) While children may possess a kind of innocence, they still stand in need of salvation. That is why parents and other concerned adults must do all they can to bring children face to face with the unique and universal claims of the gospel. It is not our duty to save them, but it is our duty to expose them to the Word of God and facilitate encounters with Christ. Timothy's mother and grandmother were believers and he came to faith as a child: 'But as for you, continue in what you have learned and have firmly believed, knowing from whom you learned it and how from childhood you have been acquainted with the sacred writings, which are able to make you wise for salvation through faith in Christ Jesus.'–2 Timothy 3:14-15.

This incident regarding children coming to Jesus was used by our Lord to illustrate the way all believers must come to him. Jesus says, "whoever does not receive the kingdom of God like a child shall not enter it" (v.15). Here he is indicating that all who come to him must come as a little child. He is referring to the special characteristics that distinguish children from adults. Children are trusting, innocent and dependent.

They are so trusting, that they have to be warned not to talk to strangers. They are so humble that they will readily accept what they are told. They are so dependent, that they simply rest in the ability and willingness of those around them to meet their needs. They do not worry about food, clothing or shelter. They do not worry about mortgage and utility bills or who will pay for groceries, fuel, heating, transport, education, health insurance, medical expenses and a host of other miscellaneous household overheads. They are oblivious to all of this.

Children in loving homes do not doubt that their family members love them. Children simply accept profound things by faith. They do not look beyond the obvious. They just believe. Those are the requirements for a person to come to Jesus. For a person to be saved, regardless of their age, they must be willing to humble themselves before God. They must be willing to lay down their pride over the life they have lived and the achievements of that life. They must humble themselves by acknowledging their sins before God. They must be willing to admit that their works and religious activity can never save them. They must come to the place where they, like a little child, simply look to Jesus in pure faith, trusting that he will do everything he has promised to do. Contrast this image of childlike faith with the very next passage where the rich young ruler came to Jesus proud of his money and his self-righteousness. He left with all his possessions, but he left without Jesus.

A person must look to Jesus by faith, trusting him and his finished work on the cross completely for their soul's salvation, acknowledging that all our righteousness is worthless in terms of achieving salvation is humbling. This requires the childlike qualities of trust, humility and dependence. This is the only way anyone ever receives salvation. This passage teaches us something about Jesus. The way Jesus ministers to these children gives us an insight into his true nature. Jesus was displeased with the behavior of the disciples in trying to exclude children from access to him. In this we see the disposition of his heart which is open and receptive to children, who were essentially a marginalized and excluded group. Jesus defends the defenseless.

In that society children were often treated with contempt and viewed as property. Female children were often just cast away and left to die. In ancient Rome, fathers held absolute power over their children. This power was called *patria potestas*. A father could condemn a child to die simply by commanding it to be done. A case where this happened was recorded as late as 60 A.D. This practice was finally outlawed in 375 A.D.

In this passage, Jesus elevates children to a place of importance. We are not to see children as potential (believers, missionaries, pastors, preachers...). We are to see them as inherently precious, for what they are, not what they might become. Jesus touched these children. No matter how insignificant you may feel you can come to Jesus for that blessed touch. We can come to him as a child and trust, accept and rest in his care.

The rich young man (10:17-31)

It is difficult to take a fresh look at a familiar passage but we must always ask what truth is being taught here? This is a passage about the cost of discipleship. This man seems very keen. He 'ran up and knelt' before the Lord. Then he addressed Jesus as, "Good teacher". His heart seems to be open and favorably disposed to Jesus. There is enthusiasm (shown by the fact that he ran to the Lord). There is humility (evidenced by the fact that he knelt at the feet of Jesus). There is an acknowledgement that Jesus is "Good". There is recognition that Jesus is wise ("teacher"). Then the man asks Jesus a very important spiritual question: "...what must I do to inherit eternal life?" Jesus replies: "Do not murder, Do not commit adultery, Do not steal, Do not bear false witness, Do not defraud, Honor your father and mother."

The man claims to have abided by the law. If what he said is true then he was a good-living guy. Then Mark records a very interesting detail: "And Jesus, looking at him, loved him." (v. 21) There must have been something very tender in the way Jesus looked at this young man that Mark noticed. But then Jesus said to him, "You lack one thing: go, sell all that you have and give to the poor, and you will have treasure in heaven; and come, follow me." Here Jesus touches on the real issue of this man's heart. That issue is money! He was a rich man. He had possessions, power and prestige. He was so disheartened with what Jesus said that he went away sorrowful. The outcome could have been so different!

This is a passage of Scripture that makes my heart ache with sadness for this young man. He had a personal encounter with the living Lord Jesus. He wanted to inherit eternal life but was not prepared to accept the cost of discipleship. We know from Scripture that keeping the law does not make a person entitled to inherit eternal life. We also know from Scripture that selling ones material possessions and giving all that one has to the poor does not entitle a person to inherit eternal life. It is not that Jesus was making additional requirements for this man. Rather it was that Jesus looked into his heart and saw the true condition of it.

This man made a choice. He kept his possessions and walked away from Jesus. Then Jesus used the incident to teach a great truth. "How difficult it will be for those who have wealth to enter the kingdom of God!" (v.24). Jesus explains that wealth can be a great obstacle in the spiritual life. Do we ever give thanks to God that we are not wealthy? Jesus said: "It is easier for a camel to go through the eye of a needle than for a rich person to enter the kingdom of God" (v.26). Of course the rich are not excluded from the kingdom of God. Rich people don't always give as generously as they could/should. This is the point that Jesus makes about the widows offering. She gave all that she had whereas others give proportionately less out of their abundance. Hers was a sacrificial not a superficial giving.

God can change a person's heart. Many wealthy people give generously to the work of the Lord. Look at what Peter has to say: "See, we have left everything and followed you" (v.29). He is seeking affirmation from the Lord. It is a plea for reassurance. There is a cost in following Jesus. For some people there is hardly any cost, such as those who come from a Christian home. But many people have had to experience rejection, ridicule, persecution, imprisonment, torture and even death. It is a courageous thing to walk away from your religion to follow Jesus. In many instances, leaving one's religion means also being ostracized by one's family. However, Jesus promises great reward for those who have endured such persecutions. And it is not all about the afterlife and what will be inherited there. Those who leave family for the sake of the gospel are born again into the family of God. This is a universal family and the convert can enjoy fellowship with believers in many countries. Jesus then reverses expectations, as he often does: "But many who are first will be last, and the last first" (v.31). Those who have first place in society might not have the same status in the kingdom.

There is always a cost to discipleship. Some people are convinced of the truth of the gospel but walk away. It might not be because wealth is an obstacle. Many other issues prevent people from following Jesus wholeheartedly. Some people will not forsake their sinful lifestyles or their heretical religious traditions. They might even be convicted by the Holy Spirit and still walk away. Being convinced and convicted should lead to conversion but sometimes it does not work that way. For some the challenge is too great and the price is too high.

This young man was a privileged individual. The parallel passage in Matthew tells us he was young. Luke tells us that he was a ruler. (Luke 18:18) This probably means that he was an influential leader in the local synagogue. In outward appearance he had possessions, prestige, power and privilege but the reality of his heart, his spiritual condition was poor. Appearances can be deceiving! His money had left him feeling unfulfilled. His morality, his clean living and his religious activity had not been able to satisfy the deepest longing of his soul. His swift climb up the rungs of the social ladder had failed to give him what he wanted most; peace with God. Many people are like him. They have money, morals, and status in society but there is still something missing in their lives. He knows he has a spiritual need and he is not ashamed to admit it publicly. In spite of all that he had, he is still needy. From the outside it appears as if he has it all, but this is not so. It seems that he just wanted to be reassured by Jesus that he was spiritually sound. He wanted a pat on the back.

We live in a technologically advanced age. Ours is a sophisticated and intellectually advanced culture. Yet people still do not know the answer to the most basic and important question of all: "What must I do to inherit eternal life?" Man can split atoms, put men on the moon, harness the power of the sun and wind but he does not know how to get to heaven. At least this young man was concerned about his soul. He is concerned about the right issue. He approached the right person (John 14:6; Acts 4:12). He comes in the right way (in humility). But he thinks salvation can be earned. He is looking for a 'do' oriented salvation. In this he is like many people of his generation and religion and he is like so many in our culture also. He wants to get his salvation like he got everything else in his life. He seems to think of salvation as a reward - if he can do enough good things, then God will grant him eternal life. Salvation is not a reward it is the free gift of God's grace. When Jesus died on the cross he said "It is finished!" He did it all and there is nothing anyone can do to add to it. Salvation is not about what we can do but what has already been done by Christ. The Philippian Jailer had the same question for Paul and Silas: "Sirs, what must I do to be saved?" (Acts 16:30) and Paul answered him: "Believe in the Lord Jesus, and you will be saved".

Jesus confronted this man on two fronts. Firstly, his understanding of the true identity of Jesus is questioned. The man had called Jesus "good teacher". Jesus is asking him do you believe I am a good teacher or do you believe that I am God? Jesus is not one who shows the way (like John the Baptist) rather he is the way (John 14:6). Jesus gives him a list of commands but it does not imply that salvation can be earned (Titus 3:5). Jesus is trying to get this man to see that he is a sinner and to get him to be honest about his spiritual condition. Jesus wants him to see that in spite of his material riches he is spiritually bankrupt. This is where most people are isn't it? They take an external, superficial, inventory of their lives and think they are alright. A person can be a good living person but he is still a sinner who needs the Savior.

Maybe Jesus only mentioned the commandments that the young man had kept. Perhaps the Lord did not mention the ones he had broken. The commandments listed in verse 19 deal with man's relationship to man. It may be that this man was right with his fellow man, but had the view that that was all that was required for salvation. A person can be moral, religious and decent but that does not make him right with God. This man's wealth (and maybe his status too) was hindering him from following the Lord. He needs to get rid of the gods he already has before he can follow the Lord. His gods are his wealth and his pride. He is told to sell what he has and give it all away. This would demonstrate that he had no other gods before the Lord. He wanted to be justified on the basis of his own merits but this is not how one is justified before God. One is justified before God solely by trusting in the merits of Christ's atoning sacrifice. A woman once commissioned a portrait of herself. When she saw the finished work of art she was displeased and complained to the artist: "it does not do me justice". The artist replied, "Madam it is not justice you need but mercy." Justice would send us to hell, mercy invites us to heaven.

Jesus demands wholehearted commitment not half-hearted convenience. Christ may not ask us to give all that we have away. He may let us keep our stuff but he does demand that we relinquish our grip on all we have and are. Jesus is effectively saying, "Turn your back on everything but me and you will be saved." This man wanted salvation on his terms and he chose his possessions over Jesus. He loved his wealth more than he wanted to be saved. What would you not give up for Jesus? What became of this young man? I imagine him growing old, losing his health and eventually dying. How sad when we think of what might have been if he had been prepared to follow Jesus. What good are religion, reputation and riches without a real relationship with Jesus? Whatever hinders a person from wholehearted commitment to Christ must be identified. Discipleship is not on our terms but on Christ's terms. He leads and calls us to follow.

Jesus foretells his death a third time (10:32-34)

This is the third time that Jesus predicts his death (see Mark 8:31, 9:31). The disciples were amazed and afraid. This time he is very specific about the detail of his impending death. In fact the disciples were afraid even before he begins to talk to them about this. They were anxious after the encounter with the rich young ruler. So this conversation must have added greatly to their distress. Imagine if you were fearful about certain things and then somebody told you that things were going to get far worse. The disciples needed a dose of reality because their expectations were not in line with the direction Jesus was taking. Jesus is on a journey to Jerusalem to fulfill his mission. He does not drag his disciples along. He does not push them. He simply leads them: "See, we are going up to Jerusalem, and the Son of Man will be delivered over to the chief priests and the scribes, and they will condemn him to death and deliver him over to the Gentiles. And they will mock him and spit on him, and flog him and kill him. And after three days he will rise." (vs.33-34) Jesus had an agenda. His plan is selfless but James and John had another agenda.

The request of James and John (35-45)

And James and John, the sons of Zebedee, came up to him and said to him: "Teacher, we want you to do for us whatever we ask of you" (v.35). This is an outrageous thing to say to Jesus. Yet it is the attitude of many Christians today. They want a Jesus who will do their bidding like a wish-granting genie. The Lord was submitting himself to the will of his heavenly father but these men wanted to share in Christ's glory. However, Jesus points out that discipleship will involve hardship, persecution, and even death (for them). He predicts their martyrdom. A row broke out between James and John on the one hand and the other ten disciples on the other. But Jesus points out that the way to greatness is through service. They are told that they are to be servant leaders who must not lord it over others.

There are some churches with hierarchal structures where those who are in leadership are an elite dictatorship. This is not the way of the Lord. He is calling them to be like him, to model their master who "came not to be served but to serve, and to give his life as a ransom for many" (v.45). Jesus was focused now on the events that would unfold in the near future. But his followers had a different focus. Jesus had one agenda and two of his closest disciples had a different agenda. Jesus is heading for the cross with determination. He will not be distracted or dissuaded from this. His mind is made up. They were on their way to Jerusalem.

The disciples thought this would mean they were entering into that place and time when Jesus would take on the mantle of the Messiah and establish his kingdom. But Jesus was focused on the cross. The cross puts everything else into perspective. The cross was his divinely appointed destiny and we are called to the way of the cross:

Philippians 2:5-8

⁵ Have this mind among yourselves, which is yours in Christ Jesus, ⁶ who, though he was in the form of God, did not count equality with God a thing to be grasped, ⁷ but emptied himself, by taking the form of a servant, being born in the likeness of men. ⁸ And being found in human form, he humbled himself by becoming obedient to the point of death, even death on a cross.

This is the mind of Christ. This is the way of the cross. Jesus was focused on the eternal plan. The cross and the death of Jesus were not some unfortunate accident. His death was predicted in the Old Testament. His death was promised to Adam and Eve in the Garden of Eden: "I will put enmity between you and the woman, and between your offspring and her offspring; he shall bruise your head, and you shall bruise his heel." (Genesis 3:15) His death was pictured in the coats of skin God made to cover the nakedness of Adam and Eve, which involved the shedding of blood. (Genesis 3:21) His death was prefigured in every sacrifice and offering in the tabernacle and the temple. Christ's death would accomplish what the animal sacrifices could not accomplish because they were a type or shadow of the one atoning sacrifice of the

Lamb of God: 'For it is impossible for the blood of bulls and goats to take away sins' (Hebrews 10:4). Christ's death would guarantee pardon for sin and an enduring peace with God for all those who call on him for salvation. Christ's death would accomplish what Adam's fig leaves failed to do by providing an adequate covering for shame. His death on the cross would satisfy the wrath of a righteous God.

Nothing would deter Jesus from fulfilling this eternal plan to be the Lamb of God who takes away the sin of the world. But it wasn't just a place and a plan that Jesus was focused upon. His mind was fixed on a people. Before he was born the angel told Joseph: "...you shall call his name Jesus, for he will save his people from their sins" (Matthew 1:21). Jesus was focused on all those who would be given to him by the Father (John 6:37). That is all those chosen in him before the foundation of the world (Ephesians 1:4).

However, there were other thoughts on the minds of James and John. The disciples were 'afraid'. We derive the word 'phobia' from this word *phobeo*. They had an intense fear. They had good reason to fear. They knew they were reaching the critical point in Christ's ministry as they approached Jerusalem and they were concerned about how events would unfold. They knew that the Pharisees and scribes hated Jesus as they had several confrontations. The religious leaders were angry about Christ's miracles and his message. The disciples are afraid for Jesus, but they are also afraid for themselves. This is not exactly what they thought being a disciple would involve. Do you ever feel like that? We might expect Jesus to comfort them but he does not. We are very like the disciples with our doubts, fears, different expectations and different agendas.

What path are you walking? Are you following your own course? On the other hand, are you following the Lord wherever he leads? Jesus might lead us to someplace we do not want to go. Jesus cares about your doubts and fears. That is why you should be regularly 'casting all your anxieties on him, because he cares for you' (1 Peter 5:7). The writer to the Hebrews tells us that Jesus sympathizes with our weaknesses.—Hebrews 4:15

As Jesus spoke to his disciples on the road to Jerusalem, his words were not what they wanted to hear. Maybe the Lord is speaking to you but you don't want to hear what he is saying. Are you following Jesus? Jesus was on the road to rejection. The religious establishment would reject him. Many people want a respectable and acceptable religion. One of his intimate circle would betray Jesus. He would be forsaken by his disciples and even by his heavenly Father. Jesus was on the road to ridicule. As he hung on the cross, he was mocked and derided. The guards of the High Priest mocked him. (Matthew 26:67-68) The soldiers of Pilate mocked him. (John 19:1-5) The crowds mocked him. (Matthew 27:39-44) Jesus was scourged and spat on and had his beard plucked. The King of kings and Lord of lords had a crown of thorns placed on his head. He was nailed to the cross. He hung there, naked, for six agonizing hours of humiliation before he died. His body was buried in a borrowed tomb. (John 19:31-42) However, his future involved not just rejection and ridicule but also resurrection.

Jesus endured the wrath of God on the cross for us. He rose from the dead for us. He came to this world with a single goal, to accomplish our salvation. He did this when he died on the cross and rose again from the dead. He went where we could not go and he did what we could not do so that we might receive the eternal life that only he can give. Let us reaffirm our faith in the following words and urge each other on in our journey with Jesus:-

I want to walk with Jesus Christ,

all the days I live of this life on earth:
to give to him complete control
of body and of soul.

Follow Him, follow Him,
yield your life to him –
He has conquered death,
He is King of kings;
accept the joy which he gives to those
Who yield their lives to Him...[61]

Jesus heals blind Bartimaeus (10:46-52)

Jesus was leaving Jericho with his disciples. On this particular day, the roads of the city were packed with pilgrims on their way to Jerusalem for the Passover. People crowded along the roads to see Jesus as he passed by. In this story, we are presented with a man named Bartimaeus who is blind. He calls out to Jesus and recovers his sight. He is a picture of all of us. We were once blind but now we see. We too have had a transforming encounter with Jesus. The lost sinner is blind, and he cannot see God. He is deaf, and he cannot hear God. He is a spiritual cripple, and he cannot walk with God. He has withered hands, and he cannot work for God. He has a defiled mind and so he does not have a right understanding of God. He has a stammering tongue, and he cannot talk to God. He is a leper in the sense that he is unclean and defiled.

As Bartimaeus called out to Jesus, there was opposition. People tried to prevent him from doing this: 'And many rebuked him, telling him to be silent' (v. 48). It seems that many people who tried to come to Jesus had to overcome obstacles. There was the paralytic who needed to be brought. There was the leper who was forbidden to mingle with the

---

[61] C. Simmonds, 1964. *Mission Praise*, Marshall Pickering, 1999.

crowds that surrounded Jesus. There were parents with children who were obstructed by Christ's closest disciples. The religious leaders were an intimidating presence, always nearby, watching. It took courage and faith to come to Christ. Those who came, like those with demon-possessed children, were desperate and determined. Priests and doctors could not help them. They understood their condition and knew that only a miracle could help.

One day a Christian and a Communist were sitting on a park bench watching the world go by. As they watched, a poor beggar walked by dressed in rags. The Communist said: "Communism would put a new suit on that man!" To which the Christian responded: "Maybe so, but Jesus Christ can put a new man in that suit." The transformation that Jesus brings about is not merely external. It is important for people to realize their own helplessness before they come to Christ. Many who came to Jesus realized that conventional approaches had failed to produce the desired result. When people are desperate enough in their condition, they will overcome opposition in coming to Christ. There is always opposition.

Bartimeaus was determined and did not let others bully him into silence and so 'he cried out all the more' (v.48). Although Bartimaeus was physically blind, he had spiritual sight or insight. He calls Jesus "Son of David". The Messiah was long promised in the line of David. Many people can see physically but they are spiritually blind. He was blind and he was a beggar. These things are connected. This was possibly the only way he could make a living. These were days before equal employment opportunities and policies of positive discrimination. There were no welfare programs or secular charitable institutions that could help him. This man depended on charity. He needed the generosity of others in order to survive. In his condition, Bartimaeus is a picture of all who are lost in sin: '...the god of this world has blinded the minds of the unbelievers, to keep them from seeing the light of the gospel of the glory of Christ, who is the image of God' (2 Corinthians 4:4). Elsewhere Paul says: 'They are darkened in their understanding, alienated from the life of God because of the ignorance that is in them, due to their hardness of heart.' (Ephesians 4:18) They are blind to their condition, to their sin and to their impending eternal doom. They need Jesus to open their eyes. Like Bartimaeus, the lost are also spiritual beggars. They can do nothing, and they have nothing within themselves to produce salvation. We are all in this condition until we call out to Jesus.

However, this man was determined. He recognized who Jesus was. He probably heard about the miracles performed by Jesus: the lepers, the lame, the demon possessed, even the dead that Jesus had restored to life. He knew that what Jesus had done for others he could do for Bartimaeus. There is a level of understanding here that is evident in the lives of many who come to Christ for salvation. They first recognize who Jesus is. They know what he has done in the lives of others and they believe that he can do the same for them. Bartimaeus exercised faith in Jesus. He knew what Jesus could do. He was aware that his greatest opportunity had come. He was in a helpless and hopeless condition but he realized that as Jesus passed by this was a day of great opportunity. So he began to cry out to the Lord for mercy.

Though he was blind, he was able to see an opportunity when it stared him in the face. He not only saw this opportunity but he seized it! The appropriate maxim in relation to calling upon Jesus is *carpe diem* (seize the moment) not *manana* (tomorrow). 'Behold, now is the favorable time; behold, now is the day of salvation' (2 Corinthians 6:2). The gospel is both important and urgent and procrastination is a wrong attitude. Bartimaeus understood that this opportunity could easily pass him by. If Bartimaeus had remained silent on that occasion then he would have remained in his pitiful condition as a blind beggar. If he had not called out to Jesus for mercy that day then the next day would have been like all the others before. He would have sat by the road begging until he died. Some people have had the opportunity to call out to Jesus for mercy but let the moment pass. Although he was blind he could see that unless he called on the Lord he would be doomed to a life of misery and darkness. If he was content in his condition he would not have cried out to Jesus. Many are content in their condition but a sense of desperation and discontent is needed before one comes to Jesus.

Has there ever in your life been an opportunity that passed by? It is a sad thing that leaves a person with regrets. It is important to call on the Lord while he is near, 'Seek the LORD while he may be found; call upon him while he is near' (Isaiah 55:6). Notwithstanding the fact that God is always near in one sense there are nevertheless critical moments in a person's life. There are crucial junctures when it is time to recognize who Jesus is and have some understanding of one's own miserable condition. It is important to understand that what Christ has done for others he can do for you, to see the opportunity and to seize the moment by calling out for mercy. There is a time when the Lord calls and we need to respond to those overtures of grace. Jesus said, "No one can come to me unless the Father who sent me draws him" (John 6:44).

Jesus healed Bartimaeus and said, "Go your way" but he followed Jesus "...glorifying God. And all the people, when they saw it, gave praise to God" (Luke 18:43). God is glorified both by Bartimaeus and those who witness the miracle. This is the acid-test of any true miracle, God will be glorified. He rejoiced in his new condition. There was such a contrast. When a person receives spiritual sight, there is also a radical transformation: "if anyone is in Christ, he is a new creation. The old has passed away; behold, the new has come" (2

Corinthians 5:17). His joy was a testimony. So it should be with all those who have had a transforming encounter with Christ. This man found a new direction. He followed Jesus. The Lord has wrought a great miracle in our lives and we have found a new direction. We follow him giving praise and glory to God and others who witness this cannot help but acknowledge that God is in it.

This man persistently cried out. Others tried to stop him but he was not hindered by the opinions of others. People take the opinions of others too much to heart. How tragic when it keeps them from crying out to Jesus for mercy and from following him. Jesus responded to this man's cry for mercy. Such a heart-cry will not fall on deaf ears. The text says: 'And throwing off his cloak, he sprang up and came to Jesus' (v.50). Everyone who comes to Christ has to cast off something. Bartimaeus was healed, Jesus told him to go his way but he wanted to be near the Lord. This is like the Gadarene demoniac (Mark 5) who wanted to be with Jesus after he was set free. When the Lord touches our lives, we will want to walk with him. We will want to be around other disciples.

Bartimaeus lived in darkness before he met Jesus but after he met Jesus, he lived in the light of God's glorious grace. He reflected/radiated that light. Scripture tell us that those who look to him are radiant. (Psalm 34:5) He was a beggar who lived in wretched poverty. There are people all around us who see just fine with their physical eyes, but they cannot see with their spiritual eyes. According to the Bible, they are blind! They cannot see the ugliness of sin or the beauty of the Lord. Those who call out to the Lord have their eyes opened by Jesus and they follow him rejoicing and praising God for what he has done for them. Their radically changed condition and the joy it arouses are a public testimony.

Chapter 11

The triumphal entry (11:1-11)

This is a turning point in Mark's Gospel. The fullness of time is approaching. People lined the streets to pay royal homage to Jesus as he entered the city and there were shouts of "Hosanna" which means 'save now'. Certain events are set in motion that will lead to the cross and the resurrection. Before the sun sets the next Friday, Jesus will have been crucified and buried. Before the sun rises on the next Sunday morning Jesus will have conquered death, hell and the grave by rising from the dead. How fickle the crowd can be.

He would be betrayed by one in his closest circle, arrested, forsaken by those he invested in for three years, denied by Peter, falsely tried, mocked, spat on, flogged, have a crown of thorns put on his head, stripped naked and nailed to a cross where he hung for six agonizing hours being insulted.

Jesus is about to fulfill an ancient prophecy. As he enters Jerusalem he is about to present himself to the nation of Israel as their king. Hundreds of years earlier the prophet Zachariah speaking about the coming king of Zion said: 'Rejoice greatly, O daughter of Zion! Shout aloud, O daughter of Jerusalem! Behold, your king is coming to you; righteous and having salvation is he, humble and mounted on a donkey, on a colt, the foal of a donkey.' (Zechariah 9:9) Jesus is about to fulfill that prophecy in detail. This is not the action of a political activist. He did not come with pomp and ceremony riding a chariot with six white steeds. There was no fanfare of trumpets announcing his arrival. Security personnel did not surround him. His disciples were not his bodyguards. The action of the crowd was completely spontaneous. They proclaim "Hosanna" as a customary greeting or blessing to welcome pilgrims during the Passover festivities. It is taken from Psalm 118:26, which is a liturgical psalm.

Imagine this scene. It is early in the morning and Jesus is making preparations to go to Jerusalem. He is moving through two little villages near the top of the mountain. He is in Bethphage, which means 'house of unripe figs' and Bethany, which means 'house of dates'. Jesus had some dear friends at Bethany, namely: Mary, Martha and Lazarus, with whom he stayed during his last days on earth. In fact, Jesus had performed one of his most astonishing miracles when he raised Lazarus from the dead in that place. (John 11) Now he stands on the top of the Mount of Olives, preparing to descend into the city below. From the top of that mountain, which stands some 2,600 feet above sea level, Jesus could see the beautiful city spread out before him. These events occurred during the week leading up to the Passover. Historians tell us that the population of Jerusalem was around eighty-thousand at this time. During the Passover, between two and three million people would crowd into the city for the celebration.

Jesus sends two of his disciples to a village to get a young donkey colt. He tells them exactly where they will find it and what the people there will say to them. He tells them what to say if asked why they are taking it. Jesus anticipates that the actions of the disciples might be questioned so he instructs them how to answer. He is always ahead of us. They carry out his instructions in detail. This is always the right thing to do. They set off on this errand and find that everything is just as Jesus had said. How did Jesus know this? Some commentators suggest that Jesus had pre-arranged this; that he had talked to the owners of this little donkey and arranged to use the animal. It is possible that Jesus pre-arranged the use of this donkey but not necessarily. On one occasion the collectors of the temple tax approached Christ's disciples for two drachma. Jesus said: "...go to the sea and cast a hook and take the first fish that comes up, and when you open its mouth you will find a shekel" (Matthew 17:27). This was not pre-arranged in any duplicitous sense. But in God's sovereign will these things were set up beforehand. The two disciples were instrumental in fulfilling the Lord's will. They were doing something far more important than they realized. Often when we obey the Lord we are engaged in something far bigger than we realize. Jesus refers to himself as "Lord" in this passage. He is still Lord today whether people recognize him and bow to him or not. There will come a day when they will.–Philippians 2:9-11.

Jesus was popular at this point in his ministry. He had raised Lazarus from the dead. He was a local celebrity. When the owners heard that it was Jesus who wanted the colt, they immediately sent it. Look at that statement in verse 3: "The Lord has need of it". That was the paradox of our Lord's earthly life. He was rich, yet he became poor (2 Corinthians 8:9). He owned all things, yet he possessed nothing. He created the universe with its stars and yet he had nowhere to lay his head. (Matthew 8:20) He had to borrow a boat from which to preach the Gospel. He created every drop of water that exists in the world, yet he cried, "I thirst" as he was dying on the cross. (John 19:28) He created the forests that included the tree that became his cross. He created the mountains and yet he was buried in a borrowed cave (tomb). In a psalm that talks about the greatness of God, we are told: "...he makes the clouds his chariot; he rides on the wings of the wind." (Psalm 104:3) Yet he had to borrow a donkey as his mode of transport.

The Lord needed that donkey to fulfill his mission here on earth. Is that not amazing? Jesus is God but he chose to use that little donkey. He is still using little donkeys to get his work done on earth. He uses you and me in spite of our stubborn wills and even our stupidity. He could have assigned the task to angels, but he chose to work through human instruments. I am glad to be a part of the Lord's business. I am glad he can use a little donkey like me! The following poem is an inspirational piece of imaginative literature that comments on that creature:

The Donkey

When fishes flew and forests walked
And figs grew upon thorn,
Some moment when the moon was blood
Then surely I was born.

With monstrous head and sickening cry
And ears like errant wings,
The devil's walking parody
On all four-footed things.

The tattered outlaw of the earth,
Of ancient crooked will;
Starve, scourge, deride me: I am dumb,
I keep my secret still.

Fools! For I also had my hour;
One far fierce hour and sweet:
There was a shout about my ears,
And palms before my feet.[62]

That donkey had to be redeemed: "Every firstborn of a donkey you shall redeem with a lamb, or if you will not redeem it you shall break its neck." (Exodus 13:13; 34:20)[63] That little donkey was alive and useful to the Lord because the blood of a lamb had redeemed it. Praise God that is why I have spiritual life today! That is the only reason you and I

---

[62] G. K. Chesterton, *The Rattle Bag*, London & Boston: Faber and Faber, 1982. ©Selection Seamus Heaney and Ted Hughes.
[63] If it was first-born.

have any usefulness to the Lord today. Praise God for the redeeming power of the blood of Jesus! That donkey had to be released. It was bound and had to be set free before the Lord could use it. Before we can be of any use to Jesus the chains of our sins have to be broken and we have to be set free. That is what he does for his saints: "...if the Son sets you free, you will be free indeed." (John 8:36). That donkey had to be ruled. Verse 2 tells us that the donkey had never been broken to ride. Yet it submitted itself to the Lord Jesus and yielded to his control. That is what the Lord expects of us! He is looking for total submission and total surrender: 'Submit yourselves...to God.'–James 4:7.

We are frail human instruments that the Lord deigns to use. When we are like that donkey (redeemed, released and ruled), the Lord can use us too. V.3 says, "The Lord has need of it and will send it back here immediately." When that donkey came back, it was better than it was when it left. When it left, it was unbroken and untried. When it came home, it was ready for the saddle. That is just what the Lord does. He takes what we give and he gives back far more. Give him an Abram, from a pagan culture, and he will change him into Abraham, a mighty man of faith. Give him Jacob, a schemer and a trickster, and he will change him into Israel, a prince of God. Give him Saul of Tarsus, a persecutor of Christians, and he will change him into Paul, a mighty apostle of God. Give him Simon, a weak, wavering man, and he will change him into Peter, a rock for Jesus. Give him your broken, sin-scarred life and he will give you back a new start, a new life and a home in heaven!

We see a humble man on the back of a humble beast, making a humble declaration of his identity. Imagine this procession. Jesus is on a donkey and throngs of common people surround him. It was a procession of paupers. The people are waving palm branches and not swords. He is riding a little donkey and not a mighty stallion. He is surrounded by ordinary men and not by soldiers.

The Roman soldiers who saw this parade must have laughed at Jesus. It must have appeared like a joke, so unlike the Roman *triumphus.* In those great celebrations, victorious Roman generals would return from the battlefields with the spoils of war. Defeated kings and soldiers would be paraded through town. The victorious army would walk past cheering crowds. Elephants, tigers and lions would be paraded past. The victorious general would be riding in the finest of chariots pulled along by handsome, well-groomed horses. Thousands would cheer and Rome would vibrate with the shouts of people praising Caesar and the Roman gods. A Roman general could only have a *triumphus* if he had killed over 5,000 enemy soldiers in battle. Very soon, King Jesus would claim over 8,000 new believers 3,000 and 5,000.– Acts 2:41; 4:4.

Who is in the crowd that day, waving palm branches before Jesus and paving the road with their clothing? I imagine Bartimaeus is there and Lazarus along with Mary and Martha. I imagine that crowd was full of people Jesus had healed and delivered. They are practicing antiphonal singing. The people in front would say a part and the people in back would answer them. We are told what they said in verses 9-10. As already noted the word "Hosanna" means 'save now'. It was a cry for the Messiah to deliver his people. It had come to be used as a shout of praise, much like "Hallelujah". Mark does not mention this but Jesus weeps over Jerusalem at this point:

Luke 19:41-44

⁴¹ And when he drew near and saw the city, he wept over it, ⁴² saying, "Would that you, even you, had known on this day the things that make for peace! But now they are hidden from your eyes. ⁴³ For the days will come upon you, when your enemies will set up a barricade around you and

surround you and hem you in on every side ⁴⁴ and tear you down to the ground, you and your children within you. And they will not leave one stone upon another in you, because you did not know the time of your visitation."

Why did Jesus weep? The Jews would reject the Messiah. He saw the future of Jerusalem and he knew that within forty years, the Romans (led by the General Titus) would besiege the city. The Romans would conquer the city and the temple and the city would be utterly demolished. Over thirty-thousand Jews would be crucified as the Legions marched toward the city. The city would hold out for months while the people died by the thousands from disease and starvation. They would throw the bodies of the dead over the walls of Jerusalem. The people would be scattered. Jesus knew all these things and Jesus wept over the city.

At this point, the people are shouting, dancing, singing, praising God and welcoming Jesus. They are vocal in their excitement. Jesus, however, is a man with a broken heart, 'a man of sorrows' (Isaiah 53:3). Have you ever wondered what Jesus sees when he looks at our city, town or village? He sees people who are going to a lost eternity. We need to see the people of our town as Jesus sees them. When we do, we too will cry over them as he wept over Jerusalem. The last thing Jesus did on that day was to visit the temple. He would have perhaps seen the beauty of the temple building with its gold and all the trappings of religion. Perhaps he saw the priests carrying out their rituals. Maybe he saw the people bringing their sacrifices to the priests. However, did they see him? Surely, they saw his physical body, but did they see the Messiah?

The King had entered the temple and they do not seem to be aware of it. The Lord of Glory had visited his house and they were ignorant of his presence. He saw they had no place for him in their temple so he left. What does Jesus see when he comes to our church? Does he see people who come looking for him, or does he see people just going through the motions? Does he see people who are worshiping him and praising him, or does he see people just caught up in the rituals? What does Jesus see in the church today? More importantly, what does Jesus see in our hearts? Does he see his face reflected back to him? Does he see a heart filled with love for him? Does he see an earnest worshiper? The big question is: do we see him?

Zechariah told Israel to be ready: "Behold, your king is coming to you". He came to them and they were unprepared for his coming. A few received him, but as a whole, the nation of Israel rejected their King. They turned him away and they crucified him. Do you know that the King is passing by right now? He is here to receive those who will come to him in faith, to restore those who will come home, to refresh those who are weary, to reward those who are faithful and to revive those who are hungry for more. He is coming again. Are we prepared for that?

Jesus curses the fig tree and the lesson thereof (11:12-14; 20-21)

This passage is difficult to interpret. It is the only miracle of its kind in the gospels and it is probably best understood as an acted-out parable. It is a negative miracle, in the sense that it ruins rather than restores. Christ demonstrated his constructive power on many occasions but in this incident his destructive power is evident. In a sense it is like the cleansing of the temple incident which also showed Jesus acting in righteous anger. The phrase, "because it was not the season for figs" presents some problems in terms of interpretation. Fig trees in Jerusalem usually leaf-out in March or April but do not produce fruit until June.

Fig trees were and are very common in Israel. There are several kinds of trees mentioned in the Bible, including the fig tree. The fig tree or fig leaves or figs are mentioned over sixty times in the Bible. It is first mentioned in Genesis 3:7 when Adam and Eve used its broad leaves to make garments to cover their nakedness. Figs were a vital part of the Middle-Eastern diet and fig trees were valued for the shade they provided. It was a sign of peace and prosperity to sit in the shade of a fig tree (1 Kings 4:25; Micah 4:4). Fig trees can grow quite big, to a height of twenty to thirty feet with a trunk about three feet in diameter. The spread of a fig tree's branches can be twenty-five to thirty feet. It was under a fig tree that Jesus first saw Nathanael (John 1:48). Fig trees are unusual in that they can produce as many as three crops in a single year.

The disciples heard Jesus when he cursed the fig tree (v.14). The next day, as they passed by, they saw that the fig tree was dead. The Lord demonstrated his sovereignty over all things, including nature. Here was the message of John the Baptist to Israel: "Even now the axe is laid to the root of the trees. Every tree therefore that does not bear good fruit is cut down and thrown into the fire" (Matthew 3:10). The fig tree was used as a symbol of the nation of Israel:

Jeremiah 24:2-10

[2] One basket had very good figs, like first-ripe figs, but the other basket had very bad figs, so bad that they could not be eaten. [3] And the Lord said to me, "What do you see, Jeremiah?" I said, "Figs, the good figs very good, and the bad figs very bad, so bad that they cannot be eaten."

[4] Then the word of the Lord came to me: [5] "Thus says the Lord, the God of Israel: Like these good figs, so I will regard as good the exiles from Judah, whom I have sent away from this place to the land of the Chaldeans. [6] I will set my eyes on them for good, and I will bring them back to this land. I will build them up, and not tear them down; I will plant them, and not pluck them up. [7] I will give them a heart to know that I am the Lord, and they shall be my people and

I will be their God, for they shall return to me with their whole heart.

⁸ "But thus says the Lord: Like the bad figs that are so bad they cannot be eaten, so will I treat Zedekiah the king of Judah, his officials, the remnant of Jerusalem who remain in this land, and those who dwell in the land of Egypt. ⁹ I will make them a horror to all the kingdoms of the earth, to be a reproach, a byword, a taunt, and a curse in all the places where I shall drive them.¹⁰ And I will send sword, famine, and pestilence upon them, until they shall be utterly destroyed from the land that I gave to them and their fathers."

The judgment of God was once again about to unfold for Israel (AD 70). They had rejected their Messiah and they would ultimately pay a terrible price. There is also a word of warning here for us. The Lord examines our lives, looking for genuine spiritual fruit in our lives. In this passage, the Lord hungers for fruit. If he finds that fruit he is pleased and if he does not find it, he is displeased.

Jesus is hungry. When Jesus was born in to this world, he laid aside his heavenly glory for a time to live in this world as a man: "For you know the grace of our Lord Jesus Christ, that though he was rich, yet for your sake he became poor, so that you by his poverty might become rich" (2 Corinthians 8:9). The fact that Jesus was hungry is evidence of his humanity. When Jesus was born into this world, he remained fully God, but he became fully man: "Have this mind among yourselves, which is yours in Christ Jesus, who, though he was in the form of God, did not count equality with God a thing to be grasped, but made himself nothing, taking the form of a servant, being born in the likeness of men." (Philippians 2:5-8) This is seen in many areas of his life. Jesus experienced hunger (Mark 11:12), thirst (John 19:28), weariness (John 4:6; Mark 4:38), pain (Matthew 27:35), rejection (John 1:11; John 7:3-5), loneliness (Matthew 26:56) and poverty. (Matthew 8:20) Because Jesus experienced life from a human perspective he is able to extend compassion and help to his people: "For we do not have a high priest who is unable to sympathize with our weaknesses, but one who in every respect has been tempted as we are, yet without sin. Let us then with confidence draw near to the throne of grace, that we may receive mercy and find grace to help in time of need".–Hebrews 4:15-16.

Jesus sees a fig tree in leaf in the distance and goes to it hoping to find some figs to eat but the tree has no fruit. The text says "for it was not the season for figs". Fig trees, which have retained their leaves through the winter usually, have figs also. It was still too early for new leaves or new fruit. However, this particular tree was all leaves with no fruit. This fig tree was deceptive because its leaves promised something the tree did not deliver. It grew in good soil and enjoyed the sunshine and the rain but did not bear fruit. This tree was fit for nothing but to be cut down and fed to the fire. We must consider this text in context. In verses 1-11 Jesus presented himself to Israel as her King but Israel would reject him. Israel was just like this fruitless fig tree, which had all the signs of spiritual life, but bore no fruit. They were keeping the letter of the Law. They were carrying out the temple ceremonies. They were observing the ancient feasts and the sacrifices. They were religious in every detail, but they had no spiritual fruit. Israel looked alive, but she was spiritually barren. Israel had been given every advantage that could be afforded to a people. They had received the personal attention of Almighty God. They had been planted in a good land. They had the Word of God, the prophets of God and the temple of God. They had everything they needed for a spiritual bumper crop, but they remained fruitless. Israel had no fruit now and there would be none in the future. They were useless spiritually and fit for nothing but the fire of judgment.[64]

---

[64] Individual Jews and even large numbers of Jews would come to saving faith in Christ but as a nation they rejected the Messiah.

However, there is a message here for us. When the Lord examines our lives, what does he see? Does he see us bearing fruit to the glory of God or, does he see a tree that has just leaves and no fruit? Are we all show and no substance? We too have been given every spiritual advantage God has to offer. We have his Word, his church and his Spirit. He has blessed us in abundance. There is no excuse for us being fruitless. We have all the appearances of life. We use the Bible and sing hymns. When people look at the church from a distance, they can see our leaves. However, is there any fruit? Are we really in love with Jesus? Are we really in love with one another? What about in our individual lives? Are we all leaves or do we have fruit? Is his will, his worship and his work first priority in our lives? Do we have all the trappings of religion and salvation, but no real commitment to God? Do we sing hymns and play the worship game while harboring resentments in our hearts? Do we look like saints from afar but under close inspection from the Lord are we bountiful or barren? Do you have any real fruit in your life?

Jesus said: "I am the vine; you are the branches. Whoever abides in me and I in him, he it is that bears much fruit, for apart from me you can do nothing" (John 15:5). What kind of fruit? We should bear the fruit of a changed life (2 Corinthian 5:17) and be a vibrant witness (Acts 1:8). The fruit of the Spirit is evidence of God's work in our lives. (Galatians 5:22-23) Therefore, what does Jesus see when he looks at our lives?

When Jesus cursed (condemned) this fig tree it was not an outburst of anger from a hungry and cranky man. The tree is a picture of the nation of Israel. They had the outward appearance of health but had a barren dead religion. If we have the appearance of life but bear no fruit the Lord will discover that on closer inspection. Those who know the Lord are expected to be fruitful. He will chastise us (to teach and train us) to become more fruitful for his glory:

Hebrews 12:5-11

⁵ And have you forgotten the exhortation that addresses you as sons?

"My son, do not regard lightly the discipline of the Lord,
  nor be weary when reproved by him.
⁶ For the Lord disciplines the one he loves,
  and chastises every son whom he receives."

⁷ It is for discipline that you have to endure. God is treating you as sons. For what son is there whom his father does not discipline? ⁸ If you are left without discipline, in which all have participated, then you are illegitimate children and not sons. ⁹ Besides this, we have had earthly fathers who disciplined us and we respected them. Shall we not much more be subject to the Father of spirits and live? ¹⁰ For they disciplined us for a short time as it seemed best to them, but he disciplines us for our good, that we may share his holiness. ¹¹ For the moment all discipline seems painful rather than pleasant, but later it yields the peaceful fruit of righteousness to those who have been trained by it.

In Revelation, we read: "Those whom I love, I reprove and discipline, so be zealous and repent." (Revelation 3:19) If we obey him and serve him, he will bless us in wonderful ways. If we refuse to obey and serve him, he will chastise us. The Lord is looking for fruit in the lives of his people as individuals and as a church. When he examines us may he find what he seeks!

Remarks about faith and prayer (11:22-25)

Here are some remarks about faith and prayer. The source of spiritual power is God, who may be accessed through prayer. The greatest difficulties can be resolved if we have faith. The greatest obstacles can be overcome if we have faith. James tells us that when we ask we must believe and not doubt (James 1:6). A strong faith is a praying faith dependent on God's will and power. The effective prayer must be offered in faith to the all-powerful God who works miracles. But it must be offered in a spirit of forgiveness. Faith and the willingness to forgive are the two conditions of efficacious prayer.

Jesus cleanses the temple (11:15-19)

This passage is sandwiched between the incident of Jesus cursing the fig tree and the passage dealing with lessons derived from that incident. Wherever Jesus went he provoked a response (astonishment, anger, fear). It is appropriate that believers would want Jesus to be present in their places of worship. On this occasion Jesus showed up and it was not a pleasant experience for some people. He did not bless what was being practiced there, rather he condemned it. Jesus is always present when people gather in his name. (Matthew 18:20) In Revelation, Jesus is pictured walking among candlesticks. (1:12-13) The candlesticks represent churches. Jesus is always present with believers when they come together. His presence is not in doubt. However, what does Jesus see when he comes amongst his people? Does he like what he sees or does he want some things to change? There was trouble in the temple. People were selling and buying things and exchanging currency there. It was the week of Passover so it was a time when many needed to exchange money and buy doves for sacrifice.

The temple complex sat on top of Mount Zion covering an area of about thirty-five acres. The outer walls of the temple grounds were between 1,000 and 1,300 feet in length. When a person entered the temple grounds, they came first into the court of the Gentiles. This area was open to all people who wanted to worship God. Jews and Gentiles alike were allowed to enter this area to pray and meditate. (Luke

18:9-14) Farther into the temple grounds, there was a low wall. Beyond this wall was the court of women. On this wall were signs that warned Gentiles to stay out of this courtyard. Only Jewish men and women could enter here. Beyond that was the court of the Israelites. Jewish women could enter this court only if they were bringing a sacrifice to give to the priests. Jewish men were allowed here at any time. Beyond that was the court of the priests. This was where the priests worked and ministered. Beyond the court of the priests was the temple itself with the holy place and the holy of holies. The events recorded in this passage took place in the court of the Gentiles.

As mentioned previously the population of Jerusalem was approximately eighty-thousand. During this time of the year, at Passover, the population swelled to over two million. These people came to Jerusalem from all over the ancient world and entered the temple to worship God. Jewish worship involved the sacrifice of animals. Mark mentioned those 'who sold doves'. Doves were the sacrifice of the poor. Those who could not afford sheep, goats or bulls could offer these inexpensive birds. (Leviticus 5:6-7; 14:22) Doves were what Mary, the mother of Jesus, brought as her sacrifice when Jesus was presented in the temple as a baby. (Luke 2:24) Other items used in temple worship were also sold here, such as wine, oil, flour, and salt that had been pronounced clean. It was very convenient! The money changers also provided a valuable service to temple worshipers. Every Jewish male was required to pay a half-shekel ransom at each census of Israel. When the Jews returned from captivity under Nehemiah the fee became yearly and was fixed at one-third of a shekel. A shekel is about half an ounce of silver (not a large amount). This tax was called 'the shekel of the sanctuary' and it had to be paid in Jewish money, other currencies were not accepted. The money changers seemed necessary because the pilgrims from around the world would be in possession of various currencies that would not be accepted in the temple. Therefore, at a superficial level it seemed like reasonable transactions were taking place to facilitate Passover pilgrims.

Verse 16 talks about those who were carrying vessels through the temple. The temple courtyard provided a quick path between the eastern part of the city of Jerusalem and the Mount of Olives and many people who were on business in the city would take this shortcut through the court of the Gentiles. To most people the things that were taking place at the temple were necessary and fine. Most people had no problem at all with the system and the way things worked.

But Jesus disliked it intensely. He came to the temple that morning knowing exactly what he would find. He had been there the day before and had seen what was happening. He returned to do something about the situation. In this scene Jesus is not a meek lamb but the fierce Lion of the Tribe of Judah. He took control of the situation and dealt with those violating the sanctity of his house. It is a violent scene where he drove people out of the temple, overturned tables and refused to allow people to pass through its courts. Imagine the scene with people and animals running around trying to get away from Jesus and money rolling along the floor. Some people might think this is uncharacteristic of Jesus, an aberration or an intemperate outburst. This incident does not fit with their understanding of the character of Christ as humble and gentle. Such zeal is usually deemed fanatical.

Jesus seeks to restore the temple to a place of worship, holiness and spirituality. Perhaps you feel that what was going on in the temple does not seem very bad. After all, the sellers and the moneychangers are providing what some might call a necessary service for the worshippers. What could be so wrong here that would drive Jesus to such drastic and violent actions? In the midst of it all he was teaching them, saying, "Is it not written: 'My house shall be called a house of prayer for all the nations'? But you have made it a den of robbers." (v.17) Here he quotes two Old Testament passages: "...my house shall be called a house of prayer for all peoples" (Isaiah 56:7) and "Has this house, which is called by my name, become a den of robbers in your eyes?" (Jeremiah 7:11) The first problem has to do with the very function of the temple itself. The house of God was intended to be a place of worship not a place of commerce.

When the first temple was built, the glory of God filled it. (2 Chronicles 7:1-3) God promised his people that he would meet with them in the temple. He promised to hear the prayers that were prayed in that place. (2 Chronicles 7:15-16) It was designed to be a place of worship but now it had ceased to be about the Lord and had become a house that was man-centered and not God-centered. The temple was no longer God's house; it had become a house devoted to the needs of men and this angered Jesus. The temple was designed as a house of prayer. The true believer, whether he was a Jew or a Gentile, could come to the temple to pray. The only place a Gentile could approach God had become a marketplace.

I was in a pet shop recently and it was smelly so I can imagine the smells and sounds of the marketplace filling that once hallowed space. Imagine the haggling going on in this place. It was hardly conducive to prayer or meditation on the things of God. The Jews had effectively closed the doors of the temple to the Gentiles and this angered Jesus.

Business was being conducted under a cloak of holiness. The sale of doves and exchange of money might seem harmless (even helpful) but it was not innocent. Those who traded in doves as well as the moneychangers who charged a 10-12 percent exchange rate were charging the people who came to worship grossly inflated prices. The High Priest was paid a percentage of the profits on top of the fee the sellers had to pay to gain permission to sell in the temple. Most of the praying that was going on in this temple was preying on the poor! It was a big money racket.

Jesus would not allow people to use the temple grounds as a shortcut. The Jewish oral law, or the *Mishnah*, actually forbade the Jews from using the temple in this way. The *Mishnah* says, "A man may not enter the temple mount with his staff or his sandal or his wallet, or with the dust upon his feet, nor may he make of it a short by-path." It seems that the Jews had lost all respect for the holiness and sanctity of the temple and treated its grounds as if it was any other place. The Jews were defiling the temple so that reverence for God was not evident in that place as it should have been.

People were amazed by what they saw Jesus do and by what they heard him say. No doubt, many of the people there that day were sincerely trying to worship God. They were interested in the reforms Jesus was trying to make in the temple. The temple had been defiled, the Lord was offended and judgment was unfolding. The whole issue in the temple was a problem of the heart. The Jews had abandoned authentic worship. Empty worship was the trouble at the temple the day Jesus visited. Empty worship brought divine judgment to that place.

Worship was strictly regulated in the Old Testament. It was very restricted. However, the Lord no longer dwells in temples made with human hands. (1 Corinthians 3:16; 6:19-20; 2 Corinthians 6:16) The Lord dwells by his Spirit in the lives of believers as individuals and as spiritual communities. It can easily be taken for granted that: 'There is neither Jew nor Greek, there is neither slave nor free, there is no male and female, for you are all one in Christ Jesus.' (Galatians 3:28) The Christian might not fully appreciate the wonderful privileges of the priesthood of all believers: 'But you are a chosen race, a royal priesthood, a holy nation, a people for his own possession.'–1 Peter 2:9.

Some people think the church exists for their convenience. Nothing in our lives should come before the Lord and his work. We should treat him, his business, his Word, his worship, and his church like they are the most important things in our lives. When God is first in our lives it will show and when he is not it will be evident. What does your life show about the place God holds in your heart? What does he see when he looks into the temple of our heart? The Lord wants authentic, Christ-centered, Spirit-filled worship. He wants a true heart worship based on truth, not camaraderie. He has the right to be at the center of it all. May God protect the church from allowing it to ever become anything else! This passage calls the believer to true spirituality. So let us guard our hearts, the temple of the Lord.

The authority of Jesus questioned (11:27-33)

The authority of Jesus is still questioned, doubted or denied altogether. Some say he was a good man, a prophet, a teacher but stop short of acknowledging him as the Son of God (or God the Son). Many people today are not interested in religion and would describe themselves as 'spiritual' rather than religious. They make up their own personal spirituality in an age of pick-and-mix values. Even within the Christian church this *a la carte* approach to truth can prevail, so that people select what they like and ignore what they do not like from the Bible.

In the passage, that we call the Great Commission Jesus said, "All authority in heaven and on earth has been given to me." (Matthew 28:18) This is the basis of the commission entrusted to us. Jesus went on to say: "Go therefore and make disciples of all nations, baptizing them in the name of the Father and of the Son and of the Holy Spirit, teaching them to observe all that I have commanded you." (Matthew 28:18-20) Here the tri-unity of God is presented in unequivocal terms (Father, Son and Holy Spirit). Notice the authoritative language in this passage of Scripture. Jesus did not say, "Perhaps you would consider getting involved in this mission and spreading the message I entrusted to you." He did not say: "Some of you should really think about doing this." He told them to "Go". Furthermore he refers to his teaching as commands not advice: "...teaching them to observe all that I have commanded you." But I want you to notice something from the passage that we call the 'Great Commission'. We have read from verse eighteen to verse twenty, but take a look at the preceding two verses: "Now the eleven disciples went to Galilee, to the mountain to which Jesus had directed them. And when they saw him they worshiped him, but some doubted." (16-17) Even at that point (the very end of Matthew's Gospel) some of his closest disciples doubted. After all that he taught them and all that they had witnessed.

For believers there is a constant battle between faith and doubt. Doubt is not exactly the same as unbelief. Unbelief is lack of belief but doubt is uncertainty. Some people are unable or unwilling to believe and will not put their trust in God. There are many people who trust in their religion no matter what. They prefer their traditions to the truth because it is their cultural identity and they will not change under any circumstances. However, Scripture must regulate theology. That is why convincing people of the truth of Scripture and consequently the error of some religious views will make no difference to their religious allegiance. How many times have we shown others that salvation is by grace alone, through faith alone in Christ alone and yet not seen people converted? An evangelical movement must not be allowed to fossilize into an evangelical monument to the past.

Many cults today deny the deity of Jesus even though the Bible clearly teaches it. Jesus returned to the temple and the religious leaders try to discredit him. These custodians of the truth approach Jesus and demand to know by what authority he is doing these things. Even within the Christian church today there are liberal religious leaders who deny the authority and inerrancy of Scripture. In the world, many people who are skeptical and cynical have questioned authority. In the church, the authority of the Bible has also been called into question. Sadly, even a translator for the American Bible Society's *Good News for Modern Man* has said:

> Only willful ignorance or intellectual dishonesty can account for the claim that the Bible is inerrant and infallible. No truth-loving, God-respecting, Christ-honoring believer should be guilty of such heresy."[65]

In the passage under review the religious leaders are literally asking, "Who do you think you are?" "What right do you have to come here and undo everything we have done?" Jesus had already overturned the tables of the moneychangers in the temple court. Now he turns the tables on these men. He asks them a simple question concerning John the Baptist. All they have to do is tell Jesus what authority John operated under and he will tell them by what authority he does what he does (vs.29-30). Jesus knew what authority John had operated under. Jesus operated under the same power: the power of God! This does not elevate John to deity or reduce Jesus to the level of a prophet. However, Jesus also knew that these men would never admit that. These religious leaders clearly demonstrate their hypocrisy by seeking an answer that made them look good. Their religion was merely an external observance of rites and rituals that had nothing to do with real relationship with God. This kind of ticking boxes is a ticking bomb that will ultimately lead to

---

[65] Robert Bratcher, *Inerrancy: Clearing Away Confusion*, *Christianity Today*, May 29, 1981, p.12.

the destruction of their souls. They were interested in power and public relations, not truth. If they said that John was sent from God, then Jesus would expose their hypocrisy, because they had rejected the message and ministry of John. If they said that John was operating under his own power, they would lose face with the people, because the majority believed that John was a true prophet sent from God. (31-32) Their answer was evasive and dishonest and so Jesus refused to answer them. (33) Jesus welcomes genuine seekers but despises insincerity.

Chapter 12

Parable of the tenants (12:1-12)

That was not the end of the matter. Jesus went on to expose the religious leaders for the hypocrites they were. In the Parable of the Tenants Jesus teaches that those who reject the grace of God will eventually face the wrath of God. It is a message directed at them. A man planted a vineyard and built a hedge around it to keep wild animals out. He dug a pit for the winepress to collect the juice that would be harvested from the grapes. He built a tower so that a watchman might keep a diligent eye on the vineyard so that it would be protected. He placed his vineyard in the hands of men assigned to work it and then he left it in their care. In this parable, the Lord of the vineyard is God. The vineyard is Israel. The husbandmen are the Jewish religious leaders. The servants are the prophets God sent to Israel. The beloved son of the lord of the vineyard is the Lord Jesus.

With this in mind, it is clear that verse 1 refers to the goodness of God toward Israel. The nation of Israel was often pictured as a vine (Isaiah 5:1-7). Jesus is sharing the parable while standing in the court of the Gentiles. God had tenderly preserved his vine in Egypt and then transported it and planted it in Canaan. There it took root and flourished. God had given his vine a good land in which to grow. They had the power, presence and protection of God. God continued to care for his vine; to bless his people. Thus, the psalmist proclaimed, 'Truly God is good to Israel.' (Psalm 73:1) This is the testimony of all believers. One day God came to us in our Egypt, dug us up by the roots, and transplanted us in a new land. Add to our salvation all the blessings he has given us; all the prayers he has answered. We too have his presence, protection and power and as such are a very privileged people. Having planted the vineyard and done everything necessary for it to succeed, the Lord sent his servants to gather his portion. The Lord is looking for fruit from his investment in his people. When this landowner sent his servants, the farmers cruelly treated them. The first one was beaten. (v.3) The next one was stoned and wounded in the head. (v.4) The next one was killed (v.5). After that, he sent several servants to get what was rightly his but they were all either beaten or killed by the men trusted to care for the vineyard. (v.5) After all the servants had been murdered, the landowner sent his son. They also killed his son (v.8). They believed that by killing the son they could claim the vineyard for themselves. (v.7) The religious leaders had been entrusted with the spiritual wellbeing of Israel. Repeatedly they led the nation astray. God sent them prophets to lead them back to the right path. Israel frequently refused to hear and heed these servants of the Lord and rejected prophet after prophet, culminating in John the Baptist.

The same thing is true today! God's witness is all around us calling people to him. (Psalm 19:1-4) Thus, people are without excuse. (Romans 1:20) God's witness is within us. (Romans 2:14) His Law is written on our hearts. Again, people are without excuse! The Jews thought that by killing the Son they could have the vineyard for themselves. They were self-serving. They wanted wealth, glory and power. Because they have rejected his servants and killed his son, he will come in wrath and destroy them. Jesus had demonstrated his deity to the Jews on many occasions through his miracles and his message. Yet, these men wanted the vineyard for themselves and they were willing to kill Jesus to get what they wanted.

In verses 10-11 Jesus changes the imagery. He stops talking about a vineyard and he starts talking about a building. (quoting Psalm 118:22) The key to a good foundation is a perfectly straight cornerstone. A straight cornerstone will ensure that the building is straight. If the stone were not right, the building would not turn out right. The Jewish leaders looked at Jesus and decided that he was not a fit cornerstone. In their eyes, he did not have the right pedigree, education, or credentials. Jesus simply did not square up to their expectations so they rejected him. They did not want to submit to his authority. Faced with the challenge to repent they chose rather to retaliate. When Jesus finished the parable, the Jews wanted to arrest him but they were afraid to do anything because the people respected Jesus as a great rabbi. Jesus was (is) God's final messenger. When they rejected him, they were saying no to God for the very last time. There was nothing left for them but judgment.

The same is true today! Jesus is God's last word to humanity: 'Long ago, at many times and in many ways, God spoke to our fathers by the prophets, but in these last days he has spoken to us by his Son, whom he appointed the heir of all things, through whom also he created the world.' (Hebrews 1:1-2) There are, therefore, no subsequent prophets. Those who reject him have no more hope of salvation. One day everybody will appear before Jesus and face him as either Savior or Judge: 'Note then the kindness and the severity of God.' (Romans 11:22) On the one hand, God is good to those who come to him in faith. He forgives them, saves them and gives them everlasting life. (Romans 10:13) On the other hand, those who reject him will face him in judgment. (Revelation 20:11-15) We will face the Lion or the Lamb.

The application is clear: beware of becoming rigidly set in a conventional pattern of behavior, beliefs, and attitudes that is a self-serving institution. Rather, see to cultivate a living, dynamic relationship with God. Submit to the authority of Scripture. Give the Lord of the vineyard the fruit that is his due, protect, and promote the truth of the gospel.

Paying taxes to Caesar (12:13-17)

Tension is mounting in Jerusalem. Jesus has offended the religious powers and they are out to get him (Mark 11:18). Therefore, they try to trap him. They are very determined either to discredit him or to have reason to accuse him before the state. The Lord's answer to the question asked shows that God has a claim on people's lives and that they have an obligation to serve him. We are his creation and we owe him worship as creator. Those who trust in him for salvation are his redeemed people and owe him worship as Savior.

The conspirators who approached Jesus came from two different groups that held opposing beliefs. First, there were the Pharisees who were the religious conservatives of the day. They were legalistic. The word 'Pharisee' has come to be synonymous with 'hypocrite' but it actually originally meant 'separatist'. This elite group of people was marked by pride and self-righteousness. Jesus often rebuked them because their religious activities were merely external. They were very nationalistic in their political views, hated being under Roman rule and wanted to be free from it. Secondly, there was the Herodians. They were a political party among the Jews who supported King Herod. Herod supported the Romans and sought to bring Roman culture to Israel. Normally, these two groups had nothing to do with one another, as they were polar opposites and detested one another. Yet they united for the common goal of trying to destroy Jesus.

There are two forces that have the power to unite people for either good or evil. Those forces are love and hatred. Love can unite people for the common good. Hatred can unite people in a quest to discredit or destroy others. These men were brought together in their common hatred of the Lord because they saw him as a threat to their way of life. These men were trying to outsmart and trap Jesus. They wanted to get him to say something that would get him in trouble with either the Roman authorities or the ordinary people. If they could get Jesus to offend Rome, they could accuse him of stirring up insurrection. Thus Rome would take care of their problem for them. If they could discredit Jesus with the people, he would lose his influence. Either way, their problem would be solved.

When a person listens to the words and watches the actions of another in an effort to find fault with them, that person has a serious spiritual problem. That is not the way of love. Love does not look for fault in others. If this attitude were practiced in the church, it would solve much of any church's troubles.

They compliment Christ on his ability as a teacher (they refer to him as "Master") and his fearless integrity. They acknowledge that he is not swayed by the opinions of men and that he speaks the truth. This was sincere praise. They were merely buttering him up and their intentions were evil. Everything they said about Jesus was true, but they didn't believe a word of it. Their own words condemn them. This is nothing more than insincere flattery designed to catch Jesus off guard. But Jesus knew their motives and he could see the condition of their hearts: 'But, knowing their hypocrisy, he said to them, "Why put me to the test? Bring me a denarius and let me look at it" (v.15). However, Christ's enemies had a coin in their possession, which was in a sense a tacit acknowledgement of Rome's right to rule.

Beware of flattery. We are vain and susceptible to it but Jesus was not. Adlai Stevenson said: 'Flattery is all right so long as you don't inhale.' Antisthenes (an ancient Greek Philosopher) said: 'It is better to fall among crows than flatterers; for those devour only the dead – these, the living.' The real danger with flattery was summed up well by Dale Carnegie: 'Flattery is telling the other person precisely what he thinks about himself.' Jesus could have believed everything good they said about him because it was all true.

They ask Jesus about paying tribute to Caesar. The tribute was a poll tax that every Roman subject was required to pay each year. The poll tax was a denarius (a day's pay for a laborer). The Pharisees believed that religion was superior to the state. The Herodians believed that the state was superior to religion. The Herodians probably did not mind paying the tax because they liked all the benefits they received from Rome. The Pharisees hated the tax because they detested Roman rule and they recoiled against using a coin that bore a graven image of the Emperor. They come to Jesus to ask him if paying this tax is right. This is the kind of trick question, which one might expect from a barrister. If Jesus said "no", they could label him an insurrectionist and have him arrested for opposing Roman law. If he said "yes" he would lose face with the common people who hated paying the tribute money to Rome. People who ask us questions about faith are not always seeking information. Sometimes they are seeking confrontation. Jesus knew they had no respect for him or for his ministry and he exposes their words as nothing more than insincere flattery.

Jesus knows the condition of our hearts also and his words expose us to the truth about ourselves:

Hebrews 4:12-13

12 For the word of God is living and active, sharper than any two-edged sword, piercing to the division of soul and of spirit, of joints and of marrow, and discerning the thoughts and intentions of the heart. 13 And no creature is hidden from

his sight, but all are naked and exposed to the eyes of him to whom we must give account.

We may deceive one another, but we will never deceive the Lord. To answer their question Jesus asked for a denarius and asked, "Whose likeness and inscription is this?" They said to him, "Caesar's." Jesus said to them: "Render to Caesar the things that are Caesar's, and to God the things that are God's" (vs.16-17). On the front of the denarius was an engraving of the head of Caesar Tiberius. In Latin on the front were the words: *Tiberius Caesar, divine son of Augustus.* On the back, in Latin, were the words *Pontifex Maximus, High Priest of the Roman nation.* The coins claimed divinity for Caesar and they claimed that Caesar was the High Priest of the Roman Empire. Jesus had to borrow a coin to use as an illustration. These men come to Jesus asking him about money and he doesn't even have any. Jesus became poor so that we might become spiritually rich through the free gift of salvation he offers to all who turn to him in repentance and faith: 'For you know the grace of our Lord Jesus Christ, that though he was rich, yet for your sake he became poor, so that you by his poverty might become rich.' (2 Corinthians 8:9) Jesus did not need to have money to be content. He trusted his heavenly Father to meet all his needs. That would be a great lesson to learn today.—Matthew 6:25-33; Philippians 4:19.

Jesus answers their question but not in the way they expected: "Render to Caesar the things that are Caesar's, and to God the things that are God's". The denarius bore the image and inscription of Caesar. Coins that bore the image of a ruler were considered the property of that person. So, in paraphrase, Jesus is effectively saying, "This coin belongs to Caesar, give it back to him if he asks for it." In this statement, Jesus recognizes the legitimacy of the state. In this we are reminded that we have an obligation to honor the authority of the state in our lives. (Romans 13:1-7; 1 Timothy 2:1-6; 1 Peter 2:13-17) The people who lived in ancient Rome enjoyed many benefits by being in that Empire. They enjoyed peace, protection, justice, safe travel, good roads, and many other things.[66] All of that had to be funded. Therefore, Rome taxed the people. The same is true today. We enjoy certain things in our society that require revenue, such as roads, schools, police and fire protection, clean water and so on. All have to be financed by taxes. The coin bore the image of Caesar and thus it belonged to him.

However, some things do not belong to Caesar. Just as the coin bore the image of a man all mankind bear the image of God. Jesus is essentially saying, "Give Caesar his money, because it bears his image. It is his. But your *devotion* belongs to God because you bear his image. You are his." Every human being in this world was created in the image of God. (Genesis 1:26-27) Just as Caesar has the right to demand what is his, God has the right to demand what belongs to him. Therefore, we have an obligation to give God our worship, obedience, praise, love and gratitude. We owe him that for being who he is and for all that he gives to us. Have we yielded the totality of our lives to the control and dominion of the Lord? Are we giving to God the things that are his: our love, devotion, time, and labors?

The Sadducees ask about the resurrection (12:18-27)

The Sadducees were a religious movement at the time of Christ's ministry in Israel. It would be neither inaccurate nor unfair to describe them as a cult because they distorted the Scriptures and as such, they were a false religion. Little is known about the Sadducees. No documents (that are clearly

---

[66] Although subjugated peoples might well object to the statement that they enjoyed peace! Justice was denied to Jesus and many other believers who died at the behest of this evil empire.

Sadducean) have been preserved. At the time of Christ they were small in number but exerted influence politically and religiously. They represented the urban, wealthy, sophisticated and aristocratic class, based in Jerusalem. When Jerusalem was destroyed in AD 70 they disappeared from history. Mark identifies them as those 'who say that there is no resurrection.' (v.18) They held this position because they accepted as Scripture primarily the first five books of the Old Testament. Thus, they rejected all beliefs and practices not found there. Since they claimed to be unable to find clear teaching about the resurrection in the books of Moses, they rejected the doctrine. This set them against the Pharisees who considered the oral tradition as authoritative as the written Scriptures.

They address Jesus as "Teacher" but they had no intention of learning from him. The case cited arose out of a provision in the Mosaic Law. (Deuteronomy 25:5-6) This provision required that if a man died without children his brother had to marry his widow. The purpose of the law was to protect the widow and guarantee the continuance of the family line. The Sadducees present a hypothetical case in which a woman married seven brothers in succession who all died childless. In the resurrection whose wife would she be? The case is so ludicrous it may well have been a Sadducean joke that poked fun at the Pharisees belief in the resurrection.

In his answer, Jesus accused the Sadducees of ignorance of the Scriptures and the power of God. In heaven marriage will not exist as it does in this world but all life will be like that of the angels. It will be characterized by service for God and fellowship with God. The mention of angels here is significant because the Sadducees did not believe in angels as Scripture elsewhere affirms: 'For the Sadducees say that there is no resurrection, nor angel, nor spirit, but the Pharisees acknowledge them all.' (Acts 23:8)[67] Therefore, Jesus is correcting that theological error as well. In addition, since in heaven there will be no more death, the need for marriage and the propagation of the human race will not exist. Jesus then focused on the cause of their erroneous thinking, identifying it as ignorance of the teaching of the Old Testament. He directed them back to the story of Moses and his encounter with God at the burning bush (Exodus 3-4). Four times in the passage God says: "I am the God of your father, the God of Abraham, the God of Isaac, and the God of Jacob." (Exodus 3:6, 14-16; 4:5) This was a part of the Old Testament Scriptures accepted as authoritative by the Sadducees. Abraham, Isaac and Jacob had long since died when God said this at the burning bush. God did not say "I was" but "I am". The present tense indicating that they are very much alive! Jesus says, "He is not God of the dead, but of the living." (v.27) and concludes by saying, "You are quite wrong." (v.27) He did not say, "You believe part of the Scripture, that's okay."

This is not the kind of language that is politically correct. Jesus would not fit in with the inter-faith agenda that emphasizes commonalities and ignores differences. Virtually every culture that has ever existed possesses some type of belief in life after death. The ancient Egyptian *Book of the Dead* is full of tales of life after death. The tomb of Pharaoh Cheops, who died about five-thousand years ago, contained a solar boat that was designed to carry him through the heavens in eternity. Ancient Greeks were often buried with a coin in their mouths to pay their fare to cross the River Styx into the land of the dead. Some Native Americans were buried with their bows, arrows and ponies, so they would be ready to hunt when they arrived at the happy hunting

---

[67] This is extraordinary in light of the appearance of angels in Genesis, one posted with a flaming sword at the entrance to Eden and the mention of angel's intimacy with women in Genesis chapter 6.

ground. The ancient Vikings believed in a place called Valhalla where they believed they would fight all day. The dead would be raised and the wounded healed every evening. Then they would feast and drink the night away, then go out to fight again. Muslims look forward to their version of heaven where every sensual, physical pleasure can be indulged throughout eternity. In our own era, nearly all non-Christian cults and religions hold to some view of life after death. Even some who have refused to believe in Jesus for salvation have felt a sense of eternity. God has put that sense of eternity into people's hearts.

The ancient Jews were no exception. They also believed in life after death. The Talmud, which contained their written and oral traditions, is filled with references to life after death. That is the issue in these verses. When the Pharisees and the Herodians failed to trap Jesus in his words, another group of religious Jews thought they would try it. The Sadducees wanted to discredit Jesus with the people. They were a minority sect among the Jews. They were few in number but a powerful and influential Jewish group. They controlled all the buying and selling that went on at the temple. Thus, they were angry with Jesus because he had interrupted their business enterprise when he cleansed the temple. (Mark 11:12-19) The Sadducees also controlled the priesthood. Not all priests were Sadducees but all Sadducees were priests. All the high priests and chief priests were Sadducees. The Sadducees also formed a majority of the Sanhedrin (the Jewish Supreme Court). They, along with the Pharisees and the Herodians, hated Jesus.

The Sadducees were extreme literalists in their interpretation of Scripture. All they accepted as truly authoritative was the Pentateuch (the five books of Moses: Genesis, Exodus, Leviticus, Numbers and Deuteronomy). They believed that one could not base doctrine on what the prophets or the other Old Testament writers said. They denied all things supernatural. They believed in the existence of God, but they rejected everything else that was of a supernatural nature. They did not believe in demons, angels or the devil, they did not believe in miracles.[68] They did not believe in heaven, hell or a future judgment. They did not believe in life after death, nor did they believe in the resurrection of the dead. They could not find these doctrines in their reading of the Pentateuch, so they rejected them out of hand. Because they did not believe in life after death, a resurrection or a future judgment, they tended to live for the moment. They lived their lives for power and profit.

These men appeal to Moses, the great lawgiver and spokesman for God universally respected by all Jews. Their aim is to embarrass and discredit Jesus as they present him with this puzzle. So they present this hypothetical case and refer to the law in Deuteronomy. They were probably trying to mock Jesus. They thought their question revealed the absolute absurdity of the resurrection. Jesus confronted them head on by accusing them of error. Jesus points out that they were ignorant of God's Word. If they had accepted the whole counsel of God's Word they would have read passages about the resurrection (Job 19:25-27; Isaiah 26:19. Daniel 12:2) The truth of the resurrection is contained in the Old Testament.

These men were like so many in our day. They knew just enough of the Bible to be dangerous. They went about saying: "The Scriptures say this and that" but they were wrong about what they believed it said. They were ignorant of God's power in spite of its obvious manifestations in the Pentateuch (Exodus). God created the universe out of nothing. God formed Adam out of the dust of the earth. God is all-powerful. There is nothing beyond the realm of possibility with him (Ephesians 3:20). Jesus corrects the errors

---

[68] The miracles recounted in, for example, Exodus, such as the parting of the Red Sea and the feeding with manna, were understood by the Sadducees as explicable as extraordinary but natural phenomena.

in their belief system. Jesus refers to the nature of heavenly relationships. While the relationship of marriage is a wonderful and divinely ordained institution, it is an earthly (temporary) institution. Marriage was designed for companionship (Genesis 2:18), continuation of the species (Genesis 1:22) and the fulfillment of legitimate sexual needs. (1 Corinthians 7:2) When we get to heaven, we will be like the angels in the sense that we will be spiritual beings that will have no need for the physical necessities of this earthly life. Much of the nature of our existence in heaven will remain a mystery until we arrive there. In heaven, like the angels, we will be deathless, sinless, glorified and eternal. But, unlike the angels, we will be like Jesus.–1 John 3:2.

The Sadducees came to Jesus talking about Moses, so Jesus turns to Moses to answer their question. This is what the disciple of Christ needs to do when confronted with hostile questions which are intended to ridicule and undermine the believer. Many people today are ignorant of the teaching of Scripture (like the Sadducees). It is a time when cults and false religions are growing. They say the Scriptures say this and that and that it has errors, inaccuracies, contradictions and ambiguities. The only worthwhile answers to such assertions are to be found in the pages of the Bible itself, which contains no errors.[69]

The philosophy of the Sadducees could be described as one of: "Eat, drink and be merry, for tomorrow we die." This same mentality prevails today. Some people do not believe in the supernatural in this scientific age. Many people believe in a supernatural world that they just make up themselves, which has no basis in Scripture. It is the product of their imaginations. Many people today reject the authority and

---

[69] All translations are to some extent interpretations. Some are more literal (verbatim) than others that are more paraphrased (dynamic equivalents) and as such may have errors. But as originally given the Scriptures contain no errors.

relevance of Scripture. They have no hope of life after death, no hope of resurrection. They have no fear of a future judgment (or so it seems). They do not believe in hell. So they live as they please. (Romans 1:18-31) Many people misinterpret and misrepresent what Scripture actually teaches. The Christian has a duty to study the Word of God (2 Timothy 2:15) to know what to believe and why to believe it (1 Peter 3:15) so as not to be ignorant of either the Scriptures or the power of God!

The great commandment (12:28-34)

In the Jewish books of the Law (the first five books of the English Bible), there are 613 laws. Of these laws, 248 are considered positive in nature while 365 are considered negative. In other words, some laws compel people to do certain things while others forbid people from certain activities. These 613 Laws formed the basis for Jewish belief and practice. It seems that the Pharisees and scribes spent much time debating which of these 613 laws was the greatest in importance. Therefore, this lawyer's question seems to have at least been legitimate.[70] Jesus takes all 613 rules and regulations and sums them up in two great statements. In this he identifies the essence of the Law. He summarizes the Commandments in one word: "Love". This kind of love is defined and explained by the Apostle Paul in 1 Corinthians 13:1-13.

In these verses, Jesus tells us that our first and foremost duty is to love God and that this love is to engage all our faculties (emotions, intellect and will). Jesus starts by quoting

---

[70] In Mark's account the motives of the man who asked Jesus this question seem to be genuine. He seems to be seeking information but Matthew tells us that he came to 'test' (ESV) Jesus. This word can refer to one person seeking to test another in a malicious sense or it can be used to speak of finding out what another person thinks about a matter.

the *shema* (a quotation of Deuteronomy 6:4-5). This passage was quoted by every Jew every day during his prayer time, thus reminding them that there is no other God but Jehovah and that anything which occupied first place in their lives ahead of God was idolatrous. All Disciples of Christ must be certain that God occupies first place in their lives, ahead of every other love or allegiance. It is easy to profess that he is the first but actions speak louder than words!

The heart is the seat of the emotions and this implies that loving God with all the heart will mean loving the Lord intensely, passionately and without pretense. To love the Lord with all the soul means that such love should engage us at the deepest level of our being. Loving God with all the mind is a missing message today. I have heard numerous messages about loving God with all the heart but never heard anybody preach on loving God with our minds. We are to involve the intellect in our love for the Lord. This love that God desires is not mindless and empty-headed. Many people in the world think Christians are naïve and foolish people who believe in a fairytale. Sadly, many Christians have given them cause to think that. We should not love God just because the preacher says so. We should love him because of who he is and what he has done for us. Loving the Lord with all our strength speaks of the quality of the love that is expected in terms of a determined resolve and commitment. When all of these things are taken together, it is clear that the Lord is telling us to love God with sincerity, fervency, the fullest exercise of an enlightened reason and with the entire energy of our being. This is the spirit of the greatest commandment.

True love for Jesus manifests itself in every area of life. Faith cannot and should not be compartmentalized so that it is a private thing. Do we love God this way? Do we love God's people this way? Do we love the people of the world this way? We are to love his Word, his church, his work, his world.[71] The Bible states that:

1 John 4:19-21

[19] We love because he first loved us. [20] If anyone says, "I love God," and hates his brother, he is a liar; for he who does not love his brother whom he has seen cannot love God whom he has not seen. [21] And this commandment we have from him: whoever loves God must also love his brother.

Love is to be the regulating principle in the spiritual life. We should not think that loving our neighbors is secondary. This is misleading because both of these are so closely intertwined that it is difficult if not impossible to separate them. In giving us what he called the second great commandment, Jesus quoted from Leviticus 19:18. Jesus is simply telling us that we are to love others with the same love which we bestow upon ourselves. We are to place others in such a position that we are constantly looking out for their best interests, their welfare and their best good. (Philippians 2:3; Romans 12:10) This love will be made manifest in forgiving attitudes, unity, compassion and witnessing.

In the English language when I say "I am" that is the "first person." When I say "you are" that is the "second person." When I say "he/she is" that is the "third person." In English, we always have 'self' first. However, in Hebrew, it is just the opposite, where the first person is "he is"; second person is, "you are" and the third person is, "I am". Therein is contained the formula for joy in this life. If we will learn to place God in the first person, others in the second person and ourselves

---

[71] Loving the world will involve loving the people of the world and having their welfare in holistic terms (body, mind, spirit) as our concern. It will also involve loving the planet and taking an interest in the ecology of the physical creation.

in the third person, then we will have our lives in order. The true formula for joy is, **J** for Jesus, **o** for others and **y** for yourself.

Mark uses the word *agape*, which refers to a never-ending, unchanging, all-consuming love for someone. This is not the kind of feeling that appears for a time then changes or disappears. *Agape* love is forever. It is the kind of love with which God loves sinners. It is a genuine, heartfelt, all-encompassing love that cannot and will not be changed by circumstances. It is a love that loves without regard for the worth of the object being loved. This is more than simple affection or some emotional feeling. It is a decision of the will. This is the kind of love that can be seen, '...but God shows his love for us in that while we were still sinners, Christ died for us.'–Romans 5:8.

Our love for Christ is to be visible as well: "If you love me, you will keep my commandments." (John 14:15) "This is my commandment, that you love one another as I have loved you." (John15:12) How is your love life? Is our love evident in our deeds and lifestyles?

Jesus said that all the other commandments hang on these. (Matthew 22:40) If we love the Lord as we should we will not sin against him. If we love our neighbor as we should we will not offend him.[72] If we are going to fulfill this great commandment, we need to be aware that it will cost us something. If I am going to love God with all my heart, soul, mind and strength, then it is going to mean that I am going to have to place his will ahead of mine. It means that I may have to say "no" to some things that I might want to do. It means that I am going to have to seek the Lord's will and make it paramount in my life.

The 613 commands were then subdivided into two groups: heavy and light. The problem was that the scribes

---

[72] See 1 John 1:8-9.

could not agree on which commands were heavy (more binding) and which were light (less binding). Some people still try to play with the Word of God. They love to argue about the Bible. They love to devise riddles and puzzles based on the Bible. They try to figure out what they can and can't get away with. Some people are always looking for a loophole. In these verses, Jesus tells us how to honor the whole law. We need to be reminded that according to the law the only way anyone will ever see God is to perfectly keep every command, both positive and negative. One slip, one broken commandment, and we are as guilty in God's eyes as if we had broken every Law of God. (James 2:10; Galatians 3:10) Jesus said that we have to be more righteous than the cleanest most religious men living if we want to go to heaven. (Matthew 5:20) The truth is, we are all guilty in the eyes of God.—Romans 3:10-23; Romans 5:12.

We are not inherently good by nature and we cannot produce anything good (Isaiah 64:6; Romans 3:12). The only hope we have of being accepted by God is for his perfect righteousness to be given to us. When we come to Jesus by faith, we are given the imputed righteousness of the Lord Jesus Christ. (Romans 4:24-25) When we believe in Jesus, we are regarded by God as having kept the full letter of the Law. He sees us as righteous (Romans 10:4) even though we are still sinners. This is possible because Jesus perfectly kept the Law of God. When he died, he died as an innocent man dying for guilty sinners. (2 Corinthians 5:21) Those who trust him by faith are given his righteousness.

The great transaction

Salvation is not a matter of who can keep the Law. Salvation is simply a matter of who believes in Jesus. (John 14:6; 1 John 5:12) To believe in him means to trust in his atoning sacrifice for salvation. The *shema* (quoted by Jesus) was written on small strips of paper and placed in leather boxes called 'phylacteries'. These leather boxes were worn on the forearms and on the foreheads (Matthew 23:6). This was an effort to literally fulfill the command of Deuteronomy 6:8, where the Lord said: "You shall bind them as a sign on your hand, and they shall be as frontlets between your eyes." Orthodox Jews around the world today still use these phylacteries. The *shema* was also written down and placed in a small round box called a *mezuzah* and placed on all the doors in the home. This served to remind the Jews of God in their going out and coming in. Most orthodox Jews still use the *mezuzah* today. This is an effort to fulfill the command of Deuteronomy 6:9: "You shall write them on the doorposts of your house and on your gates." The *shema* can be found in Deuteronomy 6:4-9; 11:13-21 and Numbers 15:37-41. It always began with an affirmation of the existence of God and a reminder that he alone is God. Thus, Jesus began in the traditional way by saying: "Hear, O Israel: the Lord our God, the Lord is one." Then Jesus took all 613 commands in the Law and condensed them into two commandments. We are to love (*agape*) in an intentional and intelligent way, showing commitment. In this sense, it is a reflection of the love God has for us. Although we can never attain such pure love, which is unconditional, perfect, eternal and changeless, we are nevertheless called to strive toward such a standard and to be imitators of Christ.

Thus the love to which we are called is utterly unselfish. It is love that gives with the expectation of nothing in return. This is the kind of love that caused Jesus to go to the cross and to give his life for us. (Romans 5:8) Therefore, we are to love the Lord wholeheartedly and sacrificially. The word 'Lord' used here is *kurios*. It speaks of one who owns another, a master. We cannot truly love the Lord until we see him as Lord. Thus, Lord is not just a title. Rather it is a title that speaks of his status. He is the superior and we are the subordinates. His title speaks of his function, to rule. We do not truly love him until we have surrendered all to him and acknowledged that he is our master. This is a call for a life of absolute submission and surrender.—Romans 12:1; Matthew 16:24.

The very core of our being should throb with love for the Lord. When the Lord possesses a person, he also possesses all that person has. The Jews quoted the *shema* twice a day. In doing this they thought they were expressing their love for the Lord. For most of them, it was merely an empty ritual, much as church is for many people.

The second commandment builds on the first. The scribe had not asked about anything beyond the first commandment. Jesus goes a step farther to teach the truth that genuine love for God also manifests itself in love for one's fellow man. Who is my neighbor? Jesus answered this question in the Parable of the Good Samaritan (Luke 10:30-37). According to Jesus, my neighbor is anyone who wears a suit of skin, irrespective of the color of that skin. We are to love our neighbor as ourselves. When self is hungry, we find it something to eat. When self is thirsty, we find it something to drink. When self gets sick, we get self some medical treatment. In other words, we always seek to meet the needs that pertain to self. We are to love those around us with the same kind of love. This does not mean that we love them with a mere sentimental or emotional love. No, we are to love them with a love that is practical. We are to do more than talk about love, we are to demonstrate genuine love to those who live around us. (James 2:16; 1 John 3:17-18) If we loved like this, there would be no problems in the church, the home or the community! Love would solve the problems and meet the needs that exist all around us.

Jesus put these two commandments together to give a summary of the law. If we loved God like he commanded us to, we would never break the first four of the Ten Commandments. If we loved our neighbor, as we should, we would never break the other six commandments. Sadly, our ability to love like that is imperfect. Jesus stated that the whole Old Testament could be summarized in these two commands. (Matthew 22:41) Getting those two things, right would change our churches, our homes, our communities and our world.

The law of God is more than a religious system to follow. It is essentially spiritual. The law exists to draw people to a faith relationship with God. (Galatians 3:24) This is a truth that eludes many people. God is not reached through empty worship and external rituals. External religion and its rituals will never be enough to save the soul. Right relationship is far more important than religion. Religious works will not save the soul. (Titus 3:5) It is grace that saves the soul.–Ephesians 2:8-9.

Jesus said to this scribe, "You are not far from the kingdom of God." What does Jesus mean? He means that this man was close, but he still had a distance to go. He was standing at the door of salvation and was looking in on the things of God, but he had yet to take the step of faith across the threshold. We need to understand the implications of this statement. Jesus was speaking to a decent, religious man. This was a man who kept the Law to the best of his ability. It is possible for a person to have a religious upbringing and still be lost. It is possible to know the truth and still be lost. It is possible to be within an inch of heaven and still die and go to hell. How is your relationship with God? If it is all it should be, you love him with all your heart, soul, mind and strength and you love others as you love yourself. Is that true about you? Or do you need to make improvements in that area of your life?

Whose son is the Christ? (12:35-37)

This is about the identity of Jesus. He is in the temple teaching the Word of God. The Pharisees, Sadducees and scribes are still looking for a way to discredit Jesus in the eyes of the people and the Roman authorities. We have seen how these groups questioned Jesus. Their questions were designed to trap him and undermine his authority. But Jesus answered well and outsmarted these deceitful and dangerous people. He gave his enemies no legitimate cause to bring a charge against him. All along Jesus had been on the defensive as he responded to their questions. Now Jesus goes on the offensive. He takes the initiative. The question he asked the scribes and Pharisees goes to the heart of what they believe about the identity of Christ. This is a relevant and important question today.

Jesus countered every attack his enemies used against him. He answered their question about paying tribute money to Caesar (12:13-17), the resurrection and the nature of life in heaven (12:18-27) and which commandment in the Law was the greatest. (12:28-34) Each time Jesus was asked questions that were designed to make him look foolish in the eyes of the people. Every question they asked was an attempt to prove his ignorance of the Word of God. They tried their best to unmask Jesus and prove that he was an imposter.

Now Jesus asks in what sense the Messiah was the Son of David. He did not receive an answer. It is not clear if Jesus waited for an answer but it is likely that there was some silent pause. Whether that silence was the result of ignorance, fear, inability or unwillingness to answer is not certain. The fact remains that Jesus did not receive an answer. Therefore, the Lord answered his own question and in doing so confirms the messianic usage of this psalm. David called the Messiah "My Lord". How could he be both David's son and David's Lord? The Messiah, though David's descendant is also the Son of God and therefore, senior in rank and authority.

I can imagine the crowds enjoying Jesus running rings around the scribes. He would have been perceived as the underdog in these battles. The crowds usually love the underdog. Not all scribes were frauds but many used their position and influence in a greedy and unscrupulous manner. They liked being addressed by honorific titles (rabbi and master). In the synagogue, they sat in a prominent position on a bench in front of the arc that contained the sacred scrolls. Jesus condemned them for seeking honor for themselves instead of God, whom they professed to serve. He also criticized them for their long prayers and hypocrisy. Scribes were not allowed to be paid and so they depended on the gifts of patrons. The more unscrupulous among them preyed on widows.

Jesus had answered all their questions. (12:34) Now he had a question for them. That question was meant to focus their attention on the person of the Messiah. When Jesus responded to the scribe who asked him the question about the greatest of the commandments, he complimented the man on his understanding. Then, Jesus said, "You are not far from the kingdom of God." Every scribe and Pharisee in the crowd must have thought, "I believe that love for God and for one's fellow man is the greatest demonstration of faith and obedience possible, so what more could I possibly need to be saved?" Christ's question is designed to address this issue. Jesus asked them, "How can the scribes say that the Christ is the son of David?" Every Jew believed that the Messiah would be a physical descendant of King David. They believed that the Christ would be a great political and military leader who would deliver Israel from those who oppressed them. They believed that the Christ would be a great king. The Jews were looking for a human being. Jesus is about to show them that the Messiah will be human but he will also be God.

He confronts them about their beliefs concerning the nature and identity of the Messiah. Many people in the Western world are like the scribes and the Pharisees. They know the Bible stories about Jesus. They love the image of that baby in his manger. They have heard about Jesus feeding multitudes, healing the sick, preaching sermons, raising the dead and walking on water. They know the story of the cross and the resurrection. However, many people in our culture cannot grasp the truth that Jesus Christ is more than a baby in a manger, or a man who was crucified. They cannot seem to grasp the truth that he is God in human flesh. People will go so far, but they often will not go far enough. Like that scribe, some people are "not far from the kingdom of God." They are on the threshold of belief. But being not far means you are lost. It is like being nearly saved! I would prefer to be nearly drowned than nearly saved! Wouldn't you? Not far is not where a person needs to remain. A person should not remain undecided about the identity of Jesus. A person should not remain on the threshold of faith. We need to come to Jesus Christ and call on him for salvation.

He is the door that leads to eternal life (John 10:9). With him, you are saved; without him you are lost (1 John 5:12). This is an unpalatable truth. Many are willing to believe Jesus was a great teacher, a prophet, a good man, but stop short of believing in his divine identity. They will not accept his unique and universal claims. This has serious consequences.

As Jesus confronts these men, he asks them about Psalm 110:1. That verse was acknowledged by all Jews to be a reference to the coming Messiah. Jesus points out that a careful reading of that verse reveals the truth that the Messiah will be more than a man. The first "Lord", in Psalm 110:1, is the Hebrew word *Yahweh*. The second "Lord" in that verse is the Hebrew word *Adonai*. The idea in this verse is that "the Lord (*Yahweh*) said to my (David's) Lord (*Adonai*)..." In other words, David addresses the Messiah as his Lord. The implication is clear. The Messiah is to be a man, but he will be more than a man. He is to be God as well. Jesus is very clearly declaring the deity of the Messiah. David was speaking under the inspiration of the Holy Spirit: 'The LORD says to my Lord, "Sit at my right hand, until I make your enemies your footstool."'

He placed the Messiah in a position of authority that was co-equal with Almighty God. The word "sit" in that verse speaks of a continuous sitting. The Messiah has a place of equal exaltation with God. (Philippians 2:9-11) The Messiah must be God because he will be in a position of absolute equality with God in his honor, power and glory. The clear implication of this can be seen in what Jesus said next: "David himself calls him Lord. So how is he his son?" In that, society a father would never call his son Lord! A father never rendered that kind of honor to a child. Children were considered subordinate and never superior to their fathers. Yet, David looks at the one who is to be his son and David calls him Lord. This is a declaration that the Messiah is to be more than a man. He is to be God and man. When the Jews heard this, they were dumbfounded. They had no answer. This unlearned carpenter had put them to shame in the very area where they were supposed to be the experts. Jesus had interpreted the Scriptures in an accurate, clear way that they could not refute.

They did not believe Jesus was the Messiah. But Jesus had proven his identity time and again. His place of birth fulfilled prophecy. His triumphal entry into Jerusalem fulfilled prophecy (in detail) concerning the Messiah. He arrived in the precise way that the prophet Zechariah said the Messiah would come. (Zechariah 9:9) His words, works and wisdom proved his identity. He fulfilled every Old Testament prophecy that predicted what the Messiah would do when he came. (Isaiah 29:18-19; 35:3-6; 61:1-2) He healed the sick, raised the dead, forgave sins, walked on water, calmed a storm and cast out demons. The Messiah was to be the Son of David. (2 Samuel 7:8-16; Isaiah 9:7; Jeremiah 23:5) According to the genealogies (Matthew and Luke) Jesus was a direct descendant of David. On many occasions, Jesus was called "Son of David."

Jesus was a man. He had a human mother. (Luke 1:31; Galatians 4:4) He had a human body, soul, and spirit. (Matt. 26:12; 38; Luke 23:46)[73] He had flesh and blood. (Hebrews 2:14). He grew (Luke 2:52) He asked questions (Luke 2:46) and increased in wisdom. (Luke 2:52) He prayed. (Mark 1:35; Luke 11:1) He was tempted. (Matthew 4:1; Hebrews 2:18; 4:15) He learned obedience. (Hebrews 5:8) He hungered (Matthew 4:2; 21:18) and thirsted. (John 4:7; 19:28) He was weary (John 4:6) and slept. (Matthew 8:24; Mark 10:21) He had compassion. (Matthew 9:36) He was angered and grieved. (Mark 3:5) He wept. (John 11:35; Luke 19:41) He was troubled. (John 11:33; 12:27; 13:21; Mark 14:33-34) He suffered (1 Peter 4:1) and bled. (John 19:34) He died (Matthew 27:50; 1 Corinthians 15:3) and was buried.– Matthew 27:59-60.

Jesus was also God. When Jesus came into this world, he was God born as a male child. That is the clear teaching of the Word of God. (John 1:1; 14; Philippians 2:5-8) The evidence from his life proves this too. He is omnipresent. (Matthew 18:20; 28:20) He is omnipotent. (Matthew 28:18; Hebrews 1:3) He has authority over disease (Matthew 4:23), over Satan (Matthew 4:10; John 12:31; Hebrews 2:14), over demons (Matthew 8:16), over men (John 17:2), over nature (Matt. 8:26-27), over sin (1 John 3:5), over the Sabbath. (Matthew 12:8) He has authority over death itself. That is over both physical death (John 5:28-29) and spiritual death. (John 5:24; Hebrews 2:15) He knew the history of the Samaritan woman. (John 4:29) He knew what the scribes and Pharisees were thinking. (Matthew 9:3-4; 12:25) He knew the true nature of Judas.–John 6:70; 13:11.

---

[73] The soul is the essence of the human being, it is who we are. The spirit is that aspect of the human being that connects with God.

Jesus receives worship from the angels (Hebrews 1:6), from the magi (Matthew 2:11), from the apostle Thomas. (John 20:28) He forgives sin. (Mark 2:5; John 8:24) He possesses all authority. (Matthew 7:29) This was reflected in his teaching, which was more than a confident style. He is the source of life itself. (John 1:4; John 5:26) He is creator of all things. (John 1:3; Colossians 1:16; Hebrews 1:2) He is preserver of all things. (Colossians 1:17; Hebrews 1:3) He receives our prayers. (Acts 7:59) He is the final judge (Matthew 25:31-32; John 5:22, 27; Acts 17:31). He is both the Lord of Glory and King of kings—Revelation 19:16.

Jesus proved his identity. Yet many Jews refused to accept him. They refused to acknowledge him as their Messiah. (John 1:11, Luke 19:14; John 19:15) Israel had all the evidence they needed to believe in Jesus. They had all the Old Testament prophecies that he had fulfilled to the letter. They had the proof in the temple records that Jesus was a descendant of King David. They had the evidence of changed lives all around them. There were people who had been sick that were now well. Blind people could see. Deaf people could hear. There were demoniacs who had been delivered. And, most amazing of all, there were a few people walking around that used to be dead! The Jews ignored that evidence

We have far more evidence than they had. We have a completed Bible (Old and the New Testaments). We can see where prophecies were made and fulfilled. We too can look around us and we can see lives changed by the amazing grace of God. We have every reason to believe that he is who he claims to be. Believe it and be bold about it in bearing true testimony to him. Luke speaks of: 'the church of God, which he obtained with his own blood.' (Acts 20:28)[74] This verse nails his deity to the cross.

---

[74] For additional information, Christian Publishing House would offer the following article.

The widow's offering (12:41-44)

This is not a parable. This is a real person observed by Jesus and commended by him. The liberal giving of this woman contrasts with the greed of the teachers who "devour widow's houses." She gives all for the Lord as the Lord gave all for us. He gives to us with an open hand, an abundance of grace, mercy and kindness. He spared not his only Son. The setting is the court of women where both men and women were allowed to gather. This is where the temple treasury was located. Jesus sat down on a bench where he could watch people bring their offerings. There were thirteen trumpet-shaped brass chests used for that purpose. It was not the rich with their large gifts which caught the Lord's attention but this poor widow. Widows were poor and vulnerable and exploited by many unscrupulous scribes. She donated two of the smallest coins in circulation in Palestine at that time. The widow's offering was greater in proportion as well as the spirit in which she gave. Jesus has something to say about the difference between superficial giving and sacrificial giving.

It is one thing to give in a formal manner out of a sense of obligation or duty but it is another thing entirely to give gladly. Giving should not be miserly, half-hearted or begrudging. Giving is an outward expression of inner faith. That is what giving to the work of the Lord is – an acknowledgement that all we have has come from his hand. Those who understand the value of the work of God will give generously. God's people should always be prepared to give liberally, voluntarily and cheerfully. Each of these qualities should feature in every gift to God. We may volunteer to give, yet not be cheerful about it. When God is our vision everything else pales into insignificance.

Acts 20:28—A Worthy Translation is Faithful
http://www.christianpublishers.org/translation-acts-20-28

The apostle Paul states clearly how God views giving:

2 Corinthians 9:6-7

[6] ... whoever sows sparingly will also reap sparingly, and whoever sows bountifully will also reap bountifully. [7] Each one must give as he has decided in his heart, not reluctantly or under compulsion, for God loves a cheerful giver.

Christians are exhorted to open-handed giving. There should be no compulsion from the church and there should be no reluctance from us when it comes to giving. It is one thing to desire God's work to be done and even to pray fervently to that end but quite another thing to contribute financially to ensure that vision becomes a reality. It is the duty of all believers to support the work of the Lord. However, a word of caution is needed here. The believer must pray, pay and play! Making a financial contribution must not become a salve to our consciences. In giving we may be excusing ourselves from going – from playing our part in the work of God. That would be a bit like the wealthy being exempt from conscription in time of war. That may have been the case in some democracies but it has no place in the divine plan.

In the church today, some people have substantial resources while others have very little. It is possible for wealthy people to be either generous or mean with what they have. The less well off, however, are not invariably generous by nature. A person of limited means may be generous or have a miserly attitude. Meanness is probably less obvious in the case of the poorer person. It is wrong to make a virtue out of either poverty or wealth.

The story of the widow's offering draws attention to something important in relation to giving. Jesus commends what some might condemn as foolish. She gave all she possessed. We might think that unless such a person develops a more sensible approach to money-management they will be trapped in poverty forever. But that is not what the Lord says. Jesus said, "Truly, I say to you". Jesus always told the truth, but whenever he uses this phrase, he is asking his disciples (then and now) to pay particular attention to the truth being taught. What exactly is the truth being emphasized here? I believe that what Jesus wants us to get hold of is this — there is a vast difference between superficial and sacrificial giving. This widow did not give from a surplus. There is nothing balanced or budgeted about her giving. It is not affordable. In fact one could say it appears reckless. But it reflects an attitude of total love and deep faith. There was nothing shallow or partial in the way she gave.

Giving must never be tokenism dressed up as thanks. It is a sad fact of life that wealth is a serious obstacle to true spirituality. Whether wealth is amassed through honest or dishonest means, one often finds that making money is the chief aim of the wealthy person. It is something to which he may have dedicated his life — a single-minded ambition, a number-one priority. Such self-made men and women are often proud and self-sufficient. They are confident in their own resources and, sadly, arrogant. These people are often the chiefs and bosses of their own commercial empires. They find it difficult to be humble. In the church, they sometimes find it difficult to follow, because they are not used to being led. Of course the Holy Spirit can transform such people into what all of us should be — generous to those in need and willing and joyful supporters of the Lord's work. A wealthy believer can make a significant contribution to the work of the local church. However, even in doing this there is a danger that he sees himself as the paymaster and expects to be in charge. However, the idea that 'he who pays the piper calls the tune' has no place in the church of Christ.

It should be remembered that God does not need our money to accomplish his purposes. Rather, he desires our cheerful willingness to give sacrificially rather than superficially. This is the biblical perspective, which needs to be preached without fear or favor. Sometimes those who can afford to contribute to a particular need say things like: "I don't want to encourage idleness" or "I wouldn't like to create false expectations." They might argue that money won't make any real difference and what is really required is better financial management and budgeting skills. On the face of it this kind of reasoning makes sense because, there is a good deal of truth in it. However, we need to be more compassionate than critical. Those who value money more than anything else are reluctant to part with it. We can rationalize our rationing but God expects us to give generously.

In the temple, Jesus observed what people were giving and he still does. He sees the motives, the excuses and the sacrifice. One very good reason for showing generosity is that God himself is generous by nature. If we desire to be truly like him, then we should not neglect to be generous. God's generosity is most evident in his willingness to cancel our great debt of sin. It is in the context of our own giving that Paul writes, 'For you know the grace of our Lord Jesus Christ, that though he was rich, yet for your sake he became poor, so that you by his poverty might become rich' (2 Corinthians 8:9). The ledger has been balanced because he paid the price in full.

Luke records the thinking of Jesus on this issue: "...give, and it will be given to you. Good measure, pressed down, shaken together, running over, will be put into your lap. For with the measure you use it will be measured back to you" (Luke 6:38). He pours a quart into a pint pot. Paul prays that the Ephesians '...may be filled with all the fullness of God' (Ephesians 3:19). Inevitably, such filling will result in overflowing.

The rich young ruler had done everything required in the law, but he was unwilling to sell all that he had and give it to the poor (Matthew 19:16-22). Ultimately, money meant more to him than obedience to the Master. Jesus could read his heart and knew how to touch the central issue. Some might suggest that Jesus' demands are unreasonable and that few of us would be prepared to follow him on these terms. But unless we are prepared to do whatever Christ asks of us we cannot count ourselves as his disciples at all. When we consider the fact that the Lord loved us and spared not his only Son how can we ever give too much? The tithe seems a small offering of thanks.

The Love of God

Could we with ink the ocean fill,
And were the skies of parchment made,
Were every stalk on earth a quill,
And every man a scribe by trade;
To write the love of God above
Would drain the ocean dry;
Nor could the scroll contain the whole,
Though stretched from sky to sky.[75]

Money is a sensitive subject. Money is essential. We depend upon it to provide the necessities of life. Money is important but the world places too much emphasis on it. Money can be used for good – to provide for the needs of the kingdom of God but it can be destructive. Paul told Timothy that: 'the love of money is a root of all kinds of evils' (1 Timothy 6:10). The writer to the Hebrews said: 'Keep your life free from love of money, and be content with what you have.'–Hebrews 13:5.

Money must be used properly. Christians have a responsibility to use the resources given to them by God to

---

[75] Frederick M. Lehman, 1917. This third verse is by Rabbi Mayer, 1096, which was anonymously altered. It was was penciled on the wall of a room in an insane asylum by a patient. The profound lines were discovered when they laid him in his coffin.

further God's kingdom upon the earth. When God's people returned from seventy years of exile in Babylon they rebuilt the temple under the leadership of Ezra and Nehemiah:

Ezra 2:68-69

[68] Some of the heads of families, when they came to the house of the Lord that is in Jerusalem, made freewill offerings for the house of God, to erect it on its site. [69] According to their ability they gave to the treasury of the work ...

We too have been delivered from captivity and we have a duty and the privilege of building for God. When we invest our money in the kingdom of God, we also place our hearts there. When we invest our finances in the world, we tie our affections to things below and not things above. Jesus said:

Matthew 6:19-24

[19] "Do not lay up for yourselves treasures on earth, where moth and rust destroy and where thieves break in and steal, [20] but lay up for yourselves treasures in heaven, where neither moth nor rust destroys and where thieves do not break in and steal. [21] For where your treasure is, there your heart will be also. ...

[24] "No one can serve two masters, for either he will hate the one and love the other, or he will be devoted to the one and despise the other. You cannot serve God and money.

Money can lead to terrible bondage: 'The rich rules over the poor, and the borrower is the slave of the lender.' (Proverbs 22:7) If we allow ourselves to fall into the slavery of debt, we are hindering our ability to follow the Lord properly. Often, our indebtedness prevents us from serving the Lord as he would have us to. Money should be used to bring glory to God. When money is properly used to glorify the Lord, then the Lord will prove his power to provide for his people:

Bring the full tithe into the storehouse...And thereby put me to the test, says the LORD of hosts, if I will not open the windows of heaven for you and pour down for you a blessing until there is no more need (Malachi 3:8-11).

When God is denied this opportunity then the child of God has forfeited a great blessing.

Jesus notices our giving. Giving is a spiritual act. In this passage about the widow's offering Jesus observed people contributing their money to the temple treasury. Jesus is still watching people give. What would he say about your giving? There are sins of commission and sins of omission. Sin is not just the bad things we do it is also the good things we fail to do: 'So whoever knows the right thing to do and fails to do it, for him it is sin.'–James 4:17.

Abram commenced tithing when he gave Melchizedeck (priest/king) a tenth of everything. Jacob continued it. Jacob resolved to give a tithe (a tenth): "And of all that you give me I will give a full tenth to you." (Genesis 28:22) Malachi commanded it: "Bring the full tithe into the storehouse, that there may be food in my house. And thereby put me to the test", says the LORD of hosts, "if I will not open the windows of heaven for you and pour down for you a blessing until there is no more need." (Malachi 3:10) Jesus condoned it: "Woe to you, scribes and Pharisees, hypocrites! For you tithe mint and dill and cumin, and have neglected the weightier matters of the law: justice and mercy and faithfulness. These you ought to have done, without neglecting the others." (Matthew 23:23) Therefore, tithing was commenced by Abram, continued by Jacob, commanded by Malachi and condoned by Christ. It was also commended by Paul: 'On the first day of every week, each of you is to put something aside and store it up, as he may prosper, so that there will be no collecting when I come.'–1 Corinthians16:2.

It is clear from this that some form of continuous giving applies to Christians. This is one of the easiest places to neglect our duty but it is also one of the most practical areas to prove our faith. We cannot fail to notice the promise of God in Malachi to those who give to God. We cannot fail to notice how God rewarded Jacob, "...for with only my staff I crossed this Jordan, and now I have become two camps." (Genesis 32:10) There is an inescapable pattern here. However, many preachers are afraid to preach it because of some who have distorted the truth in what has come to be known as, 'the prosperity gospel.'

Jesus condemned the superficial giving of some when he commended the sacrificial giving of the widow's offering. We do not give in order to gain. We do not give to God because he is needy. We give in thankfulness for his faithfulness.

There are three basic reasons why people do not tithe. Some people simply do not understand the place giving holds in the lives of believers. Many simply refuse to obey the Lord. Some people do not give even though they know they should. God has a rightful claim to our resources. All that we have belongs to God. It is not just ten-percent that belongs to God it is one-hundred-percent. We need to examine ourselves about the matter, the manner and the measure of our giving.

As the metal coins were cast into these trumpets, they made a loud noise and the more money that was cast in, the louder the sound. Those who wanted to put on a show could easily do so. This was a practice that was condemned by Jesus:

Matthew 6:2

2 "Thus, when you give to the needy, sound no trumpet before you, as the hypocrites do in the synagogues and in the streets, that they may be praised by others. Truly, I say to you, they have received their reward.

When the widow gave her two small coins, they sound small compared to the offerings of the rich. But this widow's testimony still stands as a great example of sacrificial giving. The tithe is a fair way of giving proportionately. We do not all give the same sum of money but the same percentage and the Lord sanctifies it: "Every tithe of the land, whether of the seed of the land or of the fruit of the trees, is the LORD's; it is holy to the LORD."—Leviticus 27:30.

Tithing did not originate with the Law. Abel brought the Lord the first-fruits of his flocks. (Genesis 4:4) Four-hundred-and-thirty years before the Law was given Abraham offered the Lord a tithe of all his increase. (Genesis 14:20) We are not to give only when we have a windfall or some excess or unexpected bonanza. We are not to give only out of guilt --- out of conviction, yes! People who give out of a sense of guilt stop doing so when the feeling of guilt stops. If you are wondering whether the tithe (ten percent) refers to gross pay (before tax and other deductions) or net pay (after tax and other deductions) I cannot help you there. Ask the Lord about it.

We are to give of our first-fruits. When we make the first part holy, then the rest becomes holy as well: 'If the dough offered as firstfruits is holy, so is the whole lump, and if the root is holy, so are the branches' (Romans 11:16). When we tithe we are declaring that everything else belongs to the Lord as well. We are to consider not just the matter of giving (i.e. the fact that we should give) we are also to consider the manner of our giving (i.e. cheerfully). However, we must also consider our motives.

The trumpets must have sounded very impressive when a large donation was given. They impressed men but the widow's offering impressed God. It is not the sum of money that makes the offering worthy. It is the heart of the giver. We should give from thankful hearts. We should give cheerfully: 'God loves a cheerful giver' (2 Corinthians 9:7).

We should give liberally. We are not to be stingy when it comes to giving to the Lord's work or his people. God blesses us in proportion to the level of our giving. I know that might sound controversial but '...whoever sows sparingly will also reap sparingly, and whoever sows bountifully will also reap bountifully' (2 Corinthians 9:6). The context of this verse is financial giving. Remember Jesus said: "...give, and it will be given to you. Good measure, pressed down, shaken together, running over, will be put into your lap. For with the measure you use it will be measured back to you."–Luke 6:38.

There will be some who will protest that they cannot afford to give. That is not true! Regardless of what comes into your life, you can always give. We cannot afford not to give. We should give sacrificially. If you wait to start giving until you have plenty, you will face two problems. First, you'll never get to where you think you have plenty. Second, when you do have extra, it will seem like too much to give. The rich gave out of their surplus but the widow gave all that she had. That got the Lord's attention! It still does!

Chapter 13

The beginning of the end (13:1-8)

Jesus talks about the end of time and the events, which characterize the end of the world.[76] This prophecy covers a tremendous expanse of time. These verses contain prophecies that have been partially fulfilled and that will be completely fulfilled in the future. Therefore, we will be looking backwards and forwards at the same time.

The temple in Jerusalem was one of the most spectacular wonders of the ancient world. The original temple constructed by Solomon was a magnificent building that took seven years to build and at great expense. But that temple was completely destroyed by Nebuchadnezzar and the Babylonians in about 600 BC. When the Jews returned from seventy years exile in Babylon, they constructed the second temple under Ezra and Nehemiah. This temple served the Jews for nearly five-hundred years, but by the time of the New Testament, it had suffered great damage due to the passage of time.

When King Herod assumed the throne in Israel, he wanted to gain favor with the Jews. Therefore, he offered to rebuild their temple. They accepted and in 18 BC, the work began. By the time of Jesus, the work had been underway some forty-six years (John 2:20) and would continue for

---

[76] The passage of Scripture is known as The Olivet Discourse. It is also recorded in Matthew 24-25 and in Luke 21.

another twenty years.⁷⁷ The temple that Jesus and the disciples visited was an amazing building. It was on Mount Moriah and literally dominated the skyline of the ancient city. The disciple who spoke called the Lord's attention to "the stones" and "the buildings." The stones that made up Herod's temple were enormous. Some were forty feet long, eighteen feet high and fifteen feet wide. They were cut by hand from pure white limestone. The doors, walls and even the floors of the temple were overlaid with pure gold. There were jewels, ornate carvings, and many awe inspiring sights which were dazzling in the sunshine.

Like every other Jew, this disciple was impressed by the Temple and calls the Lord's attention to some of its details. Jesus responds by telling him that the temple will eventually be dismantled and destroyed. This was literally fulfilled in 70 AD when the Roman general Titus and his army conquered the city. Titus ordered his men to preserve the temple, but it was gutted by a fire set by one of his soldiers. As a result, the general ordered the temple to be dismantled stone by stone to get to the gold that melted into the cracks during the fire. Today, there is not a single stone left from the great temple Herod built.⁷⁸

The disciples are baffled by what Jesus said about the destruction of the temple. Therefore, they come to him for an explanation. These men come asking the same questions people still ask about the end times (vs.5-8). Everyone wants to know *when* it will happen, and *what* will be the signs that it is here. Jesus answers their last question in these verses.

---

⁷⁷ A contemporary example is the Gaudi designed *La Sagrada Familia* basilica in Barcelona which has been under construction for many years.

⁷⁸ It is noteworthy that the Jews accepted the assistance of Herod in the construction of the temple and that this is in stark contrast to the Jews who returned from the Babylonian captivity as they refused help from those outside covenant relationship with the Lord. Thus the holy purpose of the temple was not compromised by Ezra and Nehemiah.

Later in the chapter, he will answer their first question. The first thing to note is the potential for deception. Jesus warned his disciples that they needed to be vigilant about this.

There will be false messiahs (v.6)

Acts 5:36-37 mentions two would-be messiahs that lived before the time of Jesus:

Acts 5:36-37

³⁶ For before these days Theudas rose up, claiming to be somebody, and a number of men, about four hundred, joined him. He was killed, and all who followed him were dispersed and came to nothing. ³⁷ After him Judas the Galilean rose up in the days of the census and drew away some of the people after him. He too perished, and all who followed him were scattered.

Theudas claimed that he could part the Jordan River. He deceived about four-hundred people and led them to their deaths. Another was named Judas the Galilean. He was a radical anti-Roman revolutionary and he founded the Zealot movement in Israel. One of the Lord's disciples, Simon the Zealot, was one of his followers. After the death and resurrection of Jesus, more would-be messiahs came to prominence. One was a man named Simon Bar-Kochba. He started a rebellion that lasted three years and cost thousands of lives in Israel. His revolt led to a harsh Roman crackdown that left Jerusalem in utter ruins. Others included Moses of Crete. He claimed that he would part the Mediterranean Sea and lead his followers across dry land from the island of Crete to Israel. Many leapt from the cliffs at his command and were drowned in the sea. In the 1100s a man named Moses al-Dar'i told his followers to sell all their possessions because the Messiah was coming at Passover in 1127. Passover came and went and his followers were left destitute. In 1666 a man named Sabbatai Zevi claimed to be the long-awaited messiah (to have heard the voice of God declaring that he was the son of God). He led his followers to the city of Constantinople and was arrested by the Turkish Sultan. The Sultan ordered him to either prove that he was the messiah or be executed. The would-be messiah and three-hundred families of his followers promptly converted to Islam.

In our own era, many so-called messiahs have paraded across the stage of history. Jim Jones, the founder and leader of the People's Temple, which is best known for the 1978 mass suicide of nine hundred and nine Temple members in Jonestown, Guyana along with the killings of five other people at a nearby airstrip. Over two-hundred children were murdered at Jonestown, almost all of whom were forcibly made to ingest cyanide by the elite Temple members. The incident in Guyana ranks among the largest mass suicides in history, though most likely it involved forced suicide and / or murder. It was the single greatest loss of American civilian life in a non-natural disaster until the events of September 11th, 2001.

In Waco, Texas in 1993 a cult called the 'Branch Davidian' at Mount Carmel were involved in a fifty-one day siege by the Alcohol Tobacco and Firearms bureau in the USA (ATF Bureau). Four ATF agents and eighty-two men, women and children died in a shoot-out and a fire.

As the end of time approaches, there will be more and more people claiming to be the savior of the world. The appearance of such people is merely a sign that the end is approaching.

There will be wars (v.7)

Our world has been marked by war since the beginning of time. However, Jesus said that wars and rumors of war would increase as the end of time approached. We are seeing that prove true in our day. Wars ravage our planet, even as man claims to be evolving into a more sophisticated social order.[79] We should not be dismayed by warfare because God is moving his pieces into place for the end game.

There will be constant upheaval in the world (v.8)

Jesus says that there will be strife among the nations. The sovereign God is preparing the world for the appearance of his Son. The saber rattling tends to cause fear but war is part of our world. As the end approaches, we will see an increase in this kind of activity.

There will be an increase in earthquakes (v.8)

This world is no stranger to earthquakes. An earthquake occurred under the Pacific Ocean in December, 2003 which spawned a tsunami that killed three-hundred-thousand people. Remember the floods in New Orleans and the tsunami in Japan, which killed fifty-thousand people. Earthquakes are increasing in their frequency and their intensity. They will continue to do so as the end of time approaches. Jesus said it would be this way.

There will be famines (v.8)

Every 3.6 seconds someone dies of starvation. Millions of people are dying of starvation and of hunger related illness. 1.3 billion people live on less than $1.00 of income per day. Another 3 billion survive on less than $3.00 per day. Famines devastate the poor nations of the world. Climate change is causing problems in the Western world. There has been a

---

[79] The notion that mankind is evolving into a more sophisticated social order is completely contrary to the teaching of Scripture which emphasizes the total depravity of man and the process of degeneration.

severe drought in the USA (2012). In Europe longer winters, later springs and more severe forms of weather are taking their toll on crop yields, the production of animal fodder and the sustainability of farming. Changes in climate can have a domino effect on a delicate eco-system where entire species of insect and animal life forms are becoming endangered and even extinct. Climates can change and the consequences could be devastating. The Western world is only a few bad harvests away from catastrophe!

There will be troubles of every kind (v.8)

Matthew's account of this conversation reveals that these troubles will be 'pestilences'. There will be an upsurge in disease and plagues as the end times approach. The 'black death' afflicted medieval Europe where whole villages were destroyed by that plague. Other plagues have swept through cities and nations leaving millions dead in their wake. Twenty-five million people died from the influenza outbreak during World War I. That is, three times more people died of the flu during World War I than were actually killed in the war itself!

We may think something like that cannot happen today. However, consider the AIDS epidemic. Huge numbers of people (especially in Africa) are HIV positive. Think of the SARS, bird flu and swine flu scares of the early twenty-first-century. One pandemic is all it will take to bring death to every continent, city, town and village on this planet. Think of the horrors of viruses like Ebola. An outbreak of deadly disease in our world has the potential to kill hundreds of millions of people in just a few weeks! An outbreak like that would shut down society, as we know it.

Jesus told his disciples some of the things that will happen as the end draws near (v.8). However, he also told them that they could not really know when the end will come. Nobody can predict that precisely. Many have tried and failed. These things will be the beginning of the end. The contractions signal the time of labor is at hand. Jesus wants people to know that he is coming again. That was his promise while he was here (John 14:1-3). That was the promise of the angels when he ascended to heaven: "Men of Galilee, why do you stand looking into heaven? This Jesus, who was taken up from you into heaven, will come in the same way as you saw him go into heaven" (Acts 1:9-11). That was the promise of the apostle Paul, writing under the inspiration of the Holy Spirit: 'For the Lord himself will descend from heaven with a cry of command, with the voice of an archangel, and with the sound of the trumpet of God. And the dead in Christ will rise first...and so we will always be with the Lord. Therefore encourage one another with these words.'–1 Thessalonians 4:16-18.

We are not to look for signs rather we are to look for the Savior. Jesus does not want his disciples to get caught up in speculating about when that day might be. Scripture says, '...the day of the Lord will come like a thief in the night.' (1 Thessalonians 5:2) Rather than getting caught up in guessing about when the Lord will return we should be busy witnessing for Jesus. Jesus Christ is coming again. As that day approaches the world will go into a time of terrible tribulation (war, disease, starvation and plagues). We must be ready for his return. May we be found working, witnessing and worshipping on that day!

Persecution for the sake of the gospel (13:9-13)

Persecution is a reality for many Christians in certain parts of the world. It is not just something that happened in the distant past. One does not hear much about it in the media but over 200 million Christians in some sixty countries are suffering intense persecution for their faith. Jesus warns his disciples of the persecution that lies ahead. He wants them to know that following him carries a high cost (Matthew 16:24). He wants them to know that they are going to be called upon to face persecution for their faith. The disciples are warned that they will be delivered up to the "councils". This is a reference to the Jewish Sanhedrin (the Supreme Court). They would also stand before "rulers and kings", who would interrogate them concerning their preaching and doctrine. They would be hunted, hounded, beaten, and some would even die, for their faith and the message they preached.

This prophecy was literally fulfilled in the book of Acts. Peter and John face the Sanhedrin and give an account of the healing of the lame man at the temple (Acts 4). Stephen is tried by the Sanhedrin and is condemned to die and stoned to death. (Acts 7) The Jews want to kill Paul for his preaching. (Acts 9:22-25) King Herod arrests James and Peter. (Acts 12) They are imprisoned and scheduled to be executed. James is beheaded, but Peter is delivered by a divine miracle. Paul is stoned and left for dead at Lystra. (Acts 14:19) Paul and Silas are imprisoned in Philippi (Acts 16:19-24). Paul is persecuted in Macedonia. (Acts 18:12-17) Paul is arrested and tried in Ephesus. (Acts 19) Paul is arrested and held for trial in Jerusalem. (Acts 21) Paul is tried before Felix. (Acts 24) Paul is tried before Festus and King Agrippa. (Acts 26) Paul is kept under arrest and sent by ship to stand trial before Caesar. (Acts 27-28) He remains a prisoner in Rome until he is executed by the Romans. That is just a brief sampling of the kind of persecution that rocked the early church. Here is Paul's own testimony concerning the things he suffered for Jesus:

2 Corinthians 11:23-29

[23] Are they servants of Christ? I am a better one—I am talking like a madman—with far greater labors, far more imprisonments, with countless beatings, and often near death. [24] Five times I received at the hands of the Jews

the forty lashes less one. ²⁵ Three times I was beaten with rods. Once I was stoned. Three times I was shipwrecked; a night and a day I was adrift at sea; ²⁶ on frequent journeys, in danger from rivers, danger from robbers, danger from my own people, danger from Gentiles, danger in the city, danger in the wilderness, danger at sea, danger from false brothers; ²⁷ in toil and hardship, through many a sleepless night, in hunger and thirst, often without food, in cold and exposure. ²⁸ And, apart from other things, there is the daily pressure on me of my anxiety for all the churches. ²⁹ Who is weak, and I am not weak? Who is made to fall, and I am not indignant?

Why did the disciples receive such treatment from the religious Jews and from secular government? They received this treatment because the gospel of the Lord Jesus Christ is a direct threat to organized religion and to corrupt human government. It is a threat to the spirit of tolerance, militant secularism and aggressive atheism. Tolerance is not a virtue. Loyalty is not a virtue. People have tolerated much that was evil in our world and shown loyalty to dictators and megalomaniacs rather than stand up for justice and human rights. The gospel calls for repentance from hedonistic and immoral lifestyles. The gospel presents the unique and universal claims of Christ. People do not like to be told that they are sinners. They do not want their sinful lifestyles to be judged, criticized or condemned. They think Christians are narrow-minded and bigoted. The gospel exposes sin and ungodliness and people react by seeking to silence the gospel and its advocates.

As the end of the church age draws closer persecution will intensify. The gospel proclaims that salvation is by grace alone, through faith alone, in Christ alone. It is a stumbling block to religious people and foolishness to many. Ironically, persecution caused the gospel to spread (it thrives in lands where it is persecuted today). When believers seal their testimony with their blood, a lost world takes notice. Approximately sixty percent of the world's Christians live in prosperity and peace. Forty percent of the world's Christians live in poverty and persecution. Many of these people suffer daily for their testimony, and many others are tortured and killed for believing in Jesus Christ. The greatest number of conversions and the greatest moves of God are being reported among our poverty stricken, persecuted church. They are suffering and dying for their faith, and millions are being influenced. The persecuted give daily testimony to the depth of their faith and commitment to the gospel.

There is a word here for the contemporary church. As the end of time, draws near, persecutions against believers will increase. We are living in an environment that is growing increasingly hostile to the gospel. Believers uphold a moral standard that the world resents and rejects. They want to be their own gods. They want to believe that everyone goes to heaven. But many think that life ends with death. They deny the immortality of the soul. The Bible teaches that there is a heaven and a hell[80] and they will face God as either friend or foe. Many want to live as though God were dead and as if they will never give an account of their actions.

The Bible teaches that: '...all who desire to live a godly life in Christ Jesus will be persecuted.' (2 Timothy 3:12) There is a war of worldviews. Liberalism has an agenda and Christians stand in the way (or should) of that. Christians are expected to tolerate sin and vice of every kind. Even people in the church expect us to tone down our message and soften our speech so that we do not offend people. But the gospel is offensive to sinners. When believers fail to go along with the

---

[80] Christian Publishing House recommends the following articles,
Hellfire - Eternal Torment?
http://www.christianpublishers.org/hellfire-eternal-torment
Hellfire - Is It Just?
http://www.christianpublishers.org/hellfire-is-it-just

expectations of this increasingly secular society they can expect to incur hostility, ridicule and rejection for their stand. Persecution separates true believers from those whose profession of faith is superficial

On April 17, 1521, the great reformer Martin Luther stood before a council to answer charges of heresy. He said:

> Unless I am convinced by Scripture and plain reason - I do not accept the authority of the popes and councils, for they have contradicted each other - my conscience is captive to the Word of God. I cannot and I will not recant anything for to go against conscience is neither right nor safe. God help me. Amen.[81]

Persecution will intensify until even the strong bonds of family are broken. Jesus said that it would be this way:

Matthew 10:34-39

34 "Do not think that I have come to bring peace to the earth. I have not come to bring peace, but a sword. 35 For I have come to set a man against his father, and a daughter against her mother, and a daughter-in-law against her mother-in-law. 36 And a person's enemies will be those of his own household. 37 Whoever loves father or mother more than me is not worthy of me, and whoever loves son or daughter more than me is not worthy of me. 38 And whoever does not take his cross and follow me is not worthy of me. 39 Whoever finds his life will lose it, and whoever loses his life for my sake will find it.

The first disciples experienced this kind of hatred, and so will the church of the end times. The world will hate believers because we stand for everything they are against and we are against everything they stand for. They are for

---

[81] Luther's Response to the Inquisition at the Diet of Worms. It is unlikely that he ever said: *"Here I stand. I can do none other."*

unrestricted liberty, the unrestrained indulgences of hedonism. Believers stand for holiness, righteousness, moderation, accountability, responsibility and moral values.

The persecution of the church will grow stronger and more public as the end approaches. Jesus tells the disciples that they will be hated for his name's sake. This is not just Christian paranoia. Jesus warned his disciples that just as the world hated him, they would hate those who follow him. (John 15:18-21) The Jews hated Jesus and his followers because he led many away from their religion. The Gentiles (especially the Greeks) hated Jesus and his followers because his teachings seemed foolish to them; intellectual cop-out. The Romans hated Christ's followers because they refused to indulge in emperor worship and accept the pantheon of other so-called 'gods'. When Christians reject the popular belief that all roads lead to heaven and the pluralist and interfaith agenda they too will be despised.

Tradition holds that Herod beheaded James. Peter was crucified upside down in Rome.[82] Andrew was crucified on an olive tree. Thomas was thrust through with pine spears, tormented with red-hot plates, and burned alive. Philip was tortured and crucified. Matthew was beheaded. Nathanael was flayed (skinned) alive and then crucified. James the Less was thrown down from the temple mount and then beaten to death with a club. Simon the Zealot was crucified. Thaddeus was beaten to death with sticks. Matthias was stoned while hanging on a cross. John the Beloved was thrown into boiling oil, but did not die. Later he was exiled to the prison island of Patmos. Paul was beheaded in Rome.

Millions down through the centuries have endured persecution, torture and death for the sake of Christ. It is still

---

[82] Christian Publishing House recommends the following articles,
1 Peter 5:13—Was Peter In Rome?
http://www.christianpublishers.org/was-peter-in-rome

happening today in places like North Korea. Many of us will never face the kind of persecution that some have faced throughout history or in other geographical locations in today's world. In the first century, the Roman Emperor Nero took Christians, coated them in tar and set them on fire to light his garden parties. Believers were sewn inside the skins of animals, thrown to wild animals to be mauled to death, and eaten alive. Many thousands went to their deaths in the Roman Coliseum to entertain the crowds and to satisfy their bloodlust. Countless believers have been burned alive at the stake, tortured to death, drowned, and mutilated because of their faith.

If we were called upon to stand for Jesus in this way are we prepared to face such a time of persecution? Certainly special grace and speech are needed at such times and only the power of the Holy Spirit will enable one to endure such trials. Persecution would do more for the church than all its programs! Persecution would purify the church:

1 Peter 1:6-8

⁶ In this you rejoice, though now for a little while, if necessary, you have been grieved by various trials, ⁷ so that the tested genuineness of your faith—more precious than gold that perishes though it is tested by fire—may be found to result in praise and glory and honor at the revelation of Jesus Christ. ⁸ Though you have not seen him, you love him. Though you do not now see him, you believe in him and rejoice with joy that is inexpressible and filled with glory,

The church would lose her appetite for worldliness and liberalism. She would see her doctrine purified and the glory of God return. A lost world would see its devotion to the Lord and many would be drawn to him. The gospel would have more influence in this world if the church that preached it were holy, pure and separated. It might seem that a message about the persecution of the believer does not make many people want to become Christians. But the reality of such sacrifice has a magnetic power to draw people to the Savior. Do we just want a comfortable religion of convenience? Is the Lord speaking to you about your level of commitment to him? Pray for the Christians who are being persecuted around the world today.

Jesus says: "...the one who endures to the end will be saved." This means that testing will be a feature of end times. He is not setting forth a doctrine of salvation by works. Rather he is emphasizing that genuine faith will manifest itself in Christian living that will endure trial and persecution. Thus Paul's words to Timothy seem particularly apt: 'if we endure, we will also reign with him; if we deny him, he also will deny us.' Such endurance is a test of the genuineness of one's faith.

The abomination of desolation (13:14-23)

So far in chapter 13 we have been considering events which were foretold by Christ to his disciples. These words were prophetic and the events he spoke about were yet to be fulfilled. The destruction of the temple was fulfilled in AD 70 and the persecution of the disciples occurred with ferocious intensity in the first century AD. So these events have been fulfilled. Because persecution is a reality today for many believers there is also an ongoing fulfillment of these words. Jesus talked about the destruction of the temple in Jerusalem, false messiahs who would deceive many, an increase in wars and natural disasters, an increase in the persecution of the followers of Christ and he issued a call to steadfastness.

What is this abomination that Jesus mentions? Luke records that that Jesus said: "But when you see Jerusalem surrounded by armies, then know that its desolation has come near." (Luke 21:20) Therefore, armies around Jerusalem precede the abomination. This prophecy involves something / someone "standing in the holy place". Clearly, the abomination is something that does not belong in the holy place. The holy place is the temple. Here Jesus speaks about the necessity of flight. The abomination of desolation is an expression taken from Daniel. (9:27; 11:31; 12:11) An abomination is something detestable to God. "Desolation" means abandoned, left alone, uninhabited, wretched and ruined. Thus, the temple will become desolate, depopulated and devastated. The time is coming, Jesus says, when it will lay in waste. True heart religion has been neglected and the temple will be deserted and destroyed.

Judaism in many parts of the world today (not exclusively but largely) is merely a cultural tradition. It is eviscerated of all spiritual meaning and value. Jesus would have been aware that the abomination that Daniel spoke about had fulfillment in the Maccabean period (167-168 BC). The profaning of the altar of burnt offering in the temple of Jerusalem by Antiochus IV (Epiphanes) in 167 BC fulfilled Daniel's prophecy. In 167 BC, Antiochus IV attempted to force the Jews to adopt Greek culture. He would not permit them to circumcise their male children, or offer the Levitical sacrifices. He forced them to offer swine to God. On one occasion, Antiochus entered the temple in Jerusalem and offered a pig on the altar. He also erected a statue of the Greek god Zeus in the Holy of Holies and he opened a brothel in the temple chambers. He so defiled the temple that the Jews abandoned it until a successful rebellion defeated Antiochus and his successors.

However, Jesus is not now talking about the incidents, which occurred at the time of the Maccabees. He is talking about a future event. In 40 AD, the insane Emperor Caligula (who thought he was a god) almost succeeded in erecting a statue of himself in the Jewish temple.[83] Then in 68 AD, Jewish Zealots took control of the temple. They desecrated it by entering the Holy of Holies and by committing murders in the temple itself. In 70 AD, Titus the Roman general entered

---

[83] Caligula made his horse a senator!

the Holy of Holies and removed many sacred items to be used in his victory procession. In A.D. 70, the Roman soldiers brought their military standards (flags) into the temple. Christ cautioned that when this abomination of desolation occurred that people should flee for their lives. Anyone on the roof of the house is not to go inside to get their belongings. Many of his hearers on this occasion would live to see the fulfillment of the events he predicted with such precision.

Anyone in the fields is not to return to the house even to get an outer garment. There is urgency stressed here as if the house is on fire and to return would be disastrous. The outer garment was used at night to keep warm and taken off during the day as it restricted movement (when working) and it was too hot. The cloak would be useful if one had to flee to the mountains for safety, as it was cold there. However, the situation would be too urgent to fetch it. A hurried flight to the mountains would be especially difficult for expectant mothers and particularly so in winter.

There will be pretenders who will perform signs and wonders and many will be deceived. However, God's people are not to be deceived. Nevertheless disciples of Christ must remain alert and on guard against such things. The best way to identify a counterfeit is not by examining the flaws in the counterfeit but by being thoroughly familiar with the real thing.

When the Zealots took possession of the temple in 67-68 AD, Christians living in Jerusalem saw it as a fulfillment of this very prophecy. Many fled the city and escaped the brutal crackdown of Rome that led to the total destruction of Jerusalem and the temple. When this sign appears, those living in Jerusalem are to leave immediately.

Jesus warns that many false Christs will emerge and attempt to lead people astray. People are looking for hope wherever they can find it. The sad truth is that false prophets and false teachers are leading many astray. The cults are flourishing, while Bible-believing churches seem to be dying (in the West). Muslims have big plans for advancing their faith, especially in areas where it has not had a traditional foothold. The Mormons, Jehovah's Witnesses, and other minority religions and cult groups are preaching their doctrines and being accepted by many. They are offering false hope and gaining acceptance. Believers are to be on guard, vigilant in protecting the truth and diligent in spreading the gospel. Christians are called to be watchful. They are called to be faithful witnesses and devoted worshippers who are working for the Lord and waiting for his return.

The second coming of Christ (13:24-27; 32-37)

Jesus promised to return (John 14:3) so it can be expected. He will come "after that tribulation." The word tribulation means trouble, difficulty and distress. As already noted it will be a time of warfare on an unprecedented scale. It will also be a time marked by earthquakes, famines, disease, and false religion and bogus messiahs. When those days are ended he will return. Mark says, "...the sun will be darkened, and the moon will not give its light, and the stars will be falling from heaven, and the powers in the heavens will be shaken." There will be signs in the heavens. The sun will not shine. Imagine the implications of that! Man cannot live without the light and heat of the sun. Temperatures will fall drastically. The earth will be plunged into utter darkness. In that darkness, even the moon will not shine because it merely reflects the light of the sun. The stars that sit poised in the heavens will fall from their places. Tides will no longer be predictable and tidal waves will sweep over the land. These verses describe a scene of utter bedlam as the universe literally disintegrates into chaos. It is a grim picture of cataclysmic horror:

Revelation 6:12-14

¹²When he opened the sixth seal, I looked, and behold, there was a great earthquake, and the sun became black as sackcloth, the full moon became like blood, ¹³ and the stars of the sky fell to the earth as the fig tree sheds its winter fruit when shaken by a gale. ¹⁴ The sky vanished like a scroll that is being rolled up, and every mountain and island was removed from its place.

A time of calamity is coming! Scripture asserts that Jesus: '...upholds the universe by the word of his power' (Hebrews 1:3). Jesus created this universe and he holds it all together. On that day, Jesus will remove his controlling hand from the universe. The disciples expected that Christ's return was imminent and lived in the light of that eschatological hope. It shaped their spirituality and lifestyles. The Lord will put out the sun and the moon. When that happens, a terrifying scene will develop in the heavens as the stars fall from the sky. Jesus will come in splendor with his glory unveiled. The psalmist says: '...he makes the clouds his chariot' (Psalm 104:3). He will come in power and no power on earth will be able to oppose him. It makes sense to be on the right side of that power. The only way to be on the right side of that power is to be in a faith relationship with the Lord Jesus Christ: 'Since, therefore, we have now been justified by his blood, much more shall we be saved by him from the wrath of God' (Romans 5:9). Jesus is coming again but not everyone will rejoice when he returns. Skeptics and scoffers deny that fact, but they cannot change the truth of it.

The lesson of the fig tree (13:28-31)

Jesus uses a fig tree to illustrate the truth. When a fig tree puts forth its leaves it is a clear sign that summer is on the way. Therefore, Jesus says, when people see the signs he has mentioned in these verses, they will know the end is near.

These signs have been identified. There will be many false messiahs. (vs.6, 21-22) There will be wars and rumors of wars. (v.7) There will be turmoil among the nations of the earth. (v.8) There will be persecution of the people of God. (v.9-13) The heavenly bodies will fall from their places, the sun and the moon will not give their light, and the universe will be plunged into darkness. (v.24-25) Even though this time is still future all the pieces are falling into place. The appearance of the signs he has mentioned will be a signal that the end is very near. Everything Jesus says will come to pass. The Word of God is an eternal book: 'The grass withers, the flower fades, but the word of our God will stand forever'– Isaiah 40:8.

What does this mean for the Christian today? It serves to remind us that we need to take the words of the Lord to heart. What he foretells will happen. This is a call for people to believe the Bible. The second coming of Christ is a hidden time. Nobody (except the Lord) knows when that event will take place. The fact is God will not put an advertisement on television to let people know that the end is near. He will not place a full-page advertisement in the newspapers. It will not be announced on the radio (even Christian radio). He will not drop flyers from the heavens or tracts through letterboxes. There will be no mailshots, emails, text-messages, tweets or notices in social network forums. We have the only warning we are going to get in the Word of God.

We are challenged to watch. The word "watch" is repeated in these verses. Jesus wants his people to be on the alert. We are to live in anticipation of his return. What does it mean to "watch"? The word means "to keep awake, to be attentive, and to be ready." It has the idea of a watchman who dares not fall asleep while he is on duty. He keeps his eyes and ears open. He stays on the alert at all times because the lives of others depend on his vigilance. The world wants to grab our attention and captivate us with its alluring treasures. Satan wants to lull us to sleep by telling us that we have plenty of time. Will we be found sleeping when he returns?

In verse 34 Jesus describes himself as a house owner who leaves his business in the hands of his servants. This man assigns each of his servants a specific task and then he takes his journey. The servants do not know when their master will return. They are encouraged to work at their tasks diligently so that they will not be found shirking their duties when their master comes back. When Jesus saved us, he saved us to go to work for him: 'For we are his workmanship, created in Christ Jesus for good works, which God prepared beforehand, that we should walk in them' (Ephesians 2:10). We should show our faith by our works (James 2:18). Do you know what the Lord wants you to do? Are you doing what he wants you to do? Are you willing to ask him what he wants you to do? Are you ready for his coming? If Jesus were to return today, would he find you faithfully serving him and carrying out his will in the world? Would he find you doing his will or doing as you will?

Chapter 14

The plot to kill Jesus (14:1-2)

The hypocrisy of the Pharisees is evident once again. Their religion had no real meaning in their lives. They could plot murder because their religion was dead. The religious leaders had been looking for a long time for a way to get rid of Jesus. (3:6; 11:18; 12:12) Now they renew and intensify their efforts. It was necessary for them to proceed with caution because of the influx of so many people into Jerusalem for the Passover. They bided their time waiting for the most opportune moment to implement the wicked scheme they had been hatching.

Jesus anointed at Bethany (14:3-9)

While this passage reveals human nature at its worst, there is also a picture here of human nature at its best. The hatred of Jesus' enemies is contrasted with the extravagant love of this woman. Here is the kind of love that every disciple of Christ should have for the Savior. Here is love that is selfless, all consuming, boundless, extravagant and conspicuous. This event occurred in the home of a man called Simon the leper. It would appear that Jesus had healed this man from leprosy and that he throws a feast in the Lord's honor to thank him for what he has done in his life.[84] Matthew, Mark and John tell this story but only John's Gospel account gives her name.

---

[84] This is speculation, but possible if not probable.

Many had come to the Lord's feet to have their needs met but she came to give him his due. It is an act of conspicuous and extravagant love for the Lord. It is also an act of sacrificial love. She had an alabaster box filled with very precious ointment of spikenard. She broke that box and poured the contents of it on the head of the Lord Jesus. John also tells us that she anointed the feet of Jesus, and wiped his feet with her hair. This box is actually a flask. Spikenard is a red-tinted ointment that is drawn from a plant that grows in India. It was a perfume used in the embalming process. It was so expensive that only the wealthy could afford to buy it. It was worth 300 denarii (v.5), a year's pay for the average worker, an extravagant gift indeed.

John's account tells us that the house was filled with the odor of the ointment (John 12:3). When she broke the flask, there was no going back! The entire contents of that vessel would have to be used. In this act she declared how much Jesus meant to her. Clearly, he meant more to her than anything else. She did not care what other people thought. Only prostitutes were seen in public with their hair down. At that moment, she did not care what anyone thought of her as she expressed her love for Jesus. Only slaves washed the feet of others. When a person entered a home, they would be offered water so they could wash their own feet, or if the household had slaves, they would perform the act. Mary took the place of a slave before the Lord. She humbled herself before him and she served him because she loved him. She had a true understanding of the value of things. Nothing in the world was as valuable to her as Jesus.

It was the custom at that time to put a few drops of perfume on the head of an honored guest when they arrived at your home but Mary broke the flask and poured out every drop on Jesus. She was making a statement about his worthiness to be worshiped and served. It is a beautiful picture of loving worship. Do not let pride hinder you from offering to the Lord the love he deserves. Don't let the opinions of others constrain you. Will you place everything you have, everything you are and everything you care about on the altar of sacrifice before him? Who will love him more than they love themselves, their own agenda, their possessions or their comfort? Who will sacrifice their pride and possessions so that their giving might honor the Lord? Who will love him extravagantly, beyond the boundaries of what convention allows and expects? Are we totally committed to Jesus?

Romans 12:1-2

¹ I appeal to you therefore, brothers, by the mercies of God, to present your bodies as a living sacrifice, holy and acceptable to God, which is your spiritual worship. ² Do not be conformed to this world, but be transformed by the renewal of your mind, that by testing you may discern what is the will of God, what is good and acceptable and perfect.

Are you willing to suffer shame if it brings glory to him? Far too many are like the fellow who called his girlfriend up one day and said, "Darling, I love you! I would climb the highest mountain for you! I would swim the deepest river for you! I would fight a jungle full of lions for you! I love you! And, if it doesn't rain tonight, I will be over to see you." Too often, we profess great love but manifest it only when it is convenient. We love him on Sunday mornings. We love him when loving him fits within our schedule! We love him when it does not get in the way of what we want to do, where we want to go and what we want to accomplish in life

There is a story from the Middle East of four brothers who decided to have a feast. As wine was rather expensive, they concluded that each should bring an equal quantity and add it to the single container, the common supply. However, one of the brothers, thinking to escape the expense of such a contribution decided to bring water instead of wine. "It won't be noticed," he reasoned. However, at the feast when the wine was poured out it was not wine at all. It was only water. Each of the four brothers had thought alike; let the others do it. Water is less expensive.

Are we failing to serve, and hoping that our withholding of ourselves will go unnoticed? We love him to a point but very few love as Mary did on this occasion. Do we live our lives on our own terms, by our own rules and say we are living for the Lord? Mary's gift should make us ashamed of our lukewarm, self-centered, half-hearted love for the Lord.

Some who witnessed this scene were very displeased with what Mary had done. They described her act of selfless worship as wasteful. One of the disciples (according to John 12:4-5 it was Judas Iscariot) calculated that the ointment would have been worth three hundred denarii. Some said that the ointment should have been sold and the money given it to the poor. This sounds good, and it sounds spiritual but John sheds light on the heart of at least one of those who thought like this: 'He said this, not because he cared about the poor, but because he was a thief, and having charge of the moneybag he used to help himself to what was put into it.'– John 12:6.

Here is a woman who loved Jesus more than she loved her possessions. She sacrificed her pride and her precious ointment because she wanted to worship and honor Jesus. She worshiped him publicly, sacrificially and extravagantly. But she is misunderstood and misinterpreted by the Lord's disciples. Criticism will come from those who want you to conform to their ways. Their response shows that they did not have the same heart of love for Jesus that she had. This mentality is still at work today. People give themselves to all kinds of pursuits in life. Some give themselves to money and people call them a success because they have the house, the car, the clothes, and the lifestyle of people who are materially well off. Some give themselves to sports, they become star athletes, and people call them heroes. Some give themselves to politics and are called great civic leaders. Some give themselves to academia and people talk about how wonderful they are because they are intellectual. Some give themselves to intellectual and artistic pursuits and they are revered as intelligentsia and bohemians. But when a talented young man or woman give themselves to a life of service to the Lord some people will say: "What a waste!"

No matter what you do in life, if you do not do it for the glory of God and to honor the Lord it is a waste of time, money and energy!

> Only one life,
> 'Twill soon be past.
> Only what's done for
> Christ will last.[85]

No matter how much money you make or how much education you get, if you do not do it for the glory of God, it means nothing. That is what Jesus said in relation to sacrificing the spiritual for the secular: "For what does it profit a man to gain the whole world and forfeit his soul? For what can a man give in return for his soul?" (Mark 8:36-37).

These people who criticized Mary were not spiritually minded but materially minded. If you love Jesus extravagantly and conspicuously you too might be criticized. Jesus defends Mary's actions: "Leave her alone. Why do you trouble her? She has done a beautiful thing to me." (v.6) The Lord's heart is grieved by their attitude. What the disciples deemed wasteful, Jesus declared to be wonderful. What bothered the disciples was something beautiful that blessed the Lord. He said: "For you always have the poor with you, and whenever you want, you can do good for them. But you will not always have me." (v.7) Jesus is not saying that we

---

[85] From the poem 'Only One Life' by C. T. Studd.

should not help the poor.[86] Rather he is saying that Mary seized the moment. The poor would always be there, but she took advantage of the opportunity to worship him. Life is short. Soon, our lives will be over. We must learn to seize those moments when we are given opportunities to serve Jesus. The Bible challenges us to make the best use of our time.–Ephesians 5:16.

Jesus says, "She has done what she could." (v.8) She was condemned by those who witnessed her actions but she was commended by the Lord. She did what she could with what she had where she was. In this, she is a good example for all. What can we do? We cannot do everything, but we can take what we have and do what we can with it! We cannot evangelize the whole world, but we can tell one person at a time about Jesus. We cannot feed every starving person in the world, but we can feed some. We cannot help everybody, but we can help some people. We can take what we have and use it for the glory of God. That is all God asks of us. Do what you can!

A Christian businessman was traveling in Korea. In a field by the side of the road was a young man pulling a crude plow while an old man held the handles. The businessman was amused and took a photograph of the scene. "I suppose these people are very poor," he said to the missionary who was his interpreter and guide. "Yes," was the reply, "those two men happen to be Christians. When their church was being built, they were eager to give something toward it, but they had no money. Therefore, they decided to sell their one and only ox and give the proceeds to the church. This spring they are pulling the plow themselves." The businessman was silent for some moments. Then he said, "That must have been a real sacrifice." "They did not call it that," said the missionary. "They thought themselves fortunate that they had an ox to

---

[86] Jesus often expressed concern for the needs of the poor (Matthew 5:3; 6:2-4; 19:21; Luke 6:20; 36-38; 21:1-4; John 13:29).

sell!" When that businessman reached home, he took the picture to his pastor and told him all about it. Then he added, "I want to double my giving to the church and do some plow work. Up until now I have never given God anything that involved real sacrifice."

She did what she could in the area of sacrifice, service and surrender. What have you given to him and what are you keeping back? When the Spirit of God speaks to our hearts it is time to step up and serve God. Too often, we miss out on those special moments of service to Jesus when we ignore the prompting of the Holy Spirit. That is why the Bible warns us to be careful lest we quench the Spirit of God.–1 Thessalonians 5:19.

Mary would have assumed a kneeling position near Jesus, in order to anoint his head with the ointment, as he reclined at table. By kneeling to him and anointing him she was surrendering to the Lord. Are we surrendered? Do the lives we live show us kneeling before him as absolute Lord? Are there aspects of our lives that remain un-surrendered? She did what she could. I wonder if Jesus would be able to say the same thing about us.

The next few verses (10-11) record the sad betrayal of Jesus by one from among his closest disciples. The Lord was sold for an insignificant amount. What a stark contrast with the extravagant love of Mary, which raises the question: what is Jesus worth to you?

Judas betrays Jesus (14:10-11; 17-21)

These verses mention the betrayal of Jesus by Judas Iscariot. His name appears last in every list of the disciples, except in Acts 1, where his name does not appear at all. Judas was exposed to the same teaching the others heard. He saw the same miracles and was involved in the same ministries. Judas spent three years with Jesus. The other eleven disciples were used of God in amazing ways. Their lives demonstrate the truth that ordinary people can be used of the Lord in extraordinary ways. Judas, on the other hand, stands as a stark warning about the dangers of wasted opportunities, hardness of heart, being materially minded and spiritual carelessness. He played his part so well that no one but Jesus knew he was a fraud. These verses reveal Judas hatching his plot to betray Jesus into the hands of his enemies.

The lessons that come from the life of this tragic character need to be heard and heeded. It is possible to be near Jesus and still be hardened in sin. Not much is known about Judas from Scripture. He is mentioned twenty times in the Gospels and twice in the book of Acts. Every time he is mentioned he is identified as a traitor. He speaks on just two occasions. Judas was the trusted treasurer but he was a thief.[87] When Jesus was anointed in Bethany Judas raised an objection:

John 12:4-6

⁴ But Judas Iscariot, one of his disciples (he who was about to betray him), said, ⁵ "Why was this ointment not sold for three hundred denarii and given to the poor?" ⁶ He said this, not because he cared about the poor, but because he was a thief, and having charge of the moneybag he used to help himself to what was put into it.

We never really know the true condition of the hearts of those around us. Judas was a privileged person. He was chosen by Jesus to fulfill a divine plan: "Did I not choose you, the Twelve? And yet one of you is a devil." He spoke of Judas the son of Simon Iscariot, for he, one of the Twelve, was going to betray him.' (John 6:70) Jesus makes it crystal clear that when he chose Judas he knew who he was and what he would do. Old Testament prophecy should be considered, 'Even my close friend in whom I trusted, who ate

---

[87] The Lord can and does forgive thieves, such as the thief who was crucified alongside the Savior, to whom he promised paradise.

my bread, has lifted his heel against me.' (Psalm 41:9) Jesus said that this prophecy would be fulfilled in his betrayal: "I know whom I have chosen. But the Scripture will be fulfilled, 'He who ate my bread has lifted his heel against me" (John 13:18). Everything Judas did, was foreknown by God (Acts 2:23). Jesus said, "...woe to that man by whom the Son of Man is betrayed! It would have been better for that man if he had not been born."—Mark 14:21.

Judas was not forced to do anything against his will. Judas was not condemned because he betrayed Jesus. He was condemned long before that because he was a lost sinner (John 3:18, 36). Judas and the other disciples witnessed the character and compassion of Christ from close quarters. They heard his words and they witnessed his works. It is astonishing that Judas could live with Jesus for over three years and still betray him. Yet, we see the same thing happening around us all the time. People can sit in church for a lifetime under the Word of God, listening to the preaching of the gospel and the prayers of God's people, witnessing the clear evidence of his saving power in the lives of those around them and still some of those people do not come to faith in Christ. It is a sobering thought that Judas was a tare among the wheat and no one but Jesus knew it.

It seems that Judas wanted power and money. Perhaps Judas expected a secular messiah and became disillusioned when he realized that Christ's kingdom was spiritual. The Bible makes it clear that what Judas did, he did at the command of Satan (John 13:27). God foreknew it and foreordained it (by his permissive will) and Satan desired it and prompted Judas to do it but Judas willingly did it.

Judas was pilfering from the money bag. The first time he speaks in the Gospels he complains about the way resources were wasted. (John 12:4-6) Jesus rebukes Judas but he does not examine his heart and repent. He heard Jesus preach the Sermon on the Mount. He witnessed Jesus healing the sick, casting out demons, restoring sight to the blind, restoring hearing to the deaf, restoring mobility to the lame and paralyzed, calming a storm, walking on water and raising the dead.

Judas was a wolf in sheep's clothing. This is a sobering thought! A person can preach and pray, do good works, attend church but that does not mean he is saved. There must be a moment of commitment when you come to Jesus Christ by faith, repenting of sin and calling on him for salvation. If that moment is missing from your life, then you are lost! Judas betrayed Jesus for thirty pieces of silver. According to Exodus (21:32) it was the price of a slave, which is less than €50 in today's money. It is an insignificant amount. However, people sell him out for less. People betray Jesus for a few moments of illicit sexual pleasure. People betray him by choosing their way of living over his way of living. Jesus taught the disciples a much needed lesson about humility by washing their feet. He assumed the place of a servant. He even washed the feet of Judas! But Judas was unmoved by the Lord's act of love.

Jesus exposed the treachery in the heart of Judas at the last supper when he dips a morsel and hands it to Judas. (John 13:25-27) To be handed the morsel by the host was a form of respect. Thus, Jesus honored Judas and attempted to break through the hatred that gripped the man's heart. However, Judas does not turn from his plan. Though Satan choreographed the events that were unfolding, Judas was a willing participant in the devil's scheme. After Judas leaves, Jesus institutes the Lord's Supper. While Jesus instructs his disciples about the greatest act of worship given to the church Judas is out conducting the greatest act of treachery the world has ever seen.

Judas betrayed Jesus with a kiss. A kiss speaks of love, affection, tenderness, respect and intimacy, particularly in that culture. After Jesus was arrested, Judas began to have pangs of remorse. The life of Judas ended in despair and suicide. What a tragic life! He had come to the very door of heaven but never entered. When Judas returns the money, the chief priests refuse to put it back in the treasury because it is deemed to be 'blood money' and it would have been unlawful to do so. What utter hypocrisy! They showed no concern for the law when they conspired to have Jesus arrested and plotted to have him killed. They were unscrupulous.

Judas resisted every opportunity to repent and believe in Jesus. In the next section of Scripture about the Lord's Supper, Jesus drops a bombshell. He announces that one of them is going to betray him. Naturally, they are astonished and upset. They were so sure that Jesus knew all things and that he knew them better than they knew themselves, that they said, one after the other: "Is it I?" Even Judas asked this question: 'Judas, who would betray him, answered: "Is it I, Rabbi?" He said to him, "You have said so." (Matthew 26:25) Judas was physically as close to Jesus as John but he was distant from the Lord in his affections. Jesus speaks of the gravity of his betrayal: "...woe to that man by whom the Son of Man is betrayed! It would have been better for that man if he had not been born." (Matthew 26:21) Judas would have been better off to have never lived than to have lived and died unrepentant and lost.[88]

The same is true of every person in this world. To live without Jesus is a terrible thing, but to die without him is a tragedy greater than the mind can comprehend. On the other side of the door of death, hell is waiting for the lost soul but heaven is the destiny of those who are in Christ.

In his High-Priestly prayer, Jesus interceded with his heavenly Father on behalf of his disciples, "While I was with them, I kept them in your name, which you have given me. I

---

[88] See Appendix B for further discussion about Judas.

have guarded them, and not one of them has been lost except the son of destruction, that the Scripture might be fulfilled." (John 17:12) This seems to rule out any possibility that Judas was saved.

The last supper (14:12-26)[89]

When Jesus was here on earth, he often ate with the disciples. In this passage, we encounter Jesus having his last meal with this intimate group. It is often called The Last Supper but it could just as well be called the First Communion. This was the feast of Passover and Christ instituted this ordinance. It is the end of the Old Covenant (Passover) and the beginning of the New Covenant (Lord's Supper).[90] It is a meal that preaches the gospel. The text says the disciples came to Jesus wishing to know where he wanted to observe the Passover meal.

The Passover was the main feast of the Jewish religious year. It was to be held on the fourteenth day of the first month of the Jewish calendar (Exodus 12:6; Leviticus 23:5). The first month of that calendar roughly corresponds with April in the contemporary Christian calendar. The Passover was a feast designed to commemorate the night when the angel of death destroyed the first-born of Egypt during the ten plagues God sent to judge Egypt. The Passover was also called 'The Feast of Unleavened Bread' because no yeast or leavened bread was to be used or even kept in the house during the days of the feast.

The regulations for the Passover are found in Exodus 12. According to verses 1-11 of that passage, every family in Israel was to take the following steps. They were to choose a lamb, which was to be killed on the evening of the Passover.

---

[89] See previous section for exposition of Mark 14:17-21.

[90] Here is an example of both continuity and discontinuity between the Judaic and the Christian order.

(Exodus 12:3-6) They were to take the blood of the lamb and put some on the door posts of their homes (Exodus 12:7). They were to roast the lamb over a fire and eat it with bitter herbs and unleavened bread. (Exodus 12:8) They were to eat this meal dressed for a journey, with their shoes on and their walking sticks in their hands. They were to eat it in as though they were in a hurry.–Exodus 12:11.

The order of the meal is as follows. They drank a cup of red wine. There was a ceremonial washing of hands which symbolized the need for spiritual and moral cleansing. They ate the bitter herbs, which symbolized their bondage in Egypt. They drank a second cup of wine, at which time the head of the household explained the meaning of Passover. They would then sing the first two of the Hallel Psalms (Psalms 113-114). Next, the head of the household who distributed pieces of it with the unleavened bread served the cooked lamb. They drank a third cup of wine. Then, they would conclude the meal by singing the rest of the Hallel Psalms. (Psalm 115-118) The disciples were asking about this meal.

Orthodox Jews still observe the Passover the same way it has been observed for thousands of years. Sadly, they are oblivious to its symbolic Christian meaning. The Passover is a wonderful picture of the person and work of the Lord Jesus Christ. The lamb was to be without blemish (Exodus 12:5). This is a picture of perfection and purity. This lamb speaks of the Lord Jesus because he is without defect. He is the sinless Savior. (1 Peter 2:22; 2 Corinthians 5:21) John the Baptist (speaking of Jesus) declared: "Behold, the Lamb of God, who takes away the sin of the world!" The lamb was to be slain and its blood applied to the doorposts of the house. (Exodus 12:7; 22-23) The family was to gather inside the house and eat the meal. When the death angel passed through the land to kill all the first-born children, those who were in homes with blood on the doorposts would be safe. Again, this is a picture of Jesus Christ. The only shelter anyone has against the wrath of Almighty God is the blood of Christ! If you ever hope to be saved, you must come to Jesus Christ by faith and when you do; his blood washes every sin away. (Revelation 1:5; 1 Peter 1:18-19) His blood is the only shield against the wrath and judgment of God.—Romans 5:9.

The lamb was to be roasted with fire (Exodus 12:8). Fire is a picture of judgment and it reminded Israel that the judgment of God was being poured out on sinful Egypt. And the only thing that prevented Israel from being judged along with Egypt was the blood of the lamb that had died to save them. The lamb had been judged in their place. This also pictures the Lord Jesus. He was judged in the place of his redeemed ones. (2 Corinthians 5:21; Galatians 3:13; 1 Peter 3:18) The lamb had to be eaten. (Exodus 12:8) It did no good to simply select a lamb. It did no good to just kill the lamb. The lamb had to be appropriated by the individual. The same is true with Jesus. His death on the cross is meaningless for you until you receive him by faith. His death cannot save you until you turn to him and receive him into your heart and life.

Some people do not like to talk about the blood but the Bible says: '...without the shedding of blood there is no forgiveness of sins.' (Hebrews 9:22) It is the blood of Jesus, which cleanses us from sin. (1 John 1:7) 'In him we have redemption through his blood, the forgiveness of our trespasses, according to the riches of his grace.' (Ephesians 1:7) The blood of Jesus is the only thing that can reconcile a lost sinner to a holy God, 'But now in Christ Jesus you who once were far off have been brought near by the blood of Christ.' (Ephesians 2:13) Some people who call themselves Christians don't like all this talk about the blood. They must have great difficulty reading the Bible. Scripture is a blood-soaked book.

There is a fountain filled with blood drawn from Immanuel's veins

And sinners plunged beneath that flood lose all their guilty stains.[91]

However, the blood of Jesus needs to be preached and believers need to plead the blood and rejoice in the blood. I glory in that crimson tide:

What can wash away my sin?
Nothing but the blood of Jesus!
What can make me whole again?
Nothing but the blood of Jesus!
Oh precious is the flow,
That makes me white as snow,
No other fount I know,
Nothing but the blood of Jesus![92]

In response to their question about the Passover Jesus sent two of his disciples to make the arrangements for the feast. From Luke 22:8, we know that these two disciples were Peter and John. Jesus tells them to enter the city and look for a man carrying a pitcher of water. They were to follow this man and he would lead them to a house where they would find everything ready for the meal. This shows the Lord's omniscience. He knew there would be a man carrying a pitcher of water. This was unusual because that was normally deemed to be a woman's work.

The Lord knows all things. The Bible says: 'The eyes of the LORD are in every place, keeping watch on the evil and the good.' (Proverbs 15:3) It also says, '...no creature is hidden from his sight, but all are naked and exposed to the eyes of him to whom we must give account,' (Hebrews 4:13)

---

[91] William Cowper, 'There is a Fountain Filled with Blood'. Cowper penned these words not long before his death on April 25, 1800. Several years later, Lowell Mason (1792-1872), an American living in Boston set William Cowper's words to music.

[92] Robert Lowry, 'Nothing but the Blood', 1876.

While there are some things about us that we wish the Lord did not know, we may be glad that he knows our needs, our burdens and all the situations we face in life. He knows and he is ready and able to help.–Hebrews 4:15-16; Matthew 6:31-34.

If Judas had known the exact location of the meal, he could have given that location to the religious leaders. It is possible that they would have tried to take the Lord Jesus then. Jesus wanted this meal to be a special time for his disciples.[93] In those verses Jesus assumes the place of a servant / slave and washes the feet of his disciples. He teaches them a lesson in humility and servant leadership. Jesus uses the occasion of the Passover to institute a new covenant. The old covenant that had been in force since the law was given to Moses revolved around keeping rituals and symbolic sacrifices. These rituals and sacrifices looked forward to the coming of the Messiah who would be God's perfect (ultimate and final) sacrifice. The new covenant would look back to the finished work of the Messiah. Instead of keeping religious rituals and performing symbolic sacrifices, we rest by faith on what Jesus did. He died for our sins on the cross, was buried and rose again the third day.

There are times when words just are not enough. In the Old Testament, some of the prophets used dramatic action to illustrate (visually) their messages from God. For example, Ezekiel drew a picture of Jerusalem on a clay tablet and built a small enemy camp and siege works to illustrate the truth that Jerusalem would be attacked. (Ezekiel 4:1-3) Ezekiel shaved his head and beard. This was an outrageous act! No Hebrew man shaved his head and beard. It was considered offensive to people in that society. He took his hair and divided it into three piles. One pile he burned another pile he struck with a sword, and the third pile he scattered to the

---

[93] The events of John 13:3-17 took place sometime between verses 17 and 18 of Mark chapter 14.

wind. This was a picture of the judgment that was about to fall on Israel. (Ezekiel 5:1-3) Jeremiah constructed a yoke and wore it to illustrate the coming Babylonian captivity. (Jeremiah 27:1-7) The prophet Abijah tore his clothes into twelve pieces and gave ten to Jeroboam to illustrate the fact that God was about to take ten tribes from Israel and form the Northern Kingdom.–1 Kings 11:29-33.

Here, at this Passover Feast, Jesus combines words and symbols to communicate truth to his disciples. The pictures Jesus painted that day are powerful and vivid and they continue to speak to us today. The bread represents Jesus' body. When it came time to serve the bread, Jesus broke it and passed it around to those at the table. It was customary to say: "Praised be Thou, O Lord, Sovereign of the world, who causes bread to come forth from the earth." This was the traditional Jewish statement as the bread was taken. It is likely these were the words Jesus used when he gave thanks for the bread. But then Jesus added a new meaning to the bread identifying it as a symbol of his body. Bread is produced when wheat is crushed. Thirty-three years earlier, in a town called Bethlehem (the house of bread) the Bread of Life took on a human body. Jesus used the bread that night to teach his disciples what he was about to do. He was on his way to the cross to lay down his life for sin, where his body would be broken for all whom he will redeem (Isaiah 53:4-6). Calvary is an event worth remembering.

The wine represents his blood. When the time came to drink the third cup of wine Jesus passed it around. On that occasion, Jesus added a new meaning to the drinking of the wine. He said it symbolized his blood. Wine is produced when grapes are crushed. Jesus was about to be crushed by the full weight of religious Israel and mighty Rome. Jesus was about to be crushed by his Father. The full force of the awesome wrath of God was poured out on Jesus. This is the teaching of Scripture. When Jesus was crushed on the cross, his precious blood was shed. All who believe in Jesus for salvation have their sins washed away by the blood of Christ.

This is what we commemorate every time we take the cup at the Lord's Table. That cup reminds us that Jesus took our place on the cross. It reminds us that we have been made right with God. It reminds us that our sins have been washed away and we are clean in the eyes of God. It reminds us of his sacrifice for us.

When they finished the meal they sang the final Hallel Psalms and left the upper room. The disciples did not know exactly what was about to happen. They did not know that before the sun set the next day Jesus would have been arrested, tried several times, condemned to death, beaten, crucified and buried. However, Jesus knew what lay ahead and willingly submitted to it. Jesus said, "Truly, I say to you, I will not drink again of the fruit of the vine until that day when I drink it new in the kingdom of God." (v.25) Here Jesus solemnly declares that this would be the last time he would share Passover with them. It is indicated here that Jesus would die, but it is a verse, which also holds out the promise of victory and the future reality of the great banquet of the redeemed community hosted by Jesus in heaven. Thus, the believer not only looks *to* the cross but *beyond* the cross and past the grave to the glorious resurrection. As the sun sets on human history, the cross casts a long shadow. In the twenty-first-century, we still find its shade comforting in the searing heat of this infernal world.

Jesus foretells Peter's denial (14:26-31)

There are many people in the Scriptures, who have failed miserably and yet they have been restored and re-commissioned by the Lord. That is something that should console us. Such people were, in fact, assigned important tasks in the kingdom of God and achieved great things for

God by his grace. That is something that should give us hope. It is important to consider the whole notion of faith and failure from a Scriptural perspective and meet the people whose lives (including their mistakes and sins) are recorded for our instruction and edification.

Peter messed up after he was converted. On the evening of The Last Supper Jesus foretold that Peter would deny him. Peter, at that point in his experience, could not believe that such a thing would happen and so he argued with the Lord. Isn't that how it is so often with us? During times of close fellowship with Jesus, it is difficult for us to believe that it will not be long before we will disappoint the one we profess to love with all our hearts. However, inevitably in our pilgrimage such times come, all too quickly and frequently, until we eventually realize that faith and failure are part of the spiritual life. Peter's faith failed, but it was a temporary failure, which was foreknown by Christ and would, in time, be forgiven and forgotten by God. The Lord broke him in order to bless him. God knows in advance the foolish things that we are going to do in the future. These things might surprise us and shock others but they do not surprise God. Our failings disappoint the Lord but he is willing to forgive. In fact, he is eager to forgive.

A fraternity of failures

When we think of biblical characters like Jonah, King David and Simon Peter we realize that the church is a building crafted out of such peculiar stones fitted together to create a structure that glorifies God. Even our irregular shape conforms to the master plan of the divine mason. The chiseling and hammering is not meaningless, God is at work to enable us to find that special place reserved for us. Pain is profitable. Tears are the initial trickle that will ultimately bring a torrent of triumphant joy. God's grace can keep us from sin but there are times when we do not avail of it. If we are not aware that the church is a fraternity of failures then there is a danger that we may become a society of Pharisees. We can never do anything to make God love us more and we can never do anything to make God love us less. Let us cast ourselves on the mercy of God. We are accepted and loved. Consider the words of this hymn:

> Depth of mercy can there be
> Mercy still reserved for me?
> Can my God His wrath forbear?
> Me, the chief of sinners spare?
>
> Jesus, answer from above:
> Is not all thy nature love?
> Wilt Thou not the wrong forget?
> Suffer me to kiss Thy feet?
>
> If I rightly read Thy heart,
> If Thou all compassion art,
> Bow Thine ear, in mercy bow;
> Pardon and accept me now.[94]

Gethsemane (14:32-52)

The disciples have just finished the Passover celebration meal with Jesus. Then they went to a place called Gethsemane. Here Jesus may be observed at a time of intense pressure. (vs.32-34) It was a place Jesus often visited with his disciples. (Luke 22:39) Gethsemane seems to have been a refuge for the Lord. It was a place where he could find solitude from the crowds and ministry that occupied his life. It was a place where he could go to find a private moment to commune with his heavenly Father. It was a sanctuary and an

---

[94] Charles Wesley (1707-1788), *Christian Hymns*, Evangelical Movement of Wales, 1977.

oasis. It was a place of refreshment. It was a special place for the Lord and his disciples.

The name Gethsemane is Aramaic in origin. The word means 'olive press'. It was a place where olive trees grew and produced their fruit. The olives would be collected, placed in a press and the olive oil was extracted from the olives under intense pressure. When Jesus and his disciples arrive at Gethsemane he leaves eight of them at the gate to the garden. He takes Peter, James and John with him as they go deeper into the garden. For Jesus, the garden of Gethsemane would be a place of intense pressures. There were internal pressures. Jesus was in a time of intense emotional and spiritual trial. He knew what was coming, but as he looked into the cup he was about to drink he was momentarily overwhelmed with horror and sorrow. No other human has ever experienced such anguish of soul as that which came upon the Lord that night. He was in great distress and anguish.

He knows he is about to suffer intense physical pain. He knows that he is about to become sin on a cross. He knows that he is about to be judged by his Father. He knows that, for the first time in eternity, there will be a breach in the unbroken fellowship he has enjoyed with God the Father. He knows that he will be abandoned by his nation, his followers and his heavenly Father. He is aware that he is about to be tried, rejected and condemned to death by the very people he came to save. He is conscious that the most powerful human government on earth is about turn its fury upon him. The thoughts of what he is about to endure literally overwhelm his mind and heart. While Jesus Christ is God in the flesh, the body he lived in was a frail human body just like ours. His body knew weariness, felt pain, got hungry and tired and here it felt distress. Such was his anguish that an angel was sent from heaven to strengthen the Lord at this time.–Luke 22:43.

Although Jesus is under enormous pressure he may be observed in prayer at this time. (vs.35-36). He went to Gethsemane to pray. In fact it was that intense pressure that brought him to his knees. Jesus spoke to his Father. He addressed him first as "Abba", a word that is equivalent to the English word "daddy". It conveys familiarity and intimacy. It was a word used in Jewish households of the day, but it was a word that no Jew would ever use when he was speaking to God. Jesus enjoyed such intimacy with his Father that he felt comfortable talking to him in this way.

The child of God has the same privilege! When Jesus taught his disciples how to pray he used this word "Father". Paul said: 'For you did not receive the spirit of slavery to fall back into fear, but you have received the Spirit of adoption as sons, by whom we cry, "Abba! Father!" (Romans 8:15) Jesus prayed that this cup might be taken from him. He is not trying to avoid the cross. He was born for that purpose. No one was forcing Jesus to go to the cross. He told the Pharisee, "For this reason the Father loves me, because I lay down my life that I may take it up again. No one takes it from me, but I lay it down of my own accord. I have authority to lay it down, and I have authority to take it up again. This charge I have received from my Father." (John 10:17-18) Jesus is about to become sin on the cross: 'For our sake he made him to be sin who knew no sin, so that in him we might become the righteousness of God.'–2 Corinthians 5:21.

That cup symbolized the undiluted wrath of God that was about to be poured out on Jesus. Thoughts of physical suffering must have been perplexing but the thought of being judged and abandoned by God was a terrifying prospect to the sinless Son of God. Jesus was experiencing spiritual oppression but he persisted in prayer and prevailed. Jesus expressed absolute obedience to the Father's will. He never sinned but he did face temptation.—Hebrews 4:15.

Victory comes through submission to God's will. We see the Master praying in a time of pressure. We may also notice the priorities of Christ. He lived to do the will of his Father: 'For I have come down from heaven, not to do my own will but the will of him who sent me' (John 6:38). He completely fulfilled the Father's plan on Calvary and declared with his dying breath, "It is finished" (John 19:30). While Jesus is praying and wrestling with the greatest load any man ever tried to carry, the disciples are asleep. Jesus commanded them to "watch" but they were tired and they all fell asleep. They had consumed a heavy meal, had a few cups of wine and walked a distance in the evening. These same three men slept though the transfiguration (Matthew 17). They had the astonishing privilege of watching the Great High Priest of heaven as he approached the Father in the Holy of Holies. They had a privilege no other men had ever enjoyed, and they slept through it all! However, it is possible that they slept out of necessity rather than apathy or boredom. Jesus warns his disciples to be watchful and prayerful because a time of temptation and trial is coming and they will need spiritual help to make it through that time of testing. Each time Jesus returns he finds them asleep. Their failure to stand with him in his hardest hour must have added to his pain and sense of loneliness and isolation.

Jesus achieved victory because he was vigilant and diligent in prayer. If we want to live victorious lives, we need to do the same. This glimpse into the events in Gethsemane shows how the Lord fought the battle for us and prevailed. He *travailed* in his soul but he *prevailed* in prayer. This passage should cause us to awake out of our slumber and be watchful and prayerful. When Jesus finished praying he announced that the time of his betrayal had arrived.—vs.41-42.

Immediately Judas appeared with a group of soldiers and members of the temple guard. They were armed and ready for action. In all the trial of that night, the character of Christ shone brightly. Even as he was betrayed by Judas, forsaken by his disciples and arrested by his enemies, Jesus is the perfect picture of grace and love. He refers to Judas as a friend. He showed compassion to Malchus. When the soldiers arrest Jesus, one of the disciples reacts by attacking the servant of the High Priest with his sword (v.47). John tells us that this disciple was Peter and that the servant was named Malchus. (John 18:10) When Peter cut off this man's ear Jesus responded by reaching out in compassion to heal and restore the severed ear. (Luke 22:51) One wonders whatever happened to Malchus? Jesus knows what he is about to face and he faces it all with courage.

When Jesus is arrested every single disciple runs away in fear (v.50). One unnamed young man, whom many believe to be Mark (vs.51-52), runs away leaving his garment in the hands of the soldiers.[95] Peter showed some courage when he drew his sword in defense of the Lord (v.47). But when the ultimate hour of testing came they fled into the shadows and left Jesus alone with his enemies.

Jesus before the council (14:53-65)

Jesus had just observed the Passover with his disciples. He instituted what is now known as the Lord's Table. He agonized in the garden of Gethsemane. There we witness the struggle of Jesus and how he acted under pressure. We see his absolute surrender to the will of the heavenly Father. Judas Iscariot betrayed Jesus with a kiss and Christ was arrested. Much had happened but more was about to unfold.

Here is an account of the Lord's trial before the Sanhedrin. In this trial, Jesus is accused and condemned by

---

[95] It was a convention of Gospel writing for the author not to mention himself by name.

the very people he came to this world to save. They are in the presence of the promised Messiah but they do not recognize him, acknowledge him or submit to him. The account in John's Gospel reveals that Jesus was first taken to the home of Annas. (John 18:13) He was the father-in-law of the High Priest Caiaphas and a man of considerable influence. When Annas finished questioning Jesus, he sent him bound to Caiaphas.–John 18:24.

The Sanhedrin

The Sanhedrin (Hebrew: סַנְהֶדְרִין sanhedrîn, Greek: συνέδριον, synedrion) means 'sitting together', hence 'assembly' or 'council'. It was an assembly of twenty-three men appointed in every city in the biblical Land of Israel. A court should not have an even number of judges to prevent deadlocks and it must be possible for a community to vote for both conviction and exoneration. This court dealt primarily with religious matters.

The Talmud identifies two classes of rabbinical courts called Sanhedrin, the Great Sanhedrin (בית דין הגדול) and a Lesser Sanhedrin (בית דין הקטן). In the Second Temple period, the Great Sanhedrin met in the Hall of Hewn Stones in the Temple in Jerusalem. The court could convene every day except festivals and Shabbat. Each city could have its own lesser Sanhedrin of twenty-three judges. However, there could be only one Great Sanhedrin numbering seventy-one. The Great Sanhedrin acted as the Supreme Court, taking appeals from cases decided by lesser courts. The uneven numbers of judges was meant to eliminate the possibility of a tie. The last to cast his vote was the head of the court.

Function and procedures

The Sanhedrin as a body claimed powers that lesser Jewish courts did not have. As such, they were the ones to whom all questions of law were finally put. The Sanhedrin met in a building known as the Hall of Hewn Stones, which was built into the north wall of the temple mount. It was half inside the sanctuary and half outside, with doors providing access both to the temple and to the outside. The name presumably arises to distinguish it from the buildings in the temple complex used for ritual purposes, which had to be constructed of stones un-hewn by any iron implements. In some cases, it was only necessary for a twenty-three member panel (functioning as a lesser Sanhedrin) to convene. In general, the full panel of seventy-one judges was only convened on matters of national significance (such as a declaration of war) or in the event that the twenty-three member panel could not reach a conclusive verdict. In the Galilee of late antiquity (by the end of the Second Temple period) the Sanhedrin reached its pinnacle of importance and legislated for all aspects of Jewish religious and political life within the parameters laid down by biblical and rabbinic tradition.

The text deals with the Lord's trial before the Sanhedrin. The members of this body were chosen for their maturity and wisdom. They were expected to be fair and impartial in all their rulings. The High Priest was in charge of the proceedings. These people were already convinced of Jesus' guilt and merely went through the motions of securing evidence against him. They behaved like prosecutors rather than independent and impartial arbiters of justice. But this was an illegal trial.

It was illegal because of *when* it was held. Under Judaic laws, which regulated the court system, a trial at night was prohibited.[96] It was also illegal to hold a trial on a feast day and this was the Passover feast. Having a trial at such a time might prevent the entire council from gathering and it would prevent the accused from mounting an effective defense, since it would make it more difficult for witnesses to come to the trial. So this trial obviously violated this regulation since it was held at night and on the Passover. This trial was rigged. The slightest inconsistency in the evidence of witnesses should have been enough to acquit Jesus. There were insufficient grounds to convict.

Christ's condemnation was based on the testimony of false witnesses and erroneous accusations. This passage of Scripture reveals the true character and condition of the human heart. His trial took place at night but as soon as dawn begins to break, the Sanhedrin convened again to legitimize the illegal decisions they reached during the night.

But it was also illegal because of *where* it was held. Jewish law mandated that all trials conducted by the Sanhedrin were to be held in The Hall of Hewn Stones. This was located on the temple grounds. This rule was violated because the preliminary trial was first held in the home of Annas and then transferred to the private residence of the High Priest. (Luke 22:54) The Sanhedrin was behaving more like a private club than a public body elected to oversee judicial proceedings in a fair manner.

It was also illegal because of the *way* it was held. There are many problems with the trial of Jesus that night. Among the illegalities of his trial are the following. Trials were illegal on the eve of the Sabbath because Jewish law required a one day adjournment in the event of a conviction. A guilty sentence could only be handed down the day after a trial. The Sanhedrin could not bring charges against a

---

[96] Luke's account says 'daybreak' but that must refer to the second trial as other Gospel accounts put it at night. This is corroborated by Peter's denials which were before the cock crowed at daybreak.

defendant; they could only investigate charges that had been made by others. The charges against Jesus were changed during the trial. He was first charged with threatening to destroy the temple. Later, he was charged with blasphemy. Then, when he stood before Pilate, his charges were changed again. This time he was charged with claiming to be the King of the Jews and forbidding the paying of taxes to Rome. Jesus was not allowed a defense before the court. All charges against him should have been thoroughly investigated and he should have been allowed time to call his own witnesses. The Sanhedrin pronounced the death sentence (v.64) but under the law the Sanhedrin could not convict or pass down a death sentence.[97]

This trial was illegal because of *why* it was held. It was not about seeking the truth of a man's guilt or innocence. In the eyes of the Sanhedrin, Jesus was guilty before the trial ever began. He had no chance of leaving this trial with anything but a guilty verdict and a sentence of death.

This trial was illegal because of *the witnesses* they called. The Jewish leaders have a problem. The men actually went out and sought witnesses to testify against Jesus (v.55). Effectively they recruited false witnesses: '...many bore false witness against him, but their testimony did not agree.' (14:56) There were many who came forward that night willing to lie. They lied against the one who had done nothing but good and who had said nothing but the truth. Furthermore their testimonies were inconsistent with one another. According to the law, the testimony of witnesses in a trial had to be in perfect agreement:

Deuteronomy 17:6	Deuteronomy 19:15
⁶On the evidence of two	¹⁵"A single witness shall not

---

[97] Under Roman rule, they could not execute the sentence of death. Their remit only allowed them to examine the prisoner and pass judgment to be ratified by the Roman authorities.

witnesses or of three witnesses the one who is to die shall be put to death; a person shall not be put to death on the evidence of one witness.	suffice against a person for any crime or for any wrong in connection with any offense that he has committed. Only on the evidence of two witnesses or of three witnesses shall a charge be established.

Finally, some people informed the court that Jesus had threatened to destroy the temple and to build it again in three days. But again their versions of what Jesus said didn't agree. (v.59) The word 'temple' in (v.58) refers to the Holy Place, not the entire temple grounds. Therefore, they are accusing Jesus of threatening to demolish the holiest place in all of Israel. To their ears, it was utterly sacrilegious. Add to that the ludicrous claim that he would rebuild the temple in three days when it had already been under construction for forty-six years and it is evident that such crass literalism in the interpretation of Christ's words regarding the temple was a convenient and cynical ploy to destroy him. Actually, Jesus never said what they claimed he said. The Lord said, "Destroy this temple, and in three days I will raise it up." (John 2:19) He was not referring to the temple in Jerusalem. He was referring to his own body that would be destroyed on the cross and raised from the dead three days later. (John 2:21) Jesus never said that he would destroy anything. At best, this accusation was based on a misunderstanding or misinterpretation of what Jesus said. However, the Gospels make it clear that these were false accusations.

It is astonishing that not a single person came forward in the Lord's defense that night. His accusers were not looking for his friends; they were looking for those who would testify against him. It is sad to think that there were some there who could have stood up for Jesus. Peter and John were nearby (John 18:15). They were too afraid to come forward and speak up. If the Sanhedrin had searched they would have found many who could give favorable testimony about Jesus. People like, Lazarus, former lepers, a man who had been paralyzed but was restored to mobility, Jairus and his daughter, the widow of Nain and her son, the Gadarene demoniac (now in his right mind), the woman who once had an issue of blood for twelve years and others. But they were only interested in finding fault and ridding themselves of Jesus once and for all. It is amazing that with all the people Jesus had helped, ministered to, fed, healed, blessed and taught, no one stood with him on that terrible night, while many were willing to put their lives on the line to accuse Jesus falsely:

Deuteronomy 19:16-19

[16] If a malicious witness arises to accuse a person of wrongdoing, [17] then both parties to the dispute shall appear before the Lord, before the priests and the judges who are in office in those days. [18] The judges shall inquire diligently, and if the witness is a false witness and has accused his brother falsely,[19] then you shall do to him as he had meant to do to his brother. So you shall purge the evil from your midst.

If a man was proven to be a false witness, he was to receive the same punishment that would have come to the man he lied against.

Jesus stands alone among his enemies. These men did not care that Jesus was innocent. They hated him because he was a threat to their way of life and the power and status they had in society. They hated him so much that they were willing to lie, to break their own laws and to condemn an innocent man to death. It is still the same today! Many religious institutions exercise power abusively. There are still people in our world who hate the name of Jesus so much that they will do anything in their power to destroy him and all those who follow him. Atheism is becoming more aggressive and secularism more militant. Jesus said, "If they persecuted me, they will also persecute you."–John 15:20.

As the trial continues, Caiaphas has a real problem. It is impossible to convict Jesus with the testimony of conflicting witnesses, so he changes tactics. He is frustrated with the proceedings thus far, so he assumes the role of prosecutor and goes on the attack. He is mystified by the fact that Jesus has not opened his mouth to refute the lies the false witnesses have told about him. Therefore, he calls on Jesus to defend himself. In response to Caiaphas' demands, Jesus remains silent. Here Jesus fulfills the prophecy of Isaiah: 'He was oppressed, and he was afflicted, yet he opened not his mouth.' (Isaiah 53:7) Caiaphas attempts to force Jesus to declare his deity. He is trying to get Jesus to incriminate himself on record. Caiaphas asks Jesus, "Are you the Christ, the Son of the Blessed?" Jesus does not disappoint Caiaphas. He answered: "I am..." He tells them that they judge him now but he will ultimately judge them. The Sanhedrin thought they were in control that night but they were terribly wrong.

When Caiaphas hears these words from Jesus, he has heard all that he needs to hear. Caiaphas rips his own clothes. This was a dramatic reaction to what he considered blasphemy.[98] It was a symbolic display designed to convey horror in the face of a terrible crime against God. In fact it is something he ought not to have done as it was expressly forbidden: "The priest who is chief among his brothers, on whose head the anointing oil is poured and who has been consecrated to wear the garments, shall not let the hair of his head hang loose nor tear his clothes" (Leviticus 21:10). When Caiaphas ripped his garments he (unintentionally) disqualified himself from the office of High Priest. The one standing

---

[98] Anyone who doubts that Jesus claimed to be God should take note.

before him was qualified for that office as the great High Priest. What a contrast between the behavior of Caiaphas and the behavior of Christ! The whole council renders their guilty verdict. After Jesus is condemned, the true nature of these men comes out. These educated, refined, religious leaders turn on Jesus like thugs. They spit in the Savior's face.[99] But, it is the fulfillment of prophecy: 'I gave my back to those who strike, and my cheeks to those who pull out the beard; I hid not my face from disgrace and spitting' (Isaiah 50:6). Peter says: 'When he was reviled, he did not revile in return; when he suffered, he did not threaten, but continued entrusting himself to him who judges justly.'–1 Peter 2:23.

Jesus endured all this in order to redeem those who would turn to him in repentance and faith. Whether we know it or not everyone stands before Jesus in judgment. Like those religious Jews, people must decide whether they will believe him or reject him. What will you decide? When you see Jesus one day (and you will), will you see him as your Lord and Savior? On the other hand, will you face him as your Judge? Will you embrace him in gratitude for the price he paid to redeem sinners? It is time for you to decide where you stand in regard to Jesus. Is he a liar or lunatic to be rejected? Alternatively, is he to be loved and obeyed as Savior and Lord?

---

[99] It is not overtly stated that the Sanhedrin were the ones who spat at Jesus and beat him. It is clear that not only the soldiers beat him but others as well. The Sanhedrin was central to the proceedings that night and if they did not participate in this violence they permitted it. They certainly had the power to stop it if they so desired. It is very likely that they were the very ones who engaged in this physical violence against the Lord, after all they were determined to kill him and plotted to murder him and carried out that wicked scheme under the cloak of justice. They had been frustrated in many such attempts up to now and here they most likely gave vent to those frustrations through violent action.

Peter denies Jesus (14:66-72)

After the cock crowed we are told, the Lord turned and looked at Peter. It was a look that penetrated Peter's heart. Peter must have experienced a range of emotions at this point. He had been afraid and perhaps also confused, disappointed and even disillusioned. Then Jesus established eye-contact. Christ did not just look *at* him, but rather he looked *into* him. What a poignant scene. Here is Jesus, betrayed by Judas, denied by Peter, deserted by his disciples and despised by his accusers. What was conveyed to Peter in that look? Somehow, I do not think it was anger or rejection rather I suspect there was pain and pardon in that look. It is amazing that Jesus maintained sufficient focus in such circumstances to deliver a look, which pierced Peter's heart.

However, the look of Jesus would have been wasted if Peter had not been looking at Jesus. Whatever trouble we find ourselves in let us keep looking to Christ for it is only there that we will come to understand ourselves and find the grace we need so much. It was a moment of intense realization. I suspect too that these denials from his close disciple hurt Jesus more than the words of mockery and the physical blows from his avowed enemies. Surely this feeling of hurt must have registered on the face of Christ. If I could commission a painting from the greatest painter of portraits, I would ask him / her to try to capture the emotions on the faces of Christ and Peter at that moment. What a masterpiece that would be. Healing starts with looking into the loving face of Christ. We will find that his gaze is fixed on us.

Fear of failure

Peter was afraid. Fear is part of human experience: fear of rejection, fear of unrequited love. There are phobias about almost anything. In one of Charlie Brown's cartoons, Lucy (the so-called psychiatrist) is trying to diagnose Charlie's emotional problems. Assuming that his problem is fear she lists several phobias in an effort to determine which one he has. Finally she says, "maybe you have a pan-a-phobia; the fear of everything!" Not many of us have pan-a-phobia but most of us do fear something: it might be spiders, thunder and lightning, the dark, enclosed spaces etc. A common biblical exhortation is to "fear not". Some people live with the what-ifs of life. What if that happens? What if it doesn't work out? What if I am left all alone? Others are afraid of failing. Fear of failure makes some people work hard whereas it makes others afraid to try because if they do not succeed they will be labeled a 'failure'.

But failure is part of life and features in biblical history and narratives. The real question is not will we fail but what will we do when we fail? The failure rate for human beings is one-hundred percent. Nobody does what is right all the time. We do not always achieve what we want to achieve or do what we ought to do. Many people feel they have failed: as parents, husbands, wives, daughters, sons, neighbors, friends or Christians. Some feel they have let the Lord down, but to fail is not the same as being a failure. We should bear in mind that failure itself is not the end of the world. It is not fatal. Our pride is dented when we fail but the blow will shape us into what God wants us to be.

Pressing on

After thousands of failed experiments, Thomas Edison invented the light bulb. He learned from his failures and was later to say, "Many of life's failures are people who did not realize how close they were to success when they gave up." No matter how many times we fall, we must get up again and get back in the race. If we fall in a sprint there is no chance of winning, no point in trying but the Christian life is a marathon, and falling does not rule out the possibility that we can still participate. Professional runners want to win marathons because that is their career but most people who run that distance just want to finish. They are not competing against others but against themselves. We must persevere toward the finishing line. We need to learn from our failures and come to see failure as something from which we can learn. Our mistakes can potentially teach us and cause us to grow. God does not just leave us in the place of failure. Even ordinary decent parents in the natural sense do not abandon or forsake their children for their errors.

One of the most beautiful passages in Scripture is where Jeremiah goes to the potter's house and watches the potter working at the wheel. He sees the potter take the vessel that is marred and remake it. He refashions something useful and even beautiful from that same clay! That is what God can do for us! He can take our broken lives; our failures and faults, reshape them, and remake us. He does not give up on us when we fail. So let us press on knowing that our lives are in the hands of the great creator of the universe.

Chapter 15

Jesus before Pilate (15:1-20)

The Jews condemned Jesus to death, but they lacked the authority to carry out the sentence. Therefore, they bound Jesus and led him away to Pontius Pilate, the Roman governor.[100] They knew they could not accuse Jesus of blaspheme. They knew that Pilate would not intervene in a Jewish religious argument. Therefore, when they brought Jesus to Pilate, they changed the charges against him: 'And they began to accuse him, saying, "We found this man misleading our nation and forbidding us to give tribute to Caesar, and saying that he himself is Christ, a king." (Luke 23:2) This was a lie. Jesus had said, "Render to Caesar the things that are Caesar's—Mark 12:17.

Pilate rejects Jesus

Here is the judge of all the earth before the earthly judge. The great Roman Empire had thousands of provincial officials in the course of the half millennium during which it ruled the Mediterranean world. But only one is generally remembered. Millions of Christians around the world mention him whenever they confess their faith in the words of the Nicene or Apostle's Creed: '...crucified (or suffered) under Pontius Pilate'. Millions of children who have never heard of the great Tiberius, second emperor of Rome, know the name of his petty underling, Pilate, an otherwise undistinguished governor.

---

[100] For further information about Pontius Pilate in relation to this trial and his authority and attitude see Appendix C.

The question that Pilate asked is a question that every individual must ask: "Then what shall I do with Jesus who is called Christ?" All other decisions (career, business, marriage partner etc.) are temporal but this one has eternal ramifications. Many who are convinced of the truth about Jesus and convicted of their sins will still not be converted to Christ, either because of cowardice or because they cherish their sinful lifestyles too much. A time comes in our lives when we must make an investigation into Christ's claims.

Pilate was brought face to face with Jesus, and he had a decision to make. He placed his career before everyone and everything. He lived to exalt himself. He attempted to get Jesus to defend himself but Jesus stood there in regal silence. Pilate was amazed and convinced that Jesus was innocent of the charges being leveled against him. That is all the detail Mark gives of Pilate's encounter with Jesus, but the other Gospel writers fill in the gaps. Luke records that Pilate sent Jesus to Kind Herod. (Luke 23:6-12) Herod questioned Jesus and his soldiers mocked him but Jesus refused to answer so Herod sent Jesus back to Pilate. Herod was also convinced of Christ's innocence. (Luke 23:15) Pilate then took Jesus into his palace to question him privately. (John 18:33-37) Jesus told Pilate that his kingdom was not of this world. After examining Jesus, Pilate sees the accusations of the Jews as motivated by envy (Mark 15:10) He knows that Jesus is innocent. (John 18:38) and he takes steps to see that Jesus is released. This whole encounter between Jesus and Pilate comes down to what is said in John 18:37-38. In verse 37 Jesus declares himself to be the truth but Pilate flippantly says: "What is truth?" and turns his back on Jesus.

Pilate ignored the claims of Jesus. He ignored the lies of the Jews who wanted Jesus dead for their own purposes. He ignored the truth. Pilate was a weak, cowardly man who was more concerned with maintaining his position and his power than he was with knowing the truth. He was more concerned with keeping the Jews happy than he was in protecting an innocent man. Jesus was a pawn in a political game. Pilate was a coward who placed his position, his prosperity, his pride above all other considerations such as truth and justice.

There are many people like Pilate in the world today. Not too many possess the position or power that Pilate enjoyed. However, many are confronted with the truth of who Jesus Christ is. (John 14:6; Acts 4:12) They come face to face with the truth, but they don't want to displease the religious authorities. They do not want to rock the boat. There is peer pressure within families and amongst friends. Many reject Jesus because they are afraid of what others will say about them. Some reject Jesus because they love their sin more than they love the truth.

The people reject Jesus

Pilate has examined Jesus and is convinced that he is innocent. Therefore, he takes a gamble to try and free Jesus without any political backlash. It was Pilate's custom to release to the crowds a prisoner of their own choosing. He has in his custody a prisoner named Barabbas (v.7). This man was a political prisoner arrested for insurrection and murder. He was a revolutionary who was trying to overthrow the Roman government in Palestine. He has been caught and now he was headed for death on a Roman cross. Pilate offers the crowd a choice between Jesus and Barabbas (vs.8-10). He thinks the people will choose the peace-loving Jesus over the violent Barabbas. He hopes the people will choose the one who had only done good deeds over the one who had committed evil acts. Pilate was wrong. The people wanted political insurrection, they wanted a political liberator. Pilate rolled the dice and he lost. The Jewish leaders stirred up the crowds and caused them to choose Barabbas over Jesus (v.11). Pilate gives in to the will of the people and allows them to have their way with Jesus. (v. 15) As a revolutionary, who was trying to defeat Rome, Barabbas was probably popular. He was like a folk hero to these people. Jesus did not seem like the kind of Messiah they were looking for. Barabbas, on the other hand, was what they thought a Messiah should be.

Many in our world are just like the crowd that condemned Jesus. All around are people who choose the world over the Lord every day. This can be seen in the way people live their lives every day. The majority is not always right! The majority rejected Jesus. The majority condemned him to death. The majority stood against him and the majority was wrong. The majority prefer their creeds, culture and confessions of faith more than Jesus and the truth of God's Word. The majority is still against Jesus today. The world, as a whole rejects him through sheer unbelief. The world ignores the Word of God. The lost multitude chooses sin over God's salvation. The lost multitude refuses to believe in Jesus.—Matthew 7:13-14)

Pilate rejected the claims of Christ against the instinct of his own soul. He sent Jesus to a particularly cruel death and washed his hands of the matter. At his trial, Jesus had conducted himself with extraordinary self-control and dignity. Pilate knew Jesus was innocent of the charges brought against him. Jesus was a common name among the Jews of Pilate's day. The name had its roots in the Hebrew for Joshua. The name 'Jesus' means Savior. Whether Pilate knew or appreciated the meaning of the name is questionable. To the Christian, Jesus is the sweetest name on earth. To Pilate it was the name of just another Jew. Ultimately, Pilate had to choose between two names: Jesus or Tiberius --- the king of the Jews or the emperor of Rome.

In the early days of his reign, Tiberius had the reputation of being an able soldier and good administrator. But he had a vicious streak and before long he was thoroughly detested in Rome, not only for his cruelties but also for his abominable vices. It is to this debauched individual that Pilate gave his allegiance. Pilate chose Caesar rather than Christ. He chose the secular rather than the sacred path. Pilate wrote the name of Jesus without any real understanding of its significance. Pilate asked, "What is truth?" when Truth was staring him in the face (John 18.38). When Pilate sent Jesus to Herod Antipas, Herod arrayed him in mocking purple (the color of kings). Pilate went further; he let his soldiers crown this 'King of the Jews' with a crown of thorns. Pilate could have dismissed all charges against this innocent man but he signed the most infamous death warrant in history. Pilate crucified Jesus and the same day made friends with Herod Antipas. The man who mocked Christ and the man who murdered Christ were allied in evil. To the end of his days, he would carry with him the memory of eyes that had looked into his eyes and read his very soul.

Jesus was charged with sedition, a revolutionary who was politically dangerous. The Jews were grievously vexed by the yoke of the Roman oppressor and yearned to cast it off. Could Pilate really believe that the Jews were actually displeased with one of their own countrymen who sought to overthrow the authority of Rome? That, for this reason, out of love for Rome, they wanted him to be crucified! Pilate witnessed the attitude of the prisoner. He would have tried others who were vocal in their defense. Jesus is portrayed by his Jewish accusers as boisterous, troublesome and aggressive. But here he is quiet, dignified and even serene. Pilate expected the crowd to choose Jesus. The echoes of "Hosanna" at Christ's triumphal entry to Jerusalem had hardly died away. Christ's accusers were inconsistent. They asked for the release of a known insurrectionist but was this not their very accusation against Jesus? Jesus had not committed any crime, stolen, murdered, or mounted a rebellion. As already mentioned Jesus taught others to give to Caesar the things that are Caesar's. Pilate was loath to condemn an innocent man but he did not want to displease the crowd.

Many today who are confronted with the claims of Christ are not willing to displease the crowd. Only very recently Jesus had been popular because of his miracles and because he held multitudes spellbound by means of his marvelous discourses. The crowd called out for the crucifixion of Jesus, a scandalous, ignominious death. Is it not outrageous for a mob to pass sentence by acclamation? Where is the great Roman system of jurisprudence and fairness? What should have been a court of justice was turned into a lynch mob. Jesus rode into Jerusalem to shouts of praise and it seemed he had no enemies. Now the people were baying for blood and it seemed he had no friends. Pilate pronounced Jesus not guilty three times and yet he failed to acquit him. He tried to wriggle out of his responsibility to decide: "Take him yourselves and judge him by your own law" (John 18:31) he said. He tried to dismiss the issue by sending Jesus to Herod. He tried to discuss the issue but Jesus had nothing to say to him. He tried to distract the crowd by offering to release either Jesus or Barabbas. He tried to disown responsibility, by washing his hands.

He asks an important question: "Then what shall I do with Jesus who is called Christ?" (Matthew 27:22) Pilate's unhappy face peers out at us from each of the four gospels. We see how, despite himself he was forced to face eternal issues and make a personal decision regarding Jesus. He was forced to make, not just a professional, but a personal investigation into Christ's claims. There was certainly nothing very professional about the investigation and the outcome was the result of political maneuvering and pragmatism rather than principle. This led him to a personal crisis, as expressed in the desperate (and pathetic) question "What shall I do then, with Jesus?"

We all stand face to face with Jesus. Pilate did not want to condemn an innocent man but he didn't want to displease the crowd either. Today you might be presented with the same dilemma. You know Jesus deserves a fair hearing but you feel intimidated. The question he asked is a vital question tearing at the heart of Pilate. It is a personal question: a decision Pilate and others would rather avoid. Ultimately, he was willing to let the crowd decide.[101] How about you? Will you reject Jesus and follow the crowd? The responsibility for that decision rests with each individual. It is a question that demands action and though it may be obvious, it still ought to be stated clearly that it is a question about Jesus. Pilate's other decisions were dwarfed by this one. It remains a crucial question today: "What shall I do then with Jesus?" There is no more important question than this.

Jesus is mocked

This passage brings us one step closer to the death of Christ on the cross of Calvary. An entire battalion of soldiers gathered to mock Jesus. This included verbal and physical abuse. He was tortured, deprived of sleep and, apparently, food and taunted and tormented by men whose profession involved killing. They arrayed him in a purple robe and crowned him with thorns. They mockingly saluted him saying, "Hail, King of the Jews!" They struck him on the head and spat on him. Here is the one to whom every knee shall one day bow and these soldiers kneel down feigning homage to him. When they had amused themselves sufficiently in this sadistic orgy of violence they led Jesus away to be crucified.

The crucifixion and death of Jesus (15:21-39)

In some ways, people have become too accustomed to the cross. We see crosses every day of our lives. Many churches have them on top of their steeples. Like any other symbol, it can lose its power if we become too familiar with

---

[101] Letting the crowd decide was actually his decision.

it.[102] In other words, we can become desensitized to the cross. For many, the cross is nothing more than a piece of jewelry that is used to adorn the ear or the neck. For some, the cross is an icon designed for worship. This is inappropriate. Some see the cross as an amulet that contains supernatural power; they hang it over their bed or carry it around to ward off evil. This too is inappropriate.

The cross is offensive to some people. In 1 Corinthians 1:23-24 Paul calls it a 'stumbling block' and 'folly'. He says: '...we preach Christ crucified a stumbling block to Jews and folly to Gentiles, but to those who are called, both Jews and Greeks, Christ the power of God and the wisdom of God.' The phrase 'stumbling block' comes from the Greek word *skandalon* which means a 'trap' or a 'snare'. It came to mean something that trips a person up and causes them to fall. The English word 'scandal' is derived from this word. To the Jews, the cross was a scandal. They could not conceive of the Messiah being nailed to a cross. Thus they stumbled over the cross.

The cross is foolishness to some people. Paul says that the Greeks considered the cross to be 'foolishness'. This word comes from the Greek *moria*, which gives us the English word 'moron'. The sophisticated Greeks looked at the idea of a Savior dying on a cross and they declared it to be moronic foolishness.

However, for those who know and love the Lord as their personal Savior the cross (meaning the event of Calvary) is an object of power and wisdom. Paul says that those who have grasped the true message of the cross understand that it is not weak or foolish. It is instead, the power of God and the wisdom of God. It is the power of God because through the

---

[102] The cross itself has no power. It is to the Savior who died on the cross that we look for salvation. It is to him that we cling, not the old rugged cross as a piece of wood but what it symbolizes, the atoning sacrifice of Jesus.

cross God forever destroyed the kingdom of Satan and broke the grip of sin.

The message of the cross is a message of pain, suffering and death. Three times, we are told in these verses that Jesus was 'crucified.' (Mark 15:20, 24-25) This word means 'to nail one to a stake'. The death Jesus died was a horrible, painful death. The English word 'excruciating' comes from two Latin words: *ex* which means 'out of' and *cruciare*, which means 'the cross'. A death on the cross was so painful that it came to be associated with any pain that caused extreme suffering. I have heard several kinds of pain described as being excruciating. Childbirth and a kidney stone have been described in that fashion.

Add to this the suffering Jesus endured before he was nailed to the cross to die. He had been beaten, mocked, spat upon and scourged, had the hair of his beard plucked and crowned with thorns. Why would he endure this kind of death? There is only one answer: his love for his lost sheep: 'God shows his love for us in that while we were still sinners, Christ died for us.'–Romans 5:8.

The cross is not a trinket to be worn without thought. It is not an amulet to be used to pacify superstitions. It is not an idol to be worshiped. It is a symbol of God's love. Therefore, let us glory in his cross, and praise the Lord for what he did for us. For it is the doorway into life for all who know Jesus as Savior: 'But far be it from me to boast except in the cross of our Lord Jesus Christ, by which the world has been crucified to me, and I to the world.'–Galatians 6:14.

As Jesus hung on that cross, giving his life for the lost, his enemies circled him like a flock of hungry vultures. They hated him so much that they even made fun of him and taunted him as he died. They reproached him, telling him to come down from the cross if he was really who he claimed to be. The tragedy in the cross is seen in two different ways.

First, it is seen in the attitude of the Jews toward Jesus. He had come into this world as their Messiah. He was the embodiment of all the Old Testament prophecies. He came to redeem them and to usher in the kingdom of God. They were looking for a conqueror, not understanding that their King had to die before he could reign. The cross was never 'Plan B'. The event of Calvary is not a tragedy but a triumph! Jesus entered this world for the purpose of going to the cross. The Jews could have received him, but they rejected him instead: 'He came to his own, and his own people did not receive him.'—John 1:11.

Second, the cross is also tragic because it brings the depravity of man into sharp focus. All the pain of hell and the undiluted wrath of Almighty God were unleashed on the Person of the Lord Jesus Christ. He literally took our place on that cross.[103] A great exchange took place whereby the prince of heaven was exchanged for the prisoners of hell.[104] He died our death; he suffered our hell; he paid our price (Romans 6:23). Because he paid the sinner's debt, those who place their trust in him for salvation are delivered from the debt of sin. We are delivered from the threat of hell. We are set free from the power and penalty of sin. Our sins were transferred to him at the cross. When we receive him into our hearts, his righteousness is transferred to us: 'not having a righteousness of my own that comes from the law, but that which comes through faith in Christ, the righteousness from God that depends on faith.'—Philippians 3:9.

The cross is a message of triumph. These verses record the death of the Lord Jesus. After six hours on the cross, he dismissed his Spirit when he knew that the price for sin had

---

[103] That is he took the place of all those who trust him for salvation. This Bible does not teach that Christ died for everybody. Universalism is unscriptural.

[104] Not people actually in hell but destined to go there if they do not repent and turn to Christ in faith.

been paid and God was eternally satisfied. The words of Jesus from the cross were not the words of a victim but the words of a victor. He did not say "I am finished". He said, "It is finished!"

When Jesus died on the cross, his death signaled the defeat of three terrible enemies of lost humanity. His death signaled the ultimate defeat of Satan, it spelled the doom of Satan's dominion in this world, which will come to an end and it signaled the defeat of sin. When sin entered the world it brought with it death, devastation and damnation but Jesus forever did away with sin when he died on the cross. As John the Baptist proclaimed, "Behold, the Lamb of God, who takes away the sin of the world!"–John 1:29.

Christ's death signaled the defeat of separation. Sin had separated the sinner from God: '…your iniquities have made a separation between you and your God, and your sins have hidden his face from you so that he does not hear' (Isaiah 59:2). The death of Jesus broke down the wall of separation erected by sin. His death brings those who trust him back into fellowship with God: 'For if while we were enemies we were reconciled to God by the death of his Son, much more, now that we are reconciled, shall we be saved by his life' (Romans 5:10).

The cross puts an end to the degeneration that began with the disobedience and rebellion of Adam and Eve. It is the beginning of regeneration, restoration and reconciliation. Jesus is our Mediator. (1 Timothy 2:5) He has bridged the gap between us and God. But now in Christ Jesus you who once were far off have been brought near by the blood of Christ (Ephesians 2:13). So, the death of Jesus was not the tragedy it appeared to be on the surface. The death of Jesus was a triumph. The message of the cross is a message of testimony. The cross of Jesus was about far more than death, suffering and blood. The cross of Jesus was a place of testimony because it was here that God made his greatest declaration of love for lost humanity.

Christ's greatest work was accomplished at the cross. When he raised Lazarus from the dead, he helped one man and his family. When he healed the lepers; delivered the demoniacs; opened the blind eyes and healed diseased, twisted bodies he was helping one person and one family at a time. When he fed the five-thousand, he helped five-thousand men plus women and children. However, when he died on the cross, Jesus was making a difference for every member of Adam's family who would look to him by faith. It was not just one man; but it was 'whosoever will'.

He could have saved himself (v.31) but he stayed on the cross to save sinners. His death was not in vain. The very day Jesus died a lost thief repented, trusted and was saved. (Luke 23:40-43) That same day a hardened, pagan, Roman military officer was convicted as he gazed at the scene before him. (Mark 15:39) The cross of Christ still trumpets the love of God for lost sinners.

In our day, the testimony of the cross has become muted by the siren call of this world and its pleasures. But those who hear the testimony of the cross and heed its message will find that there is power in its message. What is the cross of Jesus to you? Is it merely a piece of jewelry? Is it just a religious symbol? Is it a talisman you hang over your bed in the futile hope that it ward off evil spirits? Is it foolishness? Or, is the cross the 'power of God unto salvation'?

All who heed the message of the cross will find that salvation is still available. They will find that God can still save souls; change eternal destinies and transform sinners into saints of God. It is to the Christ of the cross we look for salvation and sanctification.

A solar eclipse may well explain the darkness that descended on the earth at the death of Jesus but that in no way negates its symbolism and significance.[105] Jesus cried out the most heart-rending cry in Aramaic, "*Eloi, Eloi, lema sabachthani?*" which means, "My God, my God, why have you forsaken me?" (v.34) Those who were listening to him misunderstood and thought he was calling for Elijah.[106]

Mark records that someone ran and filled a sponge with sour wine and offered it to Jesus. This was wine mixed with myrrh, which acted as a painkiller.[107] Jesus declined to take it. (v.23) The person who offered Jesus this concoction said: "Wait, let us see whether Elijah will come to take him down" (v.36). These words are usually understood as derisive but it is possible that they were sincere and not scornful.

When Jesus died the curtain of the temple was torn in two, from top to bottom. It is not an insignificant detail that the tear was from the top down rather than the bottom up. This signifies a divine act rather than a human act. The curtain functioned as a screen for the Holy of Holies where only the High Priest could enter to make intercession for sin. But Christ's death made access to God available to all who call upon Jesus for salvation. Jesus would now be the High Priest and only mediator. (1 Timothy 2:5) All who are in Christ henceforth will be 'a royal priesthood'–1 Peter 2:9.

---

[105] Although the darkness of a solar eclipse would not last three hours as this darkness did.

[106] This is possibly just because they misheard or it might be that they were expecting Elijah to appear at the time of the Messiah. See earlier comments that deal with this.

[107] Myrrh was a substance from a shrub-like tree that produced a bitter gum used as a fragrance by the living and an embalming agent for the dead. When the leaves of this tree were crushed, they exuded a very fragrant odor. Myrrh was mentioned in association with the life and ministry of the Lord Jesus Christ (the Magi, Matthew 2:11). Nicodemus brought myrrh to anoint the body of Jesus for burial (John 19:39). The word myrrh means 'bitter' and it came to be associated with suffering and death.

At the moment of Christ's death the centurion at the foot of the cross said: "Truly this man was the Son of God!" (v.39). This is an astonishing acknowledgement from a most unlikely source.

There were several women looking on from a distance, among them were Mary Magdalene, and Mary the mother of James the younger and of Joses, and Salome. (v.40) When he was in Galilee, they followed him and ministered to him, and there were also many other women in the entourage who travelled with him to Jerusalem. There is only the briefest allusion to these faithful followers of Jesus. Some are identified by name. Some of these witnesses of Christ's death were to be also the first witnesses of his resurrection.

Jesus is buried (15:42-47)

The bloodied body of Jesus hangs lifeless on the cross. The crowds depart. His mother Mary and John leave the scene of his death. The soldiers are preparing to leave Calvary. It is a sad scene of death, pain and sorrow. Out of the darkness of that bleak moment at Calvary shone the light of one brave soul who was willing to identify himself with the Lord Jesus. One man was willing to claim and minister to the body of the Lord. His name is Joseph of Arimathaea. His courageous actions challenge all disciples to take a stand with Jesus as well.

All four of the Gospel writers tell us about this man named Joseph. Their descriptions reveal a man of character and integrity. He was from a place called Arimathaea. In Old Testament times, the city was called Ramah, or Ramahthainzophim (the latter sounding rather like a form of medication). It was located twenty miles northwest of Jerusalem and was the hometown of the prophet Samuel (1 Samuel 1:1). He was a wealthy man. (Matthew 27:5) His ability to purchase an expensive tomb near the city of

Jerusalem bears this out. He is called a 'good' and a 'just' man. (Luke 23:50) This means he had a good moral character and set an excellent example.

He is also called an 'honorable counselor' (Mark 15:43). The word 'counselor' indicates that Joseph was a member of the Sanhedrin. This seventy-member body was the supreme ruling court of the Jews. They possessed ultimate power in all matters of the Jewish religion and social life. They were immensely powerful men. This was the very body that condemned Jesus to death. The word 'honorable' means he was in good standing and an influential and respected member of that body of men. Literally, Joseph was a leader among leaders. He would have been well known and well respected by the Pharisees, the Sadducees and the scribes.

He waited for the kingdom of God. Joseph, like Simeon and Anna, who confessed their faith in Jesus in the temple when he was a baby (Luke 2:22-28), was a man with genuine faith in God. Joseph was more than just a cultural Jew. His faith was real and he looked for and longed to see the Messiah. Most of the Jewish leaders possessed a religion that was dead. They denied God by the way they lived and by the way they practiced their religion. Joseph, on the other hand, had a genuine faith that affected the way he lived.

Though we may not have positions of influence we can all strive to possess the same kind of moral and spiritual qualities that Joseph demonstrated in his life. We can, by God's grace be good and just. We can never be good in the sense of being perfectly righteous, but we can be like Joseph, available and ready to serve the Lord at all times.[108] We can all be like Joseph by possessing a genuine faith in the Lord Jesus Christ. What made Joseph different was his faith in the Lord Jesus Christ. That is what separated him from the dead

---

[108]The Christian is perfectly righteous in terms of justification. I am talking here about sanctification and holy living.

co-religionists that lived around him. All they had were their rituals, their rules and their self-righteousness. Joseph, on the other hand, possessed a living faith that changed his life.

But he was a secret disciple. Joseph had come to embrace the truth that Jesus was the long awaited Messiah that was to come and save Israel. While he was a believer, he kept his faith a secret. The Gospel of John says:

John 19:38

³⁸ After these things Joseph of Arimathea, who was a disciple of Jesus, but secretly for fear of the Jews, asked Pilate that he might take away the body of Jesus, and Pilate gave him permission. So he came and took away his body.

Joseph was a believer, but he was afraid of what would happen to him if others found out. We don't know how long Joseph believed in Jesus, but we do know that he opposed the efforts of the Sanhedrin to condemn Jesus to death:

Luke 23:50-51

⁵⁰ Now there was a man named Joseph, from the Jewish town of Arimathea. He was a member of the council, a good and righteous man, ⁵¹ who had not consented to their decision and action; and he was looking for the kingdom of God.

Joseph was a wealthy man, but he had not, up to this time, been willing to pay the price of identifying himself with the Lord Jesus Christ. The poor have less to lose! Joseph had many commendable qualities, but his failure to publicly declare his faith in Jesus is not one of them. In this aspect of his life, Joseph is not someone we want to emulate. Sadly, many believers fit the same profile as Joseph of Arimathaea. They are so deeply undercover that the CIA couldn't identify them as a child of God! Their neighbors do not know they are saved. Their co-workers do not know they are saved. Their classmates do not know they are saved. If you watched them day in and day out, there would be little evidence that they are saved. Their lives are not all that different from the world around them. They use some of the same coarse language and do the same things as the lost around them. They intentionally hide their faith because they are afraid of what people will say about them. On the other hand, maybe they do not intentionally hide their faith but never intentionally reveal it. If you were accused of being a Christian, would there be enough evidence to convict you?

The Bible says: 'The fear of man lays a snare, but whoever trusts in the LORD is safe.' (Proverbs 29:25) Fear of others is the trap Satan sets to ensnare the timid saint of God. Satan wants to silence the testimony of believers. Fear is a trap to be avoided at all costs. The Christian is expected to take a bold stand for their Lord. Our testimony for him is commanded, expected and well deserved: 'Let the redeemed of the LORD say so, whom he has redeemed from trouble.' (Psalm 107:2) We can do no better than to openly declare our faith in, love for and allegiance to the Lord Jesus Christ, for his grace, love, mercy, forgiveness and salvation. Saints of God, renounce the secret service and openly embrace him!

Joseph had purchased a tomb near the city of Jerusalem probably because he planned to be buried in it one day. Tombs that were carved out of the rocks were expensive. Only the wealthy could afford one. That tomb would be the earthly monument to his wealth, his power and his accomplishments during his life. A tomb of that kind was a way of making a mark for posterity. That tomb was designed to declare his glory.

When Joseph saw Jesus dying on the cross, his priorities changed. As Joseph watched Jesus die that day, he made a decision. He would be silent no more. He would hide his faith no longer. When Jesus was dead, Joseph went boldly to Pilate to ask for the body of his Lord. After determining that Jesus was indeed dead, Pilate gave the body to Joseph and allowed him to take it away for burial. So Joseph asks for and tenderly cares for the Lord's body. To him, it was a precious thing that deserved to be treated with compassion and care. (v.43, 46) To Pilate, the body of Jesus was merely a corpse, a piece of rubbish to be disposed of.

The Jews had already made a deal with Pilate that the bodies would be taken down from the crosses. (John 19:31-34) The next day was the Passover and the Jews wanted the bodies taken down and disposed of before the holy day dawned. That is why Pilate ordered his soldiers to break the legs of the crucified men. With their legs broken, the condemned men could no longer push themselves up in order to breathe. Without that ability, they would die of suffocation within minutes. Therefore, the soldiers took a wooden mallet and broke the legs of the dying men with brutal blows. When they came to Jesus, however, he was already dead. To confirm this, they thrust a spear into his side and water and blood came out. This signaled the fact that death had taken place. The plasma and the platelets in his blood had already separated.

The text says that Joseph 'went in boldly' to ask for the body of Jesus. Pilate is amazed that Jesus is already dead. He sends for the centurion, who confirms the fact that Jesus is dead. Pilate releases the body to Joseph and he, along with Nicodemus, begin the burial preparations (John 19:38-42). It seems that believers now surround Pilate! Maybe Nicodemus was influenced by the courage he saw in Joseph. Remember he once came to Jesus by night. (see John 3) They may have been there that day as part of the delegation set by the Sanhedrin to observe the death of Jesus. If so, these men came to Calvary representing a dead religion but they would become ambassadors of the living Lord!

When Jesus died on the cross, Joseph was no longer concerned with his own glory. He is now emboldened to step up and openly declares his association with Jesus. Joseph could have lost power, prestige and popularity. By touching a dead body, Joseph defiled himself. Joseph took a risk. To be a genuine disciple of Jesus is to live a life of shame (taking up the cross). It is to live a life where you give up your rights and your will. You deny yourself, giving yourself over to the will of the one who died to redeem you from sin. It is to live a life that is out of step with the world. It is to live such a radically different life that the world looks on you with, distrust and misunderstanding and perhaps even hatred.

Hugh Latimer was raised to the bishopric of Worcester in the reign of Henry VIII. It was the custom in those days for each of the bishops to give gifts to the king on New Year's Day. Latimer went with the rest of his brethren to make the usual offering. But instead of a purse of gold he presented the King with a New Testament in which was a leaf doubled down to this passage which read 'Whoremongers and adulterers God will judge.'[109] That took courage, especially with someone as volatile and violent as Henry VIII. He was later burnt at the stake with Nicholas Ridley. He is quoted as having said to Ridley: "Play the man, Master Ridley; we shall this day light such a candle, by God's grace, in England, as I trust shall never be put out."

What kind of disciple are you? Are you vocal and bold in your witness and your testimony? Or do you tend to hold back out of fear of what others will say or think about you? Has God spoken to you about being bolder in your witness? Are you like Joseph of Arimathaea in that you are keeping your faith a secret? Is the Holy Spirit convicting you to take a public stand for your faith? The Holy Spirit emboldens for witness.

---

[109] Tan, P. L. *Encyclopedia of 7700 Illustrations : A treasury of Illustrations, Anecdotes, Facts and Quotations for Pastors, Teachers and Christian Workers*, Thirteenth printing 1996, c1979). Dallas: Texas, Bible Communications Inc.

Jesus was placed in the tomb and the stone rolled across the entrance to seal it. This section closes with the statement: 'Mary Magdalene and Mary the mother of Joses saw where he was laid.' (v.47) This shows their devotion to the Lord and explains why they were able to visit the Tomb on the day of the resurrection.

Chapter 16

The Resurrection (16:1-8)

Throughout the Bible, God used angels to make special announcements to humans. He used an angel to send a message of destruction to Lot in Sodom (Genesis 19); to announce the birth of Samson (Judges 13); to announce the birth of John the Baptist (Luke 1); to announce the conception of Christ (Luke 1:11) and to announce the birth of Christ. (Luke 2:8-14) It seems that when God has an announcement of extreme importance, he often sends that message through an angel. This passage in Mark's Gospel presents an angel who made an announcement that reverberates two-thousand years later.

On that first Easter morning, as dawn was breaking on a world that would be forever changed an angel delivered a special message. It is a message that is still vital today. It is a sad sight in my mind's eye to see these sorrowing women as they made their way through the streets of Jerusalem early that Sunday morning. They were going to the tomb of the man they had believed to be the Messiah. They were going to the tomb of a man who had promised life to all who came unto him, but who was now dead, or so they thought! Certainly, they were confused and confounded as they came near the tomb.

They were also concerned about the huge stone that covered the entrance to the tomb. How would they ever gain access to the body? How could these three women ever hope to move this massive stone? Yet they carried on determined to minister to the body of Christ. As they came within sight of the tomb, they were astounded to see the stone rolled away. Seeing this, they ran to the tomb and looked in, only to find that the body of Jesus was gone. An empty tomb does not necessarily declare a resurrection.

Whatever doubts and concerns entered their hearts they were short lived. Suddenly, the women noticed a young man sitting upon the stone. (Matthew 28:2-3) He delivered a message of hope that still has the power to change lives. It is a message of peace: "Do not be alarmed." (v.6) What grace that these first words are words of peace. Two-thousand years later the resurrection is still bringing that same message of peace to the hearts of all who believe in him. It is not only a message of peace, but it is also a message of power: "He has risen" (v.6). Jesus was not the first person to rise from the dead. Others, such as, Lazarus (John 11), the widow of Nain's son (Luke 7) and Jairus' daughter (Mark 5) had been resurrected by the Lord's power. However, Jesus was the first to ever be resurrected and to die no more. All the others were just temporary resuscitations. They had to die again. Jesus accomplished a true resurrection that first Easter morning. The Christian has a living Lord, not a dead religion.

Because he was able to conquer death, all those who receive him as their Savior become partakers of that same resurrection power. The resurrection power of the Lord Jesus is active today. Every redeemed sinner is a testimony to the life changing, life-giving power of the risen Christ. We have a living Lord. The angel says, "He has risen; he is not here!" (v.6). He is active, not just absent. This work of the risen Lord is finished forever. (Hebrews 10:12) Jesus is alive and active on our behalf. He is acting as our intercessor. (Hebrews 7:25; Romans 8:34) He is watching over us always (Hebrews 4:13). He feels our pain. (Hebrews 4:15) He is acting as our advocate. (1 John 2:2) He is preparing a place for us. (John 14:1-3) His activity is all for the benefit of his people.

Then the angel of the Lord makes a promise: "you will see him, just as he told you." (v.7) The angel closed his message to these women by reminding them of the Lord's promise. Faith is based on his Word. They would see him again. This must have encouraged their hearts. They had come to the tomb that morning expecting to see a dead body but they left it with the promise that they would look upon his living face again. Hope was rekindled in their hearts.

Believers today also have such a promise for they too shall see his face (Revelation 22:4) not in Galilee, but in glory. Heaven will be wonderful for Christ's disciples because they will get to see Jesus. This angel delivered an immensely important message. The resurrection of Jesus changed everything. The day Jesus was crucified was a dark and terrible day. His body was placed in the tomb and as the sun went down that night so did the hopes and dreams of the Lord's disciples. However, what a difference a day makes! Mark moves his readers beyond that tragic Saturday to a glorious Sunday when the world changed forever.

These women had witnessed the death of Jesus and watched as his body was placed in a tomb and a stone was rolled over the opening to seal his body inside (Mark 15:46-47). When the Sabbath ended, they set out with spices to anoint the body of Jesus. The perfume these women were intending to use would have served the purpose of masking the smells of decomposition. They set out as morticians but return as missionaries. Their intention is to go to the tomb to perform one final act of love and service to the Lord. Their devotion is evident in this labor of love.

On the way, they talked about the stone at the entrance to the tomb because they were concerned that they might not be able to gain access to the tomb. They are aware that they would be unable to move that stone by themselves. Maybe they hoped to persuade the soldiers to assist and allow them have access to the tomb. They were not going there looking for a living Lord, they were looking for a cold corpse. They were still living in Saturday. When that awful Saturday dawned, all they could see was the shattered remains of their hopes and dreams. These women, along with all the Lord's followers, had placed their faith and confidence in Jesus. Then all their fondest hopes and dreams died with Jesus on the cross. Faith turned to sorrow and hopelessness as they saw his broken body taken down from the cross and placed in that tomb. It all seemed fatal and final.

However, it was not the end. It was the dawn of a new beginning: 'And entering the tomb, they saw a young man sitting on the right side, dressed in a white robe, and they were alarmed.' (v.5) From the other Gospel accounts it can be known that this is no ordinary young man but an angel. He tells them not to be afraid. He confirms what they already know: that Jesus was crucified and died. They had witnessed the crucifixion. He wants them to know that his cry of "it is finished!" did not mean that he was finished. The angel wants them to know that the empty tomb of the Lord is not a place of despair and defeat. That empty tomb is a place of glory, a place of power and a place of hope. That was a message those women needed to hear that Sunday morning and it is the message people need to hear today. After telling the women that Jesus had risen from the dead, the angel invited them to look at the place where the body had been.[110] Their hopes were resurrected.

For two-thousand years, skeptics have tried to prove that the resurrection did not take place. They have concocted every kind of theory imaginable to account for the empty tomb. If the Jews had the body, they would have produced it when the disciples started preaching the resurrection. If the disciples had taken the body, they would not have suffered persecution and died for a lie. That empty tomb is still

---

[110] John's account reveals what they saw: strips of linen, the burial cloth (John 20:6-7).

preaching today! That tomb still tells this world that Jesus is alive and that he is able to save all who come to him by faith (Hebrews 7:25). That message brought them out of the gloom and into the glory of life.

The angel sends them away from the tomb to carry the message to the disciples who were filled with fear and in hiding. (John 20:19) God used these women to be the first disciples to proclaim the resurrection. As such they were the first to roll countless stones away from the hearts of millions. They were the first to spread the good news not just of that empty tomb but also of the risen Savior. What they encountered at the tomb was not what they expected as they traveled there. What they encountered changed their lives forever. Mark says that they 'fled from the tomb, for trembling and astonishment had seized them, and they said nothing to anyone, for they were afraid' (v.8). This must mean that they told nobody along the way because it is known from the other Gospel writers that they did run to find the disciples and tell them (e.g. Matthew 28:8; John 20:1).

This news affected the disciples too. Peter and John ran to the tomb. John looked in and saw the evidence and he believed. (John 20:8) Later that day, Jesus would appear to more of the disciples. Because of their testimony, many were brought out of the darkness and gloom of Saturday into the wonder and glory of Sunday. Such is the power of the resurrection. When the resurrection is first encountered and believed, it fills the heart with amazement. When the Lord's resurrection is embraced by faith, it brings about a change in the life of the person who receives its truth. Today can be a new beginning of faith and hope for all who will live in the power, peace and promises of the resurrection.

Jesus appears to Mary Magdalene (16:9-20)[111]

In these verses Mark summarizes the events of (Luke 24:13-35). In that section of Scripture, details are recorded of Christ's encounter with the two downhearted disciples on the road to Emmaus. Then Jesus appears to the disciples prior to his ascension.

As we are nearing the end of our journey through the Gospel of Mark the text says: "he appeared first to Mary Magdalene". Of all the people, Jesus could have revealed himself to that morning he chose to reveal himself to Mary. Why? Was it just coincidental that she happened to be the first to be in the right place at the right time? On the other hand, did Jesus choose her to be the first to see him?

Mark emphasizes what kind of woman Mary was when she met Jesus. He states that Jesus cast seven devils out of Mary. She was trapped in the worst kind of bondage as a prisoner of Satan. She probably lived a wicked life. Then, one day, she met a man named Jesus who spoke to her and set her free. He changed her life so that from that moment on, she followed him because she loved him for all that he had done in her life. Her love for Jesus manifested itself in absolute devotion to him. Devotion to the Lord leads to

---

[111] Some of the earliest manuscripts do not include 16:9-20. Some Bible scholars do not believe that these verses were actually written by Mark. They believe some other person added them later. The reason they believe this is that the language used in these verses is different from the language used in the rest of the Gospel of Mark. In addition, the three oldest manuscripts in existence do not include these verses. However, they are part of the canon of Scripture. The early church fathers mention them being in Mark toward the end of the first century.

Christian Publishing House does not accept that verses 9-20 were a part of the original text. They were a second-century interpolation by a charismatic group. For a full explanation of this, please see the article,

Was Mark 16:9-20 Written by Mark?
http://www.christianpublishers.org/textual-mark-16-9-20

significant encounters with God. The Lord honored that devotion by allowing her the privilege of being the first to see him after the resurrection. Those who have been forgiven most seem to love him most in return. (Luke 7:36-50) Mary got to see Jesus first because she was at the tomb.

The Lord appeared to Mary to console her broken heart. It was a ministry of love and grace on his part to help a wounded woman through a time of heartache. I see evidence of the resurrection all around me in the lives of those he has changed by his power. I do not need to go to Jerusalem and look into a tomb to know that Jesus is alive. I need to look no farther than those all around me, who have been changed by his power, to know that he lives.

The day Jesus rose from the dead there was flurry of activity. From sunrise to sunset, the Lord was actively ministering to his followers. He wanted them to know that he was alive. He wanted them to know that the resurrection was a reality. Jesus used his time to minister to those he cared about the most. He took the time to minister to those who would have the task of ministering to others. He wanted those who would call on others to believe in Jesus to believe in him first. So, he spent the day building faith in the hearts of those who mattered most to him. In order to get a full understanding of the events of that resurrection day it is necessary to look at the accounts of all four Gospel writers. Each writer gives different details of that wonderful morning. They do not contradict one another. They simply supply different details about the events of that morning.

Several women come to the tomb early in the morning (Matthew 28:1; Mark 16:2-3; Luke 24:1, 22; John 20:1). An angel rolled away the stone from the tomb. (Matthew 28:2-3) The Roman guards panic and flee. (Matthew 28:4; 11-15) The women arrive at the tomb, finding it open and empty. (Matthew 28:1; Mark 16:4; Luke 24:2-3, 23; John 20:1) Two angels appear to the women inside the tomb. They tell the women that Jesus is alive and to go tell the disciples. (Matthew 28:5-7; Mark 16:5-7; Luke 24:4-8; 23) The women go to tell the disciples who do not believe their report. (Matthew 28:8; Mark 16:8; Luke 24:9-11) Peter and John run to the tomb, find it empty and return home. (Luke 24:12, 24; John 20:3-10) Mary Magdalene comes back to the tomb. She remains there alone crying when she sees an angel, and then she sees the risen Savior.

Christ comforts and consoles the brokenhearted. Jesus confirms the meaning and significance of the resurrection with the disciples on the road to Emmaus. He did this through the Scriptures. Later that evening he appeared to his disciples as they were eating their evening meal. Jesus appeared in their midst as they were receiving the report of his resurrection appearance from the two disciples from Emmaus. (Luke 24:36) The disciples were locked in the upper room because they were afraid of the Jews. (John 20:19) Apparently, Jesus was able to pass through the walls of the room where they were. He simply materialized in their presence and revealed himself to them.–John 20:20.

Mark says that Jesus reprimanded them for their unbelief. He wanted the disciples to accept the message of the resurrection by faith. They failed to believe his Word, even when he told them he would arise from the dead. They did not believe the eyewitness testimony of people that had seen the risen Lord. They did not even accept the evidence they had seen with their own eyes. (John 20:1-10) If they had all this evidence and still did not believe how could they expect people to believe them when they preached about the resurrection? Jesus knew that this group of people was in a unique position. They could go to the empty tomb. They could talk with the risen Lord. They could see him and touch him. Jesus knew that he was going away to heaven. He knew that these men would be called on to preach about the resurrection without one shred of physical evidence to back up their preaching. Jesus knew that the next generation of Christians, those who would be saved through the preaching of the apostles, would not have the benefit of all this evidence. They needed to be fully convinced. They would need that conviction to preach the resurrection.

Early believers lived in a day when many had seen the risen Savior for themselves. (1 Corinthians 15:3-8; 1 John 1:1) We are two-thousand years removed from the events of that day. We cannot go see the tomb or the grave clothes. We cannot go and talk to Peter or Mary Magdalene and ask them about all they saw. We must accept the message by faith. We believe that Jesus died and rose again because the Word of God says so.

Parting words (16:15-18)

Jesus commissioned these men to: "Go into all the world and proclaim the gospel to the whole creation". The day Jesus rose from the dead he began to prepare his disciples for his departure. He knew that he would be ascending back into heaven forty days after he arose. He knew that when he left, his followers would be tasked with the mission of continuing his work in the world. They would have the task of carrying the message of salvation to the ends of the earth. If they were going to carry out that mission, they needed to understand exactly what that mission would require. They needed to know that there would be successes and that there would be failures. Some people would believe the message, while others would reject it. They needed words of comfort, hope and instruction. That is exactly what they heard from Jesus that day. The disciples are told to preach the gospel. They are to go into the world with the good news of salvation.

What is the message they were to preach? It is clearly articulated by the Apostle Paul:

1 Corinthians 15:3-4

³ For I delivered to you as of first importance what I also received: that Christ died for our sins in accordance with the Scriptures,⁴ that he was buried, that he was raised on the third day in accordance with the Scriptures,

The gospel is comprised of these three essential components. This is the message, the mission field is defined and the disciples are to take the good news into the entire world. No place was off limits. Whether the good news is proclaimed across the ocean or across the street, it is to be proclaimed. It is a command and disciples are called to obedience. It is not a suggestion. It is not optional. It is a call to action. Believers are to tell the story with their lives. Christians are to live in such a way that lost people will see the difference in their lives and know that God has done something in them. (Philippians 1:27; Matthew 5:16) In this sense the gospel is both verbal and visual.

Jesus says, "Whoever believes and is baptized will be saved, but whoever does not believe will be condemned." This verse has been misunderstood and misapplied by many who want to add baptism to faith as the condition for salvation. Some people feel that baptism is an essential component of salvation. These words do not teach baptismal regeneration.[112] The thief on the cross was never baptized, yet the Lord assured him of salvation. (Luke 23:43)[113] The Gentiles who believed in Caesarea were baptized after they believed. (Acts 10:44-48) Jesus himself did not baptize. (John

---

[112] I am not saying that all forms of paedo-baptism are heretical. I am a Baptist pastor and as such I believe in adult, believer's baptism by full immersion. I am in fellowship with others who hold different views about the form and modalities of the ordinance but I disagree with any who hold that it is a rite of regeneration that imparts spiritual life through the mediation of a sacramental system.

[113] One might argue that this was an exceptional situation.

4:1-2)[114] This seems strange if salvation comes from baptism. Paul told the Corinthians that he was glad that he had only baptized a few of their number. (1 Corinthians 1:14-16) Paul would not have thanked God for that, if baptism were essential for salvation.

Nearly one hundred and fifty passages in the New Testament teach that salvation is through faith alone. In the New Testament, baptism is connected closely with death and burial. (Romans 6:1-5) It is symbolic of dying to the old life of sin. Faith, on the other hand, is associated with the new birth, or new life in Christ. If Jesus is not talking about being baptized for salvation, what is he talking about? Jesus is talking about obedience to God. Those who are saved by grace will have a desire to follow the Lord in believer's baptism. They will have a desire to give a clear, public witness to their new-found faith. For many, their baptism is their first opportunity to tell a crowd that they have trusted Jesus for salvation. Jesus is saying that salvation results in obedience. The Christian is not saved by works but he / she is saved to work (Ephesians 2:10). Baptism is an outward work that speaks of an inward salvation. It is a public testimony of the salvation that occurred by faith.

Jesus said "...whoever does not believe will be condemned." If people reject Jesus they must face the consequences of that decision. Jesus tells his disciples that signs would follow the true believers. God's power would rest on them. He also said:

Mark 16:17-18[115]

---

[114] John 3:26 might seem to imply that Jesus did baptize others but that is explained in John 4:1-2.

[115] Christian Publishing House does not accept that verses 9-20 were a part of the original text. They were a second-century interpolation by a charismatic group. For a full explanation of this, please see the article,
Was Mark 16:9-20 Written by Mark?
http://www.christianpublishers.org/textual-mark-16-9-20

¹⁷ And these signs will accompany those who believe: in my name they will cast out demons; they will speak in new tongues;[116] ¹⁸ they will pick up serpents with their hands;[117] and if they drink any deadly poison, it will not hurt them; they will lay their hands on the sick, and they will recover."

These two verses have been taken out of context and misapplied and have spawned heretical movements and activities. The actions described in these verses refer to events that took place during the early days of the church. When the Lord Jesus sent out the disciples with the gospel he authenticated the message through amazing displays of his power. Every miracle (except one) mentioned by the Lord in these verses can be found in the book of Acts: the casting out demons (Acts 8:7; 6:18; 19:11-16); speaking with new tongues (Acts 2:4-11; 10:46; 19:6); taking up serpents (Acts 28:5) and laying hands on others for healing. (Acts 3:7; 19:11; 28:8-9) Drinking deadly poisons is the only one not mentioned in Acts. The early church father, Eusebius, said that Barsabbas had done this during the course of his ministry.[118] In other words, this prophecy was literally fulfilled in the first century, by the apostles.

God can still do miracles and send signs to confirm his message. However, the greatest miracle in the world today is

---

[116] Christian Publishing House would ask its readers to consider the following article,

Is Speaking in Tongues a Biblical Teaching?

http://www.christianpublishers.org/speaking-in-tongues-truth

[117] Christian Publishing House would ask its readers to consider the following article,

Is Snake Handling Biblical?

http://www.christianpublishers.org/snake-handling-biblical

[118] Obviously this is an extra-biblical source. Joseph, called Barsabbas, was one of the two men, along with Matthias, nominated to take the place of Judas Iscariot. The disciples cast lots and the lot fell on Matthias (Acts 1:25).

the lives of those he has changed through the power of the new birth. The gospel is still the single most important issue in the world today.

The significance of the ascension (16:19-20)

In our journey with Jesus through the message of Mark we have followed him through the days of his earthly ministry. We have seen how he handled opposition from the religious leaders. We have been in his company as he healed the sick, restored sight to the blind, hearing to the deaf, cast out demons and raised the dead. We have seen him perform many great miracles. We have followed him into the wilderness where he battled with Satan. We have seen up mountains, teaching, praying and touching the lives of so many. We have seen him on the sea in a boat, calming a storm, walking on water. We have observed the transfiguration. We have been impressed by his wisdom, authority, courage and power. We followed him as he went to the cross to die for our sins. We followed his body as he was carried to the tomb and sealed inside. We followed his disciples as they ran to the tomb to investigate the rumors of his resurrection. We followed the Lord as he went to his disciples and let them know that he was alive. Now we follow Jesus and his disciples to the top of the Mount of Olives. This is as far as we can go right now. There we witness his ascension back into heaven and learn what it means for us right now.

Mark's Gospel closes with Jesus going back to heaven to be with his Father. This is an event freighted with significance. Mark skips over forty days in one statement. He jumps all the way from day of the resurrection to the day Jesus ascended back into heaven (Acts 1:9-11). Some might think that the ascension is a minor event with little importance or relevance today. But the ascension is an event of profound importance and relevance. It is not just a distant and mysterious event.

The ascension made the Lord's purposes clear. While Jesus tarried with them, they still held to the hope of a temporal, earthly kingdom. When he left and sent the Holy Spirit they came to understand that Jesus had come to save sinners and not sit upon an earthly throne. When Jesus ascended to heaven the door was opened for the Spirit of God to descend to the earth (John 16:7). The coming of the Spirit made the spread of the Gospel possible and successful.

The ascension made the Lord's plan understandable. It became clear that God's plan of salvation involves all three members of the Godhead. The Father sent the Son. The Son gave his life and shed his blood on the cross. The Spirit was sent to take that message and apply it to the hearts of people. (John 16:7-11) Therefore, the ascension of the Lord Jesus Christ is an important event. When Jesus ascended into heaven and took up his place at his Father's right hand, he went there to continue his ministry on behalf of his people.

Consider the place Jesus occupies in heaven today. His mission has been accomplished. He returned bearing in his body the marks of the cross (John 20:27; Revelation 5:6; Zechariah 13:6). Many people have scars from accidents and injuries that have healed in time. Scars tell stories. But the scars of Jesus tell the greatest story ever told. He accomplished redemption on the cross for all who will believe in him by faith. He is the perfect, eternal, once-for-all-time atonement for sin.—Hebrews 9:11-14; 10:12-13.

Dr. Claude Barlow was a medical missionary to Shaohsing, China, in the early part of the twentieth century. During his ministry there, a strange disease began killing people. He could not find a remedy. In search of a cure, he filled his notebook with observations of the peculiarities he had witnessed in hundreds of cases. Then, with a small vial of the germs, he sailed for the United States. Just before he arrived, he injected himself with the deadly disease and hurried to his alma mater, Johns Hopkins University Hospital. He had become very sick and now depended on his former professors to find a cure. They were able to save his life and send him back to China with a cure for this dreaded disease. In the process, a multitude of lives was spared.

In the midst of our epidemic called 'sin', Jesus went to the cross and infected himself with our deadly disease. He then committed himself to the Father's care and returned to heaven with the cure. Death and hell are no longer our destiny, if we are trusting in Jesus for salvation. Christ conquered sin and death. He died but he rose from the grave victorious. When he ascended to heaven, it was not as a defeated and wounded warrior. He entered heaven as the conquering general who invaded the territory of the enemy, ransacked his position, spoiled him and returned in victory to his own city: 'He disarmed the rulers and authorities and put them to open shame, by triumphing over them in him.' (Colossians 2:15) Imagine the scene in heaven; Jesus has forever conquered sin and Satan at the cross. He returned to heaven as the mighty conqueror.

The Battle of Verdun was one of the major battles during the First World War on the Western Front. It was fought between the German and French armies, from 21 February to 18 December 1916, on hilly terrain north of the city of Verdun in north-eastern France. It ended with a French tactical victory. Verdun resulted in more than 700,000 casualties, an average of 70,000 for each of the ten months of the battle. Modern estimates increase the number of casualties to 976,000. The Battle of Verdun is considered the greatest and lengthiest in world history. Never before or since has there been such a lengthy battle, involving so many men, situated on such a tiny piece of land. The battlefield was not even ten square kilometers.

After World War I when many French soldiers were returning from fighting the Germans in the trenches, they would approach the city of Paris. There on the Arc de Triumph, built by Napoleon was a robed choir. As the dirty, bloody soldiers approached, some helping their crippled and blind comrades, others still covered with the blood of their fallen friends, that choir would sing out: "What right have you to enter the Arc of Triumph?" Those soldiers would stop before the choir, lift their voices together and cry, "We have been to Verdun! We have been to Verdun!" Then, the soldiers would be given a hero's welcome.

Imagine the scene in heaven that day as Jesus made his way into the city. I can hear the angelic hosts crying out: "What right do you have to enter heaven!" Then, I can hear the answer rising from the throat of the one who gave voice to the wind, "I have been to Calvary!" Then I can see the angels bow before him! I can see the Father rise to meet and greet him!

He is the captain of our salvation who has wrought a mighty victory for us. Surely we can say: 'We rest on Thee, our shield and our defender'. The hymn 'We Rest on Thee' has a sad story associated with it. In January 1956, five missionaries sang it before entering the Ecuadorian jungle to bring the gospel to the Auca Indians.[119] After the men reached the Aucas, the Indians murdered them on the Curaray River.

However, the story has a happy ending. Years later, contact with the Aucas was re-established, and many came to Christ, including the killers, which is how first hand details of the missionaries' deaths came to light.

One of the best known of the five martyrs was Jim Elliot. A number of his sayings are still quoted (e.g. "He is no fool who gives what he cannot keep, to gain what he can-not

---

[119] Their names were Nate Saint, Ed McCully, Jim Elliott, Roger Yoderian, and Peter Fleming.

lose"). Elliot's wife Elisabeth went on to considerable fame as an author and radio broadcaster. Her book *Through the Gates of Splendor* describes the encounter with the Aucas. Its title comes from a line in this hymn.

We rest on Thee, our Shield and our Defender!
We go not forth alone against the foe;
Strong in Thy strength, safe in Thy keeping tender,
We rest on Thee, and in Thy Name we go.
Strong in Thy strength, safe in Thy keeping tender,
We rest on Thee, and in Thy Name we go.

Yes, in Thy Name, O Captain of salvation!
In Thy dear Name, all other names above;
Jesus our Righteousness, our sure Foundation,
Our Prince of glory and our King of love.
Jesus our Righteousness, our sure Foundation,
Our Prince of glory and our King of love.

We go in faith, our own great weakness feeling,
And needing more each day Thy grace to know:
Yet from our hearts a song of triumph pealing,
"We rest on Thee, and in Thy Name we go."
Yet from our hearts a song of triumph pealing,
"We rest on Thee, and in Thy Name we go."

We rest on Thee, our Shield and our Defender!
Thine is the battle, Thine shall be the praise;
When passing through the gates of pearly splendor,
Victors, we rest with Thee, through endless days.
When passing through the gates of pearly splendor,
Victors, we rest with Thee, through endless days.[120]

---

[120] Edith G. Cherry, circa 1895, *Mission Praise*, Marshall Pickering, 1999.

When Jesus returned to heaven, he did not leave his people alone. He sent his Spirit into the world to indwell, fill, guide, teach and comfort the people of the Lord. (John 16:7) The Holy Spirit is the comforter who draws alongside us to give aid. Because of Jesus, we have a comforter on earth and a counselor in heaven. He is our intercessor in heaven. (Romans 8:34; Hebrews 7:25) How can we account for the transformation in Peter from the time he denied Jesus three times to the Day of Pentecost? On the night Jesus was betrayed Peter was a coward. On the day of Pentecost he preached in the power of the Holy Spirit and three-thousand people were saved. The reason for the transformation is the anointing of the Holy Spirit!

According to the Bible, Jesus confesses us before the throne of God: 'So everyone who acknowledges me before men, I also will acknowledge before my Father who is in heaven, but whoever denies me before men, I also will deny before my Father who is in heaven.' (Matthew 10: 31-32) He is our mediator. (1 Timothy 2:5) He is our advocate: '...we have an advocate with the Father, Jesus Christ the righteous' (1 John 2:2). Because he perfectly fulfilled God's plan of redemption he is the guarantee of all the promises of the new covenant. His presence in heaven is our guarantee of safe passage to eternal bliss. He guarantees our citizenship in heaven:[121]

Hebrews 6:19-20

[19] We have this as a sure and steadfast anchor of the soul, a hope that enters into the inner place behind the curtain, [20] where Jesus has gone as a forerunner on our behalf, having become a high priest forever after the order of Melchizedek.

---

[121] Christian Publishing House
Resurrection Hope - Where?
http://www.christianpublishers.org/resurrection-hope-where

The word 'forerunner' refers to a scout, a trailblazer, one who charts the course others are to follow Jesus is our forerunner because he has gone before us. He is our model, mentor and Master. He has scouted the trail, routed the enemy, cleared the way, and guarantees safe passage. When Jesus Christ ascended to heaven he did so as the risen Lord of Glory. He ascended as one who is to be worshiped, served, obeyed and loved.

Jesus promised that he was going to prepare a place for us in heaven so that we could be there with him throughout eternity (John 14:1-3). One day, we will join him in that place he is making ready for us. When Jesus was on earth, he told his disciples that he would be going away. However, he also promised that he would come again. (John 14:1-3) The angels who attended the Lord's ascension confirmed this promise: "Men of Galilee, why do you stand looking into heaven? This Jesus, who was taken up from you into heaven, will come in the same way as you saw him go into heaven."– Acts 1:11.

Heaven has been altered by the ascension of Jesus. Heaven is better than it was before Jesus left to come to the earth (if it is possible to say such a thing). Because of what Jesus did at Calvary heaven is no longer just the home of God the Father, God the Son, God the Spirit, and countless angels. The door of heaven has been opened to every person who will trust Jesus by faith.

The ascension of Jesus has implications for us on earth here and now, not just hereafter. Ten days after the ascension an amazing event took place (Acts 2). The disciples (numbering about one hundred and twenty at the time) were praying in a room in Jerusalem. While they prayed, the Holy Spirit descended on them. On that day, Peter preached in Jerusalem and three-thousand people from all over the known world were saved. The gospel message has not changed in over two-thousand years. We have the privilege of taking the same message the disciples preached to our world today. All around us are the lost who need to hear that Jesus made a way for them to be saved. His last words should be our first concern. Will they all listen? No! Will they all respond by coming to Jesus for salvation? No! While many won't, some will!

The Lord had already ascended to heaven, but we are told that he 'worked with them' (v.20). The phrase means that he was a partner in their labor. How is that possible? He is in heaven and they are upon the earth. How did Jesus work with his disciples? He did it through his intercession. As he prayed for them in heaven at the right hand of God, all the power they needed to accomplish their mission was given to them. He did it through the power of the Holy Spirit. While Jesus was here in a human body, he was limited to one geographic location at a time. When the Spirit of God came, he entered into every single one of the Lord's followers. He came into the disciples on the Day of Pentecost. He has entered into every saint of God, at the moment of their conversion, since that day (1 Corinthians 12:13; Galatians 4:6; Romans 8:9). As we labor for the Lord in this day, we can be assured that he will ever be with us. (Hebrews 13:5; Matthew 28:20) We can be certain that he will empower us and use us for his glory. He still works with his people. The ascension of Jesus was an amazing event. It opened the door of that heavenly city for all the redeemed to follow. It allowed the Holy Spirit to descend to fill and thrill the saints of God.

May every believer be filled and thrilled by the presence and power of God as they work in partnership with him in fulfilling the Great Commission to go and make disciples. That means making converts and nurturing them through teaching them the Word of God.

APPENDIX A

Who Killed Jesus?

Revisionist history might assert that it is anti-Semitic to say that the Jews are responsible for the death of Jesus. Indeed many historians believe that Jesus never existed. Such a position is so blind to the readily available data that it can only be described as something akin to holocaust denial.

Did the Jews kill Jesus?

It is politically incorrect to say the Jews killed Jesus. However, the Gospel accounts clearly portray the scribes and Pharisees plotting with the Herodians to destroy Christ. Jesus despised the Pharisees (as a group of people) and addressed them directly with these words:

Matthew 23:27-33

[27] "Woe to you, scribes and Pharisees, hypocrites! For you are like whitewashed tombs, which outwardly appear beautiful, but within are full of dead people's bones and all uncleanness. [28] So you also outwardly appear righteous to others, but within you are full of hypocrisy and lawlessness.

[29] "Woe to you, scribes and Pharisees, hypocrites! For you build the tombs of the prophets and decorate the monuments of the righteous, [30] saying, 'If we had lived in the days of our fathers, we would not have taken part with them in shedding the blood of the prophets.' [31] Thus you witness against yourselves that you are sons of those who murdered the

prophets. ³² Fill up, then, the measure of your fathers. ³³ You serpents, you brood of vipers, how are you to escape being sentenced to hell?

They were untrustworthy and unworthy leaders always on the lookout for opportunities that would allow them to accuse and kill Jesus. Christ overturned the tables of the moneychangers and the seats of the sellers of doves in the temple courtyard, which would not have endeared him to either group. (Mark 11:15-19) The enemies he made on that occasion would, most likely, want revenge. Matthew states: "The chief priests and the elders of the people gathered in the palace of the high priest, whose name was Caiaphas, and plotted together in order to arrest Jesus by stealth and kill him." (Matthew 26:4-5) After Jesus had been delivered to Pilate Matthew informs us: "When morning came, all the chief priests and the elders of the people took counsel against Jesus to put him to death." (Matthew 27:1) Later, when Pilate tried to release Jesus Christ, the crowd (probably consisting mostly of Jews in Jerusalem for the feast of Passover) vehemently insisted that he had to be killed (Luke 23:23). Therefore, they too are culpable. However, while both ordinary Jews and their religious leaders were guilty (i.e. responsible) for playing a role in Jesus' execution, a distinction may be made between these two categories of people.

About 200 years before Jesus arrival, there were certain men, who stood out and protected the nation of Israel from foreign pagan governments. After Alexander the Great had conquered the world (336-323 B.C.) his kingdom broke into four parts. Two in particular became constant oppressors of Israel - the Grecian Seleucid dynasty in Syria and the Greek Ptolemies of Egypt. The first to be corrupted by this Hellenistic influence were the Jewish priests. The extreme corruption of Jewish priests and oppressive Grecian Seleucid dynasty brought about a rebellion from men, who became known as the Maccabees (the Hasmonaeans): Mattathias, his sons Judah, Jonathan, and Simeon.

The Maccabees reinstated pure worship at the temple before the coming of the Messiah (John 1:41-42; 2:13-17). However, faith in the priesthood had been destroyed by the activities of Hellenized priests. In addition, it was maligned even further under the Hasmonaeans, that is, an ancient Judean dynasty who were descendants of the Maccabees. Undeniably, rule by politically minded priests instead of a king of David's line brought hardships on the Jewish people.– 2 Samuel 7:16; Psalm 89:3-4, 35-36.

It is from this era that the Jewish religious leaders, the Pharisees and Sadducees appear. The Hasmonaeans originated with zeal for pure worship of God, but that faded into harmful self-absorption, which involved a negative view of the Jewish people and maltreatment of them, decade after decade. Those priests had the opportunity to unite the people under the Mosaic Law, but rather led the nation into the depths of internal political strife. In this atmosphere, conflict-ridden religious views thrived. The original Maccabees (Hasmonaeans) no longer existed, but the fight for religious control between the Sadducees, the Pharisees, the Herodian dynasty, Jewish zealots and others would typify the Israelite nation now under Herod and Rome.

These corrupt, power-hungry, abusive religious leaders had control over the ordinary Jewish people for almost two hundred years. At first, they freed them from the Hellenist dynasties. However, in time they became oppressive, punishing the people mercilessly for any fraction of the Mosaic Law or the unauthorized oral law. The Jewish people worked hard while the Jewish religious leaders took much of their money in taxes, with the Roman government taking their share as well. The common Jewish people, who chanted for Jesus's death, were an oppressed people under duress and controlled by the Pharisees and Sadducees. Are they guilty of calling for Jesus' death? Yes. Yet many ordinary Jews sided with Jesus privately, some even publicly.

Did Pontius Pilate kill Jesus?

Pontius Pilate was the Roman governor of Judea. He was Caesar's representative and, as such, was the greatest authority in the land. He had power over life and death. Jesus Christ was brought to him for the final verdict. Pilate interviewed Christ and said, "Do you not know that I have authority to release you and authority to crucify you?" (John 19:10). Afterwards, he shared his obvious conclusion with the chief priests: "I find no fault in him." (Luke 23:4) He was convinced of Christ's innocence and tried to dissuade the priests and the crowd from their aim to have him killed. But he finally caved in to the blood-thirsty religious leaders and washed his hands, saying, "I am innocent of this man's blood." (Matthew 27:24) The reason why he surrendered to the will of the angry crowd is given in the Gospel of John: 'The Jews answered him, "We have a law, and according to that law he ought to die because he has made himself the Son of God." When Pilate heard this statement, he was even more afraid.' (John 19:7-8) Clearly, Pilate's decision was motivated by the fear of a potential revolt. Therefore, to keep the leaders happy, and to prevent a dangerous rebellion, he relented to their request. Although Pilate had the power to prevent Christ's death, he chose to sacrifice an innocent man to keep the peace. Pilate, therefore, was a willing participant and contributed to Christ's death. That day the judge of all the earth stood before the earthly judge but in the final judgment the roles will be reversed. Surely, on that day Pilate will realize (as Macbeth did after he murdered King Duncan and emerged from the king's bedroom chamber with bloodstained hands) the futility of water to cleanse him of such a deed: "Will all great Neptune's ocean wash this blood

Clean from my hand?"[122] Of course, the Scottish play is just a literary construction, albeit tenuously connected to history.[123]

Did Satan Kill Jesus?

The beautiful hymn, 'In Christ Alone', by Stuart Townend and Keith Getty, contains the line: 'Light of the world by darkness slain'. Is this theologically accurate? At the risk of sounding petty, I suggest it is not in accordance with what Scripture teaches. In every other respect, this is an excellent hymn and I am loath to quibble unnecessarily. I am not the first Calvinist to have cause to voice concern about some hymns and I suspect I will not be the last. Augustus Montague Toplady (1740-1778), author of 'Rock of Ages', used The *Gospel Magazine* to criticize John Wesley.[124]

The apostle Paul advised the church in Ephesus about learning to walk in love: 'addressing one another in psalms and hymns and spiritual songs, singing and making melody to the Lord with your heart.' (Ephesians 5:19) He also counselled

---

[122] William Shakespeare, *Macbeth*, Act II, Scene II, Ls.60-61.

[123] See *Holinshed's Chronicles*, Everyman's Library, (first published 1927), 1978.

[124] The Gospel Magazine is a Calvinist, evangelical magazine from the UK and is one of the longest running of such periodicals, having been founded in 1766. Toplady was sponsored by Selina Hastings Countess of Huntingdon (1707–1791) who played a prominent part in the religious revival of the eighteenth century and the Methodist movement in England and Wales. In 1739 she joined the first Methodist society in Fetter Lane, London. It was some time after the death of her husband in 1746 that Lady Huntingdon threw in her lot with John Wesley and George Whitfield in the work of the great revival. Whitfield became her personal chaplain, and, with his assistance, following problems put in her path by the Anglican clergy from whom she had preferred not to separate, she founded the " Countess of Huntingdon's Connexion". This was a Calvinistic movement within the Methodist church, as were Whitfield chapels.

the Colossians to: 'Let the word of Christ dwell in you richly, teaching and admonishing one another in all wisdom, singing psalms and hymns and spiritual songs, with thankfulness in your hearts to God' (Colossians 3:16). We absorb doctrine through the hymns we sing. They play a significant role in shaping our understanding of truth.

Some might feel that I am nitpicking and that the popularity and melody of this song are enough reason to keep using it. I certainly feel it is worth singing, notwithstanding my reservations about this one line in question. However, for many it is carry-on-karaoke at church irrespective of the words. If Christians avoid telling lies, they should also avoid singing them! However, for many: 'Thought would destroy their paradise...where ignorance is bliss 'tis folly to be wise' (lines from the last stanza of the poem, 'Ode on a Distant Prospect of Eton College' by Thomas Gray (1716 – 1771).

The second verse of this hymn expresses the truth that it was the wrath of God that Jesus bore at Calvary: "till on that cross as Jesus died, the wrath of God was satisfied'. It is a pity, therefore, to spoil this thought in the third verse. The hymn has powerful and poetic lyrics and it is certainly a stimulus to worship. However, we are to worship in spirit and truth. (John 4:24) Jesus said that, "the Father is seeking such people to worship him." (John 4:23) Perhaps one of the problems with the line is its poetic construction with the juxtaposition of light and darkness and the symmetry of such a contrast. I would humbly suggest to its authors that they might consider revising that one line so that it reflects theological truth. I would avoid the poetic intent for the sake of something more accurate, like, 'Lamb of God who for us was slain'.

Satan was no doubt the major force behind the whole gruesome scenario. He had attempted to neutralize and destroy Jesus Christ from the start, by tempting him and by trying to bring about his spiritual destruction. He continued tempting Jesus all the way to the end. No doubt, Satan stirred up the spirit of envy and bitterness in the religious leaders. Did Satan influence Pilate's decision to have Jesus scourged mercilessly? Did Satan move the unrelenting crowds to request the death penalty by crucifixion? I believe that Satan wanted Jesus to be traumatized beyond endurance, hoping that he would finally give up and surrender. Though it may be difficult to know the exact extent of Satan's contribution, he was there and he was heavily involved. It is right to consider the battle between Satan and Jesus as a cosmic struggle between light and darkness (Genesis 3:15) but wrong to conclude that Satan killed Jesus.

Did the sins of the world kill Jesus?

Humans sinned from the beginning and have needed redemption ever since. During the time of ancient Israel, God instituted a sacrificial system meant to emphasize the seriousness of sin and its demand for payment. Transgression of some of the Ten Commandments could not be paid for by any sacrifice; the penalty was death. The Bible is clear that the penalty of sin is death. (Romans 6:23) To prevent such an end for all of humanity a sacrifice was needed that would suffice as payment for all our sins. The Son of God was the only sufficient payment for the sins of the world. Was it then our sins that killed Jesus?

The ultimate cause

Who ultimately killed Jesus? Was it the Jewish leaders? Was it the Jewish people? Was it Pilate? Was it Satan? Was it our sins? Scripture is clear about this. The much loved and often quoted verse from John's Gospel spells it out: 'For God so loved the world, that he gave his only Son, that whoever believes in him should not perish but have eternal life.' (John 3:16) Who, therefore, killed Jesus? The Jewish leaders wished it. The crowd preferred the release of Barabbas. Pilate could have but did not prevent it. Roman soldiers carried it out. Satan incited it. Our sins demanded it. Jesus willingly submitted to it. In his own words: "No one takes it from me, but I lay it down of my own accord. I have authority to lay it down, and I have authority to take it up again. This charge I have received from my Father." (John 10:18). However, here also Jesus makes it clear that God the Father authorized his death. Thus, we read in the prophetic passage in Isaiah: '...it was the will of the LORD to crush him.' (Isaiah 53:10) Here, indeed, is love 'vast unmeasured, boundless, free'.[125]

---

[125] From the hymn, 'Here is love vast as the ocean'. Words: William Rees (1802-1883), verses 1-2. William Williams possibly wrote verses 3-4; translated from Welsh to English by William Edwards in *The Baptist Book of Praise*, 1900. Cited here from *Mission Praise*, Marshall Pickering, 1999.

APPENDIX B

Judas

Judas forever bears the stigma of his actions and is loathed and consigned to damnation. His name is anathema in the Christian church and his infamous act of betrayal is forever mentioned in the church's commemoration of the ordinance of communion, where the words of the apostle Paul are frequently cited: '...that the Lord Jesus on the night when he was *betrayed* took bread...' (emphasis added by italics).

All the Gospel writers who refer to him as the one who betrayed the Lord note the treachery of Judas (Matthew 10:4; Mark 3:19; Luke 6:16; John18:2). His dishonesty is also noted as John refers to him as a thief (John 12:6). Thus, he is depicted as avaricious, covetous, treacherous and deceitful.

Satan entered into Judas (John 13:2, 27). Satan had also spoken through Peter on one occasion for the Lord had to rebuke him with the words: 'Get behind me, Satan' (Mark 8:33). Although Peter later denied the Lord he was forgiven, restored to right relationship with Jesus and re-commissioned in the Lord's service.

The suicide of Judas is usually understood as the last act of a tormented and damned soul. It is possible that in his mind (in some perverse way) he thought that terminating his life would be an act of repentance. When a person is overwhelmed with sorrow and realizes the horror of his actions a distressed mind can produce distorted thought processes that lead to inappropriate actions.

He was undoubtedly remorseful. He changed his mind, confessed that he had sinned in betraying Jesus and tried (unsuccessfully) to return the thirty pieces of silver. (see Matthew 27:3-4) However, it seems that the "woe" statement of Jesus (Matthew 26:21) rules out any possibility of redemption for Judas?

When the one hundred and twenty disciples gathered to select a replacement for Judas Peter said: "to take the place in this ministry and apostleship from which Judas turned aside to go to his own place" (Acts 1:25). This seems to suggest that the apostate Judas had gone to the destiny reserved for him.

John's Gospel records that Jesus prayed for his disciples (John 17) where he referred to Judas as the, "son of destruction". In that prayer the Lord says of his disciples: "not one of them has been lost except the son of destruction, that the Scripture might be fulfilled." (John 17:12) This raises the question as to whether Judas was never saved or saved and subsequently lost. This begs the question: 'is it possible to lose one's salvation?' The best comment on that question is the words of Jesus:

John 10:27-29

27 My sheep hear my voice, and I know them, and they follow me. 28 I give them eternal life, and they will never perish, and no one will snatch them out of my hand. 29 My Father, who has given them to me, is greater than all, and no one is able to snatch them out of the Father's hand.

If Judas is lost it is because he was never saved.

What motivated Judas? Was it love of money?[126] Was he jealous of the other disciples? Perhaps he understood that Jesus would be executed and his instinct for self-preservation determined his actions. Maybe he was disappointed and

---

[126] The thirty pieces of silver he received may have been a deposit on a larger sum.

angry that his worldly hopes would not be fulfilled and, therefore, his actions were spiteful.

Any psychological profile of Judas is speculative and futile. It may be noted that he called Jesus 'Rabbi' (Matthew 26:25) but never 'Lord'. His presence among the Lord's disciples shows that there can be, not only uncommitted 'followers' of Jesus, but charlatans, unscrupulously dishonest rogues and even those who collaborate with Satan.

APPENDIX C

Pontius Pilate

Little is known about the life and career of Pontius Pilate before he was appointed governor of Palestine. It is likely that he held a series of political and military positions as he climbed the Roman political ladder. The Bible and other ancient historical accounts of Pilate's life and actions paint him as being incompetent and heavy-handed.

Pilate was the governor of Palestine from 26-36 AD. According to the Jewish historian Josephus, Pilate was responsible for much of the turmoil that marked his career as governor of Palestine. On one occasion, he permitted his soldiers to enter Jerusalem with flags bearing the image of Caesar. This insulted the Jews and nearly led to a bloody rebellion. On another occasion, he confiscated the treasury of the temple (*corban*) to pay for an aqueduct he was building. The *corban* was to be used for God's service alone. Jews who objected to this insult were severely beaten by plain clothed soldiers.

Pilate killed some Galileans as they offered their sacrifices (Luke 13:1). He lost his position when he ordered his cavalry to attack some Samaritans who had gathered at Mount Gerizim as part of a religious quest. After being deposed as governor, Pilate was exiled to northern Europe, where tradition says that he committed suicide. When he lost his power, his position and his pride, he had nothing for which to live. This is the petty, self-centered man Jesus faced in trial.

Pilate's ancestors were Roman nobles of the equestrian order. He had served a tour of duty in Syria as an administrative military tribune with the Twelfth Legion and had earned the reputation of being a tough commander. His wife, Claudia Procula, is said to have been the granddaughter of Caesar Augustus, so Pilate had the highest connections in Rome. Pilate ignored the claims of Jesus and he ignored a clear warning from his wife.–Matthew 27:19.

As procurator of Judea, Pilate carried a heavy responsibility. Judea was the capital of the seven million Jews who lived in the Roman Empire – seven percent of its entire population. Moreover, Judea commanded the trade routes and lines of communication between Syria and Egypt. Judea was also important because it was the only outpost preventing Parthia from moving in and blocking Roman access to Egypt. Rome depended on Egypt for her grain supply, so Egypt itself could not be allowed to fall into hostile hands either. In addition, the ships that carried their precious cargoes of wheat to Rome must never be endangered. Therefore, the governorship of Judea was a trust of some magnitude.

Pilate was not going to allow some local 'messiah' to imperil his position as guardian of Rome's Egyptian gate, so he caved in to political expediency. If he let Jesus go, he would incur the wrath of the Sanhedrin. If he let Jesus go, he would in effect be endorsing Christ's claim to be a king --- the King of the Jews. He rejected the claims of Christ against the advice of his wife and the instinct of his own soul and signed the death warrant that consigned Jesus to a particularly cruel and horrible death.[127]

Then Pilate gave Jesus a title. As was customary in the case of a public execution, the governor wrote a placard

---

[127] I am not sure that there was an actual death warrant that was signed. I am speaking metaphorically.

naming both the criminal and the crime. Much to the annoyance of the Jews, Pilate wrote, JESUS OF NAZARETH, THE KING OF THE JEWS (John19:19-20). The placard was written in Latin, the language of government; in Greek, the language of culture and in Hebrew, the language of religion. The title was written in all three languages so that all could read it and he would not change the wording: "What I have written I have written," he said.

The Jews were a much older civilization than the Romans. Before Pompey marched into Jerusalem, the Jews were a great people. When the Romans were still barbarians, the Jews were already a great people. Before the story of Romulus and Remus and the she-wolf was circulated, the Jews were a great people. Before Alexander the Great was crowned king of Macedonia in 336 B.C. the Jews were a great people. Before the Athenians began building the Parthenon in 447 B.C., the Jews were a great people. The Jews were a great people before Xerxes invaded Greece, Cyrus the Persian conquered Babylon, Nebuchadnezzar rose to power, the Phoenicians founded Carthage and the Assyrians forged their cruel empire. The Jews were a great people before Ramses the Great began construction of the temple of Abu Simbel.

Their roots and their history go far back before Hammurabi of Babylon hammered out his legal code, back before the Hyksos Kings subdued Egypt. When the Bronze Age was coming to flower in Egypt, the Jews were a people to be reckoned with in this world.

Pilate despised the Jewish nation but the Hebrew nation had a legal code greater than Rome's. They had a religion greater, far greater--than Rome's. Even in Pilate's day, the Jews were the world's bankers. Before the century was over, the Jews would teach Rome a lesson it would not soon forget. To quell the Jewish revolt, the Romans were forced to assemble an army of eighty thousand men. Alexander the

Great had carved out his vast empire with thirty-two thousand men. Julius Caesar needed only twenty-five thousand soldiers to conquer Gaul and invade Britain. To fight the Jews, however, Titus was forced to mobilize ten thousand cavalrymen and seventy thousand infantrymen, and even against those odds, the Jews kept the Romans at bay for four long years. In the end, the Romans won, not because of greater skill but because of greater numbers.

After the Romans conquered Jerusalem, they still had to subdue Masada. And the Jews led by Bar Kokhba tried to resist Rome again in A.D. 135. The Jews would outlast Pilate, the Caesar he served, and the empire he represented. When the Huns and Goths and Vandals at last descended on Rome, the Jews were still a mighty people. They are a mighty people today.[128]

However, Pilate despised this people. He thought of the Jews as moneylenders and religious fanatics. He wrote 'Jesus of NAZARETH the King of the Jews.' Nazareth! Even the Jews regarded this Galilean town with a measure of contempt. They despised Galileans because they were of mixed blood and because so many Gentiles lived in Galilee, thus, in their understanding, contaminating the purity of the race. They despised Galilee because its chief city was Tiberius, named after a despised emperor and it was built on the site of an old graveyard, adding further to the notion that it was unclean and unfit for Jewish habitation. The Jews despised Galileans because they spoke the native Aramaic with a thick, north-country accent. "Can anything good come out of Nazareth?" asked Nathanael when Philip told him he had found the Messiah, a man named Jesus of Nazareth—John 1:45-46.

---

[128] Though beleaguered and much maligned in this world they are still a great nation, surrounded by enemies.

Pilate had been governor of Judea long enough to know how much Nazareth was despised by the Jews. Therefore, his inscription over the cross was intended to annoy the Jews. It was not Jesus of Jerusalem. The sophisticated Judeans spoke the name of Nazareth with a sneer. Nazareth was a place to be derided.

Ultimately, Pilate had to choose to serve Tiberius rather than Jesus. Caesar Tiberius was the adopted stepson of Caesar Augustus. He retired to the island of Capri and abandoned himself to all forms of lust. When he finally died, there was such rejoicing in Rome that people ran about shouting, "To the Tiber with Tiberius!" Others offered prayers to the infernal gods to give him no room below except among the damned.

One wonders if Pilate heard positive or poisoned reports about Jesus. The procurator persuaded himself that it was in his own best interest to stay in the good graces of Caiaphas and his crowd and to do nothing that the suspicious old tyrant back in Rome might interpret as treason.

Contrary to all appearances, the man on the center cross was the King of the Jews. However, he was more than that --- much more. In the book of Revelation, he is called 'King of kings and Lord of lords' (19:16). Three days later Pilate was faced with the news that the tomb was empty and the man he had murdered was alive.

Bibliography

Andrews, Edward D. *FOR AS I THINK IN MY HEART—SO I AM: Combining Biblical Counseling with Cognitive Behavioral Therapy.* Cambridge: Christian Publishing House, 2013.

Arndt, William, Frederick W. Danker, and Walter Bauer. *A Greek-English Lexicon of the New Testament and Other Early Christian Literature. 3rd ed. .* Chicago: University of Chicago Press, 2000.

Arnold, Clinton E. *Zondervan Illustrated Bible Backgrounds Commentary: Matthew, Mark, Luke, vol. 1.* Grand Rapids, MI: Zondervan, 2002.

Black, Allen. *THE COLLEGE PRESS NIV COMMENTARY: MARK.* Joplin: College Press Publishing Company, 1995.

Brand, Chad, Charles Draper, and England Archie. *Holman Illustrated Bible Dictionary: Revised, Updated and Expanded.* Nashville, TN: Holman, 2003.

Bratcher, Robert. "Inerrancy: Clearing Away Confusion." *Christianity Today*, May 29, 1981: 12.

Brooks, James A. *The New American Commentary: Mark (Volume 23).* Nashville: Broadman & Holman Publishers, 1992.

Chesterton, G. K. *The Rattle Bag.* London & Boston: Faber and Faber, 1982.

Cooper, Rodney. *Holman New Testament Commentary: Mark.* Nashville: Broadman & Holman Publishers, 2000.

Edwards, James R. *The Pillar New Testament Commentary: The Gospel according to Mark.* Grand Rapids: Wm. B. Eerdmans Publishing Co., 2002.

evangeliorum, Sancti Augustini Quaestiones. *Saint Augustine.* Turnhout (Belgium): Brepols, 1980.

France, R. T. *The New International Greek Testament Commentary: The Gospel of Mark.* Grand Rapids: Wm. B. Eerdmans Publishing Co., 2002.

Hendriksen, William. *New Testament Commentary: Exposition of the Gospel According to Mark (12 volume).* Grand Rapids: Baker Book House, 1975.

Henry, Matthew. *Matthew Henry's Commentary on the Whole Bible, complete and unabridged in one volume.* Peabody: Hendrickson, 1991.

Hooker, Morna D. *Black's New Testament Commentary: THE GOSPEL ACCORDING TO ST MARK.* London: Continuum, 1981, Reprinted 2001, 2003 and 2006.

Lange, John Peter, Philip Schaff, and William G. T. Shedd. *A Commentary on the Holy Scriptures: Mark.* Grand Rapids: Zondervan, 1959.

Lewis, C. S. *Christian Reflections.* Hammersmith: Collins Fount Paperbacks, 1967.

Mounce, William D. *Mounce's Complete Expository Dictionary of Old & New Testament Words.* Grand Rapids, MI: Zondervan, 2006.

Ryle, J. C. *Mark (Expository Thoughts on the Gospels).* London: Banner of Truth, 1985.

Spurgeon, Charles H. *Morning and Evening: Daily Readings.* Peabody: Hendrickson Publishers, 1995.

Stein, Robert H. *Baker Exegetical Commentary on the New Testament: Mark.* Grand Rapids, MI: Baker Academics, 2008.

Tan, P. L. *Encyclopedia of 7700 Illustrations : A treasury of Illustrations, Anecdotes, Facts and Quotations for Pastors, Teachers and Christian Workers.* Dallas: Bible Communications Inc., Thirteenth printing 1996, c1979.

Vine, W E. *Vine's Expository Dictionary of Old and New Testament Words.* Nashville: Thomas Nelson, 1996.

Walton, John H., Victor H. Matthews, and Mark W Chavalas. *The IVP Bible Background Commentary: Old Testament.* Downers Grove: IVP Academic, 2000.

www.ingramcontent.com/pod-product-compliance
Lightning Source LLC
Chambersburg PA
CBHW020728160426
43192CB00006B/156